REFORMING PUBLIC PROCUREMENT LAW

This collection of essays on the reform of public procurement law and policy honours the contribution of Sue Arrowsmith as the leading scholar in the field.

The book is divided into three main parts – on the UK, the EU and the world – and focuses on central reform themes that have characterised the evolution of public procurement law and policy in the past decades. These include sustainability, complex contracts, review and remedies, electronic procurement and defence procurement, as well as topics such as debarment, the overall development of EU procurement reform, the very nature of procurement law, or the regulation of UK procurement law after Brexit. The book also covers the dynamic reform process of the EU Procurement Directives and case law, the UNCITRAL Model Law on Procurement, the WTO Government Procurement Agreement, and national systems including the US, China, Africa, and the UK.

The chapters are written by experts in specific topics of procurement reform from Africa, Asia, the Americas and Europe with backgrounds in academia, legal practice and international organisations.

The reader is provided with a diverse set of insights into the objectives, approaches, priorities and future direction of public procurement reform.

Reforming Public Procurement Law

Liber Amicorum in Honour of Sue Arrowsmith

Edited by
Annamaria La Chimia
and
Martin Trybus

•HART•
OXFORD • LONDON • NEW YORK • NEW DELHI • SYDNEY

HART PUBLISHING

Bloomsbury Publishing Plc

Kemp House, Chawley Park, Cumnor Hill, Oxford, OX2 9PH, UK

1385 Broadway, New York, NY 10018, USA

29 Earlsfort Terrace, Dublin 2, Ireland

HART PUBLISHING, the Hart/Stag logo, BLOOMSBURY and the Diana logo are trademarks of Bloomsbury Publishing Plc

First published in Great Britain 2024

A catalogue record for this book is available from the British Library.

A catalogue record for this book is available from the Library of Congress.

ISBN: HB: 978-1-50996-797-1
ePDF: 978-1-50996-800-8
ePub: 978-1-50996-798-8

Typeset by Compuscript Ltd, Shannon

CONTENTS

LIST OF CONTRIBUTORS

Editors

Annamaria La Chimia, LLB (Hons), LLM (International Commercial Law), PhD, a Barrister and Solicitor in Italy (non-practising), is a Professor of Law and Development and serves as the Director of the Public Procurement Research Group (PPRG) at the School of Law, University of Nottingham. Additionally, she holds a Research Fellow position at Stellenbosch University. Anna is also the head and founder of the Humanitarian and Development Procurement Unit and the co-founder/co-lead of the Procurement and Human Rights Unit within the PPRG. At Nottingham, Anna is the Director of the School mentoring scheme. She served as the co-director of the School's equality and diversity committee until 2020, leading the Athena Swan team and securing the first Athena Swan award for the School. Anna has extensive experience as an Expert Senior Advisor for international, national and non-governmental organisations. She has been invited to be a speaker and keynote by both national and international institutions at numerous events and has held visiting professorships at the University LUISS, the University La Sapienza of Rome, La Statale of Milan, the University of Copenhagen and the Danish Institute of Human Rights.

Anna first met Sue in 2001 in Nottingham when she attended Sue's (and Martin Trybus's) LLM Modules on public procurement law and policy. Her association with Sue deepened when she completed her LLM dissertation with Sue and was subsequently offered a PhD scholarship (sponsored by the PPRG) to conduct research on tied-aid procurement. Anna joined the faculty as a Lecturer in Law in 2006 and achieved promotion to a Personal Chair in Nottingham in 2019. She assumed the role of Director of the PPRG in 2020 after Sue's retirement. Anna taught with Sue on the LLM course on procurement law and international trade, and has collaborated with her on various projects, including the Asia Link and the African Link. She was instrumental in establishing the Executive Programme in Public Procurement Law & Policy, devising the Programme's innovative assessment policy. Anna has co-authored publications with Sue on several occasions and contributed chapters to many of Sue's edited collections, most recently co-editing *Public Procurement in (a) Crisis: Global Lessons from the COVID-19 Pandemic* (Hart Publishing, 2021).

Martin Trybus, LLM, PhD (Wales), *Ass iur* (Düsseldorf), *Ref iur* (Berlin) is Professor of European Law and Policy, Director of the Institute of European Law, and Associate Dean at the University of Birmingham (Birmingham Law School),

United Kingdom and Visiting Professor at the University of Utrecht, The Netherlands. His research focuses on EU law, especially law and policy relating to public procurement and to defence integration. He is, inter alia, the author of *Buying Defence and Security in Europe: The EU Defence and Security Procurement Directive in Context* (Cambridge University Press, 2014, in Chinese in 2018) and numerous academic articles. Professor Trybus has been working with several international organisations, especially the OECD and the European Defence Agency, and for national governments on projects involving procurement reform and defence procurement, defence exports and state aids. Previously he worked for the universities of Nottingham and Sheffield and for OECD/SIGMA in Paris. In 2010–16 he served on the European Space Agency Procurement Review Board, serving again 2020–26, and was elected Chair in 2022. In 2017–21 he worked as Network Coordinator and Director of Research on the EU-funded Horizon 2020 project 'EU Trade and Investment Policy (EUTIP)', and is now Director of Training on a similar project on Sustainability and Procurement (SAPIENS Network).

Martin first studied procurement law as Sue's LLM student at Aberystwyth and did his LLM dissertation under her supervision. He was one of Sue's first PhD students at the University of Wales, Aberystwyth (graduated 1998), and was the Deputy Director of the PPRG in 1996–97 in Aberystwyth and in 2000–05 in Nottingham. While both at Nottingham, Sue and Martin edited *Public Procurement: The Continuing Revolution* (Kluwer, 2002), co-supervised PhD students, taught on the Nottingham LLM and co-organised Public Procurement: Global Revolution II.

Contributors

Robert D Anderson is Honorary Professor in the School of Law at the University of Nottingham and serves on the part-time external faculties of the International Master's Programme in Public Procurement Management of the University of Rome Tor Vergata and its sister programme at the University of Belgrade. Until March 2019, he was Counsellor and Team Leader for Government Procurement and Competition Policy in the Secretariat of the World Trade Organization, where he worked for 21 years. He previously served as a staff member in the Canadian Competition Bureau and the Saskatchewan (Province of Canada) Department of Finance. Mr Anderson holds a JD (*Juris Doctor*) from Osgoode Hall Law School, York University (Canada); a Bachelor of Arts with Honors in Economics from the University of British Columbia; and Executive Certificates in Public Policy and Economic Development from the John F Kennedy School of Government, Harvard University. He is editor/co-editor of three books and author/co-author of more than 100 published articles/book chapters/comments or reports on topics in public procurement policy, competition policy and/or international trade policy. He was first recruited as Honorary Professor by Sue Arrowsmith, collaborated with her on a major research volume (S Arrowsmith and RD Anderson (eds), *The WTO Regime on Government Procurement: Challenge and Reform* (Cambridge

University Press and the WTO, 2011), benefited from her participation with him as a resource person in numerous WTO technical assistance workshops and acknowledges with pleasure her important mentorship.

Roger Bickerstaff is Partner, Bird & Bird LLP, London, Dublin, San Francisco, Honorary Professor University of Nottingham School of Law, ex-Chair Society for Computers & Law (2013–16), ex-President International Federation of Computer Law Associations (2016–18). Roger's legal practice over 30 years has focused primarily on technology law, with a significant public sector element. He advises both public-sector entities and bidders on major public-sector IT infrastructure procurement processes. Roger is a part-time lecturer on the LLM course at the University of Nottingham School of Law and on the Tor Vergata, Rome International Masters in Public Procurement Management. He has a particular interest and focus on the use of technology in public procurement processes and was co-author with Sue of the e-procurement chapter in *The Law of Public and Utilities Procurement: Regulation in the EU and UK* (3rd edn). He has known Sue for over 30 years, contributing to procurement conferences organised by Sue when she worked at the University of Wales, Aberystwyth, and a wide variety of subsequent conferences in many locations.

Luke RA Butler, LLB(Hons), LLM (European Law), PhD, Pg Dip, SFHEA, Barrister (non-practising) is Professor of Public Procurement Law & Regulation, Head of the UK Public Procurement Unit within the Public Procurement Research Group and Director of the Executive Programme in Public Procurement Law & Policy, University of Nottingham. Luke specialises in all aspects of public procurement law and regulation, with a particular focus on defence and security procurement. Notable publications include *Transatlantic Defence Procurement: EU and US Defence Procurement Regulation in the Transatlantic Defence Market* (Cambridge University Press, 2017) and many specialist articles on contract-pricing regulation. Luke regularly advises, trains and consults for governments, regulators, international organisations and civil society organisations, and has acted as a UN consultant on capacity-building projects in the field. Luke regularly works closely with Sue in various roles. He serves with Sue as the joint General Editor of the *Public Procurement Law Review*. He is also co-author and editor of books that include *Public Procurement in (a) Crisis: Global Lessons from the COVID-19 Pandemic* (Hart Publishing, 2021) and a monograph on the Foundations of EU Public Procurement Law (Cambridge University Press, forthcoming). Luke and Sue have also jointly provided training, advice, and presentations to Government departments, national auditors, and inquiries.

Richard Craven is a Senior Law Lecturer at the University of Sheffield, United Kingdom. His research interests relate primarily to public law and regulatory studies. His empirical legal research has been published in leading academic journals and has received prestigious funding awards. Richard was Sue's PhD student at the University of Nottingham between 2008 and 2012.

Arwel Davies, LLM PhD (Nottingham) is an Associate Professor and LLB Programme Director at the Hillary Rodham Clinton School of Law, Swansea University. His research covers international economic law, with a focus on world trade law, international investment law and their respective dispute-settlement mechanisms. He is a co-author of *World Trade Law* (Bloomsbury, 2018) and has authored numerous academic articles. Arwel studied EU public procurement law with Sue in Aberystwyth. His PhD, under Sue's supervision, was completed in Nottingham in 2000.

Laurence W Gormley, MA (Oxon), MSc (Lond), LLD (Utrecht) FRSA is a Professor at the College of Europe, Bruges, Emeritus Professor of European law at the University of Groningen and a Bencher of Middle Temple. His research has mainly focused on the EU's internal market, particularly the free movement of goods, taxation, public procurement, and EU customs law and judicial protection in EU law. Laurence is the author of *Prohibiting Restrictions on Trade within the EEC* (1985); *EU Taxation Law* (2005) and *EU Law of Free Movement of Goods and Customs Union* (2009), myriad articles in learned periodicals, and contributions to books, including Parts 12 and 20 of volume 52 of *Halsbury's Laws of England* (4th edn). He has also edited various books. He is the joint editor of *Cambridge Studies in European Law & Policy* and joint general editor of the *Oxford Encyclopedia of EU Law*, and is a member of the editorial or advisory boards of several periodicals, including the *Public Procurement Law Review*. Prior to his appointment at Groningen (1990–2019), he was an Official at the European Commission. He has been Visiting Professor at University College London, Bremen, Bonn, Bucerius and Leuven, and a Visiting Fellow of Sidney Sussex College Cambridge and the Centre of European Legal Studies, Cambridge. Laurence was the first Chairman of the Dutch Association for Procurement Law (1985–95) and was President of the European Law Faculties Association (2015–16). He and Sue have known each other for many agreeable years.

Baudouin Heuninckx, PhD, DSc, is a Chartered Procurement and Supply Professional (MCIPS) and the former Deputy Head of Procurement of the Belgian Armed Forces. Before that, he was the Belgian Deputy National Armaments Director, Chief Counsel of the Procurement Division of the Belgian Armed Forces, and worked on the A400M military transport aircraft programme for the international organisation OCCAR. He has also an academic background, teaching public procurement law and management. He was until recently the Chairman of the Belgian inter-federal Public Procurement Commission. He has written numerous books and articles on public procurement, in particular in the fields of defence and security. His 2017 book, *The Law of Collaborative Defence Procurement in the European Union*, and his chapter on defence and security procurement in Professor Sue Arrowsmith's 2018 book *The Law of Public and Utilities Procurement* are widely considered as references in these fields.

Totis Kotsonis, Msc (Econ), PhD (London School of Economics), is a partner at the London office of Pinsent Masons LLP, where he heads the firm's procurement, subsidy control and trade law practice. He has been advising governments, regulated utilities and suppliers on all aspects of public procurement law for more than 20 years and speaks and writes regularly on the subject. He is a member of the editorial board of the *Public Procurement Law Review* and a member of the European Commission stakeholder expert group on public procurement. He has previously been involved in assisting the UK Government in the implementation of EU procurement directives, including Remedies Directive 2007/66. More recently, he has been involved in discussions with the UK Government in relation to the development of the post-Brexit procurement law regime, including as regards court procedural reform. He has known Sue since 2006, and with her encouragement wrote his first article for the *Public Procurement Law Review*, on the definition of 'special or exclusive rights' under the 2004/17 Utilities Directive, in 2007. He has been collaborating with Sue ever since, including in the context of the Public Procurement Lawyers' Association (PLA). Totis has been a member of the PLA's executive committee since the founding of the Association in 2008.

John Linarelli, JD (American), LLM (Georgetown), PhD (Law) (King's London), PhD (Philosophy) (California – Riverside) is Professor of Law at the University of Pittsburgh School of Law, where he is a member of the Center for International Legal Education. He has served in senior faculty positions on both sides of the Atlantic. He is formerly Professor of Commercial Law at Durham University in the United Kingdom, where he was co-director of Durham's Institute for Commercial and Corporate Law. Professor Linarelli is an elected member of the American Law Institute, a Fellow of the European Law Institute and a Fellow of the American Bar Foundation. Before becoming an academic, Professor Linarelli practised government contracts law in Washington, DC. His first full-time academic role was at Aberystwyth University, where he worked with Professor Arrowsmith. He was involved in work towards the first Public Procurement Global Revolution Conference with Professor Arrowsmith at the time. He has also been a longstanding friend of the Public Procurement Research Group and was an Honorary Professor of Law at the University of Nottingham, where he taught on the LLM in Procurement Law and Policy. He later served as examiner for that LLM programme and has served as examiner for PhD students writing on public procurement law. He co-authored, with Sue Arrowsmith and Don Wallace Jr, *Regulating Public Procurement: National and International Perspectives* (Kluwer, 2000). Professor Linarelli's research spans international economic law and comparative and transnational commercial law. He is author, with Margot Salomon and M Sornarajah, of *The Misery of International Law: Confrontations with Injustice in the Global Economy* (Oxford University Press), which won the European Society of International Law Book Prize in 2019. Professor Linarelli is co-editor, with Teresa Rodríguez de las Heras Ballell, of the *Hart Studies in Commercial and Financial Law* book series, published by Hart/Bloomsbury.

Caroline Nicholas led the work of the United Nations Commission on International Trade Law (UNCITRAL) in reforming its Model Law on Public Procurement, working with Professor Sue Arrowsmith, who identified the key policy developments to be reflected in the text. As Head of UNCITRAL's Technical Assistance programme, Caroline has worked with countries across the globe on public procurement reform. She teaches public procurement law and policy at the post-graduate level in several countries, publishes regularly on these subjects, and sits on university academic and editorial boards. She serves as an investigator in the United Nations and led a United Nations programme assessing war damage claims from the Government of Kuwait after Iraq's 1990 invasion and occupation of Kuwait. She is a solicitor and previously practised commercial law in England and Wales and in Hong Kong.

Geo Quinot, BA LLB (Stellenbosch) LLM (Virginia), MA (Free State), MPA (Birmingham), LLD (Stellenbosch) is Professor of Law in the Department of Public Law and the School of Public Leadership at Stellenbosch University, South Africa, and Founding Director of the African Procurement Law Unit (APLU). He is also admitted as an Advocate of the High Court of South Africa. His research focuses on general administrative law, including a particular focus on the regulation of state commercial activity such as public procurement, as well as on legal education. He has published widely in these areas and is the author, co-author and/or editor of eight published books, the most recent of which are *Public Procurement Regulation in Africa: Development in Uncertain Times* (LexisNexis, 2020) and *Administrative Justice in South Africa: An Introduction*(2nd edn, Oxford University Press, 2020). Quinot is the founding editor-in-chief of the open-access journal, *African Public Procurement Law Journal*, which is the first of its kind on the African continent. As an advocate, Quinot advises on matters relating to administrative law, and especially public procurement law, to both public buyers and suppliers to the state. Geo has collaborated with Sue on various British Academy-funded projects that laid the groundwork for the establishment of APLU in 2012, and they co-edited the first book that provided a multi-jurisdictional analysis of public procurement law on the African continent, *Public Procurement Regulation in Africa* (Cambridge University Press, 2013).

Rebecca Rees is a partner and Head of Public Procurement at Trowers & Hamlins LLP, an international law firm headquartered in London. Rebecca is a leading national expert in public procurement law and is named as a 'Top Ranked and Leader in the Field for Public Procurement (UK-wide)' by the *Chambers and Partners' Guide to the Legal Profession 2023*. She is also recognised as a Global Leader in the *Who's Who Legal Guide to Government Contracts 2023*. Rebecca has significant experience in advising clients in the public, private and third sectors on public procurement, subsidy control and building safety strategy issues.

She advises clients on procurement strategy and structures, how to conduct flexible and compliant procurement procedures, and how to compile objective and transparent evaluation models and guidance. With particular interests in value-led procurement, social value and building safety, Rebecca is a member of the UK Competency Steering Group for Procurement Competency, Department of Levelling Up, Housing and Communities' Procurement Advisory Group, and the National Social Value in Housing Taskforce, which focuses on the further development of robust measurement and management of social-value outcomes in the public sector. Rebecca is a Visiting Fellow at the Centre of Construction Law at Dickson Poon School of Law at King's College London and is currently undertaking a PhD in public procurement at the University of Nottingham, focusing on price-evaluation models. Rebecca was one of Sue's last PhD students and continues to work with Sue, collaborating on training modules for the current UK procurement reform agenda.

Mari Ann Simovart, Dr Iur (University of Tartu, Estonia) is Associate Professor of Law and Head of the Department of Public Law at the University of Tartu, Estonia. Her research focuses on EU and national public procurement law. She is the author of the commented edition of the Estonian Public Procurement Act and numerous book chapters, as well as academic articles. Simovart is editor of the academic journal *Public Procurement Law Review* and has been leading several research projects in the field of public procurement law. From 2020, she served on the European Space Agency Procurement Review Board. Sue has welcomed Mari Ann as a visiting scholar to the University of Nottingham, Public Procurement Research Group on several occasions, and is cooperating with her in her position as editor of the *Public Procurement Law Review*.

Professor Christopher Yukins teaches in the government procurement law programme at the George Washington University Law School, the leading programme of its kind in the United States. He teaches online and in person, on contract formations and performance issues in public procurement, state and local procurement, anti-corruption, foreign and comparative public procurement and procurement reform. Professor Yukins has worked on a wide array of public procurement issues throughout his career and has testified before committees of the US Congress and the European Parliament. He has lectured at universities across Europe, and he contributed to the UN's *Guidebook on Anti-Corruption in Public Procurement*. He worked – with Professor Sue Arrowsmith and co-author Caroline Nicholas – on sweeping reforms of the UN Commission on International Trade Law (UNCITRAL) Model Procurement Law; for nearly a decade, he served as an advisor to the U.S delegation to that reform effort.

Ping Wang, LLB (Peking), LLM PhD (Nottingham) is Professor of International Economic Law at Changchun University of Science and Technology, China. His research activities focus on international and Chinese public procurement law and regulation, competition law and intellectual property law, as well as EU law and its lessons for China's unified internal market initiative. Professor Wang has been working with several international organisations and government agencies, such as the WTO, the World Bank, the EU and China's Ministry of Finance and Ministry of Commerce regarding China's GPA accession and government procurement reform. Ping was one of Sue's PhD students at the University of Nottingham (graduated 2007) and the Deputy Director of the PPRG 2006–20 in Nottingham.

LIST OF CASES

European Union [Court of Justice of the European Union]

United Kingdom

Competition Appeal Tribunal

England and Wales High Court

England and Wales Court of Appeal

Court of Session (Outer House)

The Supreme Court of the United Kingdom

Canada

France

Taiwan

LIST OF STATUTES AND INSTRUMENTS

International Instruments

National Statutes, Rules and Other Instruments

Botswana

Canada

China

Congo Braza

Estonia

European Union Statutes

European Union Regulations and Directives

United Kingdom

1

Introduction

Sue Arrowsmith – The Champion of Procurement Reform

ANNAMARIA LA CHIMIA AND MARTIN TRYBUS

This edited collection on the reform of procurement law and policy celebrates the contribution of Professor Sue Arrowsmith, KC (Hons), BA (Oxon), D Jur, to the understanding and reform of public procurement law and policy in the United Kingdom (UK), the European Union (EU) and beyond. Public procurement, the process of the public sector buying goods and services from private companies, has been subject to regulation and policy at least since the eighteenth century, but it is only since the 1980s that what Arrowsmith/Davies and Arrowsmith/Trybus called a 'revolution' has been unfolding. Organisations such as the World Trade Organization (WTO) and the EU, but also major countries like the UK or Germany, introduced binding procurement laws for the first time. This development also brought with it a new procurement infrastructure, ranging from new procuring agencies, tribunals dealing with appeal cases, law firms specialising in procurement law, and bodies specialising in training those needing to learn about procurement law and policies. More recent major aspects of what requires a continuous reform effort include the necessity to include sustainability in the procurement process (environment, labour rights, climate change and more), the emergence of electronic procurement and its centralisation, the Covid-19 pandemic and Brexit. The Public Procurement Research Group (PPRG) at the University of Nottingham (founded by Arrowsmith and now led by La Chimia), the University of Utrecht Centre for Public Procurement, the procurement chairs at the Universities of Copenhagen and Munich, the Government Contract Programme at the George Washington University or the African Public Procurement Regulation Research Unit at the University of Stellenbosch, are all groups of academics dedicated to the research of public procurement law. Research networks such as the Procurement Law Academic Network (PLAN) created by Arrowsmith, Sustainability and Procurement in International, European and National Systems (SAPIENS NETWORK), or the European Procurement Law

Group are dedicated to specific aspects of procurement research. Dedicated journals such as the *Public Procurement Law Review* (founded by Arrowsmith), the *Public Contract Law Journal* or the *European Procurement and Public Private Partnerships Law Review* cover research in the area, as do specific conference series, such as *Public Procurement: Global Revolution* (University of Nottingham) launched by Arrowsmith, the *International Public Procurement Conference* (Florida Atlantic University) or the *Global Procurement Conference* (University of Rome II Tor Vergata). Dedicated master programmes are offered by, inter alia, the universities of Nottingham (launched by Arrowsmith and her colleagues at the PPRG), Stellenbosch, Bangor, Turin and ITC/ILO, and Rome II Tor Vergata, and George Washington University. And these are only examples from the discipline of law and programmes taught in English. Procurement is also taught in business and political science schools and in many countries and languages, and Arrowsmith texts are read across borders and disciplines.

Sue Arrowsmith read jurisprudence at the University of Oxford (Somerville College) from which she graduated with a first-class honours degree and won several university and college law prizes, including the prestigious Gibbs Prize. She then proceeded to a postgraduate research degree on a Commonwealth Scholarship at the Osgoode Hall Law School of York University in Toronto, graduating with a D Jur. Her first book, *Government Procurement and Judicial Review* (Carswell, 1988), was based on her doctoral thesis, the keystone of her research on public procurement. Sue's first appointment (Tutor 1987–88, Lecturer 1988–91) and chair (1991–98) were at what was then the University (College) of Wales, Aberystwyth (now University of Aberystwyth). Here she established the *Public Procurement Law Review* (1991) as first editor-in-chief, founded the PPRG as first Director (1997), organised the first *Public Procurement: Global Revolution* conference (1998), and generally established public procurement as a taught subject and as a separate research subject in Great Britain and Northern Ireland. The co-editor of this collection Martin Trybus was one of her first PhD students there (PhD Wales, 1998). The year 1998 saw the beginning of her time at Nottingham, where she started, together with her PPRG colleagues, the Executive LLM in procurement law, and where Sue not only supervised but inspired dozens of PhD students in public procurement law and policy (including the co-editor of this collection Annamaria La Chimia). In Nottingham, Sue continued (with Trepte from 2011) the conference series with *Public Procurement: Global Revolution II–IX*.

In 1992, Sue launched the first international academic procurement journal, *Public Procurement Law Review* (PPLR), and has been editing the *Review* for more than 30 years. She remains General Editor, now alongside Luke Butler who has contributed to this book, as did assistant editor Mari Ann Simovart. The board membership has rapidly expanded and now includes dozens of members, reflecting the breadth of the work published by the *Review*. Nottingham colleagues – Professor Annamaria La Chimia, Dr Aris Georgopoulos and Dr Peter Trepte – are all Board Members of the *Review*, and Dr Paula Bordalo Faustino is the Book

Reviews Editor. The Board Members Peter Trepte, Laurence Gormley, John Linarelli, Caroline Nicholas, Robert Anderson, Roger Bickerstaff, Geo Quinot and Baudouin Heuninckx all contributed to this book, all of them also regular contributors to the *Review*. The PPLR includes a section dedicated to journal articles and another on news and current issues. It has become a leading publication outlet for procurement experts and scholars, a blind peer-reviewed, Scopus-indexed journal, and is featured within the A-rated list of journals in major national academic accreditation systems, such as the Italian Anvur. The PPLR is published by Sweet & Maxwell and contains many Arrowsmith articles.

As already noted, in 1997, Sue founded the PPRG, which she served as Director until her retirement in 2020. One co-editor of this collection (Trybus) acted as her Deputy Director in Aberystwyth and Nottingham, and the other co-editor (La Chimia) succeeded her as Director of the PPRG in Nottingham in 2020. The PPRG has been the first British centre dedicated to the study, research and teaching of public procurement law and policy. It is recognised by scholars as a leading research centre across Europe and globally. The PPRG now includes nine Units specialising in different research activities, each led or co-led by different PPRG members. Many events and activities are associated with the PPRG and its members, including conferences, seminars and lectures, some of which, such as the Global Revolution series of conferences, will be discussed further below. Notably, there is the active PPRG Visiting Scholar Scheme, which has facilitated the hosting of scholars from around the world. This Scheme has strengthened collaboration among procurement scholars and fostered a community of experts in the field. Once again, it was Sue's vision that enabled the establishment of this Scheme in 2006. Originally run by Georgopoulos and La Chimia since 2006, it is now carried forward by La Chimia in her role as the new Director of the PPRG. The Scheme has hosted over 40 scholars from Asia, Africa and Europe in the past 15 years, and continues to be sought after by scholars who wants to spend a period of research in the UK. Quinot and Simovart, who contributed to this book, have both twice been visiting scholars of the PPRG.

In 1996, Sue initiated the world-leading series of conferences, *Public Procurement: Global Revolution*, in Aberystwyth and then continued them in Nottingham throughout her career. In 2010 a *Global Revolution* conference was also held in Copenhagen, co-organised and hosted by the late Steen Treumer, who sadly passed away before completing his contribution to this book. Since 2011, the conference has been organised in collaboration with Trepte, a contributor to this collection. After Sue's retirement in 2020, the conference has been taken forward by her successor, La Chimia (with Trepte), with the latest event held at the East Midlands Conference Centre in June 2022. This series of conferences has become a firm event in the agenda of the procurement community. Over the years, the series has brought together an impressive array of public procurement experts and talent from all over the world, with the latest event in 2022 attracting well over 200 participants, including 38 sessions and hosted over 100 speakers. *Global Revolution XII* will be held on 17 and 18 June 2024 in Nottingham.

Sue has been a prolific writer. Her numerous books and other publications have been extensively cited in courts in the UK, in other parts of Europe and the Court of Justice of the EU and in Asia, Africa, the Caribbean and the Americas. Her major treatise *The Law of Public and Utilities Procurement* (3rd edn, Sweet & Maxwell, 2014 (vol 1) and 2018 (vol 2)) was described in 2018 by the domestic High Court as 'the leading academic authority' and 'highly persuasive' for courts in making decisions, and it has also been cited in at least 10 other European countries. Her other authored books include (with J Linarelli and D Wallace Jr) *Regulating Public Procurement: National and International Perspectives* (Kluwer, 2000) and *Government Procurement in the WTO* (Kluwer, 2003). Her most recent edited collections include (with Luke R Butler, Annamaria La Chimia and Christopher R Yukins) *Public Procurement in (a) Crisis? Global Lessons from the COVID-19 Pandemic* (Hart Publishing, 2021); (with Peter Kunzlik) *Social and Environmental Policies in EC Procurement Law: New Directive and New Directions* (Cambridge University Press, 2009); (with RD Anderson) *The WTO Regime on Government Procurement: Challenge and Reform* (Cambridge University Press, 2011); (with S Treumer) *Competitive Dialogue in EU Procurement Law* (Cambridge University Press, 2012); and (with Geo Quinot), *Public Procurement Regulation in Africa* (Cambridge University Press, 2013). These works, as well as numerous other Arrowsmith publications, are cited repeatedly in the contributions to this book. While Sue held the title of Achilles Professor of Public Procurement Law and Policy while at the University of Nottingham, her contribution to specific aspects of EU law and international trade law would equally have merited titles in these disciplines. A constant awareness of the interplay of the national, EU and international levels of procurement law and policy are apparent in her work. Common or overarching themes of many of her contributions to our knowledge and understanding of public procurement law and policy include an emphasis on the importance of procurement training for procurement officers and a certain weariness of 'over-regulation', advocating a less regulated procurement system based on general principles combined with, again, training of the stakeholders. Moreover, she often reacted very quickly but still rigorously to major developments, such as the COVID pandemic.

Sue has taught university modules on procurement since 1995, at postgraduate and undergraduate levels. Her teaching has always fully reflected her passion for procurement law and policy; she applied to teaching the same rigour and professionalism that she applied to research, combining critical legal analysis with practical examples and case studies. Her teaching has been innovative and participatory, exhorting students to share their experiences and learn from each other, engaging them through in-class group work and presentations. She has contributed to developing the teaching of procurement around the world. She was Project Leader of the EU-funded project for developing a global academic network on procurement regulation, known as PLAN, which included setting up several university centres for teaching and research in procurement in Europe and Asia (2008–12). She also received awards from the British Academy, including a Newton Fellowship, to develop, with Quinot, this work in Africa, leading to the creation and development of a further procurement centre in Africa. Together with her colleagues at Nottingham, she set up a pioneering part-time, distance-learning programme on public procurement law and policy. The course soon became a world-leading programme, attracting students from all over the world and recognised by the EU Commission as an example of excellence. Students included high-level practitioners, policy makers, civil servants and officials of international organisations such as the World Bank and UNCITRAL. Sue was the director of the programme until her retirement, continuing to contribute to teaching and offering her assistance to the course as mentor to the new programme Director.

Sue has been supervising many research students, including the editors of this collection and many of the contributors (Davies, Craven, Heuninckx). Her students have benefited from her knowledge and guidance, often having the opportunity to work as her research assistants, gaining valuable insights into how to carry out research and organise events. For example, La Chimia was Sue's research assistant for over two years when she started her PhD in 2002, followed by others, including Ama Eyo, Silvia De Mars, Richard Craven, Paula Faustino and Serban Filipon. Sue was a conscientious supervisor, generously dedicating her time to students, never making students wait for comments on their chapters; the editors of this collection often remember submitting their chapters late at night and finding comments the next day as they switched on their PCs (La Chimia at 9:00 am, Trybus at 8.00 pm), given her well-known habit of rising early (switching on her PC at 6.00 am at the latest). While we would see our colleagues allowing themselves some rest while patiently waiting for their supervisors' comments, we were, if we wanted, ready to work on our corrections the next day. Sue often went above and beyond her role as a supervisor. In fact, she never limited herself to advising on a thesis, encouraging students to publish their work (often co-writing articles) and providing guidance on their research paths and careers. Moreover, she would take her research students to academic conferences and other events, introduce them to her national and international networks, highlight job opportunities, write reference for academic and other positions and internships, and discuss research plans for the time after the PhD she supervised – a model supervisor in all respects, even as to patience. It is no surprise that many of her former students are now academics. Her successor at the helm of the PPLR (Butler) is even the former research student of one of her former research students (Trybus). Fostering emerging talents has undeniably been a cornerstone of her tenure as a professor, exemplifying a commitment that not only imparts knowledge but also has a lasting impact. This dedication to nurturing the potential within her students has not only defined her role but has also become the very essence of her professional legacy, shaping the trajectories of countless individuals who have, in turn, contributed to a broader intellectual and academic community. The present editors have personally reaped the rewards of this invaluable support and mentorship.

During the Nottingham years, Sue's role as the leading expert in procurement law and policy consolidated. The breadth and impact of her activities also expanded, thanks to the growing group of scholars working and collaborating with her at the PPRG in Nottingham (where most of the authors in this collection – including the editors – spent their formative academic years) and around the world, when collaboration with researchers in Africa (such as Quinot), Asia (such as Wang), the Americas (such as Yukins or Linarelli) and Europe (such as Caranta or Simovart) was enabled and facilitated by the award of important research grants by national (UK) and international (EU) funding bodies.

In 2019, Sue was awarded the title of Queen's Counsel (*honoris causa*) (now King's Counsel) by Her Majesty The Queen, in recognition of her exceptional contribution to the law of England and Wales, and in 2007 she received the CIPS Swinbank Medal for thought innovation in purchasing and supply. In 2009, she was awarded the Lord Deering Award by the University of Nottingham in recognition of her world-class contribution towards enhancing students' learning experience.

This will be a collection of chapters on the reform of public procurement law and policy, written by leading academics and practitioners in the field from across the globe, all of whom have a connection to Sue as former research students (Davies, Craven, Wang, Heuninckx), colleagues (Trepte, Butler, Wang, Linarelli), important friends in relevant international organisations (Nicholas and Anderson), in the legal professions (Kotsonis and Bickerstaff) and in other universities (Caranta, Simovart, Yukins, Quinot, Gormley), many actually fitting into more than one of these 'classifications'. Authors hail not only from the UK, but also from Austria, Italy, Estonia, Belgium, China, South Africa, the USA and Canada. An important element of each contribution will be a discussion of Sue's contribution to the aspect of procurement covered in the chapter. The UK is currently going through a major reform process that shows the strong influence of Sue's thoughts. However, she worked on the Advisory Committee of the EU for procurement for many years, and had an impact on EU procurement law, on the UNCITRAL Model Law, the WTO Government Procurement Agreement and national systems, inter alia, in the US, China and South Africa. While all the authors develop their topics further and add to our understanding of the reform of public procurement law and policy, they will show how the evolution of their respective topics has been influenced by the work of Sue Arrowsmith.

There will be separate parts, with chapters on the reform of procurement law and policy in the UK, and in the EU and internationally. Certain topics, such as remedies, sustainability and defence, will be covered in more than one part, and the main objectives of public procurement, such as efficiency, value for money, non-discrimination, equal treatment, competition and transparency, will feature across the collection.

In Part I on public procurement law in the UK, Rebecca Rees addresses the question whether social value is still a secondary consideration in the UK, before Richard Craven discusses the regulation of complex procurement in the UK.

This is followed by a chapter written by Totis Kotsonis on the post-Brexit procurement remedies system in England and Wales. Roger Bickerstaff then discusses e-procurement and procurement transparency, before Luke Butler concludes Part I with a chapter on defence procurement regulation in the UK as 'A Silent Soldier in the March for Procurement Reform'. The topics sustainability (Rees), remedies (Kotsonis) and defence (Butler) are also covered in chapters by Caranta, Simovart and Heuninckx respectively in Part II on public procurement law in the EU.

Part II starts with a general assessment of the reform(s) of EU procurement law by Laurence Gormley. Then Roberto Caranta addresses the 'never secondary, forever horizontal' promises of sustainable public procurement. This is followed by contributions by Mari Ann Simovaert, on 'Arrowsmith and the Balanced Procurement Review System under EU Law', and Peter Trepte, who specifically addresses the concepts of exclusion and debarment in EU law. Baudouin Heuninckx considers the need for further reform of defence and security procurement in the EU. The topics sustainability (Caranta), remedies (Simovart) and defence (Heuninckx) mirror the individual chapters in Part I on the UK by Rees, Kotsonis and Butler, respectively.

Part III goes beyond the UK and the EU and covers procurement regulation at the international level, on the one hand, and at the regional or national level, on the other hand. This 'out of Europe' part of the book starts with a chapter by John Linarelli on the early period of globalising procurement law and policy, followed by a chapter by Robert Anderson on the WTO Agreement on Government Procurement (GPA) as a global pillar of market access, good governance, sustainability and economic reform. Arwel Davies then addresses multilateral and plurilateral national treatment obligations and discrimination in public procurement. Caroline Nicholas and Christopher Yukins discuss the reform of the UNCITRAL Model Law on Public Procurement, followed by Geo Quinot, who covers the UNCITRAL Model Law and procurement regulation in Africa. Part III and the book itself are completed by Ping Wang, who provides a critical view of 20 years of procurement reform in China.

This edited collection is the result of a friendly collaborative project. The authors have been invited to collaborate according to their expertise and connection with Sue. We assisted the authors throughout the writing process, reviewing chapters from a very early stage to ensure consistency and avoid repetitions. We held an online workshop in early January 2023, where the authors presented and discussed their papers. Each paper was assigned to a discussant for review to avoid overlaps. The workshop was an important moment for reflection and exchange, where we took stock of what we learned and where we want to be going forward. Papers were then submitted and reviewed throughout the year.

What will emerge from reading this collection is a far-reaching perspective of a continuing reform process in public procurement regulation and policy, and the contribution that Sue Arrowsmith is making to this process. Sue Arrowsmith's work has been central in the establishment and evolution of public procurement as a discipline of law. She has inspired hundreds of academics and practitioners worldwide, and her legacy will continue for many years to come. We are part of that legacy, and we are grateful to have known her, to have been taught by her and to have worked with her on numerous projects. We have learned from her rigour, her discipline and her critical thinking; we have benefitted from her generous scholarship and her encouragement when taking our first steps in academia; and with this collection we want to express our appreciation and gratitude.

PART I

National Influence: United Kingdom Public Procurement Law

2

Social Value in the UK – Still a 'Secondary' Consideration?

REBECCA REES

I. Introduction

As for many reading this chapter, Sue is inextricably linked with my passion for public procurement law. My professional experience began in 2003, when (as a trainee solicitor at Trowers & Hamlins LLP) my supervising partner, Charles Morrish, plonked Sue's 'blue bible' on my desk and told me to 'get reading'! At that time, social value was very much viewed with an air of impotency: United Kingdom (UK) contracting authorities wanted to include horizontal policies in their evaluation models but were told that 'OJEU rules'[1] prohibited it. Paradoxically, those same contracting authorities, whilst nervous about ignoring such OJEU rules by pursuing social value agendas, honoured the rules more in their breach than their observance.

Despite this, public procurement law and its commercial significance, its *potential*, had gripped me, and I signed up to attend the Global Revolution conference at the University of Nottingham in 2004. This is where I first met Sue, and I was immediately in awe of her encyclopaedic knowledge of the procurement rules and their development, her acuity across the wide-ranging number of topics under discussion, as well as her pithy and acerbic asides, giving 'short shrift' to concepts or developments she deemed ill-conceived or short-sighted.

A. A Brief Overview

Traditionally, the consideration of 'horizontal criteria' by UK contracting authorities was limited by the European Union (EU), primarily due to the concern that it could adversely affect market integration between Member States (one of the EU's

[1] The *Official Journal of the European Union* (OJEU) is an online portal that includes rules regulating the purchase by public sector bodies and certain utility sector bodies of goods, works, services or supplies in public works contracts. 'OJEU rules' is a colloquial term used previously in the UK to refer to all of the procurement rules derived from the EU Treaty.

own horizontal policies!). To that end, the pursuit of an effective and functioning internal market restricted the discretion of a contracting authority to pursue policy objectives through its procurement practices, unless it was pursuing EU-led, rather than national or local, policies.

Significant legal developments in the early 2000s resulted in the EU's recognition of a new order: one that placed more sustainable and socially focused aims at its core, rather than simply focusing on economic, internal-market-orientated objectives.[2] Nevertheless, in practice, this new order was not seized upon enthusiastically by the UK or its contracting authorities, many of which took a risk-averse approach to the shift in emphasis and did not seek to procure horizontal objectives through their procurement procedures, as further explained in section III.

II. Horizontal Policies and Criteria in Procurement: What Are They?

When we talk about horizontal policies, we are talking about those objectives that a contracting authority chooses to pursue or secure through its procurement process, even though they are not 'inherently necessary'[3] to achieve the functional objective of a specific procurement. Primarily these will be social and environmental policies, and they may include policy areas such as upskilling and training citizens, providing fair pay and work conditions, environmental and energy policies, and equality and diversity initiatives.

As Sue has commented in order to explain the phenomenon, 'the primary objective of a procurement is seen to be the purchase on competitive terms of a product, work or service meeting a particular functional need, and factors relating to horizontal policies are designated as "secondary" in the sense that they do not relate to this need'.[4]

[2] Previously the Treaty establishing the European Community (EC Treaty) (25 March 1957) had included the principle of an 'open market economy with free competition' (Art 4(1) EC); that has now been replaced with Art 3(3) of the Treaty of Lisbon [2007] OJ C306/1, expounding on the need for 'a highly competitive social market economy, aiming at full employment and social progress'. Nevertheless, it is argued that Art 114 of the Treaty on the Functioning of the European Union (TFEU) [2008] OJ C115/13 creates the legal basis for the promotion of the internal market and nothing more. Sue notes that 'it should also be recalled that the EU may not impose obligations in any area of industrial, social or environmental policy that it chooses, but can act only on matters that are within the scope of its own legal powers. This limits intervention to certain policy areas since the power to regulate Member State public procurement for the purposes of opening up public markets clearly does not extend to imposing obligations to use procurement as a policy tool for any purposes: however it is not clear that this has always been kept in mind by the EU legislature.' See S Arrowsmith, *The Law of Public and Utilities Procurement*, vol 2 (3rd edn, Sweet & Maxwell, 2018) 721, para 20-38. See also S Arrowsmith and P Kunzlik, 'Public procurement and horizontal policies in EC law: general principles' in S Arrowsmith and P Kunzlik (eds), *Social and Environmental Policies in EC Procurement Law: New Directives and New Directions* (Cambridge University Press, 2009) 9, 38–46.

[3] Arrowsmith and Kunzlik (n 2) 13.

[4] ibid. But of course Sue would now object to the use of the term 'secondary' as it connotes that they are lesser, which is not the position she adopts. See early use of this term in S Arrowsmith, *Government*

In the UK, these horizontal policies find their way into the procurement process at all of the key stages in a procurement procedure: market consultation and/or soft-market testing; advertisement (or selection of a long list of bidders); assessment of bidders/short-listing process; tender and bid evaluation/selection of preferred bidder; and contract implementation and performance management.

III. In Context: Why are Horizontal Policies Not Enthusiastically Embraced by UK Contracting Authorities?

Procurement in the UK was previously subject to European legislative intervention for decades. Sue's position has always been that the relevant procurement regulation is primarily concerned with the effective functioning of the internal market.[5] This was achieved via the EU Treaty free-movement principles and, when awarding public contracts, the relevant Procurement Directives.[6]

The Directive position, however, conferred a significant margin of discretion on the individual contracting authority as to what it seeks to procure and how it seeks to procure it, including how it will evaluate and attribute relative importance to horizontal policies. This does not mean that a contracting authority has complete *carte blanche* over the policies it pursues via a regulated procurement process: both the Treaty and the Directives sought to limit the discretion of a contracting authority to pursue horizontal policies in order to develop a single concept and the reality of the internal market in the following ways:

- Prohibiting discrimination in the procurement process itself.
- Only allowing the award of a contract through a transparent procedure, to ensure that competition is publicised to all interested suppliers and is conducted in accordance with the rules using pre-disclosed selection and award criteria.
- Removing certain restrictions that prevent bidders from other Member States from accessing the relevant market (including those that are not necessarily discriminatory but are, instead, considered disproportionate in light of the objectives pursued).

Sue previously argued that the three limitations noted above are the scope of the EU's legal competence in this respect.[7] The Treaty and the Directive(s) simply

Procurement and Judicial Review (Carswell, 1988) 81; and S Arrowsmith, 'Public Procurement as a Tool of Policy and the Impact of Market Liberalisation' (1995) 111 *LQR* 235, fn 1.

[5] See Arrowsmith (n 2) 149, para 3-16.

[6] eg Directive 2004/18/EC of the European Parliament and of the Council of 31 March 2004 on the coordination of procedures for the award of public works contracts, public supply contracts and public service contracts [2004] OJ L134/114 ('the Consolidated Directive') and Directive 2004/17/EC of the European Parliament and of the Council of 31 March 2004 coordinating the procurement procedures of entities operating in the water, energy, transport and postal services sectors [2004] OJ L134/1.

[7] Arrowsmith and Kunzlik (n 2) 30–33.

seek to deliver up and develop an internal market: no more. For example, Sue has always been clear that neither the Treaty nor the Directives regulate to ensure value for money in purchasing decisions. Instead, she rejects this view entirely and states that procurement law is simply and only concerned with the operation of the internal market:

> [S]o far as the Treaty is concerned, the free movement provisions are concerned only with hindrances to trade … not with the competitive behaviour of purchasers … [for example], the purpose of the positive obligation to advertise is to ensure monitoring of the obligation not to discriminate – it is not to ensure value for money.[8]

Whilst there are some commentators who disagreed,[9] this position simply and succinctly explains the long-running tension between procurement law and horizontal policies in the UK: because if you apply the restrictions noted above broadly, they become, in themselves, barriers to implementing horizontal policies and a source of tension between the EU and the individual Member State and, more impactfully, an individual contracting authority's interpretation of the rules and its willingness to include horizontal policy requirements within individual contract opportunities.

For example, a broad interpretation of the legal restrictions is likely to result in a very narrow scope for a Member State to pursue horizontal policies due to the potential for such policies to favour national or local firms. This is the position that has permeated UK practice for the past 30 years: that the EU's pursuit of the effective functioning of the internal market *prevents* consideration of any horizontal policy that could favour a national or local bidder.

However, Sue is not a fan of broad interpretation and supports a limited role for the Directive in balancing the interests of the internal market with a Member State's pursuit of particular horizontal policies. She notes that 'neither the Community legislator nor the ECJ [European Court of Justice] should impose its own assessment of the values pursued by horizontal policies but at the most the EC should concern itself with questions of proportionality'.[10] In other words, Sue argues that in respect of horizontal policies, Member States have the sole role in deciding how to balance them against other national policy considerations, be they social, environmental or value-for-money policies. Furthermore, that horizontal objectives should be treated on equal terms with other policies (eg the pursuit of 'value for money'). On that basis, the EU does not need to concern itself with a Member State's decisions as to how to balance those internal/domestic policies: it may intervene only when all or any of the policies undermine the internal market.

[8] ibid 33.

[9] A Sanchez-Graells, 'More Competition-Orientated Public Procurement to Foster Social Welfare' in K Thai (ed), *Towards New Horizons in Public Procurement* (PRAcademics Press, 2010) 81, 105; and see also A Sanchez-Graells, *Public Procurement and the EU Competition Rules* (Hart Publishing, 2010).

[10] Arrowsmith and Kunzlik (n 2) 36.

On the flip-side to the limitations placed on a Member State's pursuit of domestic policies, the EU has promoted the use of procurement rules by Member States to secure social and environmental objectives on an EU-wide basis. For example, crime-fighting policies via the use of mandatory and discretionary exclusion grounds include the requirement to exclude those bidders who have been convicted of corruption[11] or fraud[12] and money laundering, etc.[13] Further, the Directives explicitly acknowledged for the first time that award criteria could include social and environmental considerations.[14]

This strategic encouragement by the EU[15] to use procurement to promote and secure social and environmental objectives, coupled with a limited interpretation of the legal restrictions on including such objectives in individual contract opportunities, should have led to a more pro-active embracing of such policies within the UK procurement process. However, this has not been the case. The introduction of the Public Services (Social Value) Act 2012, which came into force on 31 January 2013, requires public sector commissioners in England (and some in Wales) to consider how they could improve the economic, environmental and social well-being of their local area through their procurement activities. This legislation has not, in practice, had a significant impact on the willingness of contracting authorities to secure social value through procurement. This is likely because the provision under the Act merely amounted to a requirement for a contracting authority to 'consider' social-value delivery in the context of public service contracts.

Whilst this consideration has assisted in raising the profile of securing social value through procurement in the UK more generally, the more impactful and effective social-value initiatives have largely been achieved through public *works* contracts (not covered by the 2012 Act). This is largely because of the long-term duration and value of such contracts, as well as the nature of the works delivered (eg, in the locality of the contracting authority's business, lending themselves to employment and skills initiatives).

Despite the introduction of the Public Services (Social Value) Act 2012, securing social value through procurement in England has been slow and patchy, and this is likely to account (at least in part) for the continued emphasis and encouragement by the UK Government (most recently in domestic circles via the post-Brexit National Procurement Policy Statement (discussed in section IV)[16] and its simple change in terminology (rather than substance) from 'Most Economically

[11] Directive 2014/24/EU of the European Parliament and of the Council of 26 February 2014 on public procurement and repealing Directive 2004/18/EC [2014] OJ L94/65, Art 57(1)(b).

[12] ibid Art 57(1)(c).

[13] ibid Art 57(1)(e).

[14] eg, see Recital 46 of the Consolidated Directive.

[15] For more in-depth analysis on the approach adopted by EU in this respect, see ch 8 of this collection.

[16] Procurement Policy Note 05/21: National Procurement Policy Statement at www.gov.uk/government/publications/procurement-policy-note-0521-national-procurement-policy-statement (3 June 2021) (accessed 23 April 2023).

Advantageous Tender' (MEAT) to 'Most Advantageous Tender' (MAT) under the Procurement Bill[17]) on UK contracting authorities' use of procurement to secure social and environmental outcomes.

IV. Where Does this Leave Us in the UK in 2024?

Notwithstanding the existing ability of contracting authorities to consider social value in their tendering practice, the post-Brexit UK Government has been keen to label a more flexible stance regarding social value as a 'post-Brexit dividend', using the move away from the 'internal market' of the EU to harness the power of public procurement and the perceived post-Brexit flexibilities to re-state the 'art of the possible' in terms of securing social and environmental outcomes and impact through public procurement.[18] This move to embrace greater flexibility was not precluded by the EU Directives, and in any event it started before the UK's withdrawal from the EU. In its (pre-Brexit) 2019 consultation,[19] the Government stated:

> The public sector must maximise social value effectively and comprehensively through its procurement. It cannot afford not to; a missed opportunity to deliver social value is a cost that has to be absorbed elsewhere in public services.

In line with Sue's original recommendations in relation to a reimagined public procurement law for the UK post-Brexit,[20] the Government has used soft-law vehicles and mechanisms to promote procurement practice that secures social and environmental outcomes. These are examined in further detail in the rest of this section.

A. National Procurement Policy Statement

Of key importance to the UK social-value agenda is the National Procurement Policy Statement (NPPS),[21] which sits alongside and supports the Procurement Bill, particularly in relation to the implementation of social-value objectives. In terms of social-value and environmental objectives, it includes three national

[17] See Cabinet Office, *Transforming Public Procurement*, CP 353 at www.gov.uk/government/consultations/green-paper-transforming-public-procurement (15 December 2020) (accessed 23 April 2023) 35.

[18] ibid 9.

[19] Cabinet Office, 'Social Value in Central Government Procurement: A consultation on how government should take account of social value in the award of central government contract' (March 2019) at www.gov.uk/government/consultations/social-value-in-government-procurement (accessed 19 October 2022).

[20] S Arrowsmith, *Transforming Public Procurement Law after Brexit: Early Reflections on the Government's Green Paper* (15 December 2020) at www.ssrn.com/abstract=3749359 (accessed 19 October 2022).

[21] See n 16.

priority outcomes. These are the relevant policy areas for a contracting authority to pursue as part of its social-value agenda, some or all of which are to be considered in the course of a regulated procurement:

- Creating new businesses, new jobs and new skills in the UK (for example, by helping new and/or small businesses grow, increasing employment opportunities where there are barriers or for those located in disadvantaged areas, and offering training opportunities).
- Tackling climate change and reducing waste (such as contributing to the reduction of greenhouse gas emissions to net zero and prioritising sustainable procurement).
- Improving supplier diversity, innovation and resilience (so as to better support start-ups, small and medium enterprises (SMEs) and voluntary, community and social enterprises (VCSEs), to increase innovation, and to modernise delivery and increase productivity).

The NPPS states that contracting authorities are not limited to the above outcomes, and are able to take into account more local, social-value and environmental priorities in their procurements.

B. Social Value Models: NHS and Central Government

Prior to the publication of the NPPS, the UK Government published a Procurement Policy Note mandating the use of the Social Value Model[22] for central government departments in England ('in-scope organisations'[23]) when determining what social-value priorities they should be considering and including within their procurements. The National Health Service (NHS) has published similar guidance, 'Applying net zero and social value in the procurement of NHS goods and services'.[24]

The Social Value Model provides that in-scope organisations should now 'explicitly evaluate' social value in their procurements, using award criteria that are related to and proportionate to the subject matter of the contract. This represented a significant change, given that previously, in-scope organisations only had to 'consider' social value in relation to services contracts pursuant to the Public Services (Social Value) Act 2012 (see section III).

[22] Procurement Policy Note 06/20: Taking account of social value in the award of central government contracts at www.gov.uk/government/publications/procurement-policy-note-0620-taking-account-of-social-value-in-the-award-of-central-government-contracts (24 September 2020) (accessed 29 April 2023).

[23] Procurement Policy Note 06/20 applies to procurements covered by the Public Contracts Regulations 2015 (SI 2015/102), and applies to all Central Government Departments, their Executive Agencies and Non Departmental Public Bodies. Together these are referred to in the PPN as 'In-Scope Organisations'.

[24] See at www.england.nhs.uk/greenernhs/publication/applying-net-zero-and-social-value-in-the-procurement-of-nhs-goods-and-services/ (23 March 2022) (accessed 29 April 2023).

Further, social value was made a mandatory award criterion. The Procurement Policy Note provides that a minimum weighting of 10 per cent of the total score should be applied in a procurement to the social-value-award criterion, to ensure that it carries enough weight to be a differentiating factor in bid evaluation. The Procurement Policy Note allows a higher weighting to be applied, if justified.

The Social Value Model sets out a list of five priority themes and eight corresponding policy outcomes that contracting authorities can use (although they do have discretion as to which ones they use for any single project). Given the publication date of the Social Value Model, neither the themes nor the corresponding policy outcomes are linked to the national priority outcomes set out in the NPPS (section IV.A), instead they are drafted to link in with the UN Sustainable Development Goals.[25]

The five key themes are as follows:

1. Covid-19 recovery;
2. tackling economic inequality;
3. fighting climate change;
4. equal opportunity; and
5. well-being.

Also included are comprehensive standardised information to accompany each of the outcomes, standard award criteria, delivery objectives that describe 'what good looks like', and metrics for contract management and reporting. Key to the approach adopted by the Social Value Model is the 'Golden Thread': that takes social values through from government priorities to the development of strategies and business cases for programmes and projects, through to procurement specifications.

The Social Value Model has been designed by the UK Government to create a standardised and complete approach to incorporating social value in a procurement for in-scope organisations. Significant detail has been provided as to everything required by an in-scope organisation to effectively incorporate the Model into its procurement documents, for example award criteria and sub-criteria, scoring rules, reporting metrics, questions and answers for bidders, etc.

This standardisation is meant to reduce burden on the Government Commercial Officers. However, the Procurement Policy Note states that the social-value element of a procurement can also be used as a differentiator. Regardless of the discretion a contracting authority has to pick and choose its own themes and outcomes, once the Social Value Model has been used, how much of a differentiator will it be? While it is undesirable to create an entire industry out of including social value in a public procurement, its inclusion in a procurement should not be reduced to a tick-box/output-led exercise – in-scope organisations will need to carry out a balancing act in order to maximise the effectiveness and impact of their social-value requirements.

[25] United Nations, *Transforming Our World: The 2030 Agenda for Sustainable Development* (A/Res/70/1), adopted 25 September 2015, 1–13.

C. Procurement Policy Notes

As suggested, now that the UK has moved away from the EU internal market, it seeks to find a new purpose for procurement. Both the NPPS and the Social Value Model were introduced via Procurement Policy Notes. Further, significant policy developments are being advanced through post-Brexit Procurement Policy Notes, including the support of SMEs,[26] the UK's transition to net zero carbon[27] and the promotion of bid hygiene.[28]

D. MAT v MEAT: Transforming Public Procurement

Introduced by the Consolidated Directive, as explained in section III, the use of award criteria to advance policy objectives is emphasised by the legislative provisions in the Procurement Bill and the removal of the 'Economic' ('E') criterion from 'MEAT', resulting in 'MAT'. As explained in the Green Paper *Transforming Public Procurement*:

> Adopting MAT (together with accompany guidance) should provide greater reassurance to contracting authorities that they can take a broader view of what can be included in the evaluation of tenders in assessing value for money including social value as part of the quality assessment. This approach is already provided for in the current regulations under MEAT, so this change would be about reinforcing and adding clarity rather than changing scope.[29]

E. Post-Brexit Separation of Law and Policy

During its journey through the Houses of Parliament, a substantial amount of discussion and lobbying focused on the requirements to recognise net zero, social value and ethical outcomes/inputs and criteria on the face of the Procurement Bill. Despite the evident support of such recognition in both Houses, the Government removed the majority of amendments that sought to achieve this. This is in line with Sue's original recommendations.

[26] See Procurement Policy Note 11/20: Reserving below threshold procurements at www.gov.uk/government/publications/procurement-policy-note-1120-reserving-below-threshold-procurements (15 December 2020; updated 3 September 2021) (accessed 29 April 2023).

[27] See Procurement Policy Note 06/21: Taking account of Carbon Reduction Plans in the procurement of major government contracts at www.gov.uk/government/publications/procurement-policy-note-0621-taking-account-of-carbon-reduction-plans-in-the-procurement-of-major-government-contracts (5 June 2021; updated 17 April 2023) (accessed 29 April 2023).

[28] See Procurement Policy Note 04/21: Applying Exclusions in Public Procurement, Managing Conflicts of Interest and Whistleblowing at www.gov.uk/government/publications/procurement-policy-note-0421-applying-exclusions-in-public-procurement-managing-conflicts-of-interest-and-whistleblowing (20 May 2021; updated 9 September 2021) (accessed 29 April 2023).

[29] *Transforming Public Procurement* (n 17) 35.

The benefits of siting social value and horizontal policies within soft law can be supported for two very practical reasons:

- Having streamlined numerous legal regimes into one piece of legislation, the Procurement Bill now covers the entire public sector: from large central government departments with immense annual budgets, to the smallest charitable housing associations and district councils, as well as universities and NHS Trusts. The social-value or net-zero carbon requirements of one authority may therefore not be the same as or bear any relation to the requirements of other contracting authorities – for example, the social-value requirements of a local authority are likely to be more place-based than those of the Ministries of Justice or Defence. To that end, the flexibility and overall efficacy of the legislative framework should be preserved by retaining a clear separation between policy and law.
- Post-Brexit, procurement policy resides within the NPPS and Procurement Policy Notes. This is not only because of the breadth of policy and the contracting authorities the relevant provisions need to cover, but also because policies around, for example, social value, net zero targets, recovery from Covid-19 are likely to change with any subsequent changes of government. Changes within the Conservative party during the passage of the Bill resulted in policy changes – for example, the emphasis on 'social value' changed to 'value for money competition', which subsequently changed to 'economic growth'. To this end, secondary legislation or guidance allows such policy aims to develop over time and be amended without the procedural hurdles that any change to the ensuing Procurement Act will require.

To conclude, the Procurement Act should be seen as the legal framework regulating how procurements are carried out and should be value- and policy-neutral to the greatest extent possible. In contrast, the key 'horizontal' or 'secondary' or 'policy' aims, outcomes and outputs to be achieved through procurement should be confined to the more flexible NPPS and related guidance. Practically speaking, it seems there would be little risk of such objectives being ignored or forgotten if allocated 'soft-law' status. If anything, they are more likely to be dynamically developed and incorporated into individual procurements if they are explained in helpful guidance.

V. Social Value: Further Challenges for the UK that Lie Ahead

A. Is it Time for a New Taxonomy?

Sue has pointed out the proliferation of terminology used to describe horizontal policies.[30] Terms such as 'sustainable development' and 'sustainable

[30] Arrowsmith (n 2) 693, para 20-01.

procurement',[31] or 'sustainable public procurement' are now commonly used, as well as 'ESG',[32] 'social value', 'green procurement' and 'corporate social responsibility', to describe the overall policy agenda (or different parts of it).

In practice, and in academic investigation, overlapping terms and terminology can cause confusion. Indeed, and as an example, I often find myself in conversation querying whether the 'social value' agenda includes 'environmental and sustainability' outcomes or whether they form part of a separate parallel agenda. The importance of words and a supporting taxonomy when seeking to describe and progress a new legal phenomenon should not be understated, and one of Sue's key contributions to this area of public procurement law has been to create a taxonomy of horizontal policies.[33]

B. Three Key Distinctions

Sue's taxonomy, as set out in 'Horizontal policies in public procurement: a taxonomy',[34] is independent of the subject matter (eg the detail of horizontal policies and what they comprise) and is based on three key distinctions, as follows.[35]

i. Policies that are Limited to Secure Compliance with General Legal Requirements and those that Go Beyond Legal Compliance

This first key distinction focuses on those requirements that oblige a contractor to comply with the legislation in force, as compared with those that oblige it to

[31] ibid. 'Sustainable procurement' has been defined by the UN Environment Programme, drawing on the UN's Sustainable Development Goals, as procurement that seeks to 'achieve the appropriate balance between the three pillars of sustainable development, ie economic, social and environmental'.

[32] At the time of writing (2023), 'environmental, social and governance' (ESG) is an extremely popular phrase in the UK when people seek to discuss horizontal agendas. It was used first in a 2004 report, *Who Cares Wins: Connecting Financial Markets to a Changing World* at www.google.com/url?sa=t&rct=j&q=&esrc=s&source=web&cd=&ved=2ahUKEwjh1ODbjeeEAxW0a0EAHZVGDJwQFnoECA8QAQ&url=https%3A%2F%2Fwww.unepfi.org%2Ffileadmin%2Fevents%2F2004%2Fstocks%2Fwho_cares_wins_global_compact_2004.pdf&usg=AOvVaw25KaC7dwtMO5wDkUEKSG_i&opi=89978449 (accessed 3 April 2023); see also *Recommendations by the financial industry to better integrate environmental, social and governance issues in analysis, asset management and securities brokerage*, which was a joint initiative of financial institutions at the invitation of the then UN Secretary-General, Kofi Annan, at www.unepfi.org/fileadmin/events/2004/stocks/who_cares_wins_global_compact_2004.pdf (accessed 29 April 2023).

[33] See S Arrowsmith, 'Horizontal policies in public procurement: a taxonomy' (2010) 10(2) *Journal of Public Procurement* 149. Sue explained that such a taxonomy is valuable: for understanding the policy implications of the legal rules; to provide a framework for subsequent legal analysis and critique; to set out clearly the key issues that need to be considered in designing effective regulatory policies; and to provide guidance for developing national policies within the EU framework; and (vice versa) to outline considerations that from an EU perspective should be considered when designing pan-EU policies for the positive use of procurement as a policy tool, highlighting those legitimate national interests that the EU must take into account when seeking to limit Member-State action in pursuit of such national policies. See also Arrowsmith and Kunzlik (eds) (n 2) 108.

[34] Arrowsmith, 'Horizontal policies in public procurement: a taxonomy' (n 33).

[35] See also Arrowsmith and Kunzlik (eds) (n 2) 109.

comply with more aspirational requirements, over and above what current legislation provides.

An example of this would be wages. Currently in the UK, a common contractual requirement of public-sector clients will be to oblige their contractors to pay their workers the 'national minimum wage' (ie the minimum wage applicable by law to all firms in the jurisdiction). However, we also see contractual requirements that oblige contractors to pay their workers the UK 'living wage' (ie a 'fair' wage that is an amount that goes beyond the national minimum).[36]

ii. Policies Concerned Only with the Performance of the Contract and those that are More General in Nature

This distinction extends the application of the horizontal policy to more general areas, beyond the public contract in question.

Taking the above example, a contracting authority may require its contractors to pay the living wage not only to those of its workers assigned to the public contract in question, but also to *all* of its workers, whether or not they are working on the public contract or another public-sector contract.

iii. Mechanisms for Implementing Policies

Sue's taxonomy sets out various mechanisms for implementing horizontal policies. She points out that one of the key elements involved in designing an effective policy is the choice of the most appropriate form of implementation for that policy. 'Most appropriate' will usually require a cost/benefit analysis, given that most horizontal policies will incur costs of one kind or another to the contracting authority.[37]

Sue identifies 10 different mechanisms:

1. the decision to purchase or not to purchase;
2. the decision on what to purchase;
3. contract conditions laid down by the purchaser;
4. packaging and timing of orders;
5. set-asides;
6. exclusion from contracts for non-compliance with government policies;
7. preferences in inviting firms to tender;
8. award criteria;
9. measures for improving access to government contracts; and
10. publicity and encouragement through contact with the market.

[36] For further details, see at www.livingwage.org.uk.

[37] Arrowsmith (n 2) 702, para 20-14: these costs can flow through to the contracting authority as additional costs to the contractors in providing the benefits (eg apprenticeships, etc), reduced competition (eg because a reduced pool of eligible bidders may be able to bid for the contract), costs accrued to the contracting authority in complying with the social or environmental policy, and procedural and other administration costs.

In the current UK marketplace, there are a number of social and environmental policies for which the choice of mechanism for implementation has already been prescribed by the UK Government for its central government departments,[38] and which it is therefore simply for the individual contracting authority to implement. Nevertheless, in the wider public sector in the UK, it will be for the individual contracting authority to make a choice as to what horizontal policy it wants to secure through procurement, as well as the mechanism by which it would like to pursue it.

C. The Need for a New Taxonomy?

Given this flexibility, a contracting authority's adoption of a taxonomy can provide clarity of thought and a consistency of analysis and approach that can support even the smallest, under-resourced contracting authority to get to grips with this increasingly important element of procurement. Further, the current taxonomy is at its most useful because it is universal: the taxonomy sits above the subject matter and detail of the horizontal policy agendas it seeks to describe.

But is there a need for a new taxonomy? By asking this question, I am not suggesting a refreshing or refurbishment of Sue's taxonomy: for all of the reasons noted above, such a taxonomy is essential, but nevertheless, as a practising solicitor, it seems to me that one of the most pressing needs we have in England, as a procurement community, is an agreed vocabulary and/or taxonomy of the various and varied horizontal policy agendas themselves.

For example, we do not have an accepted legal definition of 'social value'; we do not have a general agreement as to whether 'social value' also includes 'sustainability'; and we do not have a definition of what types of outcomes 'sustainability' includes. This means that most of the conversations we have in this space suffer from a lack of clarity and can end in a discussion of semantics rather than substance.

It is suggested that a legal definition of 'social value', coupled with an underpinning agreed taxonomy of the various industrial, social and environmental policies included in that definition, would address the current perceived lack of clarity as to the specific social-value outcome. It is important to address and

[38] See, eg, the UK Government's 'Social Value Model' in section IV.B, which uses award criteria to implement its preferred social-value policies in procurement. The use of award criteria is a very popular mechanism for implementing horizontal policies and has underpinned the Government's Social Value Model in England and associated Guidance, as well as the NPPS (explained in section IV.A). This mechanism of implementation has historically been limited by the EU Directives to only those policies that are within the scope of the contract. Mechanisms used elsewhere in the world that help secure policies that go beyond the scope of the contract, have not been generally permitted under EU-derived domestic legislation. Instead, such policies must be linked to the subject matter of the contract. Despite seeking to break this link in the Green Paper *Transforming Public Procurement* (n 17), under the current Procurement Act 2023 (see section 23(2)(a)) this link remains. Use of award criteria can also provide a mechanism for assessing the cost of the proposed policy outcomes, although we rarely see this used in the UK (see below at paragraph [D.ii]).

resolve this lack of clarity and confusion as to what social value comprises and how it should be delivered, not least because inconsistent application of the social-value agenda reduces its impact and contracting authorities' willingness to fully embrace it through their procurement practices.[39]

For example, 'well-being' is one of the five overall themes in the UK Government's Social Value Model. As part of the model award criteria that can be adopted for this theme, Criterion 'MAC 7.1' allows contracting authorities to include in their procurements the requirement for bidders to 'demonstrate action to support health and wellbeing, including physical and mental health, in the contract workforce', with the relevant sub-criteria touching on recruitment practices of the bidder, staff engagement and consultation. Whilst 'health and wellbeing' is one of the UN's Sustainable Development Goals,[40] are the Social Value Model's well-being award criteria and sub-criteria an accurate reflection of a social-value goal or do they in practice simply describe how all reasonable employers should be treating their employees in the twenty-first century? Is this really social value or is this, actually, simply complying with those general legal requirements Sue recognises in the first limb of her taxonomy?

This debate is important, because if different contracting authorities arrive at different conclusions, the social-value agenda cannot be seen as simple, straightforward or deliverable without risk of debate and/or dispute. Whilst the social-value policy agenda remains a developing one within the UK, it is often criticised as being woolly,[41] woke[42] and cynically applied.[43] One response to these criticisms would be to develop, alongside Sue's original taxonomy, a detailed, outcome-specific taxonomy, to clear the current obfuscation caused by vocabulary, thereby assisting contracting authorities to deliver up more social value and environmental impact through their procurements in a way that maximises efficiency and value-for-money outcomes.

D. Evaluation of Social Value

Whilst the UK Government has set out clearly *what* social-value outcomes it would like UK contracting authorities to secure, its guidance on *how* contracting

[39] See Cwmpa, *For Economic and Social Change: Welsh Government Social Value Review Summary Report* (June 2022).3.

[40] See at www.un.org/.

[41] A Slater and F Alexander, 'Social value is now a key component of public sector contracts, but how to define value-adding initiatives and then deliver and report on it is still a work in progress' at www.capgemini.com/gb-en/insights/expert-perspectives/delivering-social-value/ (7 July 2022) (accessed 18 August 2023).

[42] See 'Woke Government law is costing taxpayers billions every year according to new research' *Express* (13 August 2023) at www.express.co.uk/news/politics/1801766/ASI-woke-public-procurement-research (accessed 18 August 2023), referring to the Briefing Paper, Maxwell Marlow, Director of Research, Adam Smith Institute, 'The Price of Everything, the Social Value of Nothing'.

[43] Marlow (n 42) fn 35, pp 4–8.

authorities should evaluate social value remains incomplete, and this omission, it is argued, leaves contracting authorities with the discretion to adopt evaluation methodologies and scoring rules that fail to properly incorporate social-value obligations into the evaluation model and therefore fail to identify the M(E)AT. This is particularly germane when it comes to the issue of the *price* of social value, as explored further below.

i. Do Horizontal Policies Cost Anything?

As a practising solicitor, I currently see two key problems with horizontal policies and how their price is evaluated:

- Cost/benefit analysis: often the price of delivering the required/proposed horizontal policies is not requested in a financial model as part of the bid price and is therefore not disclosed nor evaluated.
- Price evaluation formulae: the way that a bid price is often evaluated in the UK (whereby the lowest price submitted by one of the bidders receives the highest marks, with the other, more expensive bids receiving a lower score on a pro rata basis) encourages bidders to hide costs or not include them in the bid price to ensure that the bid price is competitive (it is hoped, the lowest). Where social-value requirements tend to be significant and costly, a price evaluation formula that encourages lowest-price bidding does not incentivise bidders to provide full or accurate price information. This in turn results in putting the delivery of the social-value requirements under the ensuing contract at risk, in the event that the cost of them has not been factored into the bid by the bidders.

ii. Cost/Benefit Analysis

Procurement Policy Note 06/20[44] now mandates that central government departments must allocate social-value criteria at least 10 per cent of the total score. I have also seen public procurement processes where social value has been allocated 20–30 per cent of the total score. These weightings make a bidder's social-value bid proposals capable of being not just a differentiator (as was envisaged in *Nord pas de Calais*[45]) but the determinant of the contract award outcome: they are likely to make the difference between winning or losing a (sometimes) multi-million- or billion-pound contract.

Further, whereas 20 years ago the social-value requirement of a contract might have been to paint a community building or weed some local tenants' front gardens, now the social-value agendas of many contracting authorities are considerably

[44] See n 23.

[45] Case C-225/98 *Commission of the European Communities v France (Nord pas de Calais)* [2000] ECR I-07445.

more ambitious, comprising apprenticeships, employment appointments, training and skills development, the cost of which is significant. Such ambitious social-value programmes are now not the preserve of companies volunteering, sponsoring or donating money and resources; they require full-time employees of bidders to create and deliver the programmes, and they cost a significant amount. The sting in the tail is that many contracting authorities remain of the view that the social-value requirement of a contract is 'free' or should be delivered out of a bidder's profit margin. Neither of the assumptions is correct, but each one leads to some poor evaluation practices that undermine the delivery of social value under the ensuing contracts. Under some long-term repair and maintenance services, bidders have indicated to me that the contracting authority's social-value requirements cost approximately 2–3 per cent of the contract value to deliver. This level of cost is equal to the amount of profit a bidder might seek to earn under the contract, meaning that the social-value element either wipes out the profit return for the bidder or must be passed through to the contracting authority.

Current bid-evaluation models often fail to evaluate the cost to the bidder of delivering the social-value requirements, that is, the 'bid price' of the social-value requirement (which would enable a cost/benefit analysis by the contracting authority). Instead they deliver up a delivery/benefit analysis (eg, the type of social-value outcomes to be delivered and their proxy financial values).[46] This is in contrast to the other contract obligations, which are likely to be evaluated on both a price and a quality basis (eg, via a cost/benefit analysis).

Currently, the failure by contracting authorities to request and then evaluate the price of the social-value requirement as part of the overall bid risks:

(a) the contracting authority's being unaware whether or not the social-value requirements render the overall contract price unaffordable (see above); and
(b) non-delivery of the social-value programme. If a bidder will win the bid only if it puts in a low price (as is common in the UK – see section V.D.iii), it will often fail to include any social-value costs in its overall bid price.

iii. Relative Price Evaluation Formula

The way that price is evaluated in a significant majority of public procurements in the UK – via a relative price evaluation formula that awards the full allocation of marks to the lowest tender submitted[47] – compounds the risks that an enhanced social-value weighting presents to a contracting authority in identifying the M(E)AT.

[46] This is what the Social Value Portal's National Themes Outcomes and Measures (TOMs) enable: a delivery/benefit analysis rather than a cost/benefit analysis.

[47] When seeking to evaluate price, a 'relative price evaluation formula' uses prices from one or more of the bids received as the basis for evaluating each individual bid proposal (eg, in the UK, the comparator will usually be the lowest price received, but the calculations can depend on the highest, lowest or average prices). In contrast, an 'absolute' approach can use either a pre-established price set

Clause 23(3)(a) of the Procurement Bill provides that contracting authorities must now clearly describe the 'assessment' methodology they will adopt under a procurement procedure to underpin the relevant award criteria and weightings. Nevertheless, although the Government recommends to central government departments that 'relative price evaluation models should only be used with caution',[48] custom and practice in the UK mean that contracting authorities use scoring mechanisms that are described by experts as 'absolutely unsuitable to decide which tender is the most economically advantageous' and 'unprofessional'.[49]

In the third reading of the Procurement Bill, the Government chose to reject an amendment proposed by Lord Best that sought to

> [s]top the continued awarding of public contracts on a basis that gives priority to lowest price, not quality and long-term value. The relative price evaluation model … encourages poor behaviour by those bidding, asking them to provide a price that they guess will be low enough to win the contract rather than a price that is realistic for the contract to be performed.[50]

This amendment would have re-orientated contracting authorities into using price evaluation formulae that allow bidders to (more truthfully and accurately) balance, inter alia, the cost of a social-value proposal against the price submitted against it.

Currently, the social-value requirement is simply an additional delivery burden on the bidder. More often than not, the bidder must still put in the lowest price if it wants to score the highest marks. This 'race to the bottom' on price, often required by a relative pricing formula, therefore fictionalises the bid proposal: bidders will not include the cost of the social-value requirements in order to keep their bid prices low, so as to secure as many marks as possible pursuant to the price evaluation formula. This failure to include a price for the delivery of the social-value obligations is, in practice, less of a risk for the bidders in certain sectors of the UK public sector, where the absence of contract management procedures and oversight often means that a contractor's subsequent failure to deliver on social-value bid promises is not monitored by the contracting authority or its representatives, nor is it sanctioned under the ensuing contract.

by the contracting authority as the basis for evaluating each bid price, or the price submitted by the bid compared to the quality of the individual bid proposal itself, without reference to the other bid proposals submitted. A relative price evaluation formula therefore seeks to compare the price of one bid against the price of another bid or other bids.

[48] J Telgen and JB Timmer, 'Conditions for rank reversal in supplier selection' *Memoranda no 2055*, University of Twente, Department of Applied Mathematics (2016) at www.research.utwente.nl/en/publications/conditions-for-rank-reversal-in-supplier-selection.

[49] 'Unprofessional' in the sense that they show that the particular contracting authority does not know how important it considers certain cost differences in performance. J Telgen and E Manunza, 'Relative scoring mechanisms and the limits of the principles of equal treatment and transparency', presentation delivered on 12 June 2017 at the *Global Revolution* Conference at the University of Nottingham.

[50] HL Deb 14 July 2022, vol 823, col 504GC.

In the absence of such an amendment, and with the courts historically only interested in transparency and equal treatment (eg, with a focus on the procedural requirements and the transparent disclosure of criteria, weightings and methodologies), the social-value agenda in the UK is at risk of being under-evaluated, under-priced and therefore under-delivered. It is also at risk of preventing the correct identification of M(E)AT going forward, particularly where weightings and scoring rules emphasise the social-value element of a contract.

E. Contract Management Considerations

At 10–30 per cent of the total score, the social-value offer of a bid is likely to be substantial and (as noted above) will often mean the difference between the 'winning' and the 'losing' bids.

Notwithstanding the position that social-value benefits offered up in bids should be included as contractual requirements in the ensuing contract, along with remedies available to enforce such requirements,[51] it has long been the case in the UK, particularly in large infrastructure and construction contracts (where the social-value requirements tend to be both extensive and expensive), that the right to terminate the contract, omit works or levy damages or other penalties did not extend to the failure to provide the social-value outcomes: the lack of an apprenticeship or two could not be seen as serious as the failure to deliver up, say, the works within the required time-frame or to the required standard.[52] This lack of enforcement against failure to deliver promised social-value outcomes continues to this date.

But it is argued that this position is no longer tenable or sustainable: if the bidder has won a contract on the strength of its social-value proposal, why should those tender promises not be converted into contractual obligations and enforced accordingly? If the social-value obligations are then not delivered, why should the contracting authority not choose to terminate the relationship and reallocate the work to another delivery partner?

Under the new post-Brexit procurement regime in the UK, we have already seen the importance that the Government puts on effective contract management and the continuation of the procurement into the contract phase.[53] The determinative nature of the social-value offering in a bid process now needs to be

[51] See PPN 14/15 – Supporting Apprenticeships and Skills Through Public Procurement (August 2015) (accessed 23 April 2023).

[52] Even if Sue Arrowsmith is keen to label these outcomes and policies as 'horizontal', many within UK industry still see them as 'secondary' and therefore diminished in importance as compared to the 'primary' function of the contract.

[53] See the Government Commercial Function's Contract Management Capability Programme 2022/2023, updated 2 August 2023 at www.gov.uk/government/publications/civil-service-helping-you-with-managing-suppliers-and-contracts/the-contract-management-capability-programme-202223-about-the-programme-html (accessed 18 August 2023).

considered in light of enhanced contract management processes, and contracting authorities need to consider the relative importance of their social outcomes 'ask'. If a contracting authority is not prepared to terminate a contract for failure of the bidder to deliver on its social-value tender proposals, should it be allocating such proposals a significant impact within the scoring methodology?

VI. Concluding Remarks

As with all other areas of public procurement law, Sue's input into and influence in this area is so vast, so complete, that to describe the whole of her contribution in a short chapter will necessarily lead to significant omissions and cursory treatment of what has been included. Although, for us practising solicitors, Sue's pioneering approach to the effective implementation of social, environmental and other 'horizontal policies' has always been ahead of the curve, her exposition of the law and subsequent exhortation to use the procurement rules as a means by which to secure tangible outcomes have not been reflected in practice. Only now, with significant post-Brexit encouragement, are contracting authorities catching up and using the abilities and flexibilities that Sue has clearly explained have always been there in the rules themselves.

Encouraging, chiding, exasperated, but always enthusiastic and adamant that we recognise the power of procurement, Sue's contribution to the law on the implementation of industrial, social and environmental objectives remains ahead of the times.

3

Regulating Complex Public Procurement in the United Kingdom: A Case Study in Policy Failure and Learning?

RICHARD CRAVEN*

I. Introduction

The complex contracting topic relates mostly to the procurement of major capital projects, for instance Public Private Partnerships (PPP) – such as the major PPP investment programmes that have operated in the United Kingdom (UK), including the Private Finance Initiative (PFI),[1] BSF (Building Schools for the Future) and NHS LIFT (Local Improvement Finance Trust). An appropriate regulatory framework for procuring such complex public contracts is critical for national and local policymakers, as the procurement process is crucial for value for money. It is also an important concern for European Union (EU) policymakers – foreign firms can be expected to be more likely to want to tender for these invariably high-value contracts. Sue Arrowsmith has been at the heart of this legal and policy debate, and the EU and domestic regulatory systems governing complex procurement represent a major part of her scholarly work.[2]

* This chapter was written whilst I held a Leverhulme Fellowship (RF-2021-363), and I gratefully acknowledge that support.

[1] S Arrowsmith, 'Application of the UK Procurement Regulations to PFI Contracts: New Case Law' (2002) 11 *Public Procurement Law Review* NA84.

[2] S Arrowsmith, *The Law of Public and Utilities Procurement*, vol 1 (3rd edn, Sweet & Maxwell, 2014); S Arrowsmith, 'Modernising the European Union's public procurement regime: a blueprint for real simplicity and flexibility' (2012) 3 *Public Procurement Law Review* 71; S Arrowsmith, 'Implementation of the New EC Procurement Directives and the Alcatel Ruling in England and Wales and Northern Ireland: a Review of the New Legislation and Guidance' (2006) 3 *Public Procurement Law Review* 86; S Arrowsmith, 'An assessment of the new legislative package on public procurement (2004) 41(5) *Common Market Law Review* 1277; S Arrowsmith, 'The EC Procurement Directives, national procurement policies and better governance: the case for a new approach' (2002) 27(1) *European Law Review* 3; S Arrowsmith, 'Public Private Partnerships and the European Union Procurement Rules: EU policies in Conflict' (2000) 37(3) *Common Market Law Review* 709; S Arrowsmith, 'The Community's legal

A complex contract, in EU public procurement law, historically refers to a situation where an authority lacks knowledge about what products and/or services are available in the market to meet its procurement needs.[3] In contrast to off-the-shelf items, for procuring a complex contract, it is generally not practicable to ask a contracting authority to specify, upfront, its detailed technical requirements. To reduce and overcome information problems – to facilitate value for money in procurement – for complex contracts, flexibility is often desirable – in particular, to enable an authority to set out its requirements in output terms and to interact with market participants. Despite these practical needs, for EU lawmakers and policymakers (as well as academics), this process flexibility has proved contentious. Though there are commercially justifiable reasons for it,[4] it may run counter to separate regulatory objectives or tools – for example, fundamental EU procurement principles – and might risk opening the door to unlawful industrial policy, contrary to the Internal Market.

Despite the complexity of this area of law, policy and practice, Arrowsmith's scholarship focuses us on the core of the debate, where there are tensions:[5] EU law, especially as interpreted by the European Commission,[6] emphasises the principles of transparency, non-discrimination and equal treatment; but rubbing against this can be legitimate (given the legal concept of proportionality) domestic policy objectives, notably the desire to optimise value for money, that is the best price–quality ratio. This tension became pronounced in 2004, when, under the Public Procurement Directive,[7] the EU introduced a new procedure for awarding complex contracts: the competitive dialogue.

Against this backdrop, in arguing for a commercially sensible approach to the interpretation of competitive dialogue, Arrowsmith can be seen to hone her more wide-ranging critique of the EU's (legal) rules-based system and her advocacy for a form of principles-based regulation,[8] which has been so prominent,

framework on public procurement: "the way forward" at last?' (1999) 36(1) *Common Market Law Review* 13; S Arrowsmith, 'The problem of discussions with tenderers under the EC Procurement Directives: the current law and the case for reform' (1998) 3 *Public Procurement Law Review* 65; S Arrowsmith and S Treumer (eds), *Competitive Dialogue in EU Procurement* (Cambridge University Press, 2012).

[3] The Public Contracts Regulations 2006 (SI 2006/5), reg 18; Directive 2004/18/EC of the European Parliament and of the Council of 31 March 2004 on the coordination of procedures for the award of public works contracts, public supply contracts and public service contracts [2004] OJ L134/114, Art 1(11)(c).

[4] In relation to this point, Arrowsmith often draws attention to a relational approach that is favoured in private practice – see, eg, S Arrowsmith, 'Reimagining public procurement law: proposals for post-Brexit reform' [2021] *Public Law* 69, 71, citing D Parker and K Hartley, 'The Economics of Partnership Sourcing versus Adversarial Competition: a critique' (1997) 3 *European Journal of Purchasing and Supply Management* 115.

[5] Arrowsmith, 'Public Private Partnerships and the European Union Procurement Rules (n 2).

[6] See, eg, European Commission, Explanatory Note – Competitive Dialogue – Classic Directive (Directorate General Internal Market and Services, 2005).

[7] Directive 2004/18/EC (n 3).

[8] Arrowsmith, 'Modernising the European Union's public procurement regime' (n 2); S Arrowsmith, 'The Past and Future Evolution of EC Procurement Law: from Framework to Common Code?' (2006) 35

post-Brexit, in the debate about why and how the UK should regulate public procurement.[9]

Focusing on this UK experience, this chapter tells the story of regulatory policymaking on the competitive dialogue.[10] From a UK perspective, this is fundamentally a story about the failure of a policy approach that depended on prescriptive legal rules. It is also about policy learning and the evolution of the EU's and UK's regulatory approach.[11]

II. Rules and Discretion

At its core, the discussion in this chapter is about the appropriate balance, within a regulatory system on public procurement, between formal legal rules and administrative discretion. Before getting started properly, therefore, please allow me a brief detour from the main topic – complex contracting – to reflect on where we might situate Arrowsmith's work within the 'rules versus discretion' debate in the general scholarship on administrative law. For these purposes, Davis provides a straightforward definition of discretion:[12] it is 'the power … to make a choice among possible courses of action or inaction'.[13] By enacting legal rules, lawmakers may attempt, to varying degrees, to constrain or structure the scope for discretionary decision-making; however, discretion is inevitable and pervasive in any legal system.[14]

How we regard discretion, and how we think lawmakers should deal with discretion, depends heavily on how we conceptualise public law. Harlow and Rawlings, relating the work of Cassese[15] to the Anglo-American common law context, identify two opposing traditions in public law scholarship.[16] The first

Public Contracts Law Journal 337; Arrowsmith, 'The problem of discussions with tenderers under the EC Procurement Directives' (n 2).

[9] Arrowsmith (n 4).

[10] The chapter refers throughout to the UK, but most of the domestic legislative references are to the law in England, Wales and Northern Ireland. The legislation is different in Scotland due to the Scotland Act 1998, s 29. There are also some public procurement policy differences between England, Wales, Northern Ireland and Scotland.

[11] For an overview of this analytical approach, see C Dunlop (ed), *Policy Learning and Policy Failure* (Policy Press 2020); PJ May, 'Policy Learning and Failure' (1992) 12(4) *Journal of Public Policy* 331.

[12] K Culp Davis, *Discretionary Justice: A Preliminary Inquiry* (University of Illinois Press, 1969) 4.

[13] ibid.

[14] See in particular JL Jowell, *Law and Bureaucracy: Administrative Discretion and the Limits of Legal Action* (Dunellen, 1975); DJ Galligan, *Discretionary Powers: A Legal Study of Official Discretion* (Clarendon, 1986); K Hawkins, *The Uses of Discretion* (Oxford University Press, 1995); J Black, *Managing Discretion* (ARLC Conference Papers, 2001).

[15] S Cassese, 'Le droit tout puissant et unique de la société: Paradoxes of Administrative Law' (2010) 22(1) *European Review of Public Law* 1105.

[16] C Harlow and R Rawlings, 'Populism and Administrative Law' LSE Legal Studies Working Paper No 12/2023 at https://ssrn.com/abstract=4414379, 12, forthcoming in E Carolan, JNE Varuhas and S Fulham-McQuillan (eds), *The Making and Re-Making of Public Law* (Hart Publishing). Elsewhere, Harlow and Rawlings refer instead to what they term 'red light theory' and 'green light theory' – see C Harlow and R Rawlings, *Law and Administration* (3rd edn, Cambridge University Press, 2009).

of these, a 'control model', refers to a traditional liberal notion of public law. In the control model, public law is 'a bridle for Leviathan', representing an external protection from abuse of state power.[17] Daintith, writing in the early 1980s, noted that, for a leading textbook writer, Wade, public law 'has for its only object "to keep the powers of government within their legal bounds" and to prevent "powerful engines of authority" from "running amok"'.[18] Administrative discretion, from such a perspective, is to be regarded as 'inherently arbitrary' and a source of 'executive tyranny' and injustice.[19]

The control model, above, may be contrasted with an 'instrumentalist' model – where public law is one instrument that the state can use to implement its policy objectives. Daintith argued that, to complement and correct the control model, one must foreground the aims and activities of government.[20] This involves starting from government policy, not constitutional principles, and asking 'what demands government makes of the constitutional and legal systems in seeking to achieve its objectives, how those systems respond to those demands, and what problems those responses create for government and for the citizen'.[21] In this regard, an instrumentalist model is able to provide a public law explanation of how state power was employed to bring about the post-war welfare state. Generally, from an instrumentalist perspective, there was a preference for democratic controls rather than legal controls (the courts), and discretion – instead of a problem for public law – was appreciated as a necessary and valuable part of policy implementation.[22] Harlow and Rawlings note that, for Ganz, it was 'for Parliament to allocate decision-making functions and … this settlement should not be disrupted', and that, to enable value judgements on a case-by-case basis, 'it might be necessary "to lay down rules embodying very broad standards [and] conferring wide discretionary powers"'.[23] Recognising that the state also has recourse to non-legal regulatory instruments, these public law scholars, looking beyond the common law rules and principles, took an interest in financial tools, like subsidies[24] and procurement,[25] and informational tools, like government guidance (soft law).[26]

It is within this institutionalist tradition that I would locate much of Arrowsmith's scholarship. However, for understanding public law in modern times, Harlow and Rawlings' models lack the same conceptual appeal.[27] This is

[17] HW Arthurs, 'Rethinking Administrative Law: A Slightly Dicey Business' (1979) 17(1) *Osgoode Hall Law Journal* 1, 3, quoted by T Prosser, 'Towards a Critical Public Law' (1982) 9(1) *Journal of Law and Society* 1, 3.

[18] TC Daintith, 'Legal Analysis of Economic Policy' (1982) 9(2) *Journal of Law and Society* 191.

[19] See C Harlow, 'Back to basics: reinventing administrative law' [1997] (Sum) *Public Law* 245, 249.

[20] Daintith (n 18) 192.

[21] ibid.

[22] Harlow (n 19) 249.

[23] G Ganz, 'Allocation of Decision-Making Functions' [1972] *Public Law* 215, 216, quoted in Harlow and Rawlings, *Law and Administration* (n 16) 41.

[24] G Ganz, *Government and Industry* (Professional Books, 1977).

[25] T Daintith, 'Regulation by Contract: The New Prerogative' (1979) 32(1) *Current Legal Problems* 41.

[26] G Ganz, *Quasi-legislation: recent developments in secondary legislation* (Sweet & Maxwell, 1987).

[27] Harlow and Rawlings, 'Populism and Administrative Law' (n 16) 17–19.

primarily due to the way in which traditional public administration has been 'reinvented' since the late-1970s onwards.[28] In this time, amongst other developments, new public management reforms,[29] inspired by private corporate practices and underpinned by the logic of market liberalism, engendered a regulatory state, which, at least initially, was based upon command and control.[30] It is against this backdrop that, in the UK, public procurement law began to materialise.[31] From the 1990s onwards, public procurement regulation would grow in importance, as the European Internal Market project advanced, and formal legal rules came to be seen as the primary instrument for constraining the industrial policy space of European Member States – discretion could not be trusted.[32]

Arrowsmith's scholarship does not accept as given the appropriateness of controlling administrative discretion via hard law. Instead, in Arrowsmith's work, law is one policy instrument that has advantages and disadvantages,[33] and, as such, whether to regulate using legal rules should be decided on a context-specific basis. Thus, grounded on a thorough understanding of policy and practice,[34] Arrowsmith is critical of the level of detail and prescriptiveness of EU public procurement, expressing concerns about how, in the UK, legal compliance can often become an objective in itself – one that distracts from other legitimate procurement objectives, like value for money.[35] In keeping with an instrumentalist frame – instead of casting government as 'bumbler or villain',[36] which is typical in many models of government buying, Arrowsmith's scholarship tends to advance a less cynical view of public procurement officials: they are professionals, possessing commercial expertise, and, as such, where appropriate, it is desirable to enable them: '[limitations] upon the discretion of procurement officers … [can] have the effect of limiting the possibility for purchasers to procure in accordance

[28] ibid.

[29] C Hood, 'A Public Management for All Seasons' (1991) 69(1) *Public Administration* 3.

[30] For a recent discussion of this, see R Schmidt and C Scott, 'Regulatory discretion: structuring power in the era of regulatory capitalism' (2021) 41(3) *Legal Studies* 454. See also G Majone, 'The Rise of the Regulatory State in Europe' (1994) 17(3) *West European Politics* 77; M Loughlin and C Scott, 'The Regulatory State' in P Dunleavy et al (eds), *Developments in British Politics* (Macmillan, 1997).

[31] See, eg, the Local Government Act 1988, pt II.

[32] See P Kunzlik, 'Neoliberalism and the European Public Procurement Regime' in C Barnard et al (eds), *Cambridge Yearbook of European Legal Studies* (Hart Publishing, 2013) 283.

[33] The general literature on this is significant. See in particular W Twining and D Miers, *How to Do Things with Rules* (5th edn, Cambridge University Press, 2012); R Baldwin, 'Why Rules Don't Work' (1990) 53(3) *Modern Law Review* 321; J Black, '"Which Arrow?": Rule Type and Regulatory Policy' [1995] *Public Law* 94; T Endicott, 'The Value of Vagueness' in V Bhatia et al (eds), *Vagueness in Normative Texts* (Land, 2005) 27; J Jowell, 'The Legal Control of Administrative Discretion' (1973) 18 *Public Law* 178.

[34] See, eg, S Arrowsmith, 'The Purpose of the EU Procurement Directives: Ends, Means and the Implications for National Regulatory Space for Commercial and Horizontal Policies' in C Barnard et al (eds), *The Cambridge Yearbook of European Legal Studies* (Hart Publishing, 2012) 1.

[35] S Arrowsmith, J Linarelli and D Wallace Jr , *Regulating Public Procurement: National and International Perspectives* (Kluwer Law International, 2000) 76.

[36] J Sekera, 'The public economy: Understanding government as a producer: A reformation of public economics' UCL Institute for Innovation and Public Purpose (IIPP) Working Paper Series: IIPP WP 2020-01, 1.

with best commercial practice'.[37] Like many instrumentalists, Arrowsmith's work is also attentive to the wider regulatory system, and the alternatives to legal rules, like informational tools:

> [O]btaining value for money is not ... mainly ... a question of following the formal steps laid down for issuing and assessing bids, but requires the exercise of wise commercial discretion ... Whilst this discretion can be circumscribed to some degree by formal rules, even in the most rigid systems these can never entirely replace subjective judgment. To ensure discretion is exercised wisely, proper training and recruitment of procurement personnel is vital.[38]

This includes the importance of soft law – non-binding rules – to policy implementation in the UK context, which is particularly relevant for complex procurement, the subject of this chapter, where the application of the law to practical situations becomes more complicated. Discussing the implementation of EU public procurement law in the UK, Arrowsmith regularly reminds us that the UK Government has traditionally preferred to rely on non-binding advice and guidance over formal legal rules to achieve its regulatory policy objectives.[39]

The discussion now turns to look at the evolving balance between legal rules and discretion in the regulation of complex procurement in the UK.

III. Policies in Conflict?

The introductory discussion in sections I and II provided some of the background for understanding the policy debate on why and how governments regulate complex procurement, and specifically Arrowsmith's position – arguing for flexibility in the interpretation and application of the EU rules governing UK PPP/PFI procurement.[40]

For a straightforward procurement, where the authority has a sufficiently detailed understanding of what it wants to buy, on paper, the various procurement objectives are in harmony – in the sense that EU/UK rules pursuing transparency, non-discrimination and equal treatment can be expected to facilitate (or to not obstruct) competition and domestic value-for-money objectives. The standard award procedures – the open and restricted procedure – are designed with this in mind, and these procedures adopt a relatively rigid legal structure. In a restricted procedure,[41] for instance, an authority must, upfront, specify its precise requirements, a minimum of five bidders should be invited to submit tenders in

[37] Arrowsmith, Linarell and Wallace (n 35) 75.

[38] ibid 19.

[39] See, eg, S Arrowsmith, 'Implementation of the New EC Procurement Directives and the Alcatel Ruling in England and Wales and Northern Ireland: a Review of the New Legislation and Guidance' (2006) 3 *Public Procurement Law Review* 86.

[40] Arrowsmith, 'Public Private Partnerships and the European Union Procurement Rules' (n 2).

[41] Public Contracts Regulations 2015, reg 28.

accordance with those specifications,[42] and the scope for any pre- and post-tender negotiations is tight.[43]

The same approach to transparency, non-discrimination and equal treatment, in general, is not suitable in a complex procurement. In these situations, there is likely to be greater tension between different procurement objectives. In complex procurements, though the authority has a procurement need, it lacks knowledge about how its needs can be met. It is not well placed, at the outset of a procurement, to specify its technical, legal and financial requirements, and would benefit from flexibility to work with bidders, to develop its requirements in line with what the market is able to deliver. In addition, administering and participating in a complex procurement can be resource intensive, with a risk that high procedural costs will deter bidder participation. Consequently, it can be impracticable to expect a high number of bidders (eg at least five bidders, as the restricted procedure's rules require) to work up complete final tenders and for an authority to scrutinise each of these.[44]

Prior to 2004, UK practice developed, in accordance with a commercial approach, in such a way as to navigate the above challenges. The UK's PFI procurement practice relied on recourse to the negotiated procedure with a contract notice (henceforth 'the competitive negotiated procedure').[45] This is an unstructured procedure, compared to the open and restricted procedures, which, importantly, provides scope for authority-bidder negotiations.[46] The PFI procurement practice involved the structuring of negotiations into bidding rounds, enabling an authority to whittle down the number of bidders, round by round, to home in on its preferred bidder. Having identified its preferred bidder, with just one bidder left in the process, further negotiations would then take place to agree the final contract. A persuasive commercial justification for preferred-bidder negotiations is that, in addition to reducing the workload for contracting authorities, only one bidder, the winning bidder, need incur the cost of pulling together the details of the deal. However, understandably, these preferred-bidder negotiations were contentious. For some, like the Commission, such negotiations lacked transparency and potentially opened the door to unlawful discrimination. In practice, the negotiations, which took place under limited competitive tension, could become extensive, and because funders are typically only prepared to get involved at a late stage, changes, sometimes significant changes, would frequently be made to a preferred bidder's offer.[47]

[42] Public Contracts Regulations 2015, reg 42.

[43] Public Contracts Regulations 2015, reg 65(3).

[44] Arrowsmith, 'Public Private Partnerships and the European Union Procurement Rules' (n 2) 722; E Aspey and R Craven, 'Regulating Complex Contracting: A Socio-legal Study of Decision-Making Under EU and UK law' (2018) 81(2) *Modern Law Review* 191.

[45] See P Braun, *The Practical Impact of EU Public Procurement Law on PFI Procurement Practice in the United Kingdom* (PhD thesis, University of Nottingham, 2001).

[46] Public Contracts Regulations 2006, regs 13 and 17.

[47] See House of Commons Committee on Public Accounts, *HM Treasury: tendering and benchmarking in PFI Sixty-third Report of Session 2006–07* (2007) 5.

Dissatisfied with the transparency and openness of UK PFI procurement practice, the Commission eventually brought a challenge against the UK Government, arguing that, in the PFI context, the competitive negotiated procedure was used inappropriately.[48] It was eventually accepted, however, even by the Commission, that to better cater for complex procurement, EU public procurement law needed reform.

In 2004, EU legal reforms, transposed into UK law in 2006,[49] introduced a new award procedure: competitive dialogue. This procedure was, in essence, a compromise for 'particularly complex contracts': contracts 'where a contracting authority is not objectively able to – (a) define the technical means … capable of satisfying its needs or objectives; or (b) specify either the legal or financial make-up of a project or both'.[50] It incorporated a degree of flexibility. At the outset of the process, rather than full technical specifications, the authority was only required to publish its 'needs and requirements',[51] and could later invite a minimum of three qualifying bidders to participate in a dialogue stage, where there was scope 'to discuss all aspects of the contract with bidders'.[52] In keeping with past UK PFI procurement practice, the dialogue stage could be structured into rounds in order to reduce the number of proposals under discussion.[53] In addition, during the dialogue stage, the authority was expressly required to treat bidders equally and to respect bidder confidentiality, unless agreed otherwise.[54]

Adding greater structure to PFI procurement practice, at the end of the dialogue stage, which had to be brought formally to a close when the authority could 'identify one or more solutions … capable of meeting its needs',[55] an authority was required to hold a final tendering round. Here, tenders needed to be much more developed than in the past – containing 'all the elements required and necessary for the performance of the project on the basis of any solution presented and specified during the dialogue'.[56] After the close of dialogue, there was limited scope for further discussions, other than in relation to clarifying, specifying or fine-tuning final tenders,[57] and when the authority had identified the most economically advantageous tender, there was only scope to clarify aspects of that tender or confirm commitments.[58]

In appearing to combine the flexibility of the negotiated procedure with the structure and transparency of the standard procedures, on paper, the competitive dialogue may seem like an ideal compromise position for a complex PFI

[48] European Commission, Single Market News No 23 (October 2000).
[49] Arrowsmith (n 39).
[50] Public Contracts Regulations 2006, reg 18(1).
[51] Public Contracts Regulations 2006, reg 18(5).
[52] Public Contracts Regulations 2006, reg 18(21)(a).
[53] Public Contracts Regulations 2006, reg 18(22).
[54] Public Contracts Regulations 2006, reg 18(21)(b) and (c).
[55] Public Contracts Regulations 2006, reg 18(24).
[56] Public Contracts Regulations 2006, reg 18(25).
[57] Public Contracts Regulations 2006, reg 18(26).
[58] Public Contracts Regulations 2006, reg 18(28).

procurement. Sections IV and V, however, reflect upon the transposition of the 2004/2006 version of competitive dialogue in the UK, including the apparent deficiencies of competitive dialogue.

IV. The Rise of Competitive Dialogue

This section discusses one aspect of the UK transposition of 2004/2006 competitive dialogue: the procedure's availability. The 2006 UK rules on competitive dialogue, adopting the definition in the 2004 Directive, confined the procedure's use to the procurement of 'particularly complex contracts' when the open or restricted procedure will not allow award of the contract.[59] However, with multiple facets to a complex contract – technical, legal and financial – and with this complexity existing on a spectrum – ranging from the straightforward to the exceptionally complex – competitive dialogue's availability evidently gave rise to a significant legal grey area. The section is entitled 'The Rise of Competitive Dialogue' because, early on, practitioners took advantage of the legal ambiguity, resulting in significant uptake in the use of the procedure following its 2006 introduction into UK law. The UK quickly became one of the highest users of competitive dialogue in the EU. De Mars and Craven report that between 2006 and 2009, UK authorities published 1,380 adverts referring to contracts to be procured under competitive dialogue.[60] By comparison, whilst France had a similarly high number, 1,430, elsewhere the numbers were much lower: in the same period, in Germany there were 129 such adverts, in the Netherlands 84 and in Spain 30.[61]

In relation to PPP/PFI procurement, the Commission had provided a strong steer to discourage the use of the competitive negotiated procedure, and this fed through into UK policy, according to which the competitive negotiated procedure was to be used only in 'truly exceptional circumstances'.[62] In the UK, competitive dialogue therefore replaced the negotiated procedure as the standard procedure for PPP/PFI procurement. The use of the competitive negotiated procedure fell dramatically, whilst there was an explosion in use of competitive dialogue.[63]

In addition to replacing the negotiated procedure for PFI/PPP procurement, high use of competitive dialogue in the UK also appeared to be a result of its use for contracts that would have been procured under the restricted procedure

[59] Public Contracts Regulations 2006, reg 18(1).

[60] S De Mars and R Craven, 'An analysis of use of competitive dialogue in the EU' in Arrowsmith and Treumer (eds) (n 2) 144, 152.

[61] ibid 152.

[62] Office of Government Commerce (OGC), *Procurement policy: information note 04/06–31 July 2006: practical guidance on the use of competitive dialogue* (2006) 3; OGC and HM Treasury, *Competitive dialogue in 2008: OGC/HMT joint guidance on using the procedure* (2008) paras 3, 8 and 9.

[63] De Mars and Craven (n 60).

in the previous regime – that is, procurements with a degree of complexity that might benefit from some dialogue, but for which the negotiated procedure had been perceived to be legally unavailable. For the UK Government, this usage of competitive dialogue – where, in its view, the 'particularly complex contract' threshold was not met – was inappropriate but prevalent – amounting to close to 30 per cent of a sample of 210 competitive dialogue procurements it analysed.[64]

Aspey and Craven explain that this 'overuse' of competitive dialogue was down to strategic decision-making.[65] Authorities benefited from using competitive dialogue over the restricted procedure (eg, in terms of its flexibility), and though there may have been an element of legal risk to using competitive dialogue when it was not permitted, in general the risk of legal consequences was minimal. In the UK, the enforcement and remedies system primarily depends on the general court system, and, according to empirical research, significant obstacles act to disincentivise litigation,[66] including the cost of litigation and restrictive time limitations for initiating legal action. A bidder was unlikely to feel sufficiently aggrieved to complain, let alone commence legal proceedings, due to a questionable choice by an authority to use competitive dialogue – a technical breach of the procurement rules that would occur at an early stage in the process.

For the Government, competitive dialogue's use 'as [a] default process for all but the most straightforward procurements'[67] was problematic, leading to unnecessary meetings and lengthier and costlier procurement. To achieve efficiency savings, government policy changed, and guidance in 2012 set out a presumption against the use of competitive dialogue, pushing authorities instead towards the restricted procedure.[68]

V. The Fall of Competitive Dialogue: Why was Competitive Dialogue a Policy Failure?

The next aspect of 2004/2006 competitive dialogue to be discussed concerns the permissibility of post-dialogue negotiations. In this section, competitive dialogue is presented as an (instrumental) policy failure, in that it did not achieve, effectively, the purpose its proponents sought to achieve.

[64] Cabinet Office, *Accelerating Government Procurement* (February 2011) 7.

[65] Aspey and Craven (n 44) 201–08.

[66] D Pachnou, 'Bidder remedies to enforce the EC procurement rules in England and Wales' (2003) 1 *Public Procurement Law Review* 35; D Pachnou, 'Bidders' use of mechanisms to enforce EC procurement law' (2005) 5 *Public Procurement Law Review* 256; S Arrowsmith and Craven, 'Public procurement and access to justice: a legal and empirical study of the UK system' (2016) 6 *Public Procurement Law Review* 227.

[67] HM Treasury, *HM Treasury Review of Competitive Dialogue* (November 2010) 10.

[68] Cabinet Office, *Procurement policy note – procurement supporting growth: supporting material for departments* (May 2012).

From an EU perspective, post-tender negotiations potentially run counter to the procurement principles, transparency, equal treatment and non-discrimination – for example, because of a risk of unfairness if the negotiations either lead to changes in bidder tenders or if the call for tenders changes. Under the 2004/2006 rules, following the formal close of the procedure's dialogue stage, the bidders remaining in the process would be invited to submit final tenders. These final tenders needed to be complete, covering 'all the elements required and necessary for the performance of the project'.[69] The authority would then be able to award the contract to the most economically advantageous tender, and in theory, the conclusion of the contract could flow swiftly and straightforwardly after that. However, because of the nature of the contracts being procured, a requirement for complete final tenders was impracticable. There are legitimate commercial and practical reasons why bidders, even at a late stage in the process, must leave some aspects of proposals outstanding. From the point of view of a bidder, it is likely to be reluctant to incur the resource costs that pulling together all the detail of a proposal may entail, which might be substantial, especially when there are no guarantees that that bidder will win. There has also been a problem, where private finance is involved, that funders (banks) will only become seriously involved after the award of the contract, and for the project to go ahead, they may want to make changes to the deal that has been agreed to ensure that they are lending on terms suitable to them. Taking this into account, the rules permitted an authority to request a bidder to 'clarify, specify or fine-tune' its final tender, provided this work did not go as far as to make 'changes to the basic features of the tender or the call for tender when those variations are likely to distort competition or have a discriminatory effect'.[70] In relation to the most economically advantageous tender, there was also scope for an authority to ask for clarifications or the confirmation of commitments in the tender, so long as this did not 'have the effect of modifying substantial aspects of the tender or of the call' and did not 'risk distorting competition or causing discrimination'.[71]

The rules on post-dialogue negotiations attempt to delineate lawful changes to a winning bid from unlawful changes. The problem here, for lawmakers, is that this type of legal rule is not something that can be drafted with exact precision. Mistakes are inevitable, and in such situations, lawmakers should reflect on what type of mistake is preferable: if underinclusive, some instances of undesirable conduct may escape from the scope of rule; and if overinclusive, instances of legitimate behaviour may be caught.

In the UK, the prohibition was often interpreted in an overinclusive way, shifting negotiations that under the negotiated procedure might have been carried out at a late stage in the process, with just one bidder, to an earlier point in the competition. The consequence was that legitimate tender modifications, for example

[69] Public Contracts Regulations 2006, reg 18(25)(b).
[70] Public Contracts Regulations 2006, reg 18(26).
[71] Public Contracts Regulations 2006, reg 18(28).

that were needed through no fault on the part of the authority and for which rewinding the process would be unduly costly, were perceived to generate excessive legal risk.[72] For the most part, given the procedure's wide usage, this may have been unproblematic. However, whilst the legal framework on competitive dialogue may have been operating well for certain complex contracts, for the more complex end of the spectrum of complex contracts, the legal framework was often perceived to be insufficiently flexible. This gave rise to perceptions of non-compliance, as procurement practice could not hold to narrow interpretations of the law, and, for authorities with a low appetite for legal risk, inefficient buying.

Though on choice of procedure the risk of challenge was, in general, perceived to be low, this was not so in the latter stages of a competitive dialogue process. By this point, bidders had more to lose from a breach of the rules, having invested significant time and money in their bids, providing a stronger incentive to complain and challenge.[73] The problem with a restrictive legal framework was exposed by the financial crisis and in the recession that followed it. Aspey and Craven draw upon the notion of a 'state of exception' to capture the way in which a crisis situation made a more flexible interpretation of the legal rules practically necessary.[74] This was reflected in UK soft law, which, by 2008, promoted a pragmatic approach: there was a need to 'balance the legal requirements with the need to achieve contract signature while operating in a world where change[s] can occur'.[75]

VI. Policy Learning?

It is not inevitable that a policy failure, like that discussed in section V, will be followed by policy learning. Nevertheless, Caranta, writing about the 2014 reforms to the EU's public procurement Directives, celebrates how the participatory aspects of EU law-making enabled the practical experience of Member States and contracting authorities to feed into the evolution of the legal regulation on complex procurement.[76] Caranta points out that these practical insights are noticeable in the Green Paper ahead of the reforms: '[A]uthorities sometimes complain that the regulatory instruments provided by the EU rules are not fully adapted to their purchasing needs. In particular, they claim that leaner and/or more flexible procedures are needed.'[77] The recitals to the 2014 Directive thus recognise 'a great need for contracting authorities to have additional

[72] Aspey and Craven (n 44) 208–19.
[73] ibid 211–13.
[74] ibid 216–19.
[75] OGC and HM Treasury (n 62) para 5.5.8.
[76] R Caranta, 'The changes to the public contract directives and the story they tell about how EU law works' (2015) 52(2) *Common Market Law Review* 391, 450–55.
[77] European Commission, Green Paper: on the modernisation of EU public procurement policy: Towards a more efficient European Procurement Market (COM(2011)15 final) 12; Caranta (n 76) 451.

flexibility to choose a procurement procedure, which provides for negotiations',[78] and resultingly, in the name of 'simplification' and 'flexibilisation', the procedures for complex procurement, and the relationship between them, were reformulated.[79]

The reform package were quickly copied out by the UK Government and transposed into domestic law.[80] However, despite evident learning and policy evolution, path-dependent EU lawmakers could not shake a general cynicism towards authority–bidder negotiations, evident in the legal rules.[81] Thus, from a UK perspective, whilst EU law-makers granted flexibility with one hand – the requirement for a 'particularly complex contract' was removed and the availability of competitive dialogue was clarified by the inclusion of a series of alternative usage grounds[82] – they appeared to take with the other – the old negotiated procedure was stripped out, and competitive dialogue was twinned with a new 'competitive procedure with negotiation'.[83] The two procedures, competitive dialogue and the competitive procedure with negotiation, share the same availability grounds.[84]

With considerable overlap between competitive dialogue and the competitive negotiated procedure, and, from a UK perspective, a lack of clarity over the relationship between the two procedures – in particular, relating to what the competitive procedure with negotiation offered that was not possible under a competitive dialogue procedure – the simplification goal of the reforms was, arguably, undermined.[85] Davey, writing from the perspective of a UK legal practitioner, speculated that, in line with a tendency to 'stick with what you know', for places like the UK, where use of competitive dialogue was well established, the competitive procedure with negotiation was at risk of being shunned in favour of the familiar.[86]

Despite the ambiguity, in practice,[87] the competitive procedure with negotiation does appear to have become a procedure for contracts that, in the previous regime, might have been recognised to be at the lower end of the complex contract threshold – that is, contracts where, at the outset, an authority is not clear that negotiations are necessary.[88] This is compatible with the UK Government's lean

[78] Directive 2014/24/EU of the European Parliament and of the Council of 26 February 2014 on public procurement and repealing Directive 2004/18/EC [2014] OJ L94/65, recital 42.

[79] Directive 2014/24/EU, Arts 29 (competitive procedure with negotiation) and 30 (competitive dialogue).

[80] Public Contracts Regulations 2015, regs 29 and 30.

[81] Jonathan Davey, 'Procedures Involving Negotiation in the New Public Procurement Directive: Key Reforms to the Grounds for use and the Procedural Rules' (2014) 23 *Public Procurement Law Review* 103, 109.

[82] Public Contracts Regulations 2015, reg 26(4).

[83] Public Contracts Regulations 2015, regs 26(4), 29 and 30.

[84] Public Contracts Regulations 2015, reg 26(4).

[85] Davey (n 81); Arrowsmith, *The Law of Public and Utilities Procurement*, vol 1 (n 2) ch 9.

[86] Davey (n 81) 109.

[87] Government Commercial Function, *Guidance Note: Competitive Dialogue and Competitive Procedure with Negotiation* (May 2021).

[88] ibid 8; Arrowsmith, *The Law of Public and Utilities Procurement*, vol 1 (n 2) ch 9.

procurement policy, which was intent on reducing recourse to competitive dialogue (see section IV). Under the competitive procedure with negotiation, if, at the outset, an authority expressly reserves the right to award via a single tendering phase, it is not compelled to negotiate, and can fall back on the legal rules to refuse any bidder attempts to open a negotiation. At the same time, if, following the initial tenders, it appears that negotiations might be beneficial, flexibility remains for the authority to enter into negotiations. In a competitive dialogue, by contrast, there must be a dialogue stage that continues until the authority can identify the solution or solutions that is or are capable of meeting its needs (as in the 2006 Regulations).[89] As such, although a dialogue stage is flexible and can be structured in different ways, a competitive dialogue may be more appropriate where the need/desire for a discussion between the authority and bidders is more certain – which, in the previous regime, might have been for those contracts closer to the top end of the complexity threshold. Nevertheless, an evident attraction of competitive dialogue is that there is express legal scope relating to the further work that can be undertaken in the post-close-of-dialogue stages.[90] There is no such wording in the rules on the competitive procedure with negotiation.

Differing from the incremental learning already discussed, the decision of the UK to leave the EU, which ultimately took place in January 2020, generated a much more radical policy rethink. The 'bureaucracy' of EU public procurement law had been a prominent target of the 'Vote Leave' campaign,[91] and in the context of the EU procurement rules, then Prime Minister Boris Johnson had talked up a 'bonfire of red tape'.[92] Though this political agenda was constrained by the UK's membership of the World Trade Organization's Agreement on Government Procurement (GPA), it became a credible reform proposal, due to the Government's willingness to engage with a wide range of stakeholders ('over 500 stakeholders') via roundtable discussion and workshops (involving academics like Arrowsmith), and to consult.[93]

Broadly, consistent with her longstanding criticisms of the EU's regulatory approach, Arrowsmith argued that, for desirable simplification, the UK's regulatory regime needed to shift from one based on hard law to one that utilises high-quality soft law.[94] Arrowsmith also argued that greater procedural flexibility – discretion – was necessary to facilitate value for money and process efficiency, domestic objectives that could be compromised by prescriptive legal provisions

[89] Public Contracts Regulations 2015, reg 30(14); Government Commercial Function (n 87) 8.

[90] Government Commercial Function (n 87) 8 and 20.

[91] H Stewart, 'Vote Leave: EU rules add almost £1.7bn to costs of Whitehall contracts' *The Guardian* (26 May 2016).

[92] C Hope, 'Boris Johnson orders a "bonfire" of red tape to give small firms a bigger slice of Government contracts after Brexit' *The Telegraph* (4 November 2019), cited in Arrowsmith (n 4) 70.

[93] Cabinet Office, *Transforming Public Procurement: Government response to consultation* (December 2021) 3.

[94] Arrowsmith (n 4); S Arrowsmith 'Transforming public procurement law after Brexit: some reflections on the Government's Green Paper' (2021) 3 *Public Procurement Law Review* 103.

that prioritised the promotion of intra-EU trade.[95] To achieve this, Arrowsmith argued for 'a single and uniform regime' – doing away with a longstanding (and, from a UK perspective, commercially illogical) distinction between public contracts and concessions in EU law[96] – and, to give the UK the greatest flexibility allowable under the GPA, a procedural toolkit based on the set of procedures available under the 2004 or 1990 Utilities Directive.[97] In relation to the latter, this would mean no competitive dialogue and no competitive procedure with negotiation. Instead, contracting authorities would have free access to the open, restricted and the (old) competitive negotiated procedure.[98]

The Government's Green Paper, *Transforming Public Procurement*,[99] adopted many of Arrowsmith's proposals. The Procurement Bill, which, at the time of writing, is nearing Royal Assent, pursues procedural simplification and flexibility by replacing the existing set of procedures, with just two procedures: an 'open procedure' and a 'competitive flexible procedure'. The competitive flexible procedure is a bare-bones procedure that, consistent with Arrowsmith's proposals, gives contracting authorities the flexibility to 'design a procurement process that meets their needs and the needs of the market'.[100] Authorities will be required to set out the design of the procurement process when it commences, and, under the legal framework, it will be possible for the format to resemble familiar procedures, such as the restricted procedure or competitive dialogue. It is expected that illustrations of some of the procedural possibilities will be outlined in government guidance, serving to preserve beneficial regulatory features of the current regime, like aspects of the procedural frameworks for the restricted procedure and competitive dialogue.

In moving away from a legal regime that relies on formal legal rules, the UK must not be complacent about the risks of poor (and even corrupt) procurement. However, though I do not speak to other aspects of the reforms, there is little sign of this in relation to the proposals on procedural reform, discussed above. Rather, the reforms attempt to shift the UK's regulatory system away from an outmoded model, recognising, with the support of a significant body of regulatory scholarship,[101] that a complicated legal text can itself be a cause of poor or non-compliant decision-making. Whilst legal redress does remain – to catch egregious legal violations – a more compliance-orientated approach, which seeks to move regulated actors towards compliance through education and advice,

[95] Arrowsmith (n 4) 72.

[96] ibid 78–79; see Directive 2014/23/EU of the European Parliament and of the Council of 26 February 2014 on the award of concession contracts.

[97] Arrowsmith (n 4) 79; Council Directive 90/531/EEC of 17 September 1990 on the procurement procedures of entities operating in the water, energy, transport and telecommunications sectors.

[98] Directive 90/531/EEC (n 97) Arts 15 and 1(6).

[99] Cabinet Office, *Transforming Public Procurement*, CP 353 (December 2020).

[100] ibid 26.

[101] See, eg, RA Kagan and JT Scholz, 'The "Criminology of the Corporation" and Regulatory Enforcement Strategies' in KO Hawkins and JM Thomas (eds), *Enforcing Regulation* (Kluwer-Nijhoff, 1984) 67.

is generally more appropriate for what would otherwise be merely inadvertent or technical breaches of the rules.[102] For Arrowsmith, therefore, the regulatory reforms depend on high-quality soft law: 'increased flexibility is not acceptable without the related proposals for detailed soft law – important to ensure effective operation of the unfamiliar flexibility'.[103] In addition to acting as an interpretative aid, this soft law has an explanatory function – explaining how the law might apply in specific practical situations in straightforward terms. Elsewhere the UK Government has done this well in the past,[104] and in the procurement context, there are signs that it is improving.[105]

VII. Conclusion

This chapter has set out the recent regulatory history of complex procurement in the UK, a story of policy failure – 2004/2006 competitive dialogue – and policy evolution through learning – the reforms and European level and the UK Government's domestic reform agenda, post-Brexit. The narrative, in many ways, provides a particularly fascinating case study on the interaction between law, policy and practice – the influence of law/regulation on practice and, in turn, law and policy itself being shaped by practice.

Henry Kissinger opined that academia is 'vicious … because the stakes are so small'. Rather than low stakes, however, Arrowsmith's contribution to the policy evolution discussed in this chapter should not be understated. Sue Arrowsmith is a central figure in the above story: in interpreting, analysing and arguing about the law in the books, Arrowsmith has impacted on the law in action – influencing how practitioners and policymakers understand and interpret the law and, ultimately, the UK's policy on public procurement law reform.

In addition, though principally a world-leading doctrinal scholar, Arrowsmith has also been path-breaking in instigating and supporting empirical legal research into complex public procurement. Thus, whilst in many areas of UK commercial law empirical legal research has been slow to materialise,[106] this is less so for public procurement. In addition to supervising my doctoral studies, which looked at the operation of competitive dialogue in the UK,[107] there was Braun's empirical investigation into the application of the European Community procurement

[102] See I Ayres and J Braithwaite, *Responsive Regulation: Transcending the Deregulation Debate* (Oxford University Press, 1992).

[103] Arrowsmith (n 4) 84.

[104] See, eg, Government Legal Department, *JOYS: The Judge Over Your Shoulder* (6th edn, 2022).

[105] See, eg, Government Commercial Function (n 87).

[106] See H Genn, M Partington and S Wheeler, *Law in the Real World: Improving Our Understanding of How Law Works: Final Report and Recommendations* (The Nuffield Inquiry on Empirical Legal Research, November 2006).

[107] R Craven, *Procurement procedures under the Private Finance Initiative: the operation of the new legal framework* (PhD thesis, University of Nottingham, 2012).

rules to the UK PFI project, completed in 2001,[108] and Telles's empirical research into competitive dialogue in Portugal and Spain, completed in 2010.[109] Much of this research serves to buttress and inform the commercially sensible approach to interpreting the legal rules that Arrowsmith advances. The mix of doctrinal scholarship and empirical insight was published in 2012, in the run into the reform of the EU public procurement Directives, in *Competitive Dialogue in EU Procurement*,[110] a collection edited by Sue Arrowsmith and the late Steen Treumer.[111]

I have been fortunate to benefit from Sue's academic supervision and career mentorship. I look forward to seeing what she does next.

[108] Braun (n 45).
[109] P Telles, *The Assessment of Competitive Dialogue's Impact Both in Portugal and Spain* (PhD thesis, University of Nottingham, 2010).
[110] Arrowsmith and Treumer (eds) (n 2).
[111] C Risvig Hamer et al (eds), *Into the Northern Light – in memory of Steen Treumer* (Ex Tuto, 2022).

4

The Reform of the UK Procurement Remedies System: Unfinished Business

TOTIS KOTSONIS

I. Introduction

Ever since her thesis,[1] Sue Arrowsmith has been making a significant contribution to the specific field of public procurement review procedures and remedies, regarding the European Union (EU) system discussed in this volume by Simovart (chapter 9) and the interlinked (but now distinct) United Kingdom (UK) remedies regime, which is the subject of this chapter.[2] One of her most significant contributions on the UK system will be referenced extensively in the context of the analysis that follows.[3]

Changes to the UK remedies system for breaches of procurement legislation have been made sporadically over the past 20 years, leading to improvements in the regime. Until recently, the impetus for change has invariably been the obligation to comply with EU law. With new post-Brexit procurement legislation expected to take effect in October 2024, it is now apt to consider some of the key changes and issues that have arisen over the past 20 years, and which had a direct impact on the system's overall effectiveness. In doing so, this chapter will also discuss certain conclusions that Sue Arrowsmith and Richard Craven reached following a legal and empirical study of the UK remedies system, the results of which were published in 2016.[4] This chapter will then consider the extent to which these conclusions continue to be relevant today and whether the new post-Brexit procurement law regime might address appropriately outstanding concerns.

[1] S Arrowsmith, *Government Procurement and Judicial Review* (Carswell, 1988).

[2] And even the international level, which is not the subject of a separate chapter; see S Arrowsmith, J Linarelli and D Wallace Jr, *Regulating Public Procurement: National and International Perspectives* (London, 2000) ch 12.

[3] See n 4.

[4] S Arrowsmith and R Craven, 'Public Procurement and Access to Justice: a Legal and Empirical Study of the UK System' (2016) 25 *Public Procurement Law Review* 227.

II. Once Upon a Time in the UK …

For a long time, the remedies system that had been applicable in the event of a breach of UK public procurement legislation was subject to significant limitations. For example, for a time there was no explicit obligation on contracting authorities[5] to proactively notify their award decision to suppliers.[6] This was problematic in that, at the time, once a contract was concluded it could not normally be set aside, so that the only remedy available to an aggrieved supplier was that of damages. However, a damages award was generally seen as less satisfactory than the pre-contractual remedy of setting aside the award decision. What is more, damages were often difficult to obtain – a reflection of the practical difficulty in demonstrating to the court that the procurement breach caused loss to the claimant, not least in cases of an unlawful direct award. Ultimately, the absence of any express obligation to notify suppliers about the award decision was also inconsistent with the requirements of EU law.[7]

In February 2003, the legislation that applied to the award of public contracts was finally amended, incorporating a requirement that contracting authorities should inform suppliers about their award decisions promptly and, if so requested, in writing.[8] However, the amendment did not go far enough, in that the new 'prompt' requirement did not always lead to contracting authorities' notifying suppliers about their award decisions before the conclusion of the contract. From today's perspective, it seems surprising that the possibility of notifying a contract award after the contract's conclusion could have ever been considered appropriate.[9] And yet the introduction of the necessary change in domestic

[5] For the sake of simplification, the chapter refers to contracting authorities alone and to the public procurement rules that applied at any given time. Unless otherwise specified, the issues raised are equally applicable to public undertakings, contracting entities operating on the basis of special or exclusive rights, as well as contracting authorities subject to procurement regulation under the utilities contracts regime that applied at the relevant time. Although many of the issues raised in this chapter could also be said to be relevant to Scotland, the chapter does not deal with the position in Scotland, which has its own domestic procurement legislation and separate court system. References to the UK should, therefore, be interpreted accordingly.

[6] See the Public Works Contracts Regulations 1991 (SI 1991/2680); the Public Services Contracts Regulations 1993 (SI 1993/3228); and the Public Supply Contracts Regulations 1995 (SI 1995/201) as originally implemented. The term 'supplier' will be used throughout this chapter to denote an economic operator interested in participating in a public procurement process or bidding in such process.

[7] See European Parliament and Council Directive 97/52/EC of 13 October 1997 amending Directives 92/50/EEC, 93/36/EEC and 93/37/EEC concerning the coordination of procedures for the award of public service contracts, public supply contracts and public works contracts respectively [1997] OJ L328/1.

[8] The Public Contracts (Works, Services and Supply) and Utilities Contracts (Amendment) Regulations 2003 (SI 2003/46). The Utilities Contracts Regulations 1996 had already been amended in July 2001 to provide for this 'prompt' notification requirement, to render the legislation compliant with the specific requirements of Directive 98/04/EC of the European Parliament and of the Council of 16 February 1998 amending Directive 93/38/EEC coordinating the procurement procedures of entities operating in the water, energy, transport and telecommunications sectors [1998] OJ L110/1.

[9] It is notable that the World Trade Organization's Agreement on Government Procurement (GPA) (see Art XVIII of the 1994 GPA and Art XVI of the revised GPA) does not impose any specific

legislation to clarify the position was arduously slow, and ultimately came about only because of the need to comply with EU law obligations.

More specifically, in January 2006, a new set of procurement regulations was introduced,[10] incorporating, for the first time, provisions that explicitly required contracting authorities to inform suppliers about their award decisions prior to the conclusion of contracts. According to these, following the notification in writing of the award decision, there had to be a standstill period of at least 10 calendar days before the contracting authority could enter into the contract with the successful supplier.[11] Given that the European Commission had already commenced infringement proceedings against the UK, these changes were necessary in order to ensure that the country complied with the decision of the Court of Justice of the European Union (CJEU) in *Alcatel*[12] and the subsequent related decision in *Commission v Austria*.[13] These judgments had confirmed that national courts had to be able to review and set aside public contract award decisions, that this required that suppliers were kept informed about the award decision, and that there had to be a sufficiently long interval between that decision and the conclusion of the contract so that suppliers were given the opportunity to challenge that decision and seek to set it aside. The new provisions improved the effectiveness of the remedies system to some extent, as they afforded potential challengers a greater opportunity to seek further information about the contract award and, if necessary, seek a remedy in court before the conclusion of the contract. However, substantial problems remained.

There were several complexities associated with these rudimentary standstill period requirements, not least the fact that unsuccessful suppliers still had no automatic right to obtain information about the reasons why they were unsuccessful. Instead, they had to request this information in writing within the tight timeframe of two working days following the notification of the award decision. That then triggered an obligation on the contracting authority to provide to the requesting supplier information about the characteristics and relative advantages of the winning tender, at least three working days before the expiry of the standstill period.[14] In seeking to challenge an award decision before the expiry of the standstill period, an aggrieved supplier would then have to apply to the court within the equally tight timeframe of three working days for an interim injunction suspending the tender process.

requirements to that effect. At the same time, the conclusion that notifying suppliers about the award decision after the conclusion of the contract would be consistent with the more limited GPA requirements, would seem wrong on the basis that this practice would clearly be inconsistent with the GPA's underlying principles and express an obligation on its signatories to put in place 'non-discriminatory, timely, transparent and effective' challenge procedures.

[10] The Public Contracts Regulations 2006 (PCR 2006) (SI 2006/5) and the Utilities Contracts Regulations 2006 (UCR 2006) (SI 2006/6) as originally implemented.

[11] PCR 2006, reg 32; UCR 2006, reg 33 as originally implemented.

[12] Case C-81/98 *Alcatel Austria v Bundeministerium für Wissenschaft und Verkehr* [1999] ECR I-7671.

[13] Case C-212/02 *Commission v Austria* ECLI:EU:C:2004:386.

[14] PCR 2006, reg 32(4) as originally implemented.

Separately, since the legislation expressly provided that, in cases where the contract had already been concluded, the only remedy available would be that of damages, the possibility of pursuing pre-contractual remedies continued to be very limited in circumstances where a contract was awarded in breach of procurement legislation without any form of advertising and competitive tendering.

Even in cases where challengers sought to take action outside the standstill period – whether by choice or because a contract was awarded without one – pursuing a claim was complicated by the fact that under domestic legislation, aggrieved parties had to act promptly and in any event within three months from the date when the alleged breach actually occurred.[15] This rule meant that it was not always sufficient for claimants to bring an action within three months; they also had to demonstrate to the court that they had acted promptly.[16] The courts did have the discretion to extend this period if they believed that there was good reason for them to do so. However, this meant that in circumstances where, through no fault of their own, the alleged breach had become public knowledge only following the expiry of the three-month period, the claimant was left with no option but to depend on the court's discretion not to bar the claim. This state of affairs was all the more surprising given that since 1989, the EU public procurement remedies Directive (the 'Remedies Directive')[17] explicitly required EU Member States to take the necessary measures to ensure that contracting authority decisions could be reviewed effectively.[18]

III. Further Regulatory Reform

Ultimately, greater steps were taken towards the fulfilment of the obligation to have in place an effective remedies regime with the implementation of Directive 2007/66 (the '2007 Directive')[19] on 20 December 2009 and the further amendment of domestic procurement legislation on 1 October 2011[20] to render it consistent with the decision of the CJEU in *Uniplex*.[21] These changes seemed to transform the pre-existing public procurement law landscape in the UK. For example, supplier rights were strengthened with the introduction of the remedy of ineffectiveness. This required the courts for the first time to set concluded contracts

[15] PCR 2006, reg 47(7) as originally implemented.

[16] cf *Holleran v Severn Trent Water Ltd* [2004] EWHC 2508.

[17] Council Directive of 21 December 1989 on the coordination of the laws, regulations and administrative provisions relating to the application of review procedures to the award of public supply and public works contracts [1989] OJ L395/33.

[18] Remedies Directive, Art 1.

[19] EU Directive 2007/66/EC of the European Parliament and the Council of 11 December 2007 amending Council Directives 89/665/EEC and 92/13/EEC with regard to improving the effectiveness of review procedures concerning the award of public contracts.

[20] Public Procurement (Miscellaneous Amendments) Regulations 2011 (SI 2011/2053).

[21] Case C-406/08, *Uniplex (UK) v NHS Business Services Authority* [2010] ECR I-00817.

aside in certain (limited) circumstances, where these had been awarded in breach of procurement legislation. The UK chose, as it could under the 2007 Directive, to provide in its implementing legislation that the effect of a declaration of ineffectiveness would be to cancel only outstanding contractual obligations, without affecting the legality of any contractual obligations that had already been performed. In line with the 2007 Directive requirements, prospective cancellation was accompanied by a requirement that the defendant contracting authority should also be ordered to pay a financial penalty, which had to be 'effective, proportionate and dissuasive'. At the same time, the court was given the power not to declare a contract ineffective, despite there being grounds for it to do so, based on (narrowly defined) overriding general interest reasons. In such a case, the court had to order the shortening of the contract's term and/or the payment of a financial penalty.

Separately, the implementation of the 2007 Directive meant that the standstill period provisions were strengthened further, requiring contracting authorities not to conclude the contract for a minimum period of 10 calendar days,[22] commencing from the day after the contracting authority had notified suppliers not only of its award decision but also of the reasons for that decision, including the characteristics and relative advantages of the winning tender. If a disgruntled supplier then issued a claim against the contracting authority's award decision before the expiry of the standstill period, or indeed after it, but before the contract's conclusion, there was no longer a need to seek an interim injunction so as to prevent the contracting authority from entering into the contract. Provided that the contracting authority had been notified about the issuing of the claim, an automatic suspension applied to the award process. This had the effect of prohibiting the contract's conclusion until such time as the court decided the claim, or the contracting authority successfully sought a court order lifting the automatic suspension.

The subsequent October 2011 changes to the regime further enhanced the protection offered to suppliers. In *Uniplex*, the CJEU had considered that the requirement to bring an action 'promptly' was inconsistent with the requirement for legal certainty[23] and that, for the same reason, the limitation period had to commence from the time of actual or constructive knowledge of the breach (rather than, as was the case in the UK at the time, from the time of the breach).[24] In order to ensure consistency with *Uniplex*, the requirement for claimants to bring an action 'promptly' was therefore removed. In addition, the amended legislation now provided for a 30-day limitation period that commenced from the date when the challenger first knew or ought to have known that grounds for starting the proceedings had arisen. At the same time, the courts were given the

[22] Assuming that the communication of the award decision was by electronic means. Different rules applied where other methods were used.
[23] *Uniplex* (n 21) [29]–[32].
[24] ibid [39]–[43].

discretion to extend the limitation period, with 'good reason', up to a maximum of three months from the date of actual or constructive knowledge of the breach. There have been no further substantive changes to the domestic remedies regime since October 2011.

IV. Improved but Not Yet Effective

In line with earlier comments, the 2009 and 2011 legislative amendments were important milestones in that they rectified some of the imbalances and shortcomings of the domestic remedies regime. For example, they made it easier for disgruntled suppliers to commence proceedings before the contract's conclusion and to seek more effective pre-contractual remedies. In cases where there were concerns about the legality of a contract that had already been concluded, in addition to seeking damages, there was now also the possibility to seek to set that contract aside by seeking a declaration of ineffectiveness.

At the same time, the introduction of more robust rules, including the 'standstill period' obligation following the notification of the award decision, the requirement proactively to provide to suppliers with adequate information about the reasons for the award decision, including the characteristics and relative advantages of the winning tender, as well as the fact that an automatic suspension would apply if a claim against the award decision were to be issued, created greater compliance incentives for contracting authorities. Equally, the risk that an aggrieved supplier might bring a challenge and seek a declaration of ineffectiveness, setting aside a contract that was entered into without competition unlawfully, increased the risks of non-compliance and, again, created additional incentives for contracting authorities to consider more carefully their procurement law obligations.

Welcomed and necessary as these improvements might have been, important issues remain that continue to hamper the system's overall effectiveness. Already in 2016, Sue Arrowsmith and Richard Craven identified several concerns in a paper that set out their analysis and conclusions following an empirical study of supplier behaviour in enforcing UK public procurement law.[25] The study was based on data that had been collected from procurement lawyers, contracting authorities and suppliers. Amongst other things,[26] the authors observed that over the period 2007–14, there had been an upward trend in the incidence of procurement

[25] Arrowsmith and Craven (n 4).

[26] It is worth noting that two-thirds of the suppliers that participated in the study indicated that they did not 'perceive' any procurement law breaches. This may be interpreted in several ways, including the possibility that this merely reflected the fact that most procurements at the time did not give rise to any compliance concerns, or lack of sufficient awareness of the procurement law requirements or, indeed, a combination of the two. Ultimately, this conclusion is irrelevant to the question of whether, when concerns with procurement law compliance do arise, the remedies system is sufficiently robust to ensure that suppliers with meritorious claims may have access to effective and indeed rapid remedies.

litigation, and that the reform of the remedies system had contributed to that trend. Despite this, the number of suppliers taking legal action remained comparatively low, and the empirical study provided evidence that litigation costs, fear of reprisals and the inadequacy of legal remedies were key reasons for this situation.[27]

According to Arrowsmith and Craven, the findings on costs provided empirical support for the argument that the UK remedies system did not comply with EU law obligations to provide effective supplier remedies and that compliance required that legal aid be made available for procurement litigation.[28] If that was not feasible, the authors considered that it might have been advisable to explore alternative enforcement solutions, including a cheaper system of judicial-type address, such as a tribunal or a first-instance review body that, even if it did not comply with the standards required by the Remedies Directive, could allow for appeal to a body that did.[29]

In terms of the concerns over the inadequacy of legal remedies, Arrowsmith and Craven noted that a key issue in this context had already been addressed by legislative reform, namely, the rules on time limits for issuing court proceedings. As discussed earlier, those rules were revised in October 2011, following the CJEU's decision in *Uniplex* to bring them into line with EU law requirements.

The most significant remaining problem identified by the Arrowsmith and Craven empirical study at the time was the difficulty in securing the suspension of contract awards. This was because the courts were more likely than not to refuse to order the suspension of a procurement process following an application by a claimant, or because, post-December 2009, the courts tended to grant applications by defendant contracting authorities for the lifting of automatic suspensions. According to the Arrowsmith and Craven empirical study, in about two-thirds of cases between 2002 and 2015, suspension of the contract award was rejected. This, they concluded, was the result of the way in which the courts decided these applications, which, according to Arrowsmith and Craven, also gave rise to concerns about compliance with the Remedies Directive.[30]

V. Additional Concerns in a Different Context

Some eight years following the publication of the results of the Arrowsmith and Craven empirical study, it is perhaps striking not only that many of the key

[27] Arrowsmith and Craven (n 4) 250–52.

[28] ibid. In truth, legal aid would have dealt only with the question of costs and not any of the other issues of substance identified by the Arrowsmith and Craven study (discussed further below).

[29] In this context, Arrowsmith and Craven (n 4) 251 also raised the possibility of informal enforcement mechanisms that could relieve pressure on the EU-compliant review system and/or improve enforcement. They did not elaborate further on this idea in their paper, and it remains unclear how this could operate in practice, not least in light of strict limitation-period provisions, which are likely to require would-be claimants to take protective action in court to ensure that, if such informal enforcement mechanisms were to fail, a claim would not be time-barred.

[30] ibid 234–37.

concerns that the study had identified still need to be addressed,[31] but also that additional issues have arisen since then that further increase concerns over the effectiveness of the domestic remedies regime.

For example, bringing an action in court remains costly and time-consuming, rendering it difficult in practice for many suppliers to pursue legal action, unless they are willing and financially able to bear the substantial costs, as well as take on the substantial cost risks, that such action entails.

Separately, because of the test the courts continue to apply in determining whether or not to lift an automatic suspension – as well as because of the way in which they choose to apply it[32] – a disproportionate number of applications by defendant contracting authorities to have the automatic suspension lifted continue to be successful, thereby limiting the remedies available to the claimant to damages.[33]

At the same time, damages continue to be difficult to obtain, given the difficulty in demonstrating causation – that is, that but for the breach, the claimant stood a real chance of being awarded the contract. In fact, following the Supreme Court's 2017 decision in *Energy Solutions*,[34] it has become even harder for claimants to obtain damages, given the Court's conclusion in that case that damages should not be available unless the breach that has caused the claimant to suffer loss was sufficiently serious. As a result, demonstrating causation is no longer sufficient to guarantee that a claimant will be compensated for the loss it has suffered due to the contracting authority's breach.

This approach has already led to the unsatisfactory situation,[35] whereby a successful claimant was left without any remedy. More specifically, in

[31] It is unknown to what extent fears of reprisal continue to constitute a factor in dissuading suppliers from pursuing otherwise meritorious claims. In any event, to the extent that this is still an issue, it is submitted that the reform of the remedies system itself cannot address such concerns. Accordingly, consideration of this issue is outside the scope of this chapter on the UK remedies system.

[32] As discussed further in section IX, in deciding these applications, amongst other things, the courts seem to give disproportionate weight to the public interest in not delaying the conclusion of public contracts.

[33] The exact number changes with each new decision, and would also depend on the period being investigated. However, it would seem that on average, just over two-thirds of applications for the lifting of an automatic suspension are successful.

[34] *Nuclear Decommissioning Authority v Energy Solutions EU Ltd (now called ATK Energy EU Ltd)* [2017] UKSC 34.

[35] In this regard the author respectfully disagrees with Arrowsmith's and Craven's position that remedies, in general, should be available only in cases of a serious breach: see Arrowsmith and Craven (n 4) 228. Amongst other things, an even more permissive regulatory system would be inadequate in creating sufficiently strong incentives for contracting authorities to seek to comply with their public procurement law obligations. Indeed, from a practitioner's perspective, the author observed a marked improvement in terms of contracting authorities seeking to ensure procurement law compliance following the introduction of the 2009 and 2011 changes to the remedies regime. Separately, a robust remedies system is important in terms of creating the necessary confidence for suppliers to participate in public procurements, thereby increasing competitive tensions and leading to better value-for-money outcomes for the taxpayer. Also, the argument that procurement law is too complex would seem inappropriate, in that other laws with which public authorities must comply, such as subsidy control, are also complex, and getting it wrong can, nonetheless, have serious consequences. This approach

Braceurself,[36] the court lifted the automatic suspension, allowing the defendant contracting authority to proceed with the contract award, on the basis that damages would be an adequate remedy for the claimant if its claim were successful at trial. At trial, the claimant was in fact successful, in that the court concluded that, but for the contracting authority's breach of the procurement rules, the claimant would have been awarded the contract.[37] Despite this, the court refused to award damages to the claimant, effectively leaving it without a remedy, because the court took the view that the contracting authority's breach was not sufficiently serious.[38] The basis for this conclusion was essentially the view that the contracting authority's breach was a single, excusable and inadvertent breach in a closely fought competition and that the impact on the winner was not 'existential' for the claimant's business.[39]

It falls outside the scope of this chapter to explain why, in the author's view, the 'sufficiently serious' requirement for the award of damages in procurement cases in the domestic courts is not merely problematic as to its effects but also wrong as a matter of law.[40] For current purposes, it suffices to note the real-world effect that the adoption of this approach has in creating an additional obstacle to accessing justice. Related to this issue are the difficulties that claimants also have in obtaining a declaration of ineffectiveness in the domestic courts.

When the ineffectiveness remedy was introduced in 2009, it gave rise to the prospect that claimants would have access to an effective post-contractual remedy, at least in certain limited cases where contracts were concluded unlawfully. Indeed, the remedy of ineffectiveness was introduced by Directive 2007 partly in recognition of the 'inherent limits' of damages actions in view of the 'practical difficulty' of having to demonstrate that, but for the breach, the claimant stood a real chance of winning the contract, especially in cases of a

then leads to the problematic conclusion that public bodies should be held to lower compliance standards wherever the law is deemed complex in nature. See also related comments by the Supreme Court that are quoted in section VI that speak to the deterrent effect of effective remedies and access to justice.

[36] *Braceurself Ltd v NHS England* [2019] EWHC 3873 (TCC).

[37] *Braceurself Ltd v NHS England* [2022] EWHC 2348 (TCC).

[38] Note that previously, in *Energy Solutions EU Limited v Nuclear Decommissioning Authority (No 3)* [2016] EWHC 3326 (TCC), the court took the view that where a breach leads to a change in the outcome of the competition, it would constitute a sufficiently serious breach. See ibid [66], [69] and [72].

[39] At the time of writing, the case is on appeal.

[40] The author's views and analysis as to why the 'sufficiently serious' approach is incorrect are set out in T Kotsonis, 'Case E-16/16, Fosen-Linjen AS and AtB: the question of whether damages claims should be limited to cases of a sufficiently serious breach, the burden of proof when seeking damages and the extent of the verification requirement at tender evaluation' (2018) 37 *Public Procurement Law Review* NA60. Although the article analyses the position by reference to the UK's compliance with the Remedies Directive, that analysis does not change because of the UK's departure from the EU, in light of existing domestic and international law obligations to ensure access to justice and effective remedies. In any event, to the extent that the EU's departure from the UK is relevant, the reasoning behind the Supreme Court's decision in *Energy Solutions*, which was based on the principle of state liability under EU law, can no longer be deemed to be valid. For additional related comments and context, see also T Kotsonis, 'Case E-7/18 – Fosen-Linjen AS v AtB AS (Fosen-Linjen II): the parable of Fosen-Linjen (reprise)' (2020) 39 *Public Procurement Law Review* NA1.

direct award.[41] And yet, over the last 14 years, there have been only two cases where the domestic courts have declared contracts ineffective,[42] and one case where, although the court considered that the grounds for ineffectiveness were made out, it held that the specific circumstances justified shortening the contract's term and requiring the payment of financial penalties instead.[43]

Whilst it could be argued that the surprisingly small number of ineffectiveness declarations merely reflects the inadequate merits of claims that have reached the courts, this situation would also seem to reflect the narrow way in which the courts have considered it appropriate to apply and interpret the law. For example, in *Basingstoke*,[44] the court took the view that the question of whether a contract was concluded unlawfully without a contract notice was a 'mechanistic test'[45] that effectively did not require detailed consideration of whether subsequent amendments to the contract fell properly within the scope of the contract as advertised in the contract notice. Instead, it was sufficient that there was 'an effective notice' capable of 'being related to the procedure and the contract'.[46]

In this context, it is also relevant to note that in the handful of cases where the courts concluded that the grounds for ineffectiveness were in fact made out, they shied away from also imposing 'effective, proportionate and dissuasive' financial penalties as required by the legislation.[47] For example, in *Faraday*,[48] the only

[41] Commission Staff Working Document, Annex to the Proposal for a Directive of the European Parliament and of the Council amending Council Directives 89/665/EEC and 92/13/EEC with regard to improving the effectiveness of review procedures concerning the award of public procurements, SEC(2006) 557, para 4.3.

[42] *Lightways (Contractors) Limited v Inverclyde Council* [2015] CSOH 169; *Faraday Development Ltd v West Berkshire Council* [2018] EWCA Civ 2532 (14 November 2018).

[43] *Consultant Connect Limited v NHS Bath and North East Somerset, Swindon and Wiltshire Integrated Care Board* [2022] EWHC 2037.

[44] *AEW Europe LLP v Basingstoke and Deane Borough Council* [2019] EWHC 2050 (TCC).

[45] The 'mechanistic test' approach was originally adopted in *Alstom Transport v Eurostar International Limited* [2011] EWHC 1828 (Ch), an earlier case that, in the author's view, is equally problematic. That case related to a contract award made on the basis of a qualification system under the utilities contracts regulations applicable at the time. In justifying the light-touch mechanistic test approach, the court noted (ibid [42]) 'The benefit of such a test is that it will often be easier to apply, and since the availability or not of the ineffectiveness remedy is something which calls for clarity if the remedy is to operate sensibly in a commercial context, ease of application is important. The detriment is that it is indeed mechanical, and may not catch some instances where, on the merits, it might be thought the remedy should operate.' The court in *Basingstoke* could have distinguished *Alstom* on the basis of its very specific facts. It is, in fact, arguable that the court *should* have rejected the mechanistic test approach as incompatible with EU law, which was still applicable in the UK at the time (see in particular Case C-19/13, *Ministero dell'Interno v Fastweb SpA* [2015] PTSR 111 [50]). Instead, it considered the 'mechanistic test' as also relevant in the context of a contract award under the Public Contracts Regulations 2015, thereby confirming the broader application of this problematic test.

[46] *Basingstoke* (n 44) [41].

[47] Public Contracts Regulations 2015 (SI 2015/102), reg 102(4).

[48] *Faraday Development Ltd v West Berkshire Council* [2018] EWCA Civ 2532. In *Consultant Connect* (n 44), the court required three different NHS Trusts to pay different financial penalties in the order of £10,000, £8,000 and £4,000. It is difficult to reconcile such payments with the requirement for the imposition of an effective, proportionate and dissuasive financial penalty, especially in circumstances

case in England that has so far led to a declaration of ineffectiveness, the Court of Appeal ordered the payment of a financial penalty of only £1.

The difficulties in obtaining pre-contractual remedies, as a result of the courts' tendency to order the lifting of automatic suspensions, as well as the difficulties in obtaining post-contractual remedies, given the way in which the courts determine whether to make a damages award or issue a declaration of ineffectiveness, means that, under our domestic remedies regime, it is difficult for claimants to have access not only to effective remedies but also, in fact, to any type of remedy.

It is true of course that the context has now changed: the UK is no longer bound by EU laws. Whilst the EU-inherited procurement legislation remains largely in place in the UK, new laws, the Procurement Act 2023 and related secondary legislation, are expected to take effect in October 2024.[49] Although at the time of writing the procurement legislative reform has yet to be fully completed, the question arises as to whether the Procurement Act 2023 – the central plank of the post-Brexit procurement legislative reform – is likely to address some of the key concerns that Arrowsmith and Craven had identified in 2016 and, indeed, the additional issues of concern that have arisen since then.

At the same time, the UK's exit from the EU gives rise to another important question that merits consideration first. As noted throughout this chapter, over the past 20 years, all the modifications in the domestic remedies regime that have led to its improvement were not effected voluntary but by necessity, so as to ensure that the UK complied with its EU law obligations. Accordingly, it is fair to question whether, in a post-Brexit context, the shortcomings of the domestic remedies regime should still be deemed to give rise to legal compliance concerns, worthy of the Government's attention.

VI. The Question of the Domestic Remedies Regime's Legal Compliance in a Post-Brexit World

When Arrowsmith and Craven carried out their study, they considered the question of whether the domestic remedies system complied with access-to-justice requirements by reference to obligations that arose under the Remedies Directive and Article 47 of the Charter of Fundamental Rights of the EU (the 'Charter'). Effectively, the two pieces of legislation converge, in that the Remedies Directive seeks to ensure that effective and rapid remedies are made available for breaches of EU procurement law, whilst Article 47 of the Charter provides for the right to an effective remedy when EU law rights and freedom are violated.

where these payments were ordered in the context of the court's having concluded that it should not make a declaration of ineffectiveness despite the fact that the grounds for ineffectiveness were made out.

[49] The new Act will not apply to Scotland, which will continue with its existing legislation that largely mirrors the EU procurement directives.

Arrowsmith and Craven had concluded that the great costs associated with bringing a claim in the courts was a significant obstacle to taking legal action, noting that this finding provided empirical support for the argument that the UK remedies system did not comply with EU law requirements.[50]

At the same time, questions that relate to access to justice, and by necessary implication access to effective remedies, are relevant not merely in an EU law context. Indeed, the right of access to justice has been part of the constitutional fabric of this country ever since the Magna Carta (1215).[51] In this regard, it is relevant to note that in its 2017 decision *R (Unison) v Lord Chancellor*,[52] the Supreme Court considered the question of costs and its effect on access to justice. More specifically, the Court considered whether an order by the Chancellor of the Exchequer requiring the payment of a fee for issuing a claim at the Employment Tribunal or Employment Appeal Tribunal interfered unjustifiably with the right of access to justice. The Supreme Court unanimously concluded that as a matter of English law, and also separately as a matter of EU law, the fees order was unlawful because it had the effect of preventing access to justice. In reaching this conclusion, the Court took note of the fact that fees were the most frequently cited reason for not submitting a claim. In setting out the Supreme Court's reasoning for its decision, Lord Reed, who gave the lead judgment, noted, amongst other things, as follows:

> Courts exist in order to ensure that the laws made by Parliament, and the common law created by the courts themselves, are applied and enforced. That role includes ensuring that the executive branch of government carries out its functions in accordance with the law. In order for the courts to perform that role, people must in principle have unimpeded access to them. Without such access, laws are liable to become a dead letter, the work done by Parliament may be rendered nugatory, and the democratic election of Members of Parliament may become a meaningless charade. That is why the courts do not merely provide a public service like any other.
>
> …
>
> The value to society of the right of access to the courts is not confined to cases in which the courts decide questions of general importance. People and businesses need to know, on the one hand, that they will be able to enforce their rights if they have to do so, and, on the other hand, that if they fail to meet their obligations, there is likely to be a remedy against them. It is that knowledge which underpins everyday economic and social relations. That is so, notwithstanding that judicial enforcement of the law is not usually necessary, and notwithstanding that the resolution of disputes by other methods is often desirable.[53]

The Supreme Court's comments would seem equally relevant by analogy to the deterrent effect of costs on issuing proceedings in the High Court in relation to procurement law breaches, which the Arrowsmith and Craven paper had

[50] Arrowsmith and Craven (n 4) 251.
[51] See further *R (on the application of UNISON) (Appellant) v Lord Chancellor (Respondent)* [2017] UKSC 51 [74].
[52] ibid.
[53] ibid [68] and [71].

identified a year earlier. To be clear, in the context of procurement litigation, the deterrent effect does not arise from the court fee alone. Although, as Arrowsmith and Craven noted, that had increased substantially in 2015 from £2,000 to £10,000 (for damages claims of more than £200,000), this still represents a comparatively small part of the overall litigation costs, which also involve substantial solicitor and counsel fees. These fees reflect not merely the complex issues procurement litigation often entails, but also the cumbersome and lengthy High Court procedures that litigants must go through before the litigation culminates in the hearing of the claim. Such hearings can last for five days, and often substantially longer, with obvious cost implications. The litigation process itself can become even more complex and more costly, in circumstances where the defendant is not as forthcoming as it should be in providing the claimant 'promptly with the essential information and documentation relating to the evaluation process actually carried out, so that an informed view can be taken of its fairness and legality'.[54] This can then lead to protracted correspondence between the opposing sides, arguing over the question of what rightly falls within the scope of 'essential' information and documentation that should be disclosable. Unless resolved, such disputes can then lead to the need for the claimant to make an application for early specific disclosure, again adding to costs.[55]

The substantial costs of bringing and, indeed, defending a claim in the High Court means that, before deciding whether to issue proceedings, the would-be claimant must also consider carefully the risk that, if it were to lose, it would be liable for a substantial part of the defendant's legal costs.[56] Separately, the would-be claimant must also consider the risk that, in issuing a claim against a contracting authority's award decision before contract conclusion, the defendant authority could apply to the court for an order to lift the automatic suspension that the issuing of the claim would trigger. In the seemingly less likely event that the court were to refuse to grant such application,[57] so that the suspension is maintained, the court would likely require the claimant to provide a cross-undertaking in damages. That then means that, in the event that the claim is unsuccessful, the claimant must compensate the defendant (and depending on

[54] This is the general position in line with *Roche Diagnostics Ltd v The Mid Yorkshire Hospitals NHS Trust* [2013] EWHC 933 (TCC). See also para 7 of Appendix H (TCC Guidance Note on Procedures for Public Procurement Cases) to the Technology and Construction Court Guide. The question of disclosure is key in any procurement dispute. As noted in *Roche* [20], 'An unsuccessful tenderer who wishes to challenge the evaluation process is in a uniquely difficult position. He knows that he has lost, but the reasons for his failure are within the peculiar knowledge of the public authority.' Failure to agree on pre-action disclosure can often lead to the need for the claimant to issue costly proceedings so as to obtain early specific disclosure.

[55] See, eg, *Serco v Secretary of State for Defence* [2019] EWHC 515 (TCC). See also the preceding footnote on the related issue of failure to agree on pre-action disclosure, leading to the need to issue proceedings.

[56] There is also the risk that where the winner has joined the proceedings as an interested party, the court might order that the unsuccessful claimant should also be liable for part of the interested party's costs. See further *Bechtel Ltd v High Speed Two (HS2) Ltd ((No 2)(Costs of the interested party)* [2021] EWHC 640 (TCC).

[57] See earlier comments in section V about the disproportionate number of interim applications that are decided in favour of the contracting authority.

the specifics of the litigation, sometimes also the declared winner, who might have joined the proceedings as an interested party) for the damages suffered as a result of the delay in concluding the contract.

Compounding concerns over costs is the related issue of the amount of time it takes before the court may dispense with a procurement claim. It is not unusual for a claimant to have to wait for nine to 12 months, sometimes significantly longer,[58] before the court considers the claim. Again, that means that before commencing proceedings, the claimant must consider carefully whether it is prepared to commit at least part of its focus and resources to a lengthy and, as noted above, procedurally complex litigation process. That in itself, can also act as a deterrent to the issuing of procurement claims.

Separately, issues that relate to the effectiveness of the domestic remedies regime may also give rise to questions over the UK's compliance with its international treaty obligations. For example, the UK is required under the Agreement on Government Procurement (GPA) to provide for a '*timely, effective*, transparent and non-discriminatory administrative or judicial review procedure'[59] through which suppliers may challenge breaches of GPA obligations.[60]

In light of the above, it seems appropriate to conclude that the concerns identified and related conclusions reached in the Arrowsmith and Craven paper, as well as the additional concerns that have emerged since then in relation to the ability of potential claimants to access effective remedies, continue to be relevant from a legal compliance perspective in a post-Brexit context. Even if that were not the case, it would still seem inappropriate to ignore the real-world impact of a remedies system that continues to fail to offer adequate access and protection to those it is meant to protect, namely, suppliers interested in, or bidding for, public contracts.

The question therefore rightfully now arises as to whether the new post-Brexit procurement law regime is likely to address these concerns.

VII. The Green Paper

The Government's 2020 Green Paper on transforming public procurement (the 'Green Paper'),[61] which set out proposals on the post-Brexit reform of procurement legislation for public consultation,[62] was encouraging in that it acknowledged many of the issues that have been giving rise to concerns under current arrangements:

[58] The author is currently involved in a procurement litigation in which the hearing has been scheduled more than 24 months after the claim was issued.

[59] Revised Agreement on Government Procurement, Art XVIII (emphasis added).

[60] Failure to comply with this GPA requirement will also give rise to non-compliance concerns under Art 277 of the UK–EU Trade and Cooperation Agreement (TCA), TS 8/2021, which incorporates related GPA obligations in the TCA.

[61] *Transforming Public Procurement*, CP 353 (December 2020).

[62] ibid. Note that the remaining section of the chapter deals with the position in the UK other than Scotland, which will retain its own procurement legislation, which is likely to continue to mirror EU procurement legislation.

> An effective and well-functioning review system is central to the successful operation of any public procurement regime … Suppliers and contracting authorities tell us [that our procurement review system] is also lengthy, expensive and complex. Small businesses, charities and social enterprises in particular find the process too costly to pursue.[63]

Similarly, noting that the vast majority of procurement claims in England and Wales are dealt with by the Technology and Construction Court (TCC), the Green Paper recognised:

> The rigour and structure that contribute to its excellence can be a hindrance in cases where a quick resolution is sought or for businesses (especially small businesses, charities and social enterprises) [that] may not be able to bear the cost of a lengthy process … The lengthy process and its impact on the number of cases which reach full trial can have a detrimental effect on access to justice.[64]

Whilst the Green Paper also acknowledged that 'many groups' favoured the introduction of a tribunal system so that procurement challenges might be dealt with 'in a faster and cheaper manner', the Government's preference was to seek to achieve these aims through proposals to reform the court rules and procedures that apply to procurement challenges.[65] To that end, the Government proposed to continue to investigate whether to transfer 'a subset of procurement challenges' to a tribunal-based system,[66] with a view to retaining the flexibility to widen the scope of a tribunal's jurisdiction 'should the anticipated benefits of Court reform not be realised'.[67] As to the scope of the proposed court reform, the Government proposed to investigate further the following:

(a) a tailored fast-track system to deal with procurement challenges;
(b) a presumption that certain types of procurement claims should be reviewed on the basis of written pleadings alone;
(c) clear rules for disclosure that would help establish what additional information should be disclosed as a matter of course in a particular challenge;
(d) the employment of a designated procurement-only judge and encouraging claimants to issue claims outside London with a view to getting hearings listed more quickly;
(e) rethinking the timescales that apply to different parts of the court proceedings, with a view to expediting these where appropriate.[68]

Separately, the Green Paper noted that under the existing system, the post-contractual remedy of damages was not given 'officially' primacy or preference over pre-contractual remedies, 'although this [did] often occur in practice'.[69] In this

[63] ibid [188].
[64] ibid [194].
[65] ibid [196] and [201].
[66] ibid. Ultimately, the question that the Government put out to consultation was much more specific (emphasis added): 'Do you believe that we should investigate the possibility of using an *existing* tribunal to deal with *low value claims and issues relating to ongoing competitions*?'.
[67] ibid [202].
[68] ibid [197].
[69] ibid [203].

context, the Green Paper also acknowledged, by reference to the Arrowsmith and Craven 2016 paper, that this de facto primacy was contrary to many bidders' preference for having the opportunity to perform the contract instead of the award of damages.[70] To that end, the Government proposed that the new rules should state formally a preference for pre-contractual remedies, to reflect the introduction of streamlined procedures to shorten court timescales and the capping of post-contractual damages.[71]

Equally encouraging in this context was the acknowledgement in the Green Paper that there was an issue with the current test the courts applied to determine whether to lift an automatic suspension, noting informal statistics that indicated that around two-thirds of 'lifting' applications were successful. Accordingly, the Government proposed that the new legislation should incorporate a 'more appropriate' procurement-specific test, with a view to providing for a more balanced approach in the determination of these applications.

VIII. The Government's Response

In its December 2021 response to the consultation that followed the publication of the Green Paper,[72] the Government noted that 80 per cent of respondents were in favour of the Government's proposals to reform court rules and processes to deliver 'a faster, cheaper and more accessible review system'.[73]

At the same time, the Government did not provide any information as to concrete next steps or timescales for bringing these proposals to fruition. Instead, it noted that it recognised 'the difficulties inherent in improving access to the review system while also trying to reduce timescales for the determination of legal challenges' and that it was 'continuing to explore feasible options' for faster and more accessible routes 'for valid challenge' of procurement decisions. It also noted, but without offering any explanation as to what that might mean in practice (such as in terms of timing), that court procedural reform was intended to align with statutory reform but that it would be subject to review by the Ministry of Justice and the Civil Procedures Rules Committee.[74]

[70] ibid.

[71] The capping of damages award proved, unsurprisingly in the author's view, a controversial proposal. According to this, other than in exceptional circumstances, successful claimants would have only been entitled to damages that amounted to a 1.5 x multiple of bidding costs. This issue, including the Government's arguments in favour of this approach, are outside the scope of this chapter. Suffice it to say that in light of the public consultation responses, the Government decided not to implement this proposal.

[72] *Transforming Public Procurement, Government response to consultation*, CP 556 (December 2021).

[73] ibid [238].

[74] ibid [239].

Separately, the Government indicated its intention to 'shelve' but keep under review the idea of using an *existing* tribunal to deal with low-value claims and issues relating to ongoing procurements.[75]

As to the proposal that the legislation should formally give pre-contractual remedies primacy over post-contractual remedies, the Government noted that it no longer intended to pursue this proposal because of the related decision not to pursue a cap on damages, and because 'there will be more opportunity for pre-contractual remedies in a quicker system'.[76]

Finally, the Government noted that 60 per cent of respondents supported the review of the test that the courts applied in determining whether to lift automatic suspensions, so as to ensure greater balance between supplier and contracting authorities' interests, 'given the current test is often thought to be skewed in favour of contracting authorities'.[77] Accordingly, the Government indicated that whilst it was still working through potential options, it envisaged introducing a new 'simple, single limb test' that provided for the lifting of automatic suspensions 'where there [were] overriding consequences for the various interests concerned', including the public interest.[78]

IX. The Procurement Act 2023

The statutory procurement law reform was never intended to deal with court procedural changes.[79] At the time of writing, it is not yet clear when this process might commence or might be completed. It is also unclear how ambitious the scope of such reform might be. As regards the Procurement Act 2023 ('the Act'), the only provision that is arguably directly relevant to the question of addressing the substantive (as opposed to the procedural) shortcomings of the current remedies system is section 102. In line with what the Government had indicated following the Green Paper consultation, this provision introduces a modified test for determining interim applications, including applications for the lifting of automatic suspensions.

[75] ibid [240]–[247]. Unfortunately, the idea of setting up a bespoke expert tribunal to deal with breaches of procurement law, which, anecdotally, seems to have been the solution favoured by most practitioners, did not seem to get much traction with the Government, possibly as a result of the complexity and costs implications that the setting up of a new expert tribunal would involve.

[76] ibid [249].

[77] ibid [250].

[78] The Government's reference here effectively mirrors the wording of Art XVIII:7(a) of the GPA: 'The procedures [for the provision of rapid interim measures] may provide that overriding adverse consequences for the interests concerned, including the public interest, may be taken into account when deciding whether such measures should be applied.'

[79] To the extent to which this reform would, as expected, involve changes to or the introduction of additional Civil Procedure Rules, these must, in any event, be made by the Civil Procedures Rules Committee and approved by the Lord Chancellor (see Civil Procedure Act 1997, s 2).

Under current rules, the courts apply the *American Cyanamid* principles[80] in determining these. As noted earlier, this has proved problematic, in that it has led to the deciding of a disproportionate number of applications in favour of contracting authorities. In principle, the *American Cyanamid* test involves a staged approach, whereby the court will first consider whether there is a serious issue to be tried and, if so, whether damages would be an adequate remedy, and if not, or if there is doubt, whether the balance of convenience lies in favour of granting or refusing the interlocutory relief being sought.[81]

Ultimately, the changes the Act introduces to the test are not as extensive as might have been hoped.[82] According to section 102(2) of the Act, in considering whether to make an interim order, the court must have regard to:

(a) the public interest in, among other things:
  (i) upholding the principle that public contracts should be awarded … in accordance with the law;
  (ii) avoiding delay in the supply of the goods, services or works provided for in the contract …;
(b) the interests of suppliers, including whether damages are an adequate remedy for the claimant;
(c) any other matters that the court considers appropriate.

As should be obvious from the above, the revised test removes the need for the court to consider the question of whether there is a serious issue to be tried. That of itself is unlikely to make much of a difference in the consideration of interim applications, where the problem has been the courts' tendency to conclude that damages would in fact be an adequate remedy for the claimant or that, in any event, public-interest considerations militate against delaying the contract's conclusion when applying the balance of convenience test.[83] Both of these elements survive, albeit that they are recast with an explicit reference to the public interest in ensuring that public contracts are awarded lawfully.

[80] *American Cyanamid Co v Ethicon Ltd (No 1)* [1975] AC 396.

[81] In practice, there is some evidence that the courts would sometimes consider the question of whether damages would be an adequate remedy as part of a broader test that seeks to determine whether in all the circumstances it would be just to confine the claimant to a remedy of damages, effectively blurring the lines between the second and third limbs. See, eg, *Alstom Transport UK Limited v London Underground Limited* [2017] EWHC 1521 (TCC) [22] and *Lancashire Care NHS Foundation Trust v Lancashire CC (Lifting application)* [2018] EWHC 200 (TCC) [30]. The issue is discussed in more detail in T Pritchard, 'Automatic Confusion? A critical analysis of the application of American Cyanamid in UK procurement challenges and the implications for reform' (2022) 3 *Public Procurement Law Review* 170.

[82] See, eg, the Procurement Lawyers' Association response to the Government consultation which, amongst other things, suggested that statutory conditions should 'make clear that there needs to be *exceptional* urgency and *overwhelming* public interest to allow the suspension to be lifted' (original emphasis). See further, response to Question 34 in the *Response by the UK Procurement Lawyers' Association on the 'Transforming Public Procurement' Green Paper* (10 March 2021).

[83] See Arrowsmith and Craven (n 4) for a more detailed discussion of this issue.

Ultimately, the revised test may be said to have the effect of moving (formally)[84] away from the *American Cyanamid* staged approach and to require the court to determine which outcome will cause the least inconvenience to the parties by reference to all the factors the court considers relevant, and which must, in any event, include the public and supplier interest considerations set out in section 102(2)(a) and (b).[85] Whether these changes would be sufficient to make an appreciable difference to the outcomes of interim applications is unclear at this stage. This could partly depend on the extent of the court procedural reform.[86] As things stand, the concern remains that in the absence of a more substantial change to the way in which interim applications are determined, the courts' tendency to give disproportionate weight to the adequacy of damages for the claimant and the public interest in not delaying a public contract award would continue.[87]

A related issue in this context is the fact that the Act does not seek to address concerns over the requirement for claimants to provide cross-undertakings. As noted previously, the court may (and more often than not will) refuse to maintain an automatic suspension unless the claimant agrees to provide a cross-undertaking in damages. This condition alone can have a substantial impact on the ability of suppliers to pursue claims or to have access to more effective pre-contractual remedies.[88] The Act does not seek to modify the current position, merely providing that in issuing an interim order, the court 'may provide for undertakings or conditions'.[89]

One small but nonetheless helpful change relates to a clarification about the application of one of the conditions, which, if met, requires the court to make an

[84] See n 81.

[85] Although the revised test does not provide for an express requirement to consider whether there is a serious case to be tried, if deemed appropriate, the court can of course take that into account under s 102(2)(c).

[86] For example, if this leads to the disposal of claims much more quickly, this should then weaken the force of the argument that the delay in entering into the contract as a result of the court process would be detrimental to the public interest, making it less likely that this would be a determinative factor in the consideration of interim applications.

[87] In this regard, it is noteworthy that in a recent judgment, the Court of Appeal did not consider it likely that the new test will change much in practice, commenting as follows in relation to the provisions of the Procurement Bill, which are substantively the same as s 102 of the Act: '[T]he Procurement Bill sets out provisions on this issue which use different words and terminology from those currently used by the courts, but – as a number of commentators have pointed out – it by no means follows that, even assuming that the Bill stays in this form, the test that will be applied by the courts will be very different to that which is currently applied.' *Camelot UK Lotteries Ltd v Gambling Commission* [2022] EWCA Civ 1020 [7].

[88] In the recent high-profile case by Camelot against the Gambling Commission (n 87), Camelot decided to drop its appeal against the High Court's decision to lift the automatic suspension, allowing the Gambling Commission to proceed with an award to Alwyn. In explaining the reason for this decision, Camelot noted that 'It has become clear that the potential damages covered by the undertakings needed for the appeal to proceed would have been too large, and involved too great a commercial risk, for it to be reasonable to provide them.' See 'National Lottery: Camelot drops legal challenge over licence transfer' *BBC News* (6 September 2022) at www.bbc.co.uk/news/business-62806297.

[89] Procurement Act 2023, s 102(4).

order setting aside a contract or modification, the equivalent to making a declaration of ineffectiveness under the current rules. Although the Act essentially recasts the limited grounds that currently trigger the requirement to issue an ineffectiveness order,[90] in line with the approach in *Fastweb*,[91] it further clarifies that the requirements for a set-aside order will also be met in cases where there was an obligation to publish a notice and, although this was published, it 'did not provide accurate information in respect of the contract as entered into'.[92]

It is to be hoped that this clarification will lead to the abandonment of the 'mechanistic test' approach[93] in favour of a more substantive test. For example, that should involve considering whether, as a matter of substance, a specific post-contract award modification falls properly within the scope of what was advertised in the contract notice, as bidders would have decided whether to express an interest in the contract, and would have prepared their tenders, by reference to that notice.

Finally, it is also relevant to note that the Act provides for an oversight authority[94] that may investigate compliance with the requirements of the Act by most contracting authorities[95] and may then issue recommendations as to the action a contracting authority should take to ensure compliance within a specified timeframe.[96] The contracting authority to which the recommendation is addressed is then required to 'have regard' to it, and it might also be required to submit progress reports on action it has taken to ensure compliance.

These provisions replace and build on the functions of the Public Procurement Review Service (PPRS).[97] The new oversight functions, including the requirement for individual contracting authorities to have regard to recommendations, should help promote greater compliance. At the same time, although these functions are comparatively stronger than those available under the PPRS,[98] they continue

[90] Procurement Act 2023, s 105. The new formulation clarifies that the set-aside conditions also apply to unlawful modifications, which is useful. However, this clarification is not sufficient on its own to make any appreciable difference to concerns over the difficulty in accessing pre- or post-contractual remedies. There are several other related changes, including the removal of the current requirement for the payment of a civil financial penalty when issuing a declaration of ineffectiveness or as a partial or fully alternative remedy where the court considers that overriding public-interest considerations warrant not issuing a declaration of ineffectiveness. This effectively reduces the severity of repercussions that apply under the existing law. However, it is unlikely that this would have a substantial impact on the current position given the reluctance of the courts to date to require a payment that is 'effective, proportionate and dissuasive' as the current law requires.

[91] See *Fastweb* (n 45) [48]–[52], by reference to the publication of a voluntary *ex ante* transparency notice.

[92] Procurement Act 2023, s 105(4).

[93] See earlier comments in relation to *Basingstoke* in section V. See also the comments in n 45.

[94] In England, that would be a Minister of the Crown. See definition of 'appropriate authority' in s 123 of the Procurement Act 2023.

[95] Excluding central government bodies, devolved governments and private utilities, amongst others. See further the Procurement Act 2023, s 108(5).

[96] See further s 109 of the Act.

[97] See at www.gov.uk/government/publications/public-procurement-review-service-scope-and-remit.

[98] See the Small Business, Enterprise and Employment Act 2015, s 40.

to be limited. Accordingly, they are unlikely to provide an adequate alternative to the judicial system.[99]

X. Concluding Remarks

Well before the 2016 UK referendum on EU membership was confirmed, there were rumours that the European Commission was concerned about the way in which the procurement remedies regime was operating in the UK and had asked the Government to provide further information and explanations as to the comparatively low instances of procurement litigation in the country. Such concerns were rumoured to have been raised in the context of the European Commission's considering whether to commence infringement proceedings against the UK for not complying with the requirements of the Remedies Directive to have in place an effective remedies system.

Whether this is factually correct is ultimately now irrelevant. As argued in this chapter, real issues continue to hamper the effectiveness of the domestic remedies regime. Not only have some of the key concerns that Arrowsmith and Craven identified in 2016 yet to be resolved, but additional concerns have also arisen since then, making it increasingly difficult for claimants to access effective remedies, whether before or after the conclusion of a public contract.

As to concerns over litigation costs and their effect as a significant obstacle to access to justice, whether these would be addressed, even if partly,[100] would depend on the extent of any future court reform. For example, if, in line with the Green Paper proposals, these would involve provisions for a quick review process based on written pleadings alone, as well as arrangements that ensure that procurement claims are dealt with on an expedited basis, such reforms should improve considerably the current position.[101]

In this context, it is instructive to note the approach the Competition Appeal Tribunal (CAT) has already sought to take in relation to the review of the legality of subsidy decisions by public authorities.[102] In issuing an order for the capping

[99] For more general comments on the new procurement legislation, including related commentary on the current absence of any substantial reform of the remedies system, see T Kotsonis, 'The UK's overhaul of procurement legislation' (November 2023) at www.pinsentmasons.com/en-gb/out-law/analysis/uk-overhaul-procurement-legislation.

[100] Although the extent of any future court reform is currently unclear, it would seem less likely that this would be capable of addressing the current concerns as regards costs and timescales as effectively as the setting up of a specialist tribunal would have done. As discussed, this is not an option the Government is considering at the moment.

[101] Sue Arrowsmith's own views as to the 'guiding principles' that should be considered carefully in the context of the reform of the remedies system are set out in her Working Paper, 'Reimagining Public Procurement Law After Brexit: Seven Core Principles for Reform and Their Practical Implementation, Part 1' (January 2020) at https://ssrn.com/abstract=3523172. See esp section 4.7.3, 'Towards a more effective and balanced system: key considerations'.

[102] Since the introduction of the Subsidy Control Act 2022 in January 2023, the CAT is the judicial body primarily responsible for the review of subsidy decisions.

of costs, in the context of the first challenge against a public authority subsidy decision under the Subsidy Control Act 2022 (SCA 2022), the CAT noted, amongst other things, as follows:

> The [subsidy control] jurisdiction needs to be fast, cheap and simple. It would be highly unfortunate were the undoubted benefits of properly granted subsidies (or the equally important matter of declining to grant a subsidy) to be subsumed in [lengthy] challenges to subsidy decisions.
>
> Although it is neither appropriate nor helpful to debate whether a formal fast track order should be made in subsidy control cases … , that is the lens through which subsidy control cases generally ought to be seen …
>
> Challenges to subsidy decisions matter, and the risk of an enormous costs bills on failure should not be an undue deterrent to bringing [subsidy control] reviews … The whole point of the subsidy control regime is to give interested parties a right to challenge subsidy decisions … The critical question is to ensure that the jurisdiction that Parliament has created is effective, and costs play a critical role here … Costs that are disproportionate will have … a chilling effect.[103]

The CAT's intended approach should be applauded, albeit that it gives rise to further questions as to why similar concerns in the context of procurement challenges, which have been identified at least since 2016, have yet to be addressed in a similar way.

As noted earlier, the question of disclosure is of immense importance in the context of procurement disputes. Regulating what should be disclosable and when, including prior to commencing proceedings, would also be important in keeping costs down by doing away with the protracted disputes that regularly take place in the context of actual and potential procurement claims.

As to the substantive issues that affect supplier access to effective remedies, as this chapter has sought to explain, the Procurement Act has addressed these either not at all or not as effectively as it could have done. For example, it was noted that the revised interim review test would seem unlikely to make a substantive difference to the way in which these applications are decided – at least, not without adequate court reform.

It is also disappointing that the Act has not sought to address more extensively some of the other key issues that affect supplier access to effective remedies. For example, the new legislation could have incorporated provisions that made it clear that a remedy of damages is available in relation to all actionable breaches

[103] *Durham Company Limited v Durham County Council* [2023] CAT 14 [3(3)], [3(4)], [8(3)] and [8(5)]. The CAT's decision to impose a cost-capping order was in fact reversed by the Court of Appeal (*Durham County Council v Durham Company Limited* [2023] EWCA Civ 729). However, that was on the ground that the CAT did not have power to make the order, rather than any disagreement with the CAT's analysis quoted above. See, eg, Sir Julian Flaux's comments at [30]: 'The judge's aim of seeking to ensure that the costs of subsidy control reviews under [SCA 2022] do not become excessive, thereby discouraging challenges under the section, was an entirely laudable one, but unfortunately the tool which he employed of imposing limiting costs caps … irrespective of their actual reasonable and proportionate costs, was one which, in my judgment, he had no jurisdiction to impose.'

(subject to the usual requirement of demonstrating causation) and not only in relation to cases where there has been a 'sufficiently serious' breach. Separately, the legislation could have introduced additional amendments that clarified further the way in which the courts should determine whether the conditions for granting a set-aside order are made out, so as to render it less difficult for claimants to access this remedy. In addition, or alternatively, the legislation could have provided that, other than in exceptional circumstances, the courts must shorten the duration of *any* unlawfully concluded or modified contract (or reduce the goods, services or works supplied under such contracts) where this has led to the claimant's having been denied a proper opportunity to seek a pre-contractual remedy.[104]

As the Government acknowledged in the Green Paper, an effective and well-functioning review system is central to the successful operation of any public procurement regime. Ultimately, as this chapter has sought to explain, whether a procurement remedies regime is effective and well-functioning is not so much a question of whether, in principle, the law enables suppliers who have suffered, or risk suffering, loss or damage to *seek* a remedy by challenging contracting authority decisions. Instead, it is a question of whether, *in practice*, potential claimants have unimpeded access to the justice system, and can *obtain* effective and timely remedies.[105]

The task of achieving this important goal remains for the moment incomplete.

[104] cf ss 104 and 105 of the Procurement Act 2023.
[105] cf *R (Unison) v Lord Chancellor* (n 51).

5

E-Procurement and Procurement Transparency

ROGER BICKERSTAFF

I. Introduction

My interest in procurement law has, as with a great many people, been stimulated and shaped by Professor Arrowsmith over many years. I even remember trundling through the seemingly endless Welsh countryside to procurement conferences at Aberystwyth University before Sue moved to Nottingham University. At the time Sue emphasised to me, as a junior technology lawyer, the importance of public procurement as a key issue in technology procurement. That has stayed with me for over 30 years. Sue's constant encouragement to write and speak on technology procurement issues has provided an academic backbone to my practitioner career. Occasionally, this needed a certain amount of arm-twisting by Sue, such as when she 'invited' me to contribute to the chapter on e-procurement in the 'Bible' – *The Law of Public and Utilities Procurement*. Inevitably, this entailed a huge amount of work: far more than I anticipated, but I am grateful to Sue as it gave me a huge understanding, insight into and interest in the subject. As always, and as with so many other people in so many areas of procurement law, Sue's thinking in this area has been an important guide to my thoughts on the use of technology in procurement and the encouragement of further transparency through the increased use of technology in procurement processes. Sue's important commentary on the Green Paper, *Transforming Public Procurement*, issued by the UK Cabinet Office,[1] identified as a key priority the adoption of increased transparency through a comprehensive open-contracting regime, together with accessibility of high quality data.[2] Sue identified that primary law itself should state clearly the core

[1] Cabinet Office, *Transforming Public Procurement* (CP 353) at https://assets.publishing.service.gov.uk/government/uploads/system/uploads/attachment_data/file/943946/Transforming_public_procurement.pdf.

[2] S Arrowsmith, 'Transforming Public Procurement Law after Brexit: Early Reflections on the Government's Green Paper' (15 December 2020) at https://ssrn.com/abstract=3749359 or http://dx.doi.org/10.2139/ssrn.3749359, 4.

obligations relating to the content, manner and timeliness of publication, together with the crucially important 'limits on proactive disclosure – which is particularly important for commercially sensitive information – based on the rules already contained in the Freedom of Information Act 2000'.[3]

These thoughts on transparency and the appropriate limits of transparency are reviewed and developed in this chapter, which examines the concept of the possibility of increased transparency in procurement processes, at least as a by-product of the increasing digitisation of procurement processes. The chapter examines the development of the transparency recommendations in the Green Paper and how they have been implemented in the the Procurement Act, and comments on the extent to which these changes will have the effect that England, Wales and Northern Ireland[4] are likely to move, in practice, to a more transparent approach to their procurement activities.

II. Green Paper Proposals on Transparency

The concept of transparency flows throughout the Green Paper recommendations. As a headline, the Green Paper identifies that 'transparency by default' should be embedded on a procurement lifecycle basis, from planning through to procurement, contract award, performance, and completion. There will be a key and important change to the practice of public procurement processes: instead of transparency occurring on a 'snapshot' basis at certain points in the procurement lifecycle (contract notice, release of procurement documentation, debriefing information and award notice), the Green Paper recommends that transparency be continuous on a real-time basis throughout the procurement lifecycle. The Green Paper comments that 'contracting authorities would be required to declare in their tender documents when information would be disclosed and justify what, if any, information is to be treated as commercially sensitive'.[5] This suggests that contracting authorities will have an element of discretion in deciding what types of information will be subject to transparency.

On the issue of the publication of award and debriefing information (which is a key element in ensuring adequate transparency), the Green Paper states that contracting authorities would need to publish 'basic disclosure information, covering the information currently required by regulation 84'[6] before they will be allowed to initiate contract award and commence standstill.

[3] ibid 5.
[4] Scotland is not participating in the Procurement Bill.
[5] *Transforming Public Procurement* (n 1) para 165.
[6] ibid para 166. The reference to 'regulation 84' is to reg 84 of the Public Contracts Regulations 2015 (SI 2015/102).

The Green Paper suggestions go well beyond regulation 84. The Green Paper refers to transparency requirements as including 'Bidder Identities; Basis of award decision; Basic disclosure of tenders submitted; Evaluation reports; Basic evaluation disclosure information'.[7] This is outside of and additional to regulation 84. An obligation on contracting authorities to publicly disclose information about successful and unsuccessful tenders, evaluation reports and evaluation information before the award of contract would be a significant change to UK procurement practice. The 'transparency by default' principle suggests bidder submissions (including tender submissions) will be disclosable. This is indicated but not stated expressly in the Green Paper. The Green Paper comments that further guidance will be published on what would not be disclosable.

It is interesting to consider whether the flexibilities allowed by the UK's departure from the EU are actually necessary to enable the introduction of the transparency developments outlined in the Green Paper. In the author's opinion, these developments did not actually require the UK's departure from the EU and they could have been introduced within the scope of the EU Directives. In essence, the Green Paper proposals in this area build on the transparency obligations within the EU Directives. They do not remove or fundamentally alter any of the key transparency obligations in the EU Directives. As such, with sufficient political ambition and direction it could have been possible to build the proposed transparency developments into the UK procurement law regime. However, until the UK's departure from the EU there was relatively little political will within the UK to explore the flexibilities and opportunities that could have been available during the period of the UK's membership of the EU.

III. Procurement Act Approach to Transparency

Whilst 'transparency' as such is not identified in the Procurement Act[8] ('the Act') as an objective or a principle, the Act refers to 'sharing information for the purpose of allowing suppliers and others to understand the authority's procurement policies and decisions' as being an objective of the new approach.[9] This approach is to be contrasted with Directive 2014/24/EU, which explicitly states that transparency is one of the fundamental principles of EU procurement law.[10] Notwithstanding this discrepancy, it is clear that increased transparency is a major commitment of the Act. The UK Government has commented

[7] *Transforming Public Procurement* (n 1) para 166.
[8] Procurement Act 2023 available at www.legislation.gov.uk/ukpga/2023/54/contents/enacted.
[9] ibid s 12(1)(c).
[10] Directive 2014/24/EU of the European Parliament and of the Council of 26 February 2014 on public procurement and repealing Directive 2004/18/EC [2014] OJ L94/65, Art 18(1).

that one of the goals of the Act is to create a 'fully transparent public procurement system'.[11] The intention is to enable everyone to view, search for and understand what the UK public sector wants to buy, how much it is spending and with whom.

There will be three elements to the new focus on transparency: enhanced and extended requirements for public procurement notices at various stages in the procurement process; a new register of suppliers; and a central digital platform:

- *Procurement notices.* Contracting entities will be required to at least consider publishing procurement notices at five stages in the procurement process, as compared to mandatory notices under the current rules solely at the tender and contract award stages. The five stages are planning, tender, award, contract commencement and contract implementation. The publication of some of the notices will not be mandatory (see section III.A).
- *Register of suppliers.* A 'register of suppliers' will be established to enable suppliers to input information about their businesses, together with information that is frequently requested in procurement processes on a once-only basis, and contracting entities must use this information provided by suppliers in their procurement processes. This should reduce duplicate work for suppliers. It will also create a standard and updateable business record, which it is intended will be linked to the central digital platform. Each supplier will provide unique identifiers, which will enable more accurate analysis of public-sector contracts by size, type and location of business, and will also include beneficial ownership information.
- *Central digital platform.* All information from the procurement notices, together with limited information from the register of suppliers (identifiers and beneficial ownership), will be published to a central digital platform. The central digital platform will be an enhanced version of the current Find a Tender service. It is intended that the platform will enable much greater analysis of the procurement data held on the platform, as a result of the storage of data in machine-readable formats, utilising the Open Contracting Data Standard (OCDS).

A. Procurement Notices

The Act requires the publication of additional transparency notices, over and above those required under the EU rules. The notices required by the Act are as shown in Table 5.1.

[11] Cabinet Office, *Transforming Public Procurement – Our Transparency Ambition* (30 June 2022) at www.gov.uk/government/publications/transforming-public-procurement-our-transparency-ambition.

Table 5.1 Procurement Notices Required under the UK Procurement Act

Stage	Notice(s)	Status	Contents
Planning	Pipeline	Mandatory if spend is more than £100m	Information on (potential) future procurements with a value in excess of £2m.
	Planned procurement	Voluntary	Further information on procurements which are soon to commence.
	Pre-market engagement	Mandatory if pre-market engagement is carried out	Information on pre-market engagement events.
Tender	Tender stage, including below-threshold contracts	Mandatory	Detailed information on opportunities to bid, including links to the tender site and information on the procedure.
	Direct award transparency	Mandatory	Information stating that a contracting entity intends to award a contract directly without a competitive process.
	Procurement termination	Mandatory (not utilities) if a tender notice or a direct award transparency notice has been published	Information that a contracting entity has decided not to award a contract.
Award	Award	Mandatory	Which companies bid, which has been selected (including beneficial ownership information).
Contract commencement	Contract detail	Mandatory	Information setting out that a contract has been entered into: likely to require final value, contract duration, extension options, commercial tools used, KPIs to be used and the redacted signed contract.

(continued)

Table 5.1 ***(Continued)***

Stage	Notice(s)	Status	Contents
Contract implementation	Contract change	Mandatory (not utilities or defence and security) unless value changed by less than 10% (goods or services) or 15% (works)	Information setting out that the contracting entity intends to modify the contract and likely to require details of the modification.
	Payments compliance	Mandatory (every 6 months during term of contract)	Details of compliance of payments made within 30 days obligation.
Contract end	Termination or expiry	Mandatory (not utilities)	Information that the contract has come to an end, for whatever reason.

As can be seen from Table 5.1, the extent of the notices that contracting entities are required to issue has been considerably expanded under the Act. Under the current EU Directives/2015 UK Regulations, the primary required notices are limited to Prior Information Notices setting out a contracting entity's intentions relating to planned procurement process (Article 48 Directive 2014/24), Contract Notices initiating competitive procurement processes (Article 49 Directive 2014/24) and Contract Award Notices advertising the results of and the award of contracts pursuant to a procurement process (Article 50 Directive 2014/24). Voluntary Ex Ante Transparency (VEAT) Notices are also established under the Remedies Directive to give some measure of protection against an ineffectiveness order.[12] Whilst the notices under the EU Directives are intended to give an adequate level of transparency, both in respect of the conduct of the specific procurement exercise and in relation to information to the market in general, the notice requirements in the Act considerably add to the requirements under the EU Directives.

In particular, the approach set out in the Act focuses on enhancing the second element of the transparency requirement – the publication to the market in general of information about and resulting from the conduct of procurement processes. Crown Commercial Services' guidance on its transparency ambition comments that under the current rules, there is only 'mandatory transparency across the

[12] Directive 1989/665/EEC of the European Parliament and of the Council of 21 December 1989 on the coordination of the laws, regulations and administrative provisions relating to the application of review procedures to the award of public supply and public works contracts [1989] OJ L395/33, Art 3a.

public sector at the tender and contract stages'.[13] The guidance further comments that 'there is a lot of valuable information produced in the other stages which will now be required to be made public'.[14]

The additional information under the Act that must be published in procurement notices will broaden the market awareness of procurement activities and deepen the level of information that is provided to the market. For example, pre-market engagement notices will be mandatory if market engagement is carried out. This could considerably broaden the awareness of these activities beyond those 'in the know', and early engagement in a procurement process through pre-market engagement could lead to bids from companies that would not otherwise bid for public-sector projects. It is a frequent complaint against public-sector procurement that there is insufficient time after the publication of a contract notice for a company to develop appropriate products and solutions.[15]

The detail of content under the Procurement Act notices is considerably enhanced in some instances as compared to the content required under the EU Directives, even for those notices that are already required under the Directives. For example, under the Act, contract award notices must include details of all the companies that 'bid' in the tender process, whereas the contract notices under the EU Directives only require details of the successful tender to be included. In passing, it is assumed that the details of the companies that will need to be published in contract award notices under the Act will be limited to the companies that submitted tenders and will not include companies that merely provided an expression of interest.

The Act includes requirements for contracting entities to publish additional levels of detail in procurement notices over and above the level of detail required by the EU Directives. The contract commencement notice is key in establishing these additional publishing requirements. It requires contracting entities to publish, amongst other matters, the 'commercial tools used', the Key Performance Indicators (KPIs) and a redacted version of the signed contract.

The full details of the requirements of the contract notices will be set out in regulations that will be made under section 95 of the Act.[16] The draft Regulations relating to transparency issued by the Cabinet Office[17] establish that the intention

[13] Cabinet Office (n 11) 9.

[14] ibid 9.

[15] Informal discussions by the author with a number of US technology companies on the challenges of winning public-sector contracts in the UK.

[16] Section 95 provides that an 'appropriate authority' (Government Minister) may by regulations make provision for (a) the form and content of the notices; and (b) how such notices are to be published. These regulations may require notices to contain specified information and may require publication on a specified online system.

[17] The Procurement (Transparency) Regulations 202X at https://assets.publishing.service.gov.uk/government/uploads/system/uploads/attachment_data/file/1170260/230713___Final_version_for_consultation__Procurement_Act__Transparency__Regulations_202X.pdf.

is to expand quite considerably on the level of detail that is required under the EU Directives, but some uncertainties remain. Whilst increased transparency can be beneficial in encouraging different companies to engage in public procurement activities, there is also a distinct risk that the enhanced transparency requirements may deter companies from engaging in public procurement processes if they consider that their important commercial, technical and/or operational details may have to be publicly disclosed.

B. Register of Suppliers

The Cabinet Office has stated that it will create a 'Register of Suppliers'.[18] This will allow suppliers to input information about their businesses and answer questions they are frequently asked across different procurements. The key difference from the existing UK central government supplier registration processes[19] appears to be that contracting authorities will be obliged to use the information provided by suppliers to the Register of Suppliers in the conduct of procurement processes. The current supplier registration processes are primarily focused on raising the visibility of suppliers to purchasing personnel within the UK public sector. Supplier information is then provided by the supplier in the conduct of each procurement process.

The new Register of Suppliers will create a 'tell-us-once' system, which should:

(a) reduce duplicate work for suppliers through making use of information provided centrally by suppliers, which will then be available to public-sector purchasers without bidders have to submit the same information in each procurement process. This should make public-sector bidding easier and less time-consuming;
(b) create a standard and updateable business record, which will then be used to populate the supplier details on the central digital platform (see section III.C). Each supplier will provide unique identifiers so that it can be identified across all its UK procurement activity. This should enable more detail and better analysis of public-sector contracts by size, type and location of business. It is also intended that the beneficial ownership information of bidders will be obtained through this process.

To a certain extent, the Register of Suppliers 'mirrors' the European Single Procurement Document (ESPD) initiative under the EU Directives.[20] The ESPD is a single standard on-line form that replaces pre-qualification questionnaires and is intended to make the process of bidding for a public contract easier, as the intention is that the same form is used across the EU in all above-threshold

[18] Cabinet Office (n 11) 11.
[19] See at https://supplierregistration.cabinetoffice.gov.uk/.
[20] Directive 2014/24/EU, Art 59.

procurement processes. This means that bidders can re-use forms from one procurement in another procurement process, as long as the information is still correct, as each contracting entity will request the same information in the same format. However, except in Scotland, the ESPD initiative has not made a great deal of progress in the UK.

The proposed Register of Suppliers should further simplify the bidding process as compared to the ESPD, as it appears that the register will be available to contracting entities and the details of the suppliers will be obtained from the register without the need for suppliers to re-provide the details to the contracting entity. The Cabinet Office commented in the impact assessment for the Procurement Bill that this will be of particular benefit to small and medium-sized enterprises (SMEs), making it easier for them to bid for any public contract.[21]

C. Central Digital Platform

The third key element of the enhanced transparency reforms under the Act is the establishment of a Central Digital Platform. This platform will contain all information from the transparency notices, together with some limited information from the Register of Suppliers. The data will be held in machine-readable format, using the Open Contracting Data Standard (OCDS).

The objective is that, over time, the platform will enable the analysis of commercial procurement data, giving contracting authorities, suppliers and all interested parties the ability to see:

(a) which live opportunities and contracts the public sector has in place, how these contracts are performing, how much has been spent through them and how long they have left to run;
(b) which companies are working with the public sector, and particular organisations within it, including their contract portfolios, earnings and performance; and
(c) how procurements change during their lifecycle, that is, how the original published value of the contract compares to the amount actually spent through it.

This will include a number of registers that will enable users to get a clear picture of various elements of public procurement:

- the register of commercial tools – details of the frameworks and the dynamic markets that are available to contracting authorities and details of contracts that have been won through different commercial tools;
- the performance register – details of suppliers' performance;

[21] Cabinet Office, 'Procurement Reform Bill – Impact Assessment' (21 April 2022) at https://bills.parliament.uk/publications/46429/documents/1767, 1.

- the prompt payment register – details of the payment performance of contracting authorities; and
- the debarment list – a list of suppliers that either must or may be excluded from procurements.

There is a clear need in the UK for a Central Digital Platform for procurement-related information. The decentralised approach to the implementation of e-procurement systems for the public sector in the UK means that central (and local) government entities do not have access to considerable amounts of public procurement information, as the information is held in a variety of private-sector e-procurement systems. In contrast to most other countries, public-sector contracting entities in the UK purchase e-procurement solutions from private-sector companies, such as Bravo Solutions. This has led to the storage of digital public procurement information in a wide range of separate and, potentially, incompatible e-procurement systems, which introduces complexities into the access to and analysis of this digital procurement information by the public sector.

This contrasts with situation in a wide variety of countries that have established a central e-procurement system for the whole of the public sector in those countries. Frequently, the use of the public sector e-procurement solution by the public sector is mandatory. In some countries (eg, Finland) there is de facto centralisation through the establishment of a central framework for an e-procurement solution, which tends to be used by most contracting authorities, even though they have the right to procure an e-procurement solution on a case-by-case basis.

South Korea is probably the key example of a country with a single, centralised e-procurement solution. The South Korean – KONEPS – e-procurement system was initially developed in 2002, and has been considerably enhanced and developed over the period that it has been in use.[22] KONEPS is a single centralised e-procurement system that is mandatory for all central-government South Korean procurement processes above a threshold financial value; but in practice, KONEPS is actively used for below-threshold procurement processes as well. Other public-sector bodies must 'make efforts' to use KONEPS, but it is not mandatory for these bodies. A wide range of interfaces have been developed between KONEPS and other government and private-sector data sources. This means that a wide range of information can be obtained through these interfaces directly for the relevant data sources, without the inputting of the data by the bidders themselves.

The centralised nature of the KONEPS system means that there is a very extensive 'pool' of procurement data available within KONEPS, from which statistics can be obtained relatively easily about various aspects of public procurement in South Korea and on which data analysis can be carried out.

[22] Dae-in-Kim, 'New Electronic Procurement Legislation in Korea', paper delivered at *Global Revolution in Procurement VII*, University of Nottingham, 15 June 2015.

This compares with the relative inaccessibility of the procurement data in the private-sector, decentralised UK public sector e-procurement solutions. As an example, a Bid Rigging Indicator Analysis System (BRIAS) has been developed as part of KONEPS through analysing data that is input into KONEPS to identify on an almost real-time basis a number of corruption 'red-flags' relating to potential bid rigging and bidder collusion. One aspect of BRIAS reviews the bid price (as a ratio compared to a reference price), the number of participants and the competition method, and applies a formula that generates a potential bid-rigging score. If the score is above a certain threshold, an alert is generated, which suggests to the procurement authorities that there is a need to collect more information to check whether there has been collusion. If the further information suggests that there may be a problem, an investigation may be opened.

Given the experience of countries that already have a central digital platform, the implementation of a Central Digital Platform by the UK Government, bringing in data from the enhanced procurement notices and the Register Of Suppliers, will greatly enhance the ability of the UK public sector in respect both of the monitoring and review of UK procurement activities and the increased opportunities to carry out analysis on the data held within the Central Digital Platform.

IV. Benefits of the Transparency Reforms

The UK Government has identified a number of benefits that will result from the transparency reforms, including:

(a) lower prices through better disclosure;
(b) improved accountability in spending;
(c) reduced scope for corruption; and
(d) time savings through the 'tell us once' system.

In essence, these are the benefits that are generally identified through the increased use of technology in procurement processes and, in particular, increased transparency resulting from the increased use of technology. The UK Government has attempted to substantiate the extent to which these benefits will occur as a result of the proposed increases in transparency. The UK Government's Procurement Bill Impact Assessment[23] recognised that the costs of the increased transparency 'are expected to be higher than Option 2 [Do Minimum option], this option is expected to deliver significant benefits in a range of areas'. The Impact Assessment commented:

> Although it is challenging to accurately quantify the potential scale of impacts of improved collection and disclosure of data; empirical studies highlight that benefits

[23] Cabinet Office (n 21) 16.

> are likely by way of reduced costs to contracting authorities; potential creation of new markets; improved accountability; and reduced corruption.[24]

The Impact Assessment refers to studies into the impact of increased transparency in Slovakia and France that have shown significant improvements in the prices offered by bidders.

In the UK context, where there is already wide involvement by SMEs in public-sector bid processes, it is less clear that increased transparency will give similar benefits. For example, there are over 5,000 companies appointed to the G-Cloud 13 Framework Agreement for the provision of cloud solutions to the public sector: 90 per cent of the suppliers on G-Cloud 13 are SMEs; 72 per cent are micro and small organisations.[25] It is hard to see that more transparency will further increase the number of suppliers in this area.

The UK Government also hopes that enhanced transparency in public procurement will bring benefits to a wide range of important stakeholders, including the following:

- *Contracting authorities* – access to a more diverse range of suppliers through better visibility of procurement plans and tender opportunities; more efficient procurement and reduced costs through better data on opportunities to collaborate with other authorities; better data on available frameworks and commercial tools; more data to conduct market analysis and to identify signs of fraud and corruption.
- *Suppliers* – better visibility of procurement plans, engagement events and tender opportunities will increase the number of opportunities to bid on; better data for horizon scanning and market intelligence; use of performance data will mean suppliers will not need to compete with others who have been proved incapable of delivering but are willing to undercut on price.
- *General public, civil society and the media* – monitoring of how public funds are spent, where and with whom, in order to better hold public authorities to account.
- *Beneficial ownership data* – enabling analysis of the corporate structures of suppliers involved in the public sector.
- *Government policy* – data from the platform will enable the monitoring of compliance with the transparency requirements of the new legislation, and also enable measuring of the impacts of the wider reform programme.

The Government recognises that there will also be costs associated with the transparency reforms. These include the time contracting authorities will need to produce and publish the new notices, and the administrative costs associated with building the new system.

[24] ibid 28.
[25] See at www.crowncommercial.gov.uk/news/g-cloud-13-agreement-goes-live.

To a certain extent there is something of a trend (almost amounting to a fashion) in public-sector procurement practice to regard increased transparency as being beneficial. In some contexts, there are very clear benefits. One of the key examples of the benefits of increased transparency is the Prozorro e-procurement system developed in Ukraine by the ProZorro team, which has created a hybrid electronic system that is built on open source. As with the proposed UK system, the Prozorro system interacts between a state-owned central database and private-sector commercial systems. The software code is completely open and freely available for download and use.

The main principle of the Prozorro e-procurement system is 'everyone can see everything'. In fact, the word '*prozorro*' means 'transparent' in the Ukrainian language. In the Prozorro system, after the award of contracts there is full transparency of all procurement documentation, including all submitted proposals from all participants, decisions of the tender commission and qualification documents. This relatively extreme form of transparency originated in a desire to combat corruption in the Ukraine through increased transparency. Prozorro was initially developed as part of the Ukrainian anti-corruption agenda, with the idea that an environment should be developed where public-sector bodies could conduct procurement activities, whilst providing public access to this information so that interested parties could monitor which contracts were awarded and to which entities. Following the initial development of Prozorro, a number of monitoring tools have been developed. These modules have a wide range of functions and enable deep analysis and monitoring of public procurement.

As previously discussed, and in relation to better accessibility to data for the purposes of monitoring and review of UK procurement activities, and the increased opportunities to carry out analysis of data, there are clear benefits relating to increased transparency. However, as well as the benefits, there are risks associated with increased transparency. In the UK context, although anti-corruption is an important issue (as exemplified by the 'private lane' issues during the Covid crisis),[26] it is not such a major concern in procurement activity as compared to the Ukraine.

Yukins has commented, in the context of the anti-corruption agenda, that policymakers crafting a sound procurement system must balance several goals. In his view, the most important goals are competition, transparency and integrity. If a procurement system reflects all these three elements in a balanced way, the system is much more likely to achieve best value in procurement, and to maintain political legitimacy. In Yukins' view, integrity has frequently been addressed separately, as part of 'anti-corruption' initiatives, and should be considered as a key integral part of a sound procurement system.[27] He notes that a fully

[26] See at https://goodlawproject.org/weve-settled-a-number-of-pandemic-procurement-cases/.

[27] CR Yukins, 'Integrating Integrity and Procurement: The United Nations Convention Against Corruption and the UNCITRAL Model Procurement Law' (2007) 36(3) *Public Contract Law Journal* at https://ssrn.com/abstract=995244.

transparent procurement system is far less likely to have problems with integrity, as many stakeholders can exercise oversight in a transparent procurement system.

Taking forward Yukins' recommendation for a sound procurement system to balance several goals, the author argues that there may also be risks – particularly relating to competition and participation – associated with the adoption of a very strong transparency agenda. Whilst the adoption of strong transparency may be appropriate in the context of the fight against corruption in Ukraine, the need for a procurement system to adopt an approach of 'transparency by default' or 'everyone can see everything' in the UK is less obvious, where corruption is less of a concern.[28]

V. Analysis of the Procurement Act Approach to Transparency

The need for transparency in procurement to be considered in a measured manner has been addressed by Coppier and Piga.[29] They recommend that transparency is a principle to be pursued with pragmatism. They note that the EU rules allow for different degrees of transparency depending on the size of the tender, acknowledging implicitly that transparency has a cost.

Coppier and Piga recognise that publishing tender processes improves the knowledge of the needs of the purchaser, fosters participation and raises accountability for the procurer. This is likely to make corruption more difficult and therefore a less likely outcome. However, they note that economists can have at least a certain degree of concern that some kinds of transparency can promote collusion, for example on-line reverse auctions in a collusive environment, or have costs associated with them, for example the fixed nature of some transparency mechanisms, such as publication costs and tender committee costs.

They note – somewhat paradoxically – that some empirical research shows that by ranking countries by their inclination to corruption (Corruption Perception Index, CPI), 'the least corrupt countries choose a less transparent way of handling their tenders (lower share of total public procurement published in the Official Journal …) while countries reputed for their higher degree of corrupt behaviour appear more transparent in their procurement'.[30] The analysis was based on a composite index produced by Transparency International, drawing on 16 surveys

[28] Whilst corruption is a threat everywhere, including in the UK, on the basis of Yukins' analysis the UK's professionalism and the integrity of procurement personnel in the UK are quite high. On this basis, the UK procurement system needs to have less of an anti-corruption focus.

[29] R Coppier and G Piga, 'Why Do Transparent Public Procurement and Corruption Go Hand in Hand?' (2006) 96(1) *Rivista di Politica Economica* 185 (available at https://core.ac.uk/download/pdf/55264511.pdf).

[30] ibid 188.

from 10 independent institutions, which gathered the opinions of businesspeople and country analysts from 159 countries. The scores range from 10 ('squeaky clean') to zero ('highly corrupt').

This analysis is represented in Figure 5.1, which identifies, at least to a certain extent, that countries with a higher Corruption Perception Index, that is those that tend to have less public-sector corruption, tend to have a lower transparency in public-sector contracting. However, the authors also remind us, echoing Yukins' comments on the importance of integrity, that each country has its own culture and institutions, noting that transparency on its own might not be enough to eradicate corruption at an acceptable cost.

Figure 5.1 Corruption Perception versus Transparency

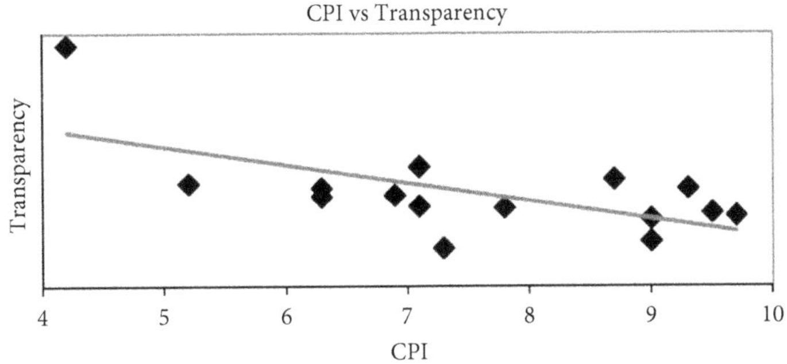

Source: R Coppier and G Piga, 'Why Do Transparent Public Procurement and Corruption Go Hand in Hand?' (2006) 96(1) *Rivista di Politica Economica* 185, 187, Graph 1.

Putting this empirical analysis to one side, and it must be viewed with a certain degree of scepticism, Coppier and Piga outline a theoretical assessment of the impact of transparency on procurement activities. Their analysis is well beyond the understanding of the author of this chapter, but their conclusions resonate with those of Yukins. They comment that 'a country with greater honesty will fix a level of transparency in its procurement lower than a country that will appear more corrupt, confirming the only apparent paradox shown by the data that less corrupt countries choose to make transparent a lower share of their total procurement through open procedures'.[31]

They also comment:

> If transparency is costly, then we have shown that countries where corruption is more pervasive and less easy to eradicate will stop short of implementing the level of transparency in procurement that would dissolve corruption. It will however find it beneficial to implement larger transparency in procurement compared to countries with a better track-record for corruption intolerance.[32]

[31] ibid 200.
[32] ibid.

Of course, transparency will always have associated costs, but the costs of transparency are likely to fall through the implementation of IT solutions, such as on-line platforms. On-line transparency is likely to be considerably cheaper and more accessible than transparency in a traditional hard-copy environment. This increases the possibility of increased transparency at a reasonable cost in the UK, but it still leaves open the question of the real benefits of strong transparency in the UK. The Government has estimated that the costs of the levels of transparency as identified in the Procurement Bill will be £36,310,991 over a 10-year period (including a '10% optimism bias'), with the costed benefits identified as £205,065,431 on a net-present-value basis. Within these costs, £17,385,114 has been allocated for the establishment and running of the Central Digital Platform. This figure appears to be rather low given the reach and sophistication of the proposed system and the relative expensiveness in practice of public-sector IT systems.[33]

Sanchez-Graells has commented on the need for public procurement systems to reach an adequate balance between their transparency requirements. He highlights the risks of collusion among tenderers or bid rigging.[34] He identifies a spectrum that goes from 'transparency-first' to 'competition-first' systems, with a number of factors that characterise these approaches, as follows:

(a) the extent to which such information needs to be identified as confidential or a business secret by its owner, or whether the need for confidentiality can be taken into account *motu proprio* by the contracting authority;
(b) the burden imposed on the owner of that information to demonstrate that it requires protection;
(c) the standard or benchmark used to assess such claims of confidentiality;
(d) applicable constraints that determine the impossibility of preventing the disclosure of specific types of information (notably, pricing), or disclosure in specific situations (eg, in the context of planned litigation); and
(e) the extent to which confidentiality granted under the procurement rules can be bypassed or nullified by more general rules on access to information and general duties to publish tender or contractual documents.

Sanchez-Graells' analysis of the state of UK transparency under the 2015 Procurement Regulations identifies that the UK has a system of protection comprising different tiers of competition-sensitive information, which include both trade secrets and commercially sensitive information, which protects the commercial interests of both tenderers and the contracting authorities and establishes a 'competition-first' system. Tenderers can protect different types of technical

[33] Cabinet Office (n 21) 25.

[34] A Sanchez-Graells, 'Transparency and competition in public procurement: a comparative view on their difficult balance' in K-M Halonen, R Caranta and A Sanchez-Graells (eds), *Transparency in EU Procurements: Disclosure within Public Procurement and During Contract Execution*, vol 9 (Edward Elgar, 2019) 33.

and financial information, including prices, and contracting authorities generally consult with tenderers before granting access to a third party. Sanchez-Graells notes that even the prices of the winning tender can be withheld as commercially sensitive information, and contracting authorities generally take steps to disguise the actual financial score received by the winning tenderer.

The transparency proposals included in the Act may well change this analysis. Whilst much of the detail of the transparency requirements in the Act remains to be determined under regulations that will be made under section 95 of the statute, it is clear that the motivation of the Act is to move towards a more transparency-led approach, with potentially less focus on the protection of bidders and successful contractors as regards confidential and sensitive information. There is an important balance to be drawn between the benefits of more transparency in public-sector procurement, which will encourage more bidders to take part in the public-sector procurement process, and the risks of excessive transparency, which can then deter bidders from taking part in procurement processes. If bidders consider that there is a possibility that their confidential and sensitive information will be disclosed, or there are requirements for that to happen, then there is a very real likelihood that potential bidders will decide not to take part in procurement processes.[35]

The guidance issued by the Cabinet Office indicates that some steps will be taken to protect the commercial and sensitive information of bidders. This guidance states that the Government will take a proportionate approach to the transparency of bidder information. However, these concerns relate primarily to the bureaucratic overhead for contracting entities in dealing with the process needed to handle the transparency requirements, rather than the bidder concerns. The guidance states that the Government is aware that 'some authorities may be worried about an increased burden on their time in order to publish this information'[36] and comments that there will be a principled approach to transparency with 'proportional levels of transparency – we want to ensure that we are only asking for the most detailed information – contract documents, performance markings etc – from the largest contracts, in order to maintain transparency without bogging procurement teams down in unnecessary bureaucracy for low-value contracts'.[37] Of course, from a bidder perspective, larger tendering processes and contracts awarded will frequently include more commercial and sensitive information than smaller tendering processes and contracts, so this principle and the Cabinet Office comments may not provide a great deal of comfort to the supplier community.

[35] The author is aware of a circumstance in which a major UK engineering consultancy decided not to take part in a procurement process in Colorado solely because the Colorado State procurement rules require the disclosure of the tenders of all bidders. The UK company decided that this would lead to too much of a risk that its commercial and sensitive information would be disclosed to the market, to its detriment.

[36] Cabinet Office (n 11) 8.

[37] ibid 9.

The Cabinet Office guidance states that 'redacted' contracts will be published pursuant to the publication of awarded contracts as part of the Contract Commencement Notice. The Act establishes that the redaction of contracts under the new procurement regime will continue to adopt at least part of the current approach of building on Freedom of Information Act (FOIA) 2000 principles. Section 94 of the Act builds on one of the two key provisions in the FOIA 2000 that have generally been regarded as being relevant in relation to the disclosure of bidder and contractor commercial and sensitive information:

- Section 41: Exemption from general duty to communicate information where the information is provided in confidence. This exemption may be relied on only where the following two conditions are satisfied:
    - the information in question must have been obtained by the public authority from any other person, including another public authority; and
    - the disclosure of the information would constitute an actionable breach of confidence actionable by the person from whom the information was obtained, or by any other person.
- Section 43: Trade secrets and other commercially sensitive information. Disclosure may be exempted where it is likely to prejudice the commercial interests of any person (including the public authority itself). In contrast to section 41, this exemption is qualified. Even if it is established that the information is a trade secret or that its release would prejudice commercial interests, the information must be disclosed unless the authority judges that the balance of public interest is in favour of maintaining the exemption.

Section 94 of the Act essentially brings section 43 of the FOIA 2000 into the new procurement regime, together with the possibility of redacting information where its non-disclosure is necessary for the purposes of safeguarding national security.[38] This is a useful clarification and gives a measure of certainty relating to the scope of commercially sensitive information that is disclosable, but it remains to be seen if the non-inclusion of section 41 of the FOIA 2000, relating to information provided in confidence, is a deterrent to companies taking part in procurement processes under the new regime. Of course, in practice establishing the grounds for the section 41 requirements relating to information provided in confidence is frequently not straightforward, but, clearly, there can be important elements of a bidder's confidential information that do not amount to a trade secrets or commercially sensitive information. Under the new regime, these elements would not be protected from disclosure in a procurement process, even though they would not be subject to disclosure under FOIA 2000 principles.

[38] Freedom of Information Act 2000, s 24.

VI. Concluding Thoughts

The Green Paper proposals and the Act clearly take England, Wales and Northern Ireland further towards the principle of 'transparency by default'. This is in line with general trends in procurement practice around the world, and in due course the author expects that the EU will follow a similar path. Of course, the UK's independent approach post-Brexit may result in differences and inconsistencies between UK and EU procurement procedures in the longer term. This will lead to additional complexities for companies looking to bid for public-sector projects in the UK and the EU, as bidders will need to take account of the two separate regimes, not least by having to monitor the separate UK and EU contract notice announcements.

Given the already significant level of interest in UK public-sector bid processes, it will be interesting to see if the increased transparency requirements set out in the Act lead to the types of improvements that have been identified in other locations.[39] The author is sceptical that there will be any 'step-change' improvements in the UK. There will inevitably be a considerable extra bureaucratic burden on contracting entities, with associated costs, but the author recognises that there is a clear need for a central digital platform that will give more opportunities for data analytics. As artificial intelligence becomes ever more wide-spread and more straightforward to use, accessibility to data is a prerequisite. Given the currently devolved and privatised nature of the existing e-procurement solutions in the UK, there is a need to create a centralised data 'pool', which can then be made available as a resource for the public and private sectors.

Going back to Arrowsmith's commentary on the UK Green Paper,[40] the Act sets out the UK Government's approach relating to the appropriate boundaries of transparency. The crucially important 'limits on proactive disclosure', as identified by Sue, have been linked to freedom of information principles. The UK Government has responded to Sue's comments that it is particularly important for commercially sensitive information to be given statutory protection in this context, based on the rules already contained in the FOIA 2000. Even though the application of these freedom of information principles in the context of the procurement process transparency will lead to considerable uncertainty in practice, it will give bidders in tendering processes under the new regime a measure of assurance that the commercially sensitive information of bidders will be afforded protection from the 'transparency by default' principle.

[39] Cabinet Office (n 21) 28.
[40] Arrowsmith (n 2) 4.

6

Defence Procurement Law and Regulation in the United Kingdom: A Silent Soldier in the March for Procurement Reform

LUKE RA BUTLER

I. Introduction and Context

Sue Arrowsmith is the ultimate procurement 'generalist', but her ubiquity is also measured by her wider impact in sub-fields such as utilities and defence. Concerning defence specifically, Sue's writings comprise, among other things, an authoritative defence chapter in her leading treatise, as well as articles on reform, the recurring theme of which is to question the justifications for distinct treatment of defence from the general part and how it might thereby be regulated.[1] Sue has also influenced a cadre of academics through commissioning articles in the *Public Procurement Law Review* and PhD supervision. Lineal descent is traceable from her student, Professor Martin Trybus, who established an academic foundation for European Union (EU) law and defence integration, to me, Martin's former student.[2] Sue also recognised early on the value of including defence on a taught syllabus.[3]

Honouring Sue's commitment to expanding the discipline's boundaries, this chapter provides a first, albeit brief, analysis of United Kingdom (UK) defence procurement law regulation. There are several motivations for this narrow domestic

[1] S Arrowsmith and B Heuninckx, 'Defence and Security Procurement' in S Arrowsmith, *The Law of Public and Utilities Procurement: Regulation in the EU and UK*, vol II (3rd edn, Sweet & Maxwell, 2018) ch 15. See most recently, S Arrowsmith, 'Reimagining public procurement law: proposals for post-Brexit reform' [2021] *Public Law* 69; S Arrowsmith, 'Transforming public procurement law after Brexit: some reflections on the Government's Green Paper' (2021) 3 *Public Procurement Law Review* 103.

[2] Procurement progeny also include Dr Aris Georgopoulos, Dr Baudouin Heuninckx and US Air Force Major Daniel E Schoeni (all former PhD students at Nottingham).

[3] Sue initially included UK single-source contract regulation on Nottingham's Executive Programme syllabus, only for it to be subsequently excluded, there being limited regulatory development in this area. As discussed in section II.B, this is now heavily regulated. EU defence procurement law has also regularly featured.

focus. First, any analysis should be welcomed. Whilst of obvious importance given the economic[4] (in particular, value for money), security and trade implications, the role of regulation in this field has been the subject of limited systematic country and comparative analysis.[5] This is an important aspect to consider given that, in addition to the many factors that affect regulation of procurement generally, the task of regulating defence is further complicated. In security terms, defence is at the centre of 'high politics' (the very survival of the state) at a time of existential geopolitical threats (from the war on terror, to Russia in the Ukraine, to China) as well as rapid technological change (cyber and AI); protection of the state significantly conditions approaches to regulating. In economic terms, defence markets are characterised by monopsonistic and oligopolistic tendencies, protectionism, difficulties in sustaining competition and historically limited prospects for international trade liberalisation. This conspiracy of factors (and others) results in contracts that are often highly sensitive, high-value, high-tech, of long duration and variable. This raises fundamental questions about the extent to which bespoke regulation is necessary, the form it should take, how it is or should be applied, and its effects on government and market behaviour.

Second, whilst perennial parliamentary inquiries repeat the same criticisms of cost and schedule overruns, and reinvent the same recommendations for political reform,[6] regulation is now increasingly given more weight as a policy tool for defence acquisition reform. The UK has experienced this at the domestic and supranational level. As an EU Member State, the UK implemented, inter alia, the 2009 EU Defence and Security Directive (EU DSD)[7] in the Defence and Security Public Contracts Regulations 2011 (DSPCR),[8] which has sought to open up national defence markets to cross-border trade. Post-Brexit, the UK has reconsidered its approach to defence procurement regulation, having introduced a Procurement Bill

[4] According to the Ministry of Defence's Equipment Plan, £242.3 billion has been allocated to defence equipment procurement and support (46% of the entire budget) for 2022–32. For an assessment, see House of Commons, *Committee of Public Accounts MoD Equipment Plan 2022–2032*, Forty-Eighth Report of Session 2022–23 Report, together with formal minutes relating to the report Ordered by the House of Commons to be printed 27 March 2023, HC 731.

[5] Contrast the United States (US), where defence procurement is a foundation of the federal procurement system and on which there is much academic commentary. See JI Schwartz, 'The Centrality of Military Procurement: Explaining the Exceptionalist Character of United States Federal Public Procurement Law', The George Washington University Law School Public and Legal Theory Working Paper No 111. For useful but dated UK literature, see K Hartley, 'Competition in defence contracting in the United Kingdom' (1992) 6 *Public Procurement Law Review* 440; and M Trybus, *European Defence Procurement Law: International and National Procurement Systems as Models for a Liberalised Defence Procurement Market in Europe* (Kluwer, 1999) ch 4.

[6] These problems date back to at least the 19th century. See, eg, SENEX, *Considerations – On the New System of Government Contracts* (Levey, Robson and Franklyn, 1856). More recently, see L Brooke-Holland, 'Defence procurement reform' (10 June 2022), Research Briefing, House of Commons Library, observing that there have been at least 13 formal reviews of defence procurement policy over the last 35 years.

[7] Directive 2009/81/EC of the European Parliament and of the Council of 13 July 2009 on the coordination of procedures for the award of certain works contracts, supply contracts and service contracts by contracting authorities or entities in the fields of defence and security, and amending Directives 2004/17/EC and 2004/18/EC [2009] OJ L216/76.

[8] Defence and Security Public Contracts Regulations 2011 (SI 2011/1848).

that will apply to public and defence procurement under a unified framework with defence-specific adaptations.[9] The UK has also adopted the Defence Reform Act 2014, extending regulation beyond contract award processes to organisation of the defence procurement function and contract management, including Single Source Contract Regulations (SSCR)[10] on pricing. The UK also envisages a specific role for reformed regulation in its new Defence and Security Industrial Strategy (DSIS).[11]

This chapter's aims and objectives are qualified in light of the constraints of space. It does not address all UK-related jurisdictions.[12] It does not rehearse the history of UK defence procurement policy in a way that would properly contextualise the role of regulation. The focus is narrowly on 'hard defence', not its equally significant counterpart 'security' procurement. It also cannot proffer an answer to the bigger question of just how effective regulation of, and for, the defence procurement market can be in improving defence outcomes, also mindful of the limits of regulation as a tool, in particular, in a highly sensitive area with an entrenched procurement culture.[13]

Rather, the modest aim is to expand the field of academic enquiry beyond the conventional focus on regulation of contract award processes to a holistic treatment of public contracting in this area, by considering wider aspects of regulated defence acquisition and provoking more fundamental thinking about the aims, objectives and tools of 'regulation'[14] in this context. There is a quiet march of defence procurement regulatory reform that could yield important insights for regulating public procurement regulation generally. This chapter is accurate at the time of writing.[15]

II. Regulation of the Defence Acquisition System

As indicated, there has been relatively limited academic focus on defence procurement regulation, specifically in the conventional sense in which it is understood,

[9] For a useful overview, see L Brooke-Holland, 'Defence procurement reform: The Defence and Security Public Contracts Regulations' (21 December 2022), Research Briefing, House of Commons Library.

[10] The Single Source Contract Regulations 2014 (SI 2014/3337).

[11] HM Government, *Defence and Security Industrial Strategy: A strategic approach to the UK's defence and security industrial sectors*, CP 410 (March 2021); Ministry of Defence, *Defence and Security Industrial Strategy: reform of the Single Source Contract Regulations*, CP 647 (April 2022).

[12] For example, the Government of Gibraltar introduced the Procurement (Defence and Security Public Contracts) Regulations 2012 (LN 2012/088) on 11 June 2012.

[13] DM O'Callaghan, 'United Kingdom's Defence Procurement: a Period of Smart Enlightenment or Halting Culture' (PhD thesis, University College London, 2001).

[14] In the interests of encouraging broad enquiry, 'regulation' could conceivably incorporate hard-law regulation through primary and secondary legislation, soft law, use of not only private law but also administrative contracts, economic regulation and regulatory economics (to capture regulation of/for the market and market failure, etc).

[15] The Procurement Bill is about to enter the Report Stage in Parliament before it receives final assent expected in June 2023. The version relied on for citation purposes is Bill 249 2022–23 (as amended in Public Bill Committee), 24 February 2023. There are likely to be further amendments of the Bill before it is finally accepted but which cannot be considered here.

that is, of processes for awarding contracts. It follows that there has been even less on defence acquisition more widely, which incorporates everything from organising the defence procurement function through to contract management. Again, there are likely many reasons for this. One is the historically limited coverage of defence in international trade instruments (eg, the World Trade Organization's Government Procurement Agreement (WTO GPA), EU Directives), which, in any event, focus on contract award. Further, aspects of contract management, in particular pricing, are even more specialist. Therefore, this short section seeks to provide a critical introduction to the UK's approach to regulating wider aspects of the defence acquisition system. The UK is a useful 'case study' of regulation, being used as a driver for defence acquisition system reform,[16] particularly where political initiatives have failed and aspects of which are certainly experimental or even globally unprecedented.

A. Regulating Defence Procurement Functions

In the UK, Defence Equipment & Support (DE&S), a trading entity of the Ministry of Defence, undertakes the procurement function.[17] Its task is complicated by many factors, not least that its customers are the Commands, each with their own procurement priorities (which may compete or conflict), budgets and timescales. As a buyer, it must organise a large civil service internally and contract with the private sector to effectively, efficiently and compliantly procure complex contracts. This must be done within an environment of changing threats and wider civil service reforms. This chapter would not begin to rehearse the systemic challenges that have been identified; suffice to state that, despite repeated attempts at reform to improve efficiency and outcomes, Parliamentary Committees have concluded that 'the Department's system for procuring equipment and managing suppliers needs an urgent rethink'.[18]

Notwithstanding, this chapter can, at least within its narrow remit, question whether there is a role for law and regulation in addressing *how* the procurement function is organised, given its impact on procurement outcomes. Instinctively, it might be thought that regulation would have no or a very limited role. However, regulatory techniques have, in fact, been applied in an attempt to render

[16] For a discussion of other drivers (but also mentioning the reforms under the Defence Reform Act 2014 as a key legal driver), see C Solar, 'Introducing Change in Public Service Organizations under Austerity: The Complex Case of Governance of the Defence in the United Kingdom' (2020) 48(4) *Politics & Policy* 700, 710.

[17] Information is available at https://des.mod.uk/ (last accessed 10 April 2023).

[18] House of Commons Committee of Public Accounts, *Improving the performance of major defence equipment contracts Twenty-Second Report of Session 2021–22 Report*, together with formal minutes relating to the report Ordered by the House of Commons to be printed 21 October 2021, HC 185. For an alternative perspective on DE&S, see A Tyler, 'Performance under Pressure' (2009) 154:5 *The RUSI Journal* 30.

organisation more 'commercial' (no doubt part of the legacy of the experiment in New Public Management[19]), although their effect in practice remains unclear. For example, the 'Defence Operating Model', which sets out the organisational structure for defence, has referred to 'contracts' entered into between the Head Office and Commands.[20] These are not contracts in the conventional legal sense of agreements entered into with external suppliers in exchange for goods or services, but rather a form of internal 'administrative contract', intended to clarify bureaucratic roles through performance-based management systems.[21] Terms such as 'SMART contracts' have also been used in this context (not to be confused with the more recently described electronic variety).[22] Again, it is beyond this chapter's scope to examine such arrangements, but the extent to which attempts to 'contractualise' internal relations between customer and buyer within government have been effective would be an interesting area for regulation-related research.

Related to the above, another considered regulatory technique is the use of contracts with the private sector to provide defence procurement services either in support of or as replacements for the state's undertaking this buyer function. Debate on whether and the extent to which to procure or manage procurement contracts in-house or through outsourced providers is not new, even in an area as sensitive as defence. Since the 1990s, the US has used major prime lead system integrators to deliver certain buying and management functions.[23]

Specifically relevant to this chapter, the UK has seriously entertained going much further. For brief context, the 2009 Levene and Gray reviews revealed that DE&S was underperforming.[24] In 2011, the MOD launched its Materiel Strategy, under which it decided to contract out a majority of DE&S operations to the private sector. The hope was that its skills would improve DE&S efficiency and incentivise delivery for less. The Government would 'contractorise'[25] DE&S through a government-owned Contractor Operated (GoCo) model. DE&S would enter into a contract with a for-profit company, which would procure on its behalf. The Government would retain overall strategic direction and ownership in the assets, with the contractor's performance incentivised by commercially negotiated fees.

The MOD recognised many risks. It wanted a 9.5 year contract covering a £100 billion spend, making it the largest GoCo of its type globally. As no single company had all the required business capabilities, consortia were expected to bid,

[19] V Lapuente and S Van de Walle, 'The effects of new public management on the quality of public services' (2020) 33(3) *Governance* 461.

[20] Ministry of Defence, *How Defence Works*, version 6.0, September 2020, 15.

[21] For a discussion of this use of contract, see generally PV Jones, *The New Public Contracting: Regulation, Responsiveness, Relationality* (Oxford University Press, 2006) 21–22.

[22] Defence Equipment and Support, Framework Document, version 1.0, 13 May 2014, 14.

[23] K Hopkins Loudin, 'Lead Systems Integrators: A Post-Acquisition Reform Retrospective' (2010) 17(1) *Defence Acquisition Review Journal* 27.

[24] *Review of Acquisition for the Secretary of State for Defence*, An independent report by Bernard Gray October 2009 ('the Gray Report'); *Defence Reform*, An independent report into the structure and management of the Ministry of Defence, June 2011 (by Lord Levene).

[25] Expression used in the Gray Report (n 24) 13.

thereby necessarily limiting the number of capable suppliers and, thus, competition. Implementing a GoCo would be complex and require transferring elements of DE&S business to Head Office and changes in the Commands to ensure they could work with the GoCo. The MOD would need to identify and mitigate conflicts of interest between GoCo bidders and existing MOD contracts in which they were existent suppliers or associates. Other countries would also need to agree that a GoCo could act as the MOD's agent on sensitive contracts. It would also take the total contracted 9.5-year term to make the savings needed to return the investment.[26]

In 2013, the MOD opened the contract to competition. There were few published details regarding the procurement process and contract.[27] It transpired that three consortia were invited, but two withdrew for lack of resources to bid and the process was halted due to the absence of competition. A National Audit Office report also found that poor governance arrangements exacerbated different expectations within the MOD and DE&S on the timing and nature of financial savings, and there remained a lack of clarity on the level of risk being transferred to the private sector. By this point, the MOD had spent £33 million, including £25 million on contractors and advisers.[28]

As the GoCo was seemingly a 'no-go' before it even began, it might be questioned why it is being considered at any length in this chapter on regulation. It is because in June 2013, the MOD nevertheless indicated that in the event that this were to be the selected option, primary legislation was needed to ensure its effective operation.[29] To confirm, even though the GoCo was not adopted, Part 1 of the Defence Reform Act 2014 has included prospective provisions for this option *if* the Secretary of State for Defence were ever to make such arrangements.[30] There do not appear to have been any public statements since regarding this sleeping leviathan, but its inclusion in legislation is nevertheless confirmation that this was formally considered a serious proposition.

The UK has also trialled other GoCo and long-term partnership arrangements with the private sector. As early as 1993, the MOD awarded a 25-year contract

[26] National Audit Office, Report by the Comptroller and Auditor General Ministry of Defence, *Defence Equipment and Support, Reforming defence acquisition* HC 946 Session 2014–15 26 February 2015, 16.

[27] A Freedom of Information Act request for further information was made by the author but limited information was provided in response. See Reference FOI2016/08287 at https://assets.publishing.service.gov.uk/government/uploads/system/uploads/attachment_data/file/557322/20160922-FOI2016-08287_GOCO_papers_response.pdf (10 April 2023).

[28] National Audit Office (n 26) 31.

[29] Ministry of Defence, *Better Defence Acquisition, Improving how we procure and support Defence equipment*, Presented to Parliament by the Secretary of State for Defence by the Command of Her Majesty June 2013, 22.

[30] These relate to: transfer of employees to that contractor; financial assistance to the contractor; financial claims against the contractor; exemptions relating to premises used by the contractor; jurisdiction of the MOD Police; 'transfer schemes' for property, rights and liabilities where the contractor is in breach of contract or the contract has come to an end; and disclosure and use of information and intellectual property rights.

to a consortium (of, amongst others, Hunting-BRAE, Lockheed Martin, Serco and Jacobs Engineering Group) to manage the Atomic Weapons Establishment (AWE). The National Audit Office has reported various failings in these arrangements over the years.[31] In 2021, the contract was terminated in favour of AWE's operating as an arm's-length body.[32] Another example, which is not a GoCo per se and which, in contrast, has actually been relatively successful, is the MOD's 25-year Long-Term Partnering Agreement (LTPA) for the provision of test and evaluation services run by QinetiQ, a privatised company but formerly part of the Defence Evaluation and Research Agency (DERA).[33]

Again, it is beyond this chapter's scope to examine the role of regulation in the context of what Defence Studies describes as the 'Defence Extended Enterprise', a public–private partnership of sorts in defence.[34] However, by way of illustration, any number of issues arise in respect of GoCos[35] that would make for an interesting study on 'government by contract' as understood in Regulation studies.[36] For example, the US procurement community will be familiar with the problem of determining the scope and exercise of the 'inherently governmental function', that is to say, which responsibilities should or should not be contracted out. Another example is 'organisational conflicts of interest', that is whether a provider should be precluded from competing for other contracts given it has inside access to government as the provider of procurement services. Indeed, US research has identified lessons learnt for the UK; this has included a recommendation that the UK should 'codify' inherently governmental functions and organisational conflicts of interests in outsourcing defence procurement services 'à la US system'.[37] More generally, the issue arises as to whether such a model would comply with international trade law regimes on public procurement, competition law and state aid. In addition to the legal issues, there are economic issues, such as the transaction costs in contracting

[31] National Audit Office, *Report by the Comptroller and Auditor General, Ministry of Defence Managing infrastructure projects on nuclear-regulated sites*, HC 19 Session 2019–20, 10 January 2020.

[32] C Mills, *Replacing the UK's nuclear deterrent: the long awaited warhead decision*, House of Commons Library Briefing Paper, Number 8941, 2 March 2021; T Plant and M Harrier, 'No Go for GOCO: The UK Renationalises Its Nuclear Warhead Factory', 6 November 2020, RUSI Commentary.

[33] Information in this regard is available at www.qinetiq.com/en/news/qinetiq-secures-13bn-ltpa-amendment-enabling-military-capability-for-the-future (10 April 2023]).

[34] J Louth and T Taylor, *British Defence in the 21st Century* (Routledge, 2018).

[35] T Taylor and J Louth, 'What the Government Must Do in Defence Procurement: The Inherently Governmental Function and the GOCO Proposal for Defence Equipment and Support', September 2013, Rusi Briefing Paper; and, relatedly, J Edwards, 'Contractorisation of UK Defence: Developing a Defence-Wide Contractorisation Strategy and Improving Implementation', 21 June 2018, RUSI Occasional Paper.

[36] On the concept of government by contract generally and its use by reference to public procurement regulation, see PV Jones, *The New Public Contracting, Regulation, Responsiveness, Relationality* (Oxford University Press, 2006) 13–16. For a discussion involving specific references to defence procurement, see H Collins, *Regulating Contracts* (Oxford University Press, 2004) ch 13; and T Prosser, *The Economic Constitution* (Oxford University Press, 2014) 233–38.

[37] WT Kirkwood, 'Inherently Governmental Functions, Organizational Conflicts of Interest, and the Outsourcing of the United Kingdom's MOD Defense Acquisition Function' (2015) 44(3) *Public Contract Law Journal* 443.

with, and overseeing, the provider, including whether it would actually reduce costs or improve efficiency, as well as security issues, such as the risk of a private provider's compromising security of the state or allies.

B. Regulating Single-Source Defence Contract Pricing

Unlike in certain other countries (eg, the US), the UK does not legally regulate the pricing of public contracts generally.[38] However, since the 1940s (but more formally since the 1960s), it has regulated (albeit through voluntary agreements) the pricing of single-source defence contracts. This was, in part, a result of the 1964 Lang Report into over-recovery on a missile contract, which identified a number of issues, including poor government estimating and over-recovery of overheads.[39] The Government has attributed some of the problems with pricing to the general consequences of market failure; that is, there are circumstances in which contracts are awarded without formal competition, reducing pressure on pricing discipline.[40] Suppliers may charge higher than market prices (or there may be no market price against which to compare), be reluctant to reveal price breakdowns, and lack the incentive to control costs once the contract is concluded and performance has commenced. A cycle of mutual dependency may also develop, exacerbating tendencies.

As indicated, since the 1960s, the UK has 'regulated' non-competitive defence contract pricing through a Government Profit Formula Agreement and Accounting Conventions. These were not put on a statutory footing but were, rather, voluntary arrangements between government and industry.[41] Their description as 'regulations' may, in part, be a reflection of established practice to incorporate reference to these arrangements in defence contract conditions (DEFCONs) as legally binding terms, which is not to say that these were necessarily always observed in practice. A Review Board for Government Contracts

[38] Similarly, there is not extensive regulation of product pricing outside the context of public procurement. An exception in this regard is pharmaceuticals. Details may be found at https://assets.publishing.service.gov.uk/government/uploads/system/uploads/attachment_data/file/675465/The_pharmaceutical_price_regulation_scheme_2014.pdf (accessed 10 April 2023).

[39] *First report of the inquiry into the pricing of Ministry of Aviation contracts* (Cmnd 2428, 1964) ('Lang Report') and *Second report of the inquiry into the pricing of Ministry of Aviation contracts* (Cmnd 2581, 1965). For a useful evaluation of the Lang Report's findings, see JF Flower, 'The Case of the Profitable Bloodhound' (1966) 4(1) *Journal of Accounting Research* 16. This received international press coverage. See 'Britain Charges Big Arms Profit; Ferranti Offers a Refund on Missile Contract' *New York Times* (29 July 1964) at www.nytimes.com/1964/07/29/archives/britain-charges-big-arms-profit-ferranti-offers-a-refund-on-missile.html (accessed 10 April 2023).

[40] See Lord Currie of Marylebone, *Review of Single Source Pricing Regulations, An independent report into the single source pricing regulations used by the Ministry of Defence* (October 2011) ('Currie Review'), paras 51 and 52.

[41] A detailed explanation of these arrangements may be found in the last Report of the Review Board for Government Contracts: Review Board for Government Contracts, *Report on the 2013 General Review of the Profit Formula for Non-Competitive Government Contracts* (February 2013).

oversaw these arrangements.[42] These were originally envisaged as applying across government, but in practice they became the exclusive province of the MOD, apparently because of the 'unusual prominence' of single-source procurement in defence.[43]

Against the backdrop of the Gray and Levene reviews, in 2011, an independent review of the regulations was conducted.[44] It identified as a serious weakness, inter alia, a tendency to focus on the appropriate profit rate (which only made up approximately 10 per cent of the contract) rather than on achieving efficiency gains in the cost base (representing 90 per cent).[45] The onus was on the MOD to show that costs were unreasonable, not for contractors to show that costs were allowable.[46] In addition, MOD policy on 'Equality of information' required open exchange between parties on costs only at the point of contract negotiation, not at conclusion.[47] Further, MOD policy on 'post-costing' also enabled a claw back of 'unconscionable profits', but only nearing the end of the contract.[48] There was also limited oversight by the Review Board, which lacked effective powers.[49] The Review proposed a new non-statutory voluntary code of conduct introducing a new pricing methodology and quarterly reporting, supported by revised contract conditions overseen by a new Single Source Regulations Office (SSRO).[50] However, the Review warned that potential lack of voluntary compliance might necessitate legislation.[51] The MOD clearly anticipated this risk.[52] In 2013, the MOD published its proposals for legislation.[53]

Part 2 of the Defence Reform Act 2014 enabled the SSCR and established the SSRO ('the 2014 framework'); the SSCR have since been amended.[54] The 2014 framework does not clearly specify its statutory aims and objectives, nor prescribe

[42] See generally S Martin, 'The review board for non-competitive government contracts: an economic evaluation' (1996) 12(2) *Defence Analysis* 205.

[43] Currie Review (n 40) 4.

[44] ibid.

[45] ibid 7, para 5, although research had previously found that in defence there was little direct evidence of excessive profits within the terms of the Yellow Book arrangements: S Martin and K Hartley, 'Comparing Profitability in the Public Utilities, Defence and Pharmaceuticals' (1997) 17(1) *Journal of Public Policy* 81, 101.

[46] Currie Review (n 40) 86, para B.65.

[47] ibid 6, para 4.

[48] ibid.

[49] ibid 24, para 84.

[50] ibid Annex E.

[51] ibid 132, E.193.

[52] The Impact Assessment to the Single Source Contract Regulations stated that such that large non-competitive contracts will always be placed with a limited number of suppliers that were unlikely to comply with non-statutory recommendations: Impact Assessment, 13 August 2014, 1.

[53] MOD (n 29).

[54] The Single Source Contract (Amendment) Regulations 2018 (SI 2018/917); the Single Source Contract (Amendment) (No 2) Regulations 2018 (SI 2018/1350); and the Single Source Contract (Amendment) Regulations 2019 (SI 2019/1106). See generally, LRA Butler, 'Single Source Wars: The Saga Continues' (2019) 28 *Public Procurement Law Review* 28; LRA Butler, 'Single Source Wars, The Saga Continues 2: The Single Source Contract (Amendment) (No 2) Regulations 2018' (2019) 28 *Public Procurement Law Review* 71.

any general legal principles.[55] The general gist is to enable industry to get a fair and reasonable price through application of a regulated pricing formula designed to 'replicate the missing competitive pressure', in exchange for providing the MOD with greater transparency over prices necessary to assure value for money through regulated reporting.[56] The 2014 framework is globally unprecedented in designating a specific regulator, but it shares certain common features with other countries (eg, US, Canada and Australia) that apply cost-and-profit principles by means of varying degrees of regulation (detailed hard law through to soft-law statements of policy). It would therefore provide a useful basis for comparative analysis of pricing regulation in other large defence trading nations. For example, recently, Canada commissioned a feasibility study on establishing similar arrangements to the UK, which was, however, ultimately not adopted due to 'key structural and application differences' that might be better understood through research.[57]

Concerning coverage, a contract must, inter alia, meet the qualifying thresholds, namely, £5 million for prime contracts and £25 million for sub-contracts, flowing the pricing and transparency requirements down the supply chain.

Concerning pricing, there are regulated pricing methods,[58] for example firm/fixed, cost-plus, etc, and a new pricing formula.[59] This has two aspects: the first is a contract profit rate, composed of a baseline profit rate subject to a six-step methodology comprising various adjustments (eg, for cost-risk and to incentivise performance);[60] the second is permitted recovery of Allowable Costs, that is those that meet the test of being appropriate, attributable to the contract and reasonable in the circumstances.[61]

Concerning transparency, contractors must provide standardised contract reports containing information that includes cost and profit breakdowns, deliverables and sub-contracts.[62] These must be provided initially on contract commencement, on an interim basis (eg, quarterly[63]) and at contract completion.[64] Further, supplier reports are required on contracts valued at £50 million or above.[65] These focus on different overhead rates and supply-chain aspects

[55] In respect of the SSRO's functions, s 13 provides that, in carrying out its functions, the SSRO must aim to ensure (a) that good value for money is obtained in government expenditure on qualifying defence contracts, and (b) that persons (other than the Secretary of State) who are parties to qualifying defence contracts are paid a fair and reasonable price under those contracts.

[56] MOD (n 29) 25.

[57] Information is available at www.tpsgc-pwgsc.gc.ca/app-acq/amd-dp/samd-dps/reponse-respond-eng.html; www.tpsgc-pwgsc.gc.ca/app-acq/amd-dp/samd-dps/resume-summary-eng.html (accessed 10 April 2023). The author requested further information on this study from the Canadian Government but received no response.

[58] SSCR, reg 10(2).

[59] Defence Reform Act, s 15(4).

[60] Defence Reform Act, s 17(2).

[61] Defence Reform Act, s 20(2).

[62] Defence Reform Act, s 24.

[63] A quarterly contract report is only required for contracts over £50 million (SSCR, reg 26(5)).

[64] SSCR, regs 23–29.

[65] Defence Reform Act, s 25; SSCR, reg 31.

(eg, engagement with small and medium-sized enterprises (SMEs) and the supplier's strategic industrial capacity). Contractors must also keep records, which the MOD may examine.[66]

Concerning oversight, the SSRO has been established as an executive non-departmental public body sponsored by the MOD.[67] The Explanatory Notes describe the SSRO as a 'regulator'.[68] The SSRO: advises the Secretary of State on setting key rates (eg, baseline profit rate) and provides statutory guidance (eg, on Allowable Costs);[69] maintains an up-to-date record of qualifying contracts; analyses reports for compliance; may give opinions and determinations on the application of the SSCR, which may lead to removal of costs or adjustments to profits; provides analysis services to the MOD; and is responsible for reviewing the 2014 framework and making recommendations.[70]

Finally, to ensure enforcement, the MOD may issue civil compliance and penalty notices for certain violations.[71]

In April 2022, the MOD published a Command Paper[72] that set out a 'significant reform agenda'. Certain of these reforms are also set out in the Procurement Bill, but are technical and not considered further here.[73]

Space precludes a fuller analysis of a complex regime that, it is suggested, would also benefit from more systematic comparison against other UK regulators (eg, in the utilities).[74] Nevertheless, some broader reflections may be provided here as a starting point.

First, the 2014 framework prompts deeper reflection on just how prevalent non-competitive procurement is generally and how should it be regulated in light of reality. The prevailing dogma often seems to be that 'competition is key' – that it should be an aim and objective of a regulated public procurement system, that public procurement already exists in a world of relatively open competitive markets and that rules enable (by design or effect) further opening of contracts to competition. It is perhaps not unfair to state that a conspiracy of optimism for competition is even present in defence, where Ministries of Defence may publicly overstate

[66] Defence Reform Act, s 23.
[67] Defence Reform Act, s 13(1).
[68] Explanatory Notes to the Act, para 46.
[69] Defence Reform Act, s 20(1).
[70] Defence Reform Act, ss 35–37.
[71] Defence Reform Act, ss 31–34.
[72] MOD (n 11) 3.
[73] For a discussion of these, see LRA Butler, 'Single Source Contract Regulation Reform under the UK Procurement Act: A Regulatory Weapon in the Defence and Security Industrial Strategy's Arsenal' (2023) 4 *Public Procurement Law Review* NA168–NA212. The Procurement Bill simply provides that sch 10 makes amendments to pt 2 of the Defence Reform Act 2014. This, in turn, enables the SSCR amendments, which will be adopted in due course. At the time of writing, there is no indication of when amended SSCRs will be adopted, along with other non-legislative proposals (eg, changes to policy and MOD and SSRO guidance) outlined in the Command Paper.
[74] The SSRO is a member of the UK Regulators Network. Details are available at www.gov.uk/government/news/ssro-joins-uk-regulators-network-ukrn.

their commitment to, and levels of, 'global competition' as the default.[75] In the UK at least, competition is probably not the reality. For instance, a Parliamentary Public Accounts Committee report concluded that around 50 per cent of MOD equipment procurement was not subject to competition at all and needed to be reduced.[76] Whilst not the norm, the sense is that non-competitive procurement is actually normal across a range of sectors and/or contracts. Indeed, the COVID-19 pandemic is also an important reminder of just how significant non-competitive procurement can become, bringing into sharp resolution the need for much closer scrutiny of how it is regulated.[77] Historically, public procurement rules have been geared primarily[78] towards addressing the ideal of market opening, not the reality of market failure.

To be clear, few would disagree that more competition is generally better than less, even if non-competitive procurement has certain distinct advantages in some cases (eg, where it can more easily enable strategic long-term partnerships with suppliers, which may not be possible through shorter transactional competitive procurement). Further, there is also the risk of regulatory myopia, that is, introducing extensive regulatory controls to address market failure where efforts could simply better focus on improving competition.

That said, using regulation to try to force some ideal of competition has its own risks,[79] and there will always be certain circumstances in which non-competitive

[75] The 2012 White Paper *National Security through Technology* set a policy of open competition in the domestic and global market, envisaging only rare exceptions when particular national security concerns applied justifying single-source arrangements. See Ministry of Defence, *National Security Through Technology: Technology, Equipment, and Support for UK Defence and Security* (Cm 8278, 2012). However, according to a House of Commons Committee Parliamentary Report, 'Across the 20 projects and programmes examined by the NAO, 14 are being procured partly or wholly non-competitively, despite the fact that "competition by default" has been departmental policy for nearly a decade. In only four of these cases was this due to "sovereignty capability" requirements, whereby the government must source capabilities from specific suppliers due to the need to protect the UK's national security interests or operational advantage. In the absence of competition, there is a risk that the Department will continue to award further contracts to poorly performing suppliers …': House of Commons Committee of Public Accounts (n 18) 13 (footnotes omitted).

[76] Public Accounts Committee, *MoD needs coherent approach to increasing competition in procurement* (23 March 2018). See also the earlier National Audit Office, *Report by the Comptroller and Auditor General, Ministry of Defence Improving value for money in non-competitive procurement of defence equipment*, HC Session 2017–2019, 25 October 2017.

[77] See generally LRA Butler, 'Regulating Single Source Procurement in Emergency Situations in the Light of the COVID-19 Pandemic: Issues in Policy and Practice'; S Arrowsmith and LRA Butler, 'Emergency Procurement and Regulatory Responses to COVID-19: the case of the United Kingdom'; and S Arrowsmith and LRA Butler, 'The Experiences and Lessons of the COVID-19 Pandemic' in S Arrowsmith et al (eds), *Public Procurement in (A) Crisis: Global Lessons from the COVID-19 Pandemic* (Hart Publishing 2021) 107, 355 and 575 respectively; and LRA Butler, *In Vitro Diagnostic Test Procurement During the COVID-19 Pandemic, Lessons Learnt and Recommendations* (University of Nottingham, 2023) ch 4.

[78] Not exclusively – regulated public procurement regimes facilitate the use of procedures that do not involve formal competition (eg, procedures permitting negotiation without any requirement for prior advertisement of a contract opportunity). However, it would be difficult to sustain that public procurement legislation truly reflects the reality of non-competitive procurement.

[79] UK experience of compulsory competitive tendering may be a salutary reminder of some of the implications of being too dogmatic. See generally S Arrowsmith, *The Law of Public and Utilities Procurement: Regulation in the EU and UK*, vol I (Sweet & Maxwell, 2014) 2–16.

procurement is necessary and even desirable. It is possible to conceive that policies and regulation may begin to reflect this reality. It is too early to say, but perhaps we may be seeing a shift in thinking in the UK, at least in defence. The post-Brexit DSIS is to move away from 'competition by default' to more strategic sourcing, that is, more 'on-shoring' of capability and closer partnerships with industry. This is accompanied by fewer and more flexible defence procurement rules, which will likely facilitate more non-competitive defence procurement, not less, in the proposed post-Brexit Procurement Bill discussed in section III.B. It is also not inconceivable that single-source contract pricing regulation of the kind adopted in the context of defence could be extended more widely, although this chapter does not consider the relative (de)merits. After all, as indicated, the original single-source pricing regime was intended to apply across government but has become the preserve of the MOD. In the Parliamentary Defence Committee, it has been questioned why the SSCR have not been extended across the public sector.[80] In any case, the SSCR regime may prompt further thinking on how non-competitive procurement is regulated generally.

A second related consideration is whether the 2014 framework is an effective regulatory model. Just as a matter of principle, the Government faces a significant challenge in trying to design a regulated pricing system for non-competitive contracts. The desire has been to use regulatory controls to 'replicate the drivers for efficiency that would exist in a market with effective competition'.[81] However, this has been done not simply through determining the comparability of prices in competitive markets in setting cost and profit allowances (itself a difficult task in economic terms) but also through extensive reporting backed by civil enforcement and regulator oversight, which is not present (at least to the same extent) in competitive markets. Further, difficulties have become apparent in trying to institute regulatory controls that, on the one hand, compensate for market failure but, on the other hand, may go too far and may end up perversely regulating to permit competitive pricing or giving contractors a competitive advantage in competitive markets. To give examples, recently the MOD has proposed permitting single-source contracts to be priced not only according to the statutory pricing formula but also by reference to open market prices in certain instances.[82] Another recurring example has been whether to permit contractors performing a qualifying single-source contract to recover costs (as indirect costs or overheads) that relate to their business overall, the effect of which might be to effectively cross-subsidise contractors on their competitive defence and non-defence contracts.[83]

[80] Defence Committee, Oral evidence: Defence Acquisition and Procurement, HC 698, Tuesday 15 November 2016, Q164, Response by Professor Trevor Taylor. For a discussion in this regard, see generally LRA Butler, 'Responsible Public Procurement: Towards A Public Service Contract Regulator?' (2019) 5 *Public Procurement Law Review* NA198–NA208.

[81] Currie Review (n 40) para 249.

[82] Ministry of Defence (n 12) 3.

[83] LRA Butler, 'Corporation Tax Relief in UK Single Source Defence Contracts: Offsetting Research and Development Expenditure Credit in Determining Allowable Costs' (2023) 2 *Public Procurement Law Review* NA94–NA109.

As a matter of form, as indicated, the Review of the former pricing regulations appeared to preference in its recommendations a voluntary code of conduct implemented through contractual terms, with oversight by a fully-fledged independent regulator, not statutory regulation subject to oversight by an arm's-length body 'sponsored' by the MOD. It would have been useful to have evaluated how the model adopted compared to that envisaged but this has not been done. As the regime has bedded down, there seems to have been a lost opportunity to revisit fundamentals in the regulatory design. Instead, current reform efforts focus largely on tweaking the regime.

As a matter of substance, a number of issues have been raised, just some of which are illustrated here. In respect of coverage, these include whether: the regime should apply to all single-source contracts, not just those above possibly arbitrary qualifying thresholds or the thresholds reduced;[84] it is appropriate to differentiate prime and sub-contract regulation, as is the case currently; certain excluded contracts should be brought within the 2014 framework; and contracts that have been amended should be subject to the 2014 framework without being subject to the parties' agreement. In respect of pricing, issues include whether: to set multiple profit rates; to treat cost risk in a certain way; and to allow certain costs but not others. Concerning civil compliance and oversight, issues include whether: there is adequate enforcement, given that civil compliance is determined by the MOD, which is also one of the contracting parties; the SSRO is sufficiently independent; and the SSRO has sufficient powers, given that it is not even able to generally require parties to provide full copies of contracts. Many of these issues have been raised by the SSRO in its reviews of the 2014 framework and its recommendations to the Secretary of State for reform since 2017,[85] but the MOD has introduced relatively few substantial reforms in response.

Overall, it is difficult to gauge whether the 2014 framework has met some of its fundamental aims, namely, to render the MOD a better-informed and intelligent customer, improve its ability to negotiate prices effectively, identify and challenge problems earlier and more robustly, and to close loopholes in the system that allow additional profits to be earned in ways that do not require cost efficiencies.[86] The Public Accounts Committee has reported that actual savings achieved have been 'very limited' to date.[87] At this stage of the 2014 framework's maturation, there continue to be more questions than answers, which may be addressed through future research.

[84] See generally LRA Butler, 'Meeting the Threshold for Effective Regulation? Contract Value Thresholds under the Single Source Contract Regulations – Rationale, Retention, Removal and Reduction' (2021) 6 *Public Procurement Law Review* 283.

[85] See, eg, Single Source Regulations Office, *Recommendations to the Secretary of State Review of Part 2 of the Defence Reform Act 2014 and the Single Source Contract Regulations 2014* (June 2017).

[86] Impact Assessment to the SSCR (n 52) 1.

[87] Public Accounts Committee, *MoD needs coherent approach to increasing competition in procurement* (23 March 2018), Conclusions and Recommendations.

III. Regulating Contract Award Procedures

Historically, the UK has not used legislation extensively to regulate the award of public-sector contracts.[88] In defence, the UK complied with the EU public-sector directives, including to the extent applicable in the field of defence and security and the EU DSD as implemented in the DSPCR. Whilst compliant, a 2015 MOD review of the DSPCR already signalled areas for reform at EU level.[89] As indicated, the post-Brexit Procurement Act will adopt a single uniform regime covering public and defence procurement in one set of rules, with defence-specific adaptations. It is beyond this chapter's scope to examine all provisions and their impact, some of which are the result of very late amendments to the Bill in Parliament. Rather, this section highlights certain key provisions, simply to contextualise the ongoing development of UK regulation. In any event, a provisional sketch here might encourage early comparative discussion of ways in which the EU DSD, or, indeed, other countries' systems of defence procurement regulation, might be reformed in view of the UK's experience.

A. Pre-Brexit Regulation

Before the EU DSD, the UK did not adopt detailed legislation to regulate defence procurement specifically. In relatively recent history, for example, the Supply Powers Act 1975 gave the Secretary of State for Defence wide powers to acquire or produce articles required for defence or the maintenance of peace and security.[90] However, there appears to be little research regarding the exercise of such broad powers in practice. Of course, the UK was also required to comply with EC law on public procurement but which principally concerned public-sector and utilities procurement.[91] More recently, MOD procurement, whether civil or military, was governed primarily by the Public Contracts Regulations 2006 (PCR 2006),[92] implementing Directive 2004/18/EC.[93] Again, there appears to be little published information and research on the UK's legal compliance with EU law in defence procurement under the EU Directives preceding the EU DSD and only some since.[94] The 2015 DSPCR Review stated that other Member States regularly

[88] C Turpin, *Government Procurement and Contracts* (Longman, 1989).

[89] Ministry of Defence, *Defence and Security Public Contracts Regulations 2011, Five Year Statutory Review* (December 2016) ('DSPCR Review').

[90] Supply Powers Act 1975, ss 1, 2 and 7(b).

[91] See generally JB Wheaton, 'Defence Procurement and The European Community: The Legal Provisions' (1992) 6 *Public Procurement Law Review* 432.

[92] The Public Contracts Regulations 2006 (SI 2006/5).

[93] Directive 2004/18/EC of the European Parliament and of the Council of 31 March 2004 on the coordination of procedures for the award of public works, public supply contracts and public service contracts [2004] OJ L134/114.

[94] LRA Butler and R Allen, 'Governing Compliance with Public Procurement Law: A View from the UK Ministry of Defence' (2020) 5 *Public Procurement Law Review* 201.

exempted procurements from the directives before the EU DSD, but does not provide detailed information on its own use of exemptions.[95] As early as 1992, there were UK Ministerial statements to the effect that the UK operated a policy of competition even where the former Article 223 of the Treaty Establishing the European Community[96] (now Article 346 of the Treaty on the Functioning of the EU (TFEU)[97]) (the essential security interests derogation) was invoked and which criticised its broad use.[98] Since, it has been stated that there was a 'culture of meeting requirements through open competition'[99] in accordance with the PCR 2006, but that standard rules did not always permit the effective acquisition of military or security capability, or deal explicitly with protecting classified information.[100]

In 2009, the EU DSD was adopted to enable suppliers in one Member State to bid for defence and security contracts in all. The intention was to reduce exclusion of defence procurement under Article 346 TFEU EU by defining the Directive's scope by reference to this provision (ie to keep procurement inside the EU treaty framework rather than outside it), with provisions adapted to the particularities of defence (eg, provisions on security of supply and information). This chapter does not rehearse existing analyses of the EU DSD[101] and the EU dimension is also examined in chapter 11 of this book by Heuninckx. As part of the transposition process of the EU DSD into the DSPCR, the MOD consulted stakeholders in two separate exercises, one on certain optional provisions that could be transposed (eg, in relation to sub-contracting), the other on the draft Regulations.[102] As the UK largely copied the EU DSD into the DSPCR, there is little to discuss concerning supplementary regulation, save to state that the UK did not transpose options that have proved to be little used (eg, the subcontracting provisions). It should be added that, unlike most central government departments, which do not publish their individual approaches to compliance with procurement legislation, the MOD has published freely available guidance on how to apply the DSPCR.[103]

[95] DSPCR Review (n 89) 4, para 1.3.

[96] Treaty Establishing the European Community (Consolidated Version) ('Rome Treaty'), 25 March 1957 [2004] OJ C325/33.

[97] Treaty on the Functioning of the European Union (Consolidated Version) [2012] OJ C326/47.

[98] Wheaton (n 91) 433.

[99] DSPCR Review (n 89) 1, para 3.

[100] ibid 4, para 1.3.

[101] For monographs on aspects of Directive 2009/81/EC, see M Trybus, *Buying Defence and Security in Europe, The EU Defence and Security Procurement Directive in Context* (Cambridge University Press, 2014); B Heuninckx, *The Law of Collaborative Defence Procurement in the European Union* (Cambridge University Press, 2016); and LRA Butler, *Transatlantic Defence Procurement, EU and US Defence Procurement Regulation in the Transatlantic Defence Market* (Cambridge University Press, 2017).

[102] Ministry of Defence, *MOD Consultation Document on the approach to implementation of Directive 2009/81/EC of the European Parliament and of the Council of July 2009*, First Consultation Document, 11 December 2009; and Ministry of Defence, *MOD Consultation Document on the approach to implementation of Directive 2009/81/EC of the European Parliament and of the Council of July 2009*, Second Consultation Document, 13 December 2010.

[103] It has produced an extensive suite of regularly updated internal Commercial Policy Statement guidance. This can be accessed via KiD at www.gov.uk/guidance/knowledge-in-defence-kid (last accessed 10 April 2023).

As indicated, the UK had undertaken a review of DSPCR implementation. This is important in itself, because it is the result of a domestic law requirement to do so, not an EU law requirement.[104] Moreover, it appears that few other Member States undertook similar reviews, as confirmed by the fact that it has been difficult to obtain information from them. The DSPCR Review reported a high level of UK compliance. It was also reported that the UK made a substantial contribution to a European Defence Equipment Market (EDEM). The UK was one of the top users of the EU DSD. By 2015, the UK value of contract award notices was £3,997 million. Its share of the market by value was 38 per cent, making the largest national value contribution.[105]

The DSPCR Review also made important general findings. First, a clear majority of MOD procurement fell under the DSPCR and PCR. It was observed that there was equal opportunity for EU suppliers, but this had not resulted in a significant increase in cross-border procurement.[106] This was said to be due not to any failings in the regulatory framework or its application, but rather to inherent difficulties of international business (language barriers, different cultures, business practices, etc), which are not unique to the defence sector.[107] This raises the issue of what, if any, measures the UK will adopt post-Brexit beyond regulation to address these issues in respect of foreign suppliers. Second, the DSPCR was considered well suited to deliver effective procurement through provisions to protect security of information and security of supply; it was observed that these have reduced the number of exempt procurements from 55 per cent to 25 per cent, although the Review did not state how exactly.[108] This is so despite the DSPCR Review's stating elsewhere that such measures could be applied under the PCR generally in any event; incidentally, the Procurement Bill does not contain such explicit provisions. It was also considered that the EU DSD represents good but not the best commercial practice that has evolved since 2009, identifying that there is no open procedure, the fact it is not as 'efficient' and 'streamlined' as Directive 2014/24/EU, and that there is scope to simplify the EU DSD to improve access and reduce the pre-qualification burden for SMEs.[109] The Review proposed: raising the contract value thresholds; permitting the open and innovation partnership procedures as is the case under the PCR 2015;[110] relaxation of rules on pre-qualification;

[104] Reg 2 DSPCR requires the MOD to review the extent to which the DSPCR's objectives had been achieved by 21 August 2016.

[105] DSPCR Review (n 89) 2, para 7.

[106] ibid 1, para 3.

[107] ibid 1, para 4. It further observed that a regulatory framework is a necessary not sufficient measure to create the market, and that non-legal factors inhibiting cross-border trade also need to be addressed: ibid 2, para 9.

[108] The MOD could not compare this reduction with the situation in other Member States as there were no figures on their use of exemptions in public domain: ibid 1, para 5.

[109] ibid 2, para 11.

[110] Although it did not identify whether this procedure was actually used by the MOD in its civil procurement, nor the precise circumstances in which it would be in the defence context.

reform of rules on repeat purchases of in-service items; and more flexible rules on contract amendments, similar to those in Directive 2014/24/EU. As discussed in section III.B, the Procurement Bill provides certain flexibilities in this regard.

There does not appear to have been any subsequent published DSPCR Review.[111] It is therefore difficult to know the extent of any impact of Brexit on compliance in this transitional phase.

B. Post-Brexit Regulation

In 2020, the Cabinet Office published its *Transforming Public Procurement* Green Paper proposals for post-Brexit reform of public procurement legislation.[112] Defence was not considered in much detail, being one of two sectors still being worked out. Nor did it feature much in the Government's response to the Green Paper.[113] The MOD did not officially publish its views on the Green Paper, despite publishing a Command Paper on SSCR reform, certain aspects of which do feature in the Procurement Bill. It is suggested that this perhaps also contributed in part to relatively limited proper parliamentary scrutiny of the defence procurement provisions during the Bill's passage.[114]

As considered briefly in section III.B.i., the DSPCR are to be repealed, with defence procurement to fall within the unform legislative regime, albeit subject to particular 'derogations' to deal with differences in the defence and security sector and to aid the delivery of the DSIS.[115] Whilst it has been stated that the Bill also introduces 'tailored rules' for defence and security procurement,[116] it may be more accurate to state that it provides more by way of exemption from rules, flexibilities and other tweaks to the application of procedural rules (eg, frameworks/modifications) than tailored rules per se (eg, there are no defence-specific rules on security of supply and information).

The following provides only a basic overview, not a systematic analysis, which may be subject to change in light of ongoing amendments.

[111] The Defence and Security Public Contracts (Amendment) (EU Exit) Regulations 2019 (SI 2019/697) do not specifically address the question of ongoing review of defence procurement prescribed in reg 2 DSPCR 2011.

[112] Cabinet Office, *Transforming public procurement*, December 2020, CP 353.

[113] Cabinet Office, *Transforming Public Procurement: Government response to consultation*, December 2021, CP 556.

[114] Much discussion largely involved rehearsing and labouring concerns made in many Parliamentary Committee inquiries over the years about overspend on defence projects, rather than addressing specific provisions. This even precipitated a probing amendment to insert a new clause requiring the Defence Secretary to commission the National Audit Office to produce a report auditing MOD procurement, but this was rejected.

[115] Procurement Bill [HL] Explanatory Notes, para 20.

[116] ibid para 5.

i. Single and Uniform Regime

In implementing the EU DSD, the UK chose to adopt separate DSPCR rather than incorporate defence within the pre-existing PCR 2006. The Bill adopts a single, uniform framework, including defence procurement, albeit with adaptations.

This decision is unsurprising. According to the 2015 DSPCR Review, one of the main reasons why the MOD adopted separate DSPCR was simply to conform to UK policy on transposition of EU law, which was to minimise the burden on government and industry and, thus, simply follow the EU's own approach.[117] However, the 2015 DSPCR Review did acknowledge complaints of having to comply with two different sets of rules, irrespective of how clear and easy each may be to follow,[118] their coexistence complicating processes, for example because of the need to use the PCR 2006 for dual-use and civil procurement, the multiplication of the amount of guidance and the increased risk of error.[119] It was further indicated that many of the different features of the DSPCR were possible under the PCR 2006 (albeit not expressly stated), for example the possibility to award contracts with conditions that protect the security of classified information despite the absence of specific rules.[120] The MOD determined that, in retrospect, it should have been possible and would have been better to draw up at the EU level a single set of rules for all procurement.[121]

In considering post-Brexit reform, presumably, it would have been open to consider whether to regulate defence primarily by other means (eg, policy). After all, unlike in the context of public-sector procurement, where UK regulation has been driven principally by international trade obligations (under EU law), defence procurement is largely excluded from international trade agreements, and the DSPCR Review identified the limited impact of the EU DSD on cross-border trade. As the Procurement Bill incorporates defence procurement within the general legislative scheme, there are clearly other reasons that justify this choice. Ultimately, whilst the EU Directives and WTO GPA are intended to reduce discrimination and open procurement markets, they may also help facilitate domestic aims and objectives, and reflect at least basic aspects of good procurement practice. Further, the continuation of detailed regulation on defence as a legacy of EU regulation does provide continuity and relative legal stability, as well as a degree of coordination in having to apply one set of rules to civil and defence procurement.

[117] DSPCR Review (n 89) 19, para 6.2. On the detail of the approach, see the Impact Assessment, Transposition of the EU Defence and Security Directive 2009/81/EC into UK Regulations (29 July 2011. On the approach to transposition generally, see HM Government, *Transposition Guidance, How to implement European Directives effectively* (February 2018).

[118] DSPCR Review (n 89) 27, para 7.26.

[119] ibid 9, para 4.9; and 27, para 7.20.

[120] Of course, it is arguable that the same could have been done under the PCR 2006, and yet, as indicated above, the MOD claimed that these were not well suited.

[121] DSPCR Review (n 89) 41, paras 10.8 and 10.9.

This rationalisation also had prominent academic support. Concerning adoption of the EU DSD, Arrowsmith had maintained that the basis for a separate defence directive was highly questionable.[122] The speculation was that the EU DSD was an exercise in symbolism or a desire to avoid opening up other aspects of the directives to amendment, but her position was also consistent with her long-standing view that, substantively, it would be preferable if the EU procurement directives were consolidated.[123] This was reiterated in her arguments for reform of UK public procurement law in the lead up to the Green Paper that preceded the Procurement Bill.[124] Most respondents to the Green Paper agreed with the need for a single set of uniform rules, believing that this would make the regulations easier for suppliers to understand and remove anomalies, citing, for example, the lack of self-cleaning provisions in the DSPCR.[125]

However, it is suggested that, whilst the basis for separate regulations for defence has been rejected, this has tended to be predicated largely on identifying the merits of uniformity. There has been less focus on whether there are still good arguments for separately regulating defence. For example, other sectors have specific regulations, for example for the National Health Service (accepting there are reasons for a distinct regime in that context). Further, there might well be areas where the MOD would like to see more regulation, or indeed less than under the general legislative scheme now proposed. In addition, there is, at least, an argument that the Procurement Bill is not necessarily the best instrument to consolidate defence-procurement regulation. It now contains a Schedule on the SSCR, such that defence procurement will be subject to a Procurement Act, a separate Defence Reform Act (which has not been amended), separate SSCR regulations, and sets of existing and future amendment regulations. There might have been good reasons for including provisions relating to the SSCR in the Procurement Act but these have not been explained.[126]

ii. Exemptions

The EU DSD contains exclusions for certain types of contracts and remains subject to Article 346 TFEU. In reality, these substantially exempt the most economically and politically significant contracts from regulation altogether. The DSPCR

[122] For the arguments generally, see S Arrowsmith, *The Law of Public and Utilities Regulation: Regulation in the EU and UK*, vol II (n 1) 15–23.

[123] S Arrowsmith, 'Modernising the European Union's public procurement regime: a blueprint for real simplicity and flexibility' (2012) 3 *Public Procurement Law Review* 71.

[124] S Arrowsmith, 'Reimagining Public Procurement Law After Brexit: Seven Core Principles for Reform and Their Practical Implementation, Part 1' (10 January 2020) at https://papers.ssrn.com/sol3/papers.cfm?abstract_id=3523172; and S Arrowsmith, 'Reimagining Public Procurement Law after Brexit: Seven Core Principles for Reform and Their Practical Implementation: Part 2' (12 August 2020) at https://papers.ssrn.com/sol3/papers.cfm?abstract_id=3672421.

[125] Government Response to the Green Paper (n 113) 6, para 15; 16, paras 66, 67.

[126] For instance, the Procurement Bill does contain provisions on procurement which may have a bearing on the status of a qualifying defence contract under the SSCR.

Review indicated that at least half of all contracts were exempt from the DSPCR.[127] However, the MOD did have a policy in place for approving recourse to Article 346 TFEU, thereby subjecting its use to some domestic controls.[128] Post-Brexit, the EU Exit Regulations included the wording of Article 346 TFEU.[129] This ensures that the MOD can still derogate from the DSPCR[130] in this interim period.

The Procurement Bill prescribes a number of exempted contracts.[131] There are certain 'counterparty exempted contracts'. For example, there is an exemption for a defence and security contract where the supplier is the government (as defined) of another state or territory.[132] There are also 'subject-matter exempted contracts', several of which do not concern defence and security contracts specifically but clearly have defence-relevant applications, and several specific to defence and security contracts. Concerning those with defence-relevant applications, there is now a distinct exemption for a contract that the contracting authority determines should not, in the interests of national security, be subject to the legislation.[133] Further, there is an exemption for contracts for the purposes of carrying out, facilitating or supporting intelligence activities.[134] In addition, there is an exemption for contracts awarded under a procedure specified in an international agreement relating to the stationing of military personnel or the implementation of a joint project between its signatories.[135] Concerning those specific to defence and security, there are exemptions for contracts: where the supplier is located where the armed forces are deployed or similarly maintain a military presence outside the UK; awarded under a procedure adopted by an international organisation; and awarded under a UK–other state or territory arrangement concerning joint development of a new product by or on behalf of the parties or its exploitation once developed.[136]

It is not clear how national security grounds and exemptions will be construed. The DSPCR Review stated the MOD's belief that the European Commission's advocacy of a strict interpretation of Article 346 TFEU may have been counter-productive to the EU DSD's aims; the MOD advocated a 'flexible' interpretation consistent with the need to develop a European Defence and Technological Industrial Base.[137] Therefore, a pre-Brexit desire for flexibility in the application

[127] DSPCR Review, p.38, para.9.5, Graph 12: Type of Exemptions used in 2015 by Value.

[128] For a discussion in this regard, see Butler and Allen, 'Governing Compliance with Public Procurement Law' (n 94) 316–19 and citations therein.

[129] Reg 6(3A)–(3C), inserted (31 December 2020) by The Defence and Security Public Contracts (Amendment) (EU Exit) Regulations 2019, regs 1, 3(3)(b) (with reg 4) (as amended by The Defence and Security Public Contracts (Amendment) (EU Exit) Regulations 2020 (SI 2020/1450), regs 1(3), 3(3)).

[130] Explanatory Memorandum to the Defence and Security Public Contracts (Amendment) (EU Exit) Regulations 2019 No 697, paras 7.1–7.7.

[131] Procurement Bill, cl 2(6).

[132] ibid sch 2, pt 1, para 4(1) and (2).

[133] ibid sch 2, pt 2, para 25.

[134] ibid para 26.

[135] ibid para 23.

[136] ibid paras 27–30.

[137] DSPCR Review (n 89) 39, paras 9.8 and 9.9.

of exemptions may be reflected in a post-Brexit desire to develop the UK defence and technological industrial base in a way that would favour a 'flexible' interpretation. There is little indication in this regard, the Explanatory Notes describing the exempted contracts as 'derogations' to aid delivery of DSIS.[138] On one hand, their characterisation as 'derogations' might suggest that exemptions are to be strictly construed, but on the other, as indicated, DSIS seems to suggest a degree of flexibility to facilitate strategic sourcing. Ultimately, the exemptions are broad and contain few terms that might otherwise act as implied conditions on use and typically indicate a strict construction.

Further, perhaps unsurprisingly, there is no apparent indication as to how any award process might be conducted pursuant to an exemption and what, if any, emphasis will be placed on encouraging competition, as was longstanding UK policy even in respect of the use of Article 346 TFEU.

iii. Coverage

The Procurement Bill excludes certain authorities, including the Security Service, Secret Intelligence Service, the Government Communications Headquarters, and the Advanced Research and Innovation Agency.[139] This raises the question of how procurement by each of these will be undertaken separately.

The Procurement Bill also defines one type of defence contract and a 'subset' thereof of covered contracts. The main type is a 'defence and security contract', which includes reference to a framework.[140] There are seven prescribed categories (eg, 'military equipment', 'sensitive equipment', etc).[141] Each is further defined (eg, 'sensitive equipment' means equipment for use for security purposes where the use or supply of the equipment may involve dealing with classified information, etc) with further sub-definitions (eg, definitions of 'supply', 'equipment' and 'classified information').[142] The subset is a 'defence authority contract', which means a defence and security contract awarded by a 'defence authority'.[143] A defence authority is to be specified in regulations made by a Minister, who may do so only if they consider that the authority exercises its functions wholly or mainly for the purposes of defence or national security.[144]

[138] Procurement Bill Explanatory Notes, HL Bill 4-EN (13 May 2022) 7, para 20.

[139] Procurement Bill, cl 2(1).

[140] ibid, cl 7(1) and (2).

[141] The others are: goods, services or works necessary for the development, production, maintenance or decommissioning of military equipment or sensitive equipment; logistics services relating to military equipment or sensitive equipment; goods, services or works for wholly military purposes; sensitive services or sensitive works; goods, services or works that are otherwise relevant to the operational capability, effectiveness, readiness for action, safety or security of the armed forces. Procurement Bill, cl 7(1)(a)–(g).

[142] ibid, cl 7(7).

[143] ibid, cl 7(4).

[144] ibid, cl 7(5) and (6).

As indicated, the types of defence and security contract are particularised in some detail through definitions. It is not clear whether such classificatory rules are an attempt to prevent issues that arose under the EU DSD in determining whether civil or defence-related rules applied to an individual contract, but there is likely to be room for interpretation.

iv. Direct Awards

For context, a European Parliament-commissioned study has previously identified the UK as having the highest percentage of competitive awards by value, with 90 per cent competitive awards as against 10 per cent non-competitive;[145] although, as already indicated, the true extent of non-competitive procurement is difficult to discern. Conversely, according to the DSPCR Review, in 2015, 67 per cent by number (173/259)[146] and 85 per cent by value (£9,023 million/£10,598 million)[147] of contracts were competitive, up from 50 per cent.[148] Thirty-three per cent by number (86/259) and 15 per cent by value (£1,575 million/£10,598 million) were non-competitive awards pursuant to the negotiated procedure without prior publication.[149] Eighty-five per cent (73/86) were national awards, a trend broadly consistent across the EU.[150]

That said, as discussed, the DSIS has replaced the 'global competition by default' policy with one focused on strategic sourcing. At this stage, it is not clear what, if any, impact this shift in policy and the new direct award provisions will have.

According to the Procurement Bill, a direct award can be made pursuant to: a direct award justification as prescribed;[151] or where a Minister has made regulations to protect life, health, public order or safety;[152] or where it is necessary to switch to a direct award.[153]

To take the first category as an illustration, a contracting authority may award a public contract directly in special cases if a direct award justification applies, and carry out a selection process or take other preliminary steps for the purpose of award. This includes an award to a supplier that should otherwise be excluded on one of the exclusion grounds, if the contracting authority considers there is an 'overriding public interest' in award to that supplier. 'Overriding public interest' includes where: (i) it is necessary in order to construct, maintain or operate critical

[145] DSPCR Review (n 89) 16–17, Table 8: Competitive and Non-Competitive Contract Awards Derived from FRS Study (%).
[146] ibid 10, para 4.10, Table 3: Number of Competitive Contract Awards.
[147] ibid Table 4: Value of Competitive Contract Awards (£ million).
[148] ibid Tables 3 and 4.
[149] ibid 10, para 4.10, Table 3: Number of Competitive Contract Awards, and Table 4: Value of Competitive Contract Awards (£ million).
[150] ibid 30–31.
[151] Procurement Bill, cl 41 and sch 5.
[152] ibid, cl 42.
[153] ibid, cl 43.

national infrastructure, for example as defined in the Government's National Cyber Security Strategy; (ii) it is necessary to ensure the proper functioning of a sector on which UK defence or security relies; or (iii) failure to award a contract to an excluded supplier would prejudice the conduct of military or security operations or the effective operation of the armed forces or intelligence services.[154] It should be observed that the EU Commission and Transparency International previously raised concerns about the proper application of exclusion grounds, for example the fact that exclusion in the context of defence contract awards is rare.[155] The Procurement Bill appears to provide broad grounds for continuing to enable excluded suppliers to participate.

Schedule 5 prescribes the direct award justifications. There are three pertaining to defence and security contracts: (i) the contract relates to supply of air or maritime transport services to the armed forces or security services deployed (or to be) outside the UK, and no reasonable supplier would be able to guarantee that all of the supply terms that would be contained in a tender would remain in effect for 10 days from submission; (ii) it is necessary for a defence authority contract to be awarded directly to enhance or maintain the armed forces' operational capability, effectiveness, readiness for action, safety or security; and (iii) a contracting authority that could rely on certain contract modification grounds (ie it would not be a substantial modification, or would be a permitted modification on unforeseeable urgency or additional works grounds) can directly award a new contract covering the same matters as a modification would.[156] As already indicated in respect of exemptions, it is not clear how strictly these justifications will be construed.

This flexibility is balanced with increased transparency. Currently, an authority can issue a voluntary transparency notice of a direct award, with a 10-day standstill period to mitigate risk of challenge on grounds of ineffectiveness; the Procurement Bill will require publication of a transparency notice before making it, thereby introducing at least some *ex ante* controls on use.

v. *Modifications*

As indicated, the DSPCR Review had previously identified the need for more flexibility in respect of modifications. The Procurement Bill provides that a contracting authority may modify a public contract, inter alia, if it is a permitted modification,

[154] ibid, cl 41(2) and (5).

[155] Commission Staff Working Document, *Evaluation of Directive 2009/81/EC on public procurement in the fields of defence and security, Accompanying the document Report from the Commission to the European Parliament and the Council on the implementation of Directive 2009/81/EC on public procurement in the fields of defence and security, to comply with Article 73(2) of that Directive* {COM(2016) 762 final}, Brussels, 30 November 2016 SWD(2016) 407 final, 67. See also Transparency International, *Evaluation of the functioning and impact of the EU Defence and Security Public Procurement Directive (2009/81/EC) across 20 EU States* (2016) 18.

[156] This is only the case for a new defence and security contract for additional goods, works or services that constitutes a qualifying defence contract within the meaning of s 14(2) of the Defence Reform Act 2014: sch 5, paras 18–20. Explanatory Notes (n 138), para 748.

as prescribed.[157] There are two permitted modifications pertaining specifically to defence authority contracts: (i) where it is necessary to enable the contracting authority to take advantage of developments in technology, or prevent or mitigate any adverse effect of those developments; and (ii) where continuous supply is necessary to ensure the armed forces' ability to maintain their operational capabilities, effectiveness, readiness for action, safety, security, or logistical capabilities and the modification is necessary.[158]

Again, increased flexibility to make modifications is balanced with increased transparency. Before modifying a public contract, a contracting authority must publish a contract change notice; however, this does not apply to defence and security contracts.[159] Therefore, again, this would appear to provide broad authority to modify contracts without many controls on use.

vi. Frameworks

The DSPCR Review called for changes to procedural rules on framework agreements but did not actually discuss them in any detail. This is surprising given their prevalence in the defence sector. The Procurement Bill has introduced significant flexibilities in respect of defence frameworks. The maximum term for a framework generally is four years but will be eight years if it is a defence and security framework, as defined; the maximum does not apply if the contracting authority considers that a longer term is required.[160] Further, whilst there is a general requirement to publish a contract award notice for contracts awarded under a framework, there is no such requirement for defence and security contracts.[161] As these are subject to so little regulation, it remains to be seen whether more extensive policy guidance will be provided on the use of frameworks and other commercial purchasing tools in the context of defence.

vii. Remedies

Historically, consistent with relatively low levels of public procurement litigation in the UK (but which is increasing in terms of reported judgments),[162] there have been few legal challenges to defence contract awards. Therefore, the case law has not provided any significant indications that the remedies system has been particularly problematic in its application to defence contracts; indeed, the High Court has given due consideration to defence and security interests, for

[157] Procurement Bill, sch 8.
[158] ibid sch 8, paras 10 and 11.
[159] ibid cl 75(1) and (6).
[160] ibid cl 47(1), (2) and (4).
[161] ibid cl 50(1) and (6).
[162] See generally, S Arrowsmith and R Craven, 'Public Procurement and Access to Justice: A Legal and Empirical Study of the UK System' (2016) 6 *Public Procurement Law Review* 227.

example in permitting contracting authorities to lift the automatic suspension on contract award.[163]

Concerning pre-contractual remedies, the Procurement Bill introduces a new test for granting interim relief, which explicitly accommodates defence and security. Thus, when considering whether to make an order, the court must have regard to the public interest, in, among other things, avoiding delay in supply, and expressly states as an example 'in respect of defence and security interests'.[164] Concerning post-contractual remedies, if there is a breach of statutory duty, the court must set aside the contract or modification, but not if it is satisfied that there is an overriding public interest in not setting it aside, again citing as an example 'in respect of defence or security interests'.[165] As in respect of the interpretation of exemptions, it remains to be seen what weight will be attributed to defence and security interests as against any countervailing considerations vis-à-vis the interests of suppliers and the broader public interest.

IV. Reflections and Conclusions

At a lunch kindly held for prospective Associate Professorships at Nottingham in 2019, I sought to move polite conversation away from the buffet[166] by casually remarking that Sue could have been the next Birks or Burrows, it perhaps being less well known that Sue had led research in Restitution early on in her career.[167] Most would have taken the compliment, given the comparison, but Sue resolutely questioned why (with due respect to those pioneers), affirming the opportunity to establish a new field. Furthering the Global Revolution in public procurement has been her calling and this book is testament to her success. Professionally, it is a great privilege to be able to work with someone whose intuitions about law and regulation in the field remain just as valid and vindicated today as they were decades ago. Sue's work is a constant point of reference, and there is no better tribute than that.

This chapter has not sought to make a substantial contribution in the space available. However, it has shed light on an area that has been greatly overlooked, especially when conceived in broader regulatory terms. As indicated, the UK has

[163] See, eg, *BFS Group Ltd v Secretary of State for Defence* [2006] EWHC 1513; *NP Aerospace Limited v Ministry of Defence* [2014] EWHC 2741; *MLS (Overseas) Ltd v Secretary of State for Defence* [2017] EWHC 3389; *Joseph Gleave and Son Ltd v Secretary of State for Defence* [2017] EWHC 238; *MSI-Defence Systems v Secretary of State for Defence* [2020] EWHC 164.

[164] Procurement Bill, cl 101(2)(a).

[165] ibid cl 103(1), (2) and (3).

[166] University catering being a constant reminder of why we are all so committed to improving procurement outcomes.

[167] S Arrowsmith, 'Ineffective Transactions, Unjust Enrichment and Problems of Policy' (1989) 9(3) *Legal Studies* 307; S Arrowsmith, 'Ineffective Transactions and Unjust Enrichment: A Framework for Analysis' (1989) 9(2) *Legal Studies* 121.

used regulation to address not only how contracts are awarded (the conventional remit of public procurement law), but also wider aspects of defence acquisition. This provokes a deeper and more holistic consideration of the aims and objectives *of* regulation (ie to achieve various policy objectives in protection of various interests) and *for* regulation (ie to ensure that regulation is effective as a matter of regulatory policy), and the forms this may take across the defence-acquisition system. This may also yield important lessons for regulating public procurement more generally.

Defence procurement in the UK is an interesting regulation 'case study' as aspects are certainly experimental. At present, there are no signs of entrusting the defence-procurement function to the private sector, but there is clearly an appetite for closer Government–industry partnerships, which will have regulatory implications. The 2014 framework on single-source contract pricing is a fascinating example of economic regulation (of sorts) in a very specific area. Finally, the post-Brexit rules on awarding defence contracts have been rationalised within a single uniform regime, but subject to adaptations that may or may not continue to give defence procurement an exceptionalist character – it remains to be seen.

Ultimately, this chapter should spur future intra- and inter- disciplinary engagement given the insights that other legal (eg Regulation) and non-legal (eg Defence Studies) disciplines may bring to bear in this context. Further, comparative discussion among defence-trading nations, in particular allies, is vital given the current threats to global security. The war in Ukraine, for example, is just the latest reminder (as if it were ever needed) that defence procurement and its regulation should be much higher on the agenda of academic discourse than it is currently.[168] This chapter is another call to arms.

[168] See, eg, the forthcoming Special Issue of the *Public Procurement Law Review* on European defence procurement responses to the war in Ukraine.

PART II

European Union Public Procurement Law

7

Reforms of EU Public Procurement Law: A Long Road to Heaven?

LAURENCE GORMLEY

I. Introduction

Sue Arrowsmith is rightly seen as the doyenne of public procurement law, not just in the United Kingdom and the European Union but on the worldwide procurement stage. Her contribution to procurement law and to the global revolution in that area has been outstanding, as has her contribution to the improvement of procurement practice.

II. Early Days

In the 1970s and early 1980s, European public procurement law was, if not in a wholly dormant state, not far short of it. The initial legislation[1] did not generate substantive litigation before the Court of Justice until Case 76/81 *SA Transporoute et Travaux v Minister of Public Works*,[2] in which the Court held that a Member State could not require that a tenderer from another Member State furnish proof by any means other than those prescribed in Articles 23 to 26 of Directive 71/305,[3] that he satisfied the criteria laid down in those provisions and relating to his good standing and qualifications, and that an opportunity to explain what appeared to be an abnormally low tender had to be given, with a reasonable time in which to furnish the relevant details. Indeed, there were only ever 13 judgments interpreting Directive 71/305, and 14 infringement proceedings, the figures for

[1] Council Directive 71/305 concerning the co-ordination of procedures for the award of public works contracts [1971] OJ English Special Edition: series I, vol II, 682; Council Directive 77/62 coordinating procedures for the award of public supply contracts [1977] OJ L13/1.

[2] Case 76/81 *SA Transporoute et Travaux v Minister of Public Works* ECLI:EU:C:1982:49.

[3] See n 1.

Directive 77/62 being two and 11 respectively.[4] The division dealing with public procurement until the late 1980s was not given much encouragement by the hierarchy, and as a result its morale was not the highest in the Commission's services. There was no explosion of activity comparable to that concerning the free movement of goods after the Commission's famous Communication on the consequences of the *Cassis de Dijon* judgment.[5]

III. New Energy

Things improved rapidly as part of the Commission's Internal Market programme, reflecting the dynamism that developed with the first Delors Commission's prioritisation of the Internal Market.[6] Clear action on public procurement was proposed,[7] with the aim of seriously implementing the existing legislation, increasing awareness of the obligations and the benefits deriving from Community rules, and enhancing the transparency of contracts concluded by the utilities.[8] Specific attention was to be paid to providing firms with advance information, limiting the use of restricted procedures and privately negotiated contracts, promoting the use of European technical standards, rationalising publication procedures and extending time limits.[9] The case law of the Court confirmed that the central freedoms of the Internal Market, such as the free movement of goods, freedom of establishment and the freedom to provide (and receive) services, and central principles of Community law, such as non-discrimination and equal treatment and transparency, applied, irrespective of whether procurement procedures are above or below the thresholds, or even outside the scope of the directives altogether.[10]

[4] Figures from Eur-Lex (Judgments on interpretation and on infringements, excluding cases decided by Orders). All links last consulted 28 August 2023.

[5] Communication from the Commission concerning the consequences of the judgment given by the Court of Justice on 20 February 1979 in Case 120/78 ('Cassis de Dijon') [1980] OJ C256/2. See LW Gormley, *Cassis de Dijon and the Communication from the Commission* (1981) 6 *EL Rev* 454, and literature cited there.

[6] Commission's White Paper, *Completing the Internal Market* COM (85) 310 Final (particularly paras 81–87); and R Bieber et al (eds), *1992: One European Market?* (Nomos, 1988); I van Bael, 'Public Procurement and the Completion of the Internal Market' (1989) 16(1) *Legal Issues of European Integration* 21.

[7] COM (86) 375 final.

[8] Commonly known then as 'the excluded sectors'.

[9] Commission's Answer to WQ 1660/86 (André), given by Lord Cockfield, [1987] OJ C124/15.

[10] See, eg, Case 45/87 *Commission v Ireland* ECLI:EU:C:1988:435; Case C-21/88 *Du Pont de Nemours Italiana SpA v Unità Sanitaria Locale No 2 di Carrara et al* ECLI:EU:C:1990:12; Case C-351/88 *Laboratori Bruneau Srl v Unità Sanitaria Locale R/M24 di Monterotondo* ECLI:EU:C:1991:304; and the Commission's Interpretative Communication on Community law applicable to contract awards not or not fully subject to the provisions of the Public Procurement Directives [2006] OJ C179/2, upheld by the General Court in Case T-258/06 *Germany v Commission* ECLI:EU:T:2010:214.

The profile of Public Procurement was raised to be dealt with at Directorate level, and new directives started to emerge: while the amendments to Directive 77/62[11] made by Directive 88/295,[12] and to Directive 71/305[13] made by Directive 89/440,[14] were already in the legislative process, as was Directive 89/665[15] on remedies in public supplies and public works contracts, the adoption of Directive 90/531[16] on procurement by the utilities (notorious for introducing compulsory Community preference over third countries, in the absence of multilaterally or bilaterally agreed comparable and effective equivalent access arrangements),[17] followed by the adoption of Directive 92/13[18] on remedies in procurement by the utilities, were of major importance. Indeed, a political link with the proposed substantive procurement regime for the utilities was already quickly made by the Italian Presidency of the Council in the second half of 1989.[19] The momentum became a stream of legislation, with the adoption of Directive 92/50[20] on the procurement of services; Directive 93/36[21] on the procurement of supplies; Directive 93/37[22] on public works contracts, and, finally, Directive 93/38[23] on the utilities. By the end of 1993, there was a brand-new box of directives, having benefited from considerable input from the European Parliament.

[11] See n 1.

[12] Council Directive 88/295/EEC of 22 March 1988 amending Directive 77/62/EEC relating to the coordination of procedures on the award of public supply contracts and repealing certain provisions of Directive 80/767/EEC [1988] OJ L127/1.

[13] See n 1.

[14] Council Directive 89/440/EEC amending Directive 71/305/EEC concerning coordination of procedures for the award of public works contracts [1989] OJ L210/1 (corr [1989] OJ L210/55).

[15] Council Directive 89/665/EEC of 21 December 1989 on the coordination of the laws, regulations and administrative provisions relating to the application of review procedures to the award of public supply and public works contracts [1989] OJ L395/83 (corr [2016] OJ L63/44), commonly referred to as the Public Sector Remedies Directive.

[16] Council Directive 90/531/EEC of 17 September 1990 on the procurement procedures of entities operating in the water, energy, transport and telecommunications sectors [1990] OJ L297/1.

[17] ibid, Art 29; P-A Trepte, *The application of procurement procedures in the hitherto excluded sectors* (1990) 1 *Utilities Law Review* 158.

[18] Council Directive 92/13/EEC of 25 February 1992 coordinating the laws, regulations and administrative provisions relating to the application of Community rules of entities operating in the water, energy, transport and telecommunications sectors [1992] OJ L76/14.

[19] The Italian Presidency made it plain that final progress on the re-examined proposal on the extension of procurement provisions to the utilities depended on the Commission's proposal on remedies for the utilities being on the table before the Council substantively discussed that re-examined proposal (COM (90) 301 Final), see LW Gormley, *Remedies and procurement by the utilities* (1990) 1 *Utilities Law Review* 166.

[20] Council Directive 92/50/EEC of 18 June 1992 relating to the coordination of procedures for the award of public service contracts [1992] OJ L209/1.

[21] Council Directive 93/36/EEC of 14 June 1993 coordinating procedures for the award of public supply contracts [1993] OJ L199/1.

[22] Council Directive 93/37/EEC of 14 June 1993 concerning the coordination of procedures for the award of public works contracts [1993] OJ L199/54 (corr [1994] OJ L111/115).

[23] Council Directive 93/38 of 14 June 1993 coordinating the procurement procedures of of entities operating in the water, energy, transport and telecommunications sectors [1993] OJ L199/84 (corr [1994] OJ L82/39 and 40).

IV. How Did the Brand-New Box Do?

The brand-new box of substantive directives lasted for over 20 years, but just as earlier legislation had to be adapted to developments in the General Agreement on Tariffs and Trade (GATT),[24] the substantive directives were adapted to international requirements stemming from the Uruguay Round GPA[25] by Directive 97/52[26] and, for the utilities, by Directive 98/4.[27] While the Commission opined that implementing measures were unnecessary, as the GPA formed an integral part of the Community legal order as an international agreement to which the Community was a party, the functioning of the Community system would be affected insofar as the GPA provisions were more favourable than the Community provisions.[28] Amendments to the substantive directives were designed to ensure that Community companies would not be subject to less favourable rules than companies from third countries relying on the GPA.[29] Particular attention was paid to ensuring that the two regimes were coherent and to the transparency requirements emanating from the GPA, especially regarding enhanced information for disappointed tenderers. Both Directives had a long, and hard-fought, gestation, in particular Directive 98/4, which had to go to conciliation before agreement was reached.[30] In relation to the utilities, the Commission succeeded in rejecting attempts to confine the changes to the regime for the utilities to public authorities and public undertakings.[31] The amount of litigation on the interpretation of the Directives was not in fact that huge,[32]

[24] eg Directive 88/295 (n 12) embraced changes required by the amendments made in 1986 to the Tokyo Round Code on Public Procurement of 1979.

[25] Agreement on Government Procurement, Annex 4(b) to the Marrakesh Agreement establishing the World Trade Organization at www.wto.org/english/docs_e/legal_e/gpr-94_e.pdf (last consulted 8 July 2023). As to the Commission's proposals, see COM (95) 107 at http://aei.pitt.edu/50230/1/COM_(95)_107_final.pdf (last consulted 8 July 2023) [1995] OJ C138. As to the Commission's amended proposal, see the very clear explanatory memorandum in COM (96) 623, final. As to the procedure in the European Parliament, see at https://oeil.secure.europarl.europa.eu/oeil/popups/printficheglobal.pdf?reference=1995/0079(COD)&l=en.

[26] European Parliament and Council Directive 97/52/EC of 13 October 1997 amending Directives 92/50/EEC, 93/36/EEC and 93/37/EEC concerning the coordination of procedures for the award of public service contracts, public supply contracts and public works contracts respectively [1997] OJ L328/1.

[27] Directive 98/4/EC of the European Parliament and of the Council of 16 February 1998 amending Directive 93/38/EEC coordinating the procurement procedures of of entities operating in the water, energy, transport and telecommunications sectors [1998] OJ L101/1.

[28] COM (95) 107, 3 (para 3); the position is more clearly stated in COM (96) 263, 3 (para 1).

[29] The Commission observed that 'The Directives, whether amended or not, deal only with the intra-Community relations, that is the relations between the European contracting entities and authorities and the European companies. They do not create rights for companies from third countries, whose rights exclusively derive from the GPA or other international agreements.' COM (96) 263, 3 (para 2).

[30] See R Williams, 'Directive 98/4 amending the utilities procurement regime' (1998) 7 *Public Procurement Law Review* 95.

[31] ibid 96.

[32] Directive 92/50, 36 interpretative judgments and 18 infringement judgments; Directive 93/36, 14 and 12; Directive 93/37, 18 and 13; Directive 93/38, 7 and 9, respectively; see n 4.

although many important cases came before the Court in this period.[33] But it was very soon clear politically that matters had to improve. The Commission moved carefully but purposively: several Member States had failed to implement all the new directives, and greater effort was needed in this area; while greater transparency had brought benefits, improvements in market access remained disappointing.[34]

This view was reiterated in the Commission's Green Paper of November 1996.[35] It observed that the primary purpose of Community procurement law was unchanged.[36] Although the aims of the Single Market remained what they had always been, the world had changed in many respects: the Commission, building on reactions to the Green Paper, identified the information revolution; changed views about the state's role in the economy; budgetary restraint, the rise of privatisation, public–private partnerships; utilities liberalisation and the internal market's success in increasing intra-EU trade.[37] The resulting increased competitiveness, and public awareness of the importance of fighting corruption and the misuse of public funds, meant that effective action was an essential political and economic priority. While fair, non-discriminatory and transparent procurement procedures made fraud and corruption in public administration more difficult, transparent procedures were not in themselves enough to eradicate fraud and corruption; an effective and dissuasive system of monitoring, procedural checks and proportional penalties would help to combat breaches of public trust.[38] Adaptation of the regulatory framework to the changed market would be essential. This meant removing utilities, which operated under conditions of effective competition, from the ambit of the directives; introducing new and flexible procurement procedures for framework contracts and for

[33] See, eg, Joined Cases C-46/93 & C-46/93 *Brasserie du Pêcheur SA v Federal Republic of Germany and R v Secretary of State for Treansport ex parte: Factortame Ltd and Others* ECLI:EU:C:1996:79; Case C-360/96 *Gemeente Arnhem et al v BFI Holding BV* ECLI:EU:C:1998:525; Case C-81/98 *Alcatel Austria AG et al v Bundesministerium für Wissenschaft und Verkehr* ECLI:EU:C:1999:534; Case C-324/98 *Telaustria Verlags GmbH et al v Telekom Austria AG* ECLI:EU:C:2000:669; Case C-390/98 *The Queen v HM Treasury, ex parte The University of Cambridge* ECLI:EU:C:2000:529; Case C-94/99 *ARGE Gewässerschutz v Bundesministerium für Land- und Forstwirtschaft* ECLI:EU:C:2000:677; Case C-513/99 *Concordia Bus Finland Oy Ab v Helsingin kaupunki et al* ECLI:EU:C:2002:495; Case 92/00 *Hospital Ingenieure Krankenhaustechnik Planungs-Gesellschaft mbH (HI) v Stadt Wien* ECLI:EU:C:2002:379; Joined Cases C-21/03 & 31/03 *Fabricom SA v Belgian State* ECLI:EU:C:2005:127; Case C-26/03 *Stadt Halle et al v Arbeitsgemeinschaft Thermische Restabfall- und Energieverwertungsanlage TREA Leuna* ECLI:EU:C:2005:5; Case C-458/03 *Parking Brixen GmbH v Gemeinde Brixen and Stadtwerke Brixen AG* ECLI:EU:C:2005:605; Case C-331/04 *ATI EAC Srl e Viaggi di Maio Snc et al v ACTV Venezia SpA et al* ECLI:EU:C:2005:718, Case C-314/09 *Stadt Graz v Strabag AG* ECLI:EU:C:2010:567; Case C-568/08 *Combinatie Spijker Infrabouw-De Jonge Konstruktie et al v Provincie Drenthe* ECLI:EU:C:2010:75; and Case C-448/01 *EVN AG and Wienstrom GmbH v Republik Österreich* ECLI:EU:C:2003:651.

[34] COM (96) 520 final, The Impact and Effectiveness of the Single Market, 15–16.

[35] COM (96) 563 final.

[36] ibid 3, para 2.3.

[37] COM (98) 143 final, Public Procurement in the European Union, 2.

[38] COM (96) 563 final, 4, para 2.4.

competitive negotiated procedures; developing procurement rules for concessions, other public–private cooperation and privatised operators; and facilitating and developing fully electronic procurement.[39] The Commission also noted that constantly changing legislation frequently did not contribute to certainty; it resolved, therefore, to issue interpretative communications, taking account of developments in the case law of the Court of Justice, in order to guide practice.[40] These documents would state or restate the law as stated by the Court, but would avoid seeking to constrain the action of Member States or contracting entities under the guise of a policy instrument.[41]

The rather open and confessional tone of the Commission's Green Paper and its response to that consultation[42] made it plain that the brand-new box was performing sub-optimally, due to the poor level of implementation and cooperation by the Member States, to inadequate supervision and enforcement by the Commission, and because the procurement legislation was perceived as somewhat cumbersome in its approach and even Delphic as far as interpretation was concerned. Yet apart from amendments necessitated through the accession of new Member States, the only substantive amendments related to new standard forms introduced by Directive 2001/78,[43] prior to the wholesale replacement of the brand-new box of directives in 2004. Any possible prospect of substituting the directives by regulations, in order to improve compliance, as in the customs field, or even of adopting a limited regulation giving the Commission supervisory and investigative powers along the lines of its powers in the competition field, got no further than action to improve control to protect the Community's financial interests in co-funded procurement by Member States and funding of projects in third countries.[44] The judgment on the brand-new box, was, unsurprisingly, 'tries hard, needs to do better'.

[39] COM (98) 143 final, 6–7, para 2.1.2.1.

[40] Perhaps the most celebrated Communication is the Interpretative Communication on Community law applicable to contract awards not or not fully subject to the provisions of the Public Procurement Directives (n 10). See also the Commission's Communications on the possibilities for integrating environmental considerations into public procurement, COM (2001) 274 final, [2001] OJ C333/12, and on the possibilities for integrating social considerations into public procurement COM (2001) 566 final, [2001] OJ C333/27; as to current guidance on the latter, see the Commission's Notice, Buying Social – A guide to taking account of social considerations in public procurement – Second edition [2021] OJ C237/1. See further, the Commission's Notice on Guidance on Innovation Procurement [2021] OJ C267/1, the Notice on tools to fight collusion in public procurement and on guidance on how to apply the related exclusion ground [2021] OJ C91/1, and Guidance from the European Commission on using the public procurement framework in the emergency situation related to the COVID-19 crisis [2020] OJ C108 I/1. In the field of defence procurement, see the Commission's Notice on guidance on cooperative procurement in the fields of defence and security [2019] OJ C157/1.

[41] The Commission had learned from the annulment of a communication in the State Aid field in Case C-325/91 *France v Commission* ECLI:EU:C:1993:245.

[42] COM (98) 143 final.

[43] Commission Directive 2001/78 of 13 September 2001 amending Annex IV to Council Directive 93/36/EEC, Annexes IV, V and VI to Council Directive 93/37/EEC, Annexes III and IV to Council Directive 92/50/EEC, as amended by Directive 97/52/EEC, and Annexes XII to XV, XVII and XVIII to Council Directive 93/38/EEC, as amended by Directive 98/4/EC (Directive on the use of standard forms in the publication of public contract notices) [2001] OJ L285/1 (corr [2002] OJ L214/1).

[44] COM (96) 583, 16, para 3.41 and 29 et seq; COM (98) 142, 30–31, para 4.6.3.

V. Twenty-First Century Blues?

The Commission's proposals for a single new directive for the classic sectors[45] responded to Arrowsmith's conversion to that approach,[46] seeking to simplify the legislation and improve its quality, to facilitate electronic procurement, a competitive dialogue in negotiated procedures, to facilitate framework agreements, to provide clarification concerning technical specifications, to strengthen award and selection criteria, and to simplify the thresholds. The European Parliament's response was notable for its emphasis on contracting authorities' being able to achieve specific environmental goals, and (demonstration of) compliance by tenderers with environmental protection requirements. After extensive ping-pong, going all the way to conciliation, the final text was adopted by the Parliament and the Council as Directive 2004/18.[47]

Some general points are striking about that that Directive (apart from the new or revised procedures themselves). First, the prominent place accorded not only to the principles of the free movement of goods, establishment and services, but also to the principles of equal treatment, non-discrimination, mutual recognition, proportionality and transparency, recognised in the case law of the Court of Justice,[48] which the second recital in the Preamble identified as flowing from the Internal Market freedoms. Trusting to principles alone, however, was not enough, hence the specific coordination provisions for procurement contracts above the specified thresholds, as opposed to providing, as in the past, for exemptions below those thresholds. These provisions were based on those principles to ensure that they would be effective and to guarantee the opening-up of public procurement to competition;[49] the 'aforementioned rules and principles' would also have to be interpreted in accordance with both the rules and principles mentioned above and other rules of the Treaty.[50] While this was clearly meant to achieve coherence, it is rather Delphic, as only principles were mentioned, not rules!

The second point is the legislative codification of the Court of Justice's case law, especially on award criteria, which clarified the possibilities for the contracting

[45] COM (2000) 275 final [2001] OJ C29E/11.

[46] S Arrowsmith, 'Future Prospects for the European Community's Regime on Public Procurement' in LW Gormley (ed), *Gordian Knots in European Public Procurement Law* (Bundesanzeiger/ERA, 1997) 88, 97.

[47] Directive 2004/18 of the European Parliament and of the Council of 31 March 2004 on the coordination of procedures for the award of public works contracts, public supply contracts and public service contracts [2004] OJ L134/114 (corr [2004] OJ L351/44).

[48] See, eg, Case C-87/94 *Commission v Belgium* ECLI:EU:C:1996:16; Case C-275/98 *Unitron Scandinavia A/S et al v Ministeriet for Fødervarer, Landbrug of Fiskeri* ECLI:EU:C:1999:567; Case C-324/98 *Telaustria Verlags GmbH et al v Telekom Austria AG* ECLI:EU:C:2000:669; Case C-92/00 *Hospital Ingenieure Krankenhaustechnik Planungs- GmbH (HI) v Stadt Wien* ECLI:EU:C:2002:379; Case C-470/99 *Universale-Bau AG v Entsorgungsbetriebe Simmering GesmbH* ECLI:EU:C:2002:746; and Case C-448/01 *EVN AG & Wienstrom GmbH v Republik Österreich* ECLI:EU:C:2003:651.

[49] See eg Case C-324/98 *Telaustria Verlags GmbH et al v Telekom Austria AG* ECLI:EU:C:2000:669; the importance of doing this was already specified in, eg, Directive 89/665 (n 14), Preamble, 3rd recital, and in Directive 93/37 (n 21), Preamble, 10th recital.

[50] Directive 2004/18 (n 47), Preamble, para 2.

authorities to meet the needs of the public concerned, including in the environmental and/or social area,[51] provided that such criteria are linked to the subject matter of the contract, do not confer an unrestricted freedom of choice on the contracting authority, are expressly mentioned and comply with the fundamental principles mentioned in recital 2.[52] The third point is the large number of recitals (60), compared with 27 in Directive 92/50, 18 in Directive 93/36 and 14 in Directive 93/37, and the 34 in the Commission's original proposal.[53] This reflects the desire – particularly of the European Parliament – to emphasise issues in the Preamble, knowing full well the Court's willingness to use it in interpreting the substantive provisions of the Directive.

In parallel with the proposal for what became Directive 2004/18, the Commission proposed a new directive for the utilities.[54] The Preamble finally agreed on in Directive 2004/17,[55] also contained 60 recitals, compared with 47 in the Commission's proposal, and 36 in Directive 90/531. Sensibly, the negotiations for both measures saw considerable alignment between them, and the utilities proposal too went all the way to conciliation.[56] The Parliament's influence was considerable. A particular triumph was the provision on monitoring mechanisms, requiring Member States to ensure implementation of the Directives 'by effective, available and transparent mechanisms', for which purpose they could, inter alia, 'appoint or establish an independent body',[57] even though the final provision was rather watered down from what the Parliament wanted.[58] A number of other issues were resolved in conciliation, for both Directives: for example, the principles referred to above must be observed in the award contracts by the public sector below the thresholds as well as above the thresholds;[59] electronic

[51] See, eg, Case C-31/87 *Gebroeders Beentjes BV v Netherlands State* ECLI:EU:C:1988:422; Case C-225/98 *Commission v France* ECLI:EU:C:2000:494; Case C-513/99 *Concordia Bus Finland Oy Ab v Helsingin kaupunki & HKL-Bussiliikenne* ECLI:EU:C:2002:495.

[52] Directive 2004/18 (n 47), Preamble, 1st recital.

[53] COM (2000) 275, [2001] OJ C29E/11.

[54] COM (2000) 276, [2001] OJ C29E/112; amended proposal: COM (2002) 235 final, [2002] OJ C203E/183.

[55] Directive 2004/17/EC of the European Parliament and of the Council coordinating the procurement procedures of entities operating in the water, energy, transport and postal services sectors [2004] OJ L134/1.

[56] The conciliation committee meetings for the two proposals were held on the same days, although a separate procedure was convened for each proposal.

[57] Directive 2004/17 (n 55), Art 72, Directive 2004/18 (n 47), Art 81.

[58] See European Parliament 2nd reading amendments to the proposed classic directive, Report – A5-0245/2003 (COD 2000/105). They were not accepted by the Commission (see COM (2002) 236 final, 2002, [2002] OJ C203E/210, 239), and it was only at the conciliation committee that the Parliament was able to obtain agreement on what became Directive 2004/17 (n 55), Art 72 and Directive 2004/18 (n 47), Art 81.

[59] This is the phrasing of the Explanatory Statement to the Parliament's Reports on the joint texts approved by the conciliation committees (Reports for Plenary A-5-0007/2004 & A-5-0008/2004), see Directive 2004/18 (n 47), Preamble, recital 2; Directive 2004/17 (n 55), Preamble, recital 9, 2nd para. The latter draws attention to the general requirements of the Treaty and the case law that these principles must be followed, even where the Directive does not apply; in Directive 2014/18, however, the approach is to state that (all) public contracting must follow those principles, but nevertheless

auctions may not be used for some works or services contracts dealing with the provision of intellectual services, like the design of works;[60] Member States may provide that tenders may be submitted electronically only if an advanced electronic signature is used;[61] and Member States may reserve participation in award procedures to sheltered workshops or require execution of contracts to take place through sheltered employment programmes.[62] Conciliation also ensured, in Directive 2004/18, that the purchase of school books would not be excluded from the scope of the Directive, while leaving intact national rules on a fixed price for school books.[63] In the prior information notice for works and services, information would have to be provided about where information could be found on the general regulatory framework for taxes, environmental and employment protection, and working conditions applicable where the contract is to be performed.[64] In Directive 2004/17, to combat social dumping, conciliation resulted in the requirement that Member States inform the Commission of any difficulties, in law or in fact, encountered and reported by their undertakings in securing the award of service contracts in third countries, and of any difficulties arising because of the non-observance of international labour law provisions.[65] Moreover, conciliation resulted in an obligation on those Member States that operate a qualification system to inform applicants as to the decision on their qualification within a period of no more than six months.[66]

Other steps had been or were also taken to simplify matters and increase transparency. A Common Procurement Vocabulary (CPV) was introduced by Regulation 2195/2002.[67] The Commission also responded to concerns about the lack of clarity about procurement in concessions,[68] particularly in relation to Public–Private Partnerships,[69] although specific legislation had to await the next round of changes.

it is desirable to make specific provisions for procurement above the thresholds established by the Directive. The Directives do not *create* an additional obligation relating to procurement outside their framework.

[60] Directive 2004/17 (n 55), Art 1(6); Directive 2004/18, Art 1(7).

[61] Directive 2004/17 (n 55), Art 48(5)(b); Directive 2004/18, Art 42(5)(b).

[62] Directive 2004/17 (n 55), Art 28; Directive 2004/18, Art 19.

[63] Directive 2004/18 (n 47), Preamble, para 47.

[64] ibid, Annex VII A.

[65] Directive 2004/17 (n 55), Art 59(1), (4).

[66] ibid, Art 49(3), 1st subpara.

[67] Regulation 2195/2002 of the European Parliament and of the Council of 5 November 2002 on the Common Procurement Vocabulary [2002] OJ L340/1.

[68] Commission Interpretative Communication on Concessions under Community law [2000] OJ C121/2. As to the earlier draft, see [1999] OJ C99/4.

[69] Green Paper on Public–Private Partnerships and Community Law on Public–Private Partnerships and Concessions, COM (2004) 327 final; Commission's Communication on Public–Private Partnerships and Community Law on Public–Private Partnerships and Concessions, COM (2005) 569 final. See further the Commission interpretative communication on the application of Community law on Public Procurement and Concessions to institutionalised PPP (IPPP) [2008] OJ C91/4.

Problems in defence procurement were initially tackled by an interpretative communication,[70] which drew attention to the problems caused by attempts to misuse the permitted exemptions for the defence sector from application of the Internal Market[71] and classic procurement rules.[72] The case law of the Court of Justice requiring that derogations from Community law had to be strictly interpreted and that their use had to be restricted to exceptional and clearly defined cases,[73] was being more honoured in the breach than in the observance by the Member States. Derogations that should be the exception according to the Treaty and the Court of Justice's case law were, in practice, the rule.[74] Accordingly, the Commission, realising that soft action by a communication was not enough, presented its proposal for a directive in this area.[75] Though the subject of fierce negotiations, the proposal's passage was relatively straightforward: the Parliament worked well, in clear cooperation with the Commission and the Council, to agree a text at first reading.[76] This approach has nowadays become the trend, as conciliation 'casts a backward shadow over the whole co-decision procedure'.[77] The resulting measure, Directive 2009/81,[78] with 79 recitals in its Preamble (compared with 48 in the Commission's proposal), addressed the shortcomings the Commission had identified, although whether various Member States realised exactly what they had agreed to has been the subject of some comment.[79] Problems with dual-use products[80] and with (the fallout from) offset contracts

[70] Commission's Interpretative Communication on the application of Article 296 of the Treaty in the field of defence procurement, COM (2006) 779; see also the accompanying Staff Working Document SEC (2006) 556, and the documents cited in n 83. See, further, D Eisenhut, 'The special security exemption of Article 296 EEC: Time for a new notion of "essential security interests"?' (2008) 33 *EL Rev* 577.

[71] Art 296 EC of the Treaty Establishing the European Community (Consolidated Version), 25 March 1957 [2002] OJ C325/33, now Art 346 of the Treaty on the Functioning of the European Union (Consolidated Version) (TFEU) [2016] OJ C202/47. See, eg, Case C-615/10 *Insinööritoimisto InsTiimi Oy* ECLI:EU:C:2012:324.

[72] Directive 2004/18 (n 47) Art 14.

[73] eg Case 13/68 *Salgoil SpA v Italian Ministry for Foreign Trade* ECLI:EU:C:1968:54, penultimate para (unnumbered), dealing with the predecessor provision, Art 224 EEC; Case C-57/94 *Commission v Italy* ECLI:EU:C:1995:150, para 23; and Case C-318/94 *Commission v Germany* ECLI:EU:C:1996:149, para 13. See further LW Gormley, *EU Law of Free Movement of Goods and Customs Union* (Oxford University Press, 2009) 529–33; M Trybus, *European Union Law and Defence Integration* (Hart Publishing, 2005) 141–66.

[74] COM (2007) 755 final, 2.

[75] COM (2007) 755 final. See the accompanying Staff Working Document, SEC (2007) 1598.

[76] European Parliament Report for Plenary A7-0030/2013.

[77] R Corbett et al, *The European Parliament* (9th edn, John Harper, 2016) 284.

[78] Directive 2009/81 of the European Parliament and of the Council of 13 July 2009 on the coordination of procedures for the award of certain works, contracts, supply contracts and service contracts by contracting authorities or entities in the fields of defence and security, and amending Directives 2004/17/EC and 2004/18/EC [2009] OJ L216/76; see M Trybus, 'The Tailor-Made EU Defence and Security Procurement Directive: Limitation, Flexibility, Descriptiveness and Substitution' (2013) 38 *EL Rev* 3.

[79] See, eg M Weiss and M Blauberger, *Judicialized Law-Making and Opportunistic Enforcement: Explaining the EU's Challenge of National Defence Offsets* (2016) 54:2 *Journal of Common Market Studies* 451, 453.

[80] See, eg, Case C-337/05 *Commission v Italy* ECLI:EU:C:2008:203, and the Opinion of AG Mazák in that case, ECLI:EU:C:2007:421, paras 54–63.

have continued to give rise to stimulating litigation.[81] However, in November 2016, the Commission's evaluation of the implementation of the Directive was less than wholly positive:

> [T]he objectives of the Directive have only partially been achieved: it led to an initial increase in competition, transparency, and non-discrimination in Europe's defence procurement market, but much more progress in Member States' consistent use of the Directive is needed to achieve fully those objectives.[82]

Against this background, the Commission's guidance notes on various facets of defence procurement in the light of the Directive have been particularly welcome.[83]

VI. If at First, You Don't Succeed …

While the 2004 package of directives was an undoubted improvement on its predecessors, it soon became clear that the regimes could be improved further. The Green Paper on the modernisation of public procurement policy[84] generated a considerable number of reactions[85] and led to the conclusion that the 2004 package was not working as efficiently as it might, and that cross-border procurement was still not as high as had been expected.[86] The proposal for a new directive for the classic sectors was based on a 'tool-box' approach, which offered Member States flexibility in adapting procedures and the tools to their situation; it was also designed to reduce considerably the administrative burden of the procurement procedures on contracting authorities and economic operators

[81] See, eg, Case C-414/97 *Commission v Spain*, ECLI:EU:C:1999:417, para 22; COM (2006) 779 (n 70) 7–8; *République Hellenique v Société Bombardier Inc*, Cour d'appel Paris Pôle 1, chambre 1 14 Avril 2015 Répertoire Général:14/07043; *Bombardier Inc v General Directorate for Defense Armaments and Investments of the Hellenic Ministry of National Defense et al*, Quebec Superior Court, 2014 *QCCS* 181; *Bombardier Inc v General Directorate for Defense, Armaments and Investments of the Hellenic Ministry of National Defense (HMOD)*, Quebec Superior Court, 2018 *QCCS* 2127; and *Eurobank Ergasias v Bombardier Inc & HMOD*, Quebec Court of Appeal, 2022 *QCCA* 802. See also the Commission's Guidance Note on Offsets, Ares (2016) 765159; D Eisenhut, *Offsets in Defence Procurement: A Strange Animal – at the Brink of Extinction?* (2013) 38 *EL Rev* 393; Weiss and Blauberger (n 79); the *ICC-ECCO Guide to International Offset Contracts* (ICC, 2019); and R Matthews and J Anicetti, 'Offset in a Post-Brexit World' (2021) 166:5 *The RUSI Journal* 50.

[82] COM (2016) 762 final, 5. See further SWD (2016) 407 final.

[83] The current guidance notes are: Commission Notice on guidance on cooperative procurement in the fields of defence and security [2019] OJ C157/1; Commission Notice on the award of government-to-government contracts in the fields of defence and security C (2016) 7727; Commission Notice on Field of Application Ares (2016) 764791; Commission Notice on Defence and Security-Specific Exclusions, Ares (2016) 764884; Commission Notice on Research and Development Ref Ares (2016) 765006; Commission Notice on Security of Supply Ares (2016) 764954; on Security of Information Ares (2016) 765061; Commission Notice on subcontracting Ares (2016) 765116, and Commission Notice on Offsets, Ares (2016) 765159 (see at https://defence-industry-space.ec.europa.eu/eu-defence-industry/defence-procurement_en).

[84] COM (2011) 15 final.

[85] See SEC (2011) 1585 final.

[86] ibid 12.

alike.[87] Unsurprisingly, a similar approach was followed in the proposal for a new directive for the utilities.[88] The third part of the package, the proposal for a specific directive relating to concessions,[89] sought to offer clarity for contracting authorities and entities, while offering economic operators some basic guarantees concerning the award procedure.[90] For all three proposals, a final version was again agreed at first reading,[91] after considerable negotiation between the Parliament, the Council and the Commission, with the Parliament again being extremely active in using the preambles to the directives to steer policy and interpretation, and in obtaining substantive modifications to the Commission's proposal.

The result was a trio of directives: Directive 2014/23 on concessions; Directive 2014/24 on classic procurement; and Directive 2014/25 on the utilities,[92] which together form the 2014 procurement package. Their preambles contain 88, 138, and 142 recitals respectively, compared with 44, 59, and 67 respectively in the Commission's proposals. An important aspect of the Parliament's activism related to the further infusion of the Directive with consideration of various special interests or values, which are indeed legitimate criteria to be considered, even more so now that the flexible criterion of the most economically advantageous tender (MEAT) has (mostly) become the norm. Nevertheless, the distinct risk of increasing still further political involvement in procurement decisions should not be underestimated. The Directives attempt to rein in the freedom of choice permitted to contracting authorities and entities, by demanding that effective competition be ensured and accompanied by specifications that enable the information provided by the tenderers to be effectively verified so as to assess how well the tenders meet the award criteria.[93] Moreover, the room for 'creativity' is diminished by the stricter criteria 'linked to the subject-matter of the (public) contract in question'.[94]

[87] COM (2011) 896 final, 6.
[88] COM (2011) 895 final, 6–7.
[89] COM (2011) 897 final.
[90] ibid 5.
[91] European Parliament Positions at First Reading: classic procurement and cf the relevant Committee proposals at www.europarl.europa.eu/doceo/document/TC1-COD-2011-0438_EN.pdf (cf European Parliament DocumentA7-0007/2013); utilities at www.europarl.europa.eu/doceo/document/TC1-COD-2011–0438_EN.pdf (cf European Parliament Document A7-0030/2013); and concessions at www.europarl.europa.eu/doceo/document/TC1-COD-2011–0437_EN.pdf (cf European Parliament Document A7-0030/2013).
[92] Directive 2014/23/EU of the European Parliament and of the Council of 26 February 2014 on the award of concession contracts [2014] OJ L94/1, corrigendum [2018] OJ L 82/17; Directive 2014/24/EU of the European Parliament and of the Council of 26 February 2014 on public procurement, and repealing Directive 2004/18/EEC [2014] OJ L94/65; and Directive 2014/25/EU of the European Parliament and of the Council of 26 February 2014 on procurement by entities operating in the water, energy, transport and postal services sectors, and repealing Directive 2004/17/EC [2014] OJ L94/243, respectively.
[93] Directive 2014/23, Art 41(1); Directive 2014/24, Art 67(4); and Directive 2014/25, Art 82(4).
[94] Directive 2014/23, Art 41(2); Directive 2014/24, Art 67(3); and Directive 2014/25, Art 82(3).

Various important extra exclusions have been inserted into the new Directives[95] at the insistence of the Parliament, responding to ferocious lobbying, such as radio media services and programme provision for radio; a number of legal services;[96] civil defence; civil protection; and danger prevention services provided by voluntary organisations or associations covered by certain CPV codes, save patient transport ambulance services.[97] The Parliament also ensured that the new Directives would not apply to certain service contracts awarded on the basis of an exclusive right enjoyed pursuant to a law, regulation or published administrative provision that is compatible with the TFEU.[98]

A number of clarifications and clear improvements are evident, such as the possibility of cooperation between contracting authorities or between contracting authorities and legal persons controlled by them,[99] and the relationship of the new Directives with the Defence and Security Procurement Directive.[100] The rules on the use of a negotiated procedure without prior publication have been tightened and better defined, as has the treatment of modern procurement methods, such as framework agreements,[101] dynamic purchasing systems, electronic procurement, the use of electronic catalogues, centralised purchasing, and occasional joint procurement and procurement involving contracting authorities or entities from different Member States.

A particularly significant feature is the considerable discretion given to contracting authorities or entities in their choice of procedures, leaving the Member States with no option but to make the choice available. This applies for innovation partnerships, and for the use of competitive dialogues.[102] There is now more flexibility about when they can be used, confirming that competitive dialogues have come of age: the Member States must give contracting authorities the option of using a competitive procedure with negotiation in specified cases.[103]

[95] Directive 2014/23, Art 10(7); Directive 2014/24, Art 10; and Directive 2014/25, Art 21.

[96] Case C-264/18 *PM et al v Ministerraad* ECLI:EU:C:2019:472.

[97] Directive 2014/23, Art 10(8)(g); Directive 2014/24, Art 10(h); and Directive 2014/25, Art 21(h). See further, eg, Case C-160/08 *Commission v Germany* ECLI:EU:C:2010:230; Case C-113/13 *Azienda sanitaria locale n. 5 'Spezzino' et al v San Lorenzo Soc coop social et al* ECLI:EU:C:2014:2440; Case C-50/14 *Consorzio Artigiano Servizio Taxi e Autonoleggio (CASTA) et al v Azienda Sanitaria Locale di Ciriè, Chivasso e Ivrea (ASL TO4)* ECLI:EU:C:2016:56; Case C-465/17 Falck *Rettungsdienste GmbH et al v Stadt Solingen* ECLI:EU:C:2019:234; Case C-796/18 *Informatikgesellschaft für Software-Entwicklung (ISE) mbH v Stadt Köln* ECLI:EU:C:2020:395; Case C-436/20 *Asociación Estatal de Entidades de Servicios de Atención a Domicilio (ASADE) v Consejería de Igualdad y Políticas Inclusivas* ECLI:EU:C:2022:559; and Joined Cases C-213/21 and C-214/21 *Italy Emergenza Cooperativa Sociale v Azienda Sanitaria Locale Barletta-Andria-Trani et al* ECLI:EU:C:2022:532.

[98] Directive 2014/23, Art 10(9); Directive 2014/24, Art 11; and Directive 2014/25, Art 22.

[99] Directive 2014/23, Arts 2(1), 2nd subpara, 17(4); Directive 2014/24, Arts 13(4), 39(5); and Directive 2014/25, Arts 28(4), 57(5).

[100] Directive 2014/23, Arts 21–23; Directive 2014/24, Arts 15–16; and Directive 2014/25, Arts 24–26; as to the new Defence and Security Procurement Directive, see Directive 2009/81 (n 78).

[101] See Joined Cases C-274/21 & C-275/21 *EPIC Financial Consulting GmbH v Republik Österreich and Bundesbeschaffung GmbH* ECLI:EU:C:2022:565.

[102] Directive 2014/24, Art 44(3); Directive 2014/25, Art 26(3), (4).

[103] Directive 2014/24, Art 26(4). The nearest equivalents are Directive 2014/23, Art 37(6) (permission to negotiate with bidders for concessions); and Directive 2014/25, Art 48(7), 2nd subpara for the utilities.

In the criteria for qualitative selection, the grounds for mandatory exclusion have been considerably widened, to include terrorist offences or offences linked to terrorism, terrorist financing, and child labour and other forms of trafficking in human beings, although there is a veritable colander of escape routes.[104] The prodigal offspring who repents and makes a binding payment arrangement may, however, be received back into the fold.[105]

The discretionary grounds for exclusion may be left open to the contracting authorities or entities, although they may be made mandatory if the Member State concerned so decides.[106] Here, too, there are escape lines:[107] exclusion for grave professional misconduct has become less one-sided – misconduct will have to be demonstrated by 'appropriate means', as opposed to by 'any means', and must be such that it renders the integrity of the economic operator questionable.[108]

The possibility or obligation to exclude an economic operator where the contracting authority or entity has sufficiently plausible indications to conclude that the operator has entered into agreements with others aimed at distorting competition has, unsurprisingly, led to litigation.[109] In relation to concessions contracts, there is a special exclusion ground, in the defence and security fields, as referred to in Directive 2009/81, if the economic operator has been found, on the basis of any means of evidence, including protected data sources, not to possess the reliability necessary to exclude risks to the security of the Member State.[110] The possibility of 'self-cleaning' offers a counterweight against arbitrary or capricious exclusion, so that if that evidence presented is considered

[104] Directive 2014/23, Art 38(4)–(10), Directive 2014/24, Art 57; and Directive 2014/25, Art 80 (by reference).

[105] Directive 2014/23, Art 38(5), Directive 2014/24, Art 57(2), and Directive 2014/25, Art 80 (1) (by reference). See also Directive 2014/23, Art 38(6), Directive 2014/24, Art 57(3), and Directive 2014/25, Art 80(1) (by reference).

[106] Directive 2014/23, Art 38(7), Directive 2014/24, Art 57(4), and Directive 2014/25, Art 80 (1) (by reference). See Case C-358/12 *Consorzio Stabile Libor Lavori Pubblici v Comune di Milano* ECLI:EU:C:2014:2063; Case C-101/18 *Idi Srl v Arcadis – Agenzia Regionale Campana Difesa Suolo* RCLI:EU:CL2019:267; Case C-41/18 *Meca Srl v Commune di Napoli* ECLI:EU:C:2019:507; Case C-395/18 *Tim SpA- Direzione e coordinamento Vivendi SA v Consip SA et al* ECLI:EU:C:2020:56; Case C-210/20 *Rad Service Srl Unipersonale et al v Del Debbio SpA et al* ECLI:EU:C:2021:445; and, particularly interesting on transposition and challenge by an unsuccessful tenderer, Case C-66/22 *Infraestruturas de Portugal SA et al v Toscca – Equipamentos wm Madeira Lda et al* ECLI:EU:C:2023:1016, paras 48–61.

[107] Directive 2014/23, Art 38(7)(b), 2nd subpara, Art 38(9); 2014/24, Art 57(4), 2nd subpara, Art 57(6), and Directive2014/25, Art 80(1) (by reference). Cf eg Directive 2004/18, Art 45(2)(d).

[108] Directive 2014/23, Arts 38(7)(c), 38(9); Directive 2014/24, Arts 57(4)(c), 57(6), and Directive 2014/25, Art 80(1) (by reference). See Case C-41/18 *Meca Srl v Comune di Napoli* ECLI:EU:C:2019:507. As to exclusion on past performance grounds, see Directive 2014/23, Art 38(7)(f); Directive 2014/24, Art 54(g); and Directive 2014/25, Art 80(1) (by reference), See further, Case C-682/21 *'HSC Baltic' UAB et al v Vilniaus miesto savivaldybės administracija* ECLI:EU:C:2023:48.

[109] Directive 2014/23, Arts 38(7)(e), 38(9); Directive 2014/24, Arts 57(4)(d), 57(6); and Directive 2014/25, Art 80(1) (by reference). See Case C-124/17 *Vossloh Laeis GmbH v Stadtwerke München GmbH* ECLI:EU:C:2018:855; Case C-416/21 *Landkreis Aichach-Friedberg v J Sch Omnibusunternehmen and K Reisen GmbH* ECLI:EU:C:2022:689; and Case C-66/22 *Infraestruturas de Portugal SA et al v Toscca – Equipamentos wm Madeira Lda et al* ECLI:EU:C:2023:1016.

[110] Directive 2014/23, Art 38(7)(i).

to be sufficient, then the operator must not be excluded from the procurement procedure.[111] The penitent prodigal offspring is again rewarded, unless there has been an exclusionary judgment against it in the Member State concerned.[112] An exclusionary judgment in one Member State does not have automatic exclusionary effect throughout the EU. The conditions relating to exclusion and proof of reliability are for each Member State to determine, having regard to EU law, but if no remedial measures have been taken to demonstrate the reliability of the operator and a final judgment did not set a period of exclusion, the maximum period is five years from the date of conviction by that final judgment for the automatically mandatory grounds of exclusion, and three years from the date of the event for the other grounds of exclusion.[113] The Directives have struck a not unreasonable balance between the interests of compliance with legal requirements and the possibility for economic operators to demonstrate that they have put their house in order.

Further aspects of clarification and improvement include greater control on the activities of subcontractors; the possibility for modification of contracts during their term;[114] and the possibility of terminating a contract during its term.[115]

While improved monitoring and individual and national reporting, as well as administrative cooperation between Member States, should facilitate improved enforcement, the development of EU law in this field seems to owe more to references for preliminary rulings than to infringement procedures.[116]

VII. Conclusions

Although there are some legitimate concerns, the overall impression is of a vast improvement, with considerably more detailed requirements building on case law and reflecting the need for greater legal certainty. This will disappoint those, like Sue Arrowsmith, who argued cogently for a principle-based system, with

[111] Directive 2014/23, Art 38(9), Directive 2014/24, Art 57(6); and Directive 2014/25, Art 80(1) (by reference). See Case C-124/17 *Vossloh Laeis* (n 109); and Case C-387/19 *RTS infra BVBA & Aannemingsbedrijf Norré-Behagel v Vlaams Gewest* ECLI:EU:C:2021:13. These provisions have direct effect, Case C-387/19, paras 43–50.

[112] Directive 2014/23, Art 38(9); Directive 2014/24, Art 57(6); and Directive 2014/25, Art 80(1) (by reference).

[113] Directive 2014/23, Art 38(10); Directive 2014/24, Art 57(7); and Directive 2014/25, Art 80(1) (by reference). See Case C-124/17 *Vossloh Laeis* (n 109).

[114] See, eg, Case 23/20 *Simonsen & Weel A/S v Region Nordjylland og Region Syddanmark* ECLI:EU:C:2021:490; and Case C-461/20 *Advania Sverige AB and Kammarkollegiet v Dustin Sverige AB* ECLI:EU:C:2022:72.

[115] See Case C-267/18 *Delta Antrepriză de Construcţii şi Montaj 93 SA v Compania Naţională de Administrare a Infrastructurii Rutiere SA* ECLI:EU:C:2019:826.

[116] All of the infringement procedures settled before judgment (ie the Member State climbed down). For Directive 2014/23, there have been four judgments on references; for Directive 2014/24, 46; and for Directive 2014/25, six. A number of cases are pending at the time of writing.

compliance demonstrated by performance indicators or by showing that the procedures applied complied with normal commercial practice; this would be backed up by national enforcement agencies within a [Union]-level framework.[117] While this type of approach had the undoubted merit of improved flexibility, it is unsurprising that the plea fell on deaf ears. A Continental suspicion of Anglo-Saxon deregulatory approaches; the fact that the early, relatively simple and straightforward directives failed to achieve the opening-up of procurement policies; the problem that not all Member States really had or have a trained profession in procurement contracting; and the view that some degree of detail is essential in harmonisation, formed a proverbial bridge too far. The call is still regularly heard that it all needs to be simpler, more flexible. Yet the first question usually asked is how to get out of the obligations in the EU rules. Underlying that question, the cloud of collusion, corruption or political interference is often not far away. In these difficult circumstances, the present Directives have struck a well-balanced line, leaving considerable discretion to the Member States. Success, however, depends on consistent compliance, vigilant market participants acting to challenge questionable decisions and actions of contracting authorities or entities, and proper enforcement by the Commission and the central and decentral judges of European law. A long road to heaven? Heaven may have to wait a long time, in pious hope and anticipation of being graced by the arrival of perfect procurement law, practices and procedures. Godot, if you come, we're in the bar!

[117] S Arrowsmith, 'The EC Procurement Directives, national procurement policies and better governance: the case for a new approach' (2002) 27:1 *EL Rev* 3, 17–23.

8

Never Secondary, Forever Horizontal: The Promises of Sustainable Public Procurement

ROBERTO CARANTA

I. Introduction

I first met Sue Arrowsmith in Berlin, on 8 December 1995. It was snowy and cold. But I was happy, fresh of professorship and having my first trip to Berlin. Being a history fanatic, I should have taken the trip before, but still, I managed to land at Tempelhof, the airport that deserved a place in history books for the action seen during the Berlin airlift. Also, I witnessed the reconstruction following the Fall of the Berlin Wall (Potsdamer Platz was still only a huge building site when I visited it). The workshop on *Public Interest Litigation before European Courts*, organised by Hans-W Micklitz and Norbert Reich, collected contributions in view of widening standing under (then) Articles 173 and 175 of the (then) EEC Treaty.[1] I was not very much a procurement law expert at the time, my focus being on judicial protection, and so I presented on indirect judicial review. Sue Arrowsmith was already the expert everyone turned to for procurement law. She had launched the *Public Procurement Law Review* a few years earlier and was putting the final touches on the first edition of her fundamental work, *The Law of Public and Utilities Procurement*.[2]

Back then, sustainability, or even green or social, was not much of a footnote in public procurement literature. In the first edition of *The Law of Public and Utilities Procurement*, Sue refers to a 'secondary condition' when discussing *Beentjes*.[3] *Beentjes* was used to exemplify the problems raised when promoting 'standards of behaviour going beyond those otherwise required by law'.[4] The internal market – or

[1] HW Micklitz and N Reich, *Public Interest Litigation before European Courts* (Nomos, 1996).

[2] S Arrowsmith, *The Law of Public and Utilities Procurement* (1st edn, Sweet & Maxwell, 1996).

[3] ibid 545 f and 825 ff; Case C-31/87 *Gebroeders Beentjes BV v State of the Netherlands* ECLI:EU:C:1988:422.

[4] ibid 820.

even a global procurement market – was where the focus was. Sue Arrowsmith was among the distinguished speakers when in 1996 the Europäische Rechtsakademie convened an expert meeting in Trier on 'GPA, Standards, Utilities, Remedies: Gordian Knots in European Public Procurement Law'.[5]

Ideologically, the Fall of the Berlin Wall had been hailed as the victory of liberal democracies and their socio-economic liberal model. International trade law changed dramatically. The old General Agreement on Tariffs and Trade (GATT) evolved into the World Trade Organization (WTO), including most countries in the world. Among the WTO agreements, the Government Procurement Agreement (GPA) is relevant here; and Sue Arrowsmith was among those taking stock of the GPA in Trier. Sue has written more than once on the GPA.[6] When considering options for reform of the Agreement, she had no doubt in identifying the functions to which the GPA is responding:

> In the context of trade agreements on procurement transparency has three main functions … – to support non-discrimination, by making it difficult to conceal discriminatory motives; to facilitate participation by suppliers unfamiliar with the system; and to improve information for market access negotiations. The first two are important in the GPA, and the third present to some extent in obligations to provide statistics on smaller, non-covered, procurements.[7]

While multiple objectives are pursued by national procurement systems, the GPA is an instrument for opening international trade: 'The GPA itself is not … concerned directly with these objectives of value for money, integrity etc, but only with removing trade barriers.'[8]

But the GPA was just a component of a wider public procurement globalisation trend insisting on market opening (non-discrimination) and transparency, and de-quoting social and environmental considerations.[9] The same approach was to be taken up by the multilateral financial institutions based in Washington (the so-called 'Washington consensus'). The 1995 World Bank Guidelines for Procurement under International Bank for Reconstruction and Development (IBRD) Loans and International Development Association (IDA) Credits clearly expounded an economic-centred approach. The responsibility for the

[5] See S Arrowsmith, 'Future Prospects for the European Community's Regime on Public Procurement' in L Gormley (ed), *Gordian Knots in European Public Procurement Law* (Bundesanzeiger, 1997) 83.

[6] Together with Robert D Anderson she edited S Arrowsmith and RD Anderson (eds), *The WTO Regime on Government Procurement: Challenges and Reform* (The World Bank, 2011); more recently, S Arrowsmith, 'Recommendations for Urgent Procurement in the EU Directives and GPA: COVID-19 and beyond' in S Arrowsmith et al (eds), *Public Procurement Regulation in (a) Crisis?: Global Lessons from the COVID-19 Pandemic* (Hart Publishing, 2021) 63.

[7] S Arrowsmith, 'Reviewing the GPA: The Role and Development of the Plurilateral Agreement After Doha' (2002) 5(4) *Journal of International Economic Law* 761, 765 (footnotes omitted).

[8] ibid 766.

[9] See P Kunzlik, 'Neoliberalism and the European Public Procurement Regime' (2013) 15 *Cambridge Yearbook of European Legal Studies* 283.

implementation of the project and the award and administration of contracts rested with the country that had borrowed money. The Bank, instead, is required by Article III, Section 5(b) of its Articles of Agreement to 'ensure that the proceeds of any loan are used only for the purposes for which the loan was granted, with due attention to considerations of economy and efficiency and without regard to political or other non-economic influences or considerations'. To this end, 'four considerations generally guide the Bank's requirements: (a) the need for economy and efficiency in the implementation of the project, including the procurement of the goods and works involved; … and (d) the importance of transparency in the procurement process'.[10]

It would be wrong to underestimate the ideological underpinning behind this approach, which was Thatcherite to its core. Section 17 of the Local Government Act 1988 had already anticipated later developments by providing that it was the duty of every contracting authority to exercise its functions in relation to its public supply or works contracts, 'without reference to matters which are non-commercial matters for the purposes of this section'.

Focusing on baseline economic value, if not even just on price, was obviously consistent with the desire to avoid discrimination based on nationality or otherwise. Economic values are easily computed, they are eminently objective and make favouring national or local suppliers difficult.[11]

To a considerable extent, this was the approach in Europe as well. Introducing then EEC public procurement law, Sue Arrowsmith remarked:

> When entities follow procurement practices which do not allow for fair competition between firms who seek to do business with that entity, these practices also operate as barriers to trade – in the Community context, they effectively prevent interested firms from having access to all parts of the Community market.[12]

Unsurprisingly, 'the opening up of public procurement has been seen as an important part of the Community's single market policy'.[13] In this context – as already recalled – social (and environmental) considerations were seen as potentially problematic.[14]

Francis Fukuyama thought the victory of liberal democracies was to mark the end of history.[15] We know it did not. Much of historical relevance has happened in the past 30 years. Like society, the law is a living organism. More often than not, it is the case law that breathes life into the law. In the European Union (EU),

[10] Guidelines Procurement under IBRD Loans and IDA Credits at https://thedocs.worldbank.org/en/doc/726081614030914180-0290021999/original/GoodsWorksandNonConsultingServices1999.pdf (rev 1999) 1 f.

[11] See S Arrowsmith, *The Law of Public and Utilities Procurement*, vol 2 (3rd edn, Sweet & Maxwell, 2018) 716. A parallel development took place concerning procurement by – or financed by – MDBs: see E Morlino, *Procurement by International Organisations* (Cambridge University Press, 2019) 121 ff.

[12] Arrowsmith (n 2) 46.

[13] ibid 50.

[14] Arrowsmith (n 7) 779 ff.

[15] F Fukuyama, *The End of History and the Last Man* (Free Press, 1992).

economic single-mindedness in public procurement suffered a big blow from *Concordia Bus*.[16] The Court of Justice firmly held that the EU law

> cannot be interpreted as meaning that each of the award criteria used by the contracting authority to identify the economically most advantageous tender must necessarily be of a purely economic nature. It cannot be excluded that factors which are not purely economic may influence the value of a tender from the point of view of the contracting authority. That conclusion is also supported by the wording of the provision, which expressly refers to the criterion of the aesthetic characteristics of a tender.[17]

Still, general public procurement principles such as transparency and non-discrimination do apply to environmental considerations in award criteria, and moreover, those criteria need to be linked to the subject matter of the contract to be awarded.[18]

II. From 'Secondary' to 'Horizontal' Considerations

Social and environmental considerations were among those then called 'secondary considerations'.[19] In Sue Arrowsmith's words, 'policies unconnected with the procurement's subject matter' pertain to 'secondary' objectives.[20]

Christopher McCrudden was the first to raise objections against referring to 'secondary' considerations or objectives. In his words:

> Describing the incorporation of social issues into procurement as involving the use of 'secondary' considerations is potentially misleading. If the subject matter of the contract can itself be the delivery of the social policy, then social issues are no longer 'secondary' to the contract, but central to it, and the use of the term 'secondary' in this context to describe them is misleading.[21]

Soon afterwards, Sue Arrowsmith joined Peter Kunzlik in editing – and writing large parts of – the first major research book on *Social and Environmental Policies in EC Procurement Law*.[22] Already in the first chapter on 'Public procurement and horizontal policies in EC law: general principles', Arrowsmith and Kunzlik took a

[16] Case C-513/99 *Concordia Bus Finland Oy Ab, formerly Stagecoach Finland Oy Ab v Helsingin kaupunki and HKL-Bussiliikenne* ECLI:EU:C:2002:495.

[17] ibid para 55.

[18] ibid paras 59 et seq.

[19] eg, J Arnould, 'Secondary Policies in Public Procurement: The Innovations of the New Directives' (2004) 13 *Public Procurement Law Review* 187.

[20] Arrowsmith (n 7) 766.

[21] C McCrudden, *Buying Social Justice: Equality, Government Procurement, and Legal Change* (Oxford University Press, 2007) 524.

[22] S Arrowsmith and P Kunzlik (eds), *Social and Environmental Policies in EC Procurement Law: New Directives and New Directions* (Cambridge University Press, 2009).

principled stance against using the 'secondary' adjective and instead argued a preference for 'horizontal'.[23] Besides the difficulty in distinguishing between 'primary' and 'secondary' in a number of situations and actual procurements, they remarked that 'even though this is not necessarily implied by the meaning of the term as it originated – there is a danger that the term "secondary policies" may carry the connotation that such policies are of secondary *importance* to other matters, and/or are of limited importance'.[24] This is again not necessarily the case, as indeed it may be that a contracting authority and its principal – be it the people or a local community – consider the social and/or economic aspects as important as, or even as more important than, the act of buying. Moreover, and this is even more relevant,

> there is a danger that the term 'secondary policies' might be taken as *de-normalising* the pursuit of horizontal policies in public procurement, by implying that in some way it is inherently not rational, normal or legitimate. This is a very important point, since it might skew the law's approach: in the trade context this might easily lead to an unwarranted assumption that these policies are suspicious and tend to cloak protectionist practices.[25]

Horizontal policies are, instead, normal – and, with a remarkable exception in the closing years of the twentieth century – they have always been so. Writing in 1972, Colin Turpin remarked:

> The volume of government procurement is such that the government's decisions on how, when and what to buy must inevitably have effects on the structure and health of industry, upon employment, and upon the economy as a whole. It would be remarkable if any government were to carry out its procurements wholly without regard to these incidental effects; in this as in other fields the decisions of government can be expected to be political decisions, which take account of the ulterior social and economic consequences of alternative courses of action.[26]

Returning a sober assessment after the worst neoliberal excesses, Arrowsmith and Kunzlik argued that

> the starting point in regulating horizontal policies in procurement should be that these policies have equal status with other governmental policies, whether these are procurement policies – such as ensuring that goods are acquired on the best possible terms, or promoting integrity in procurement – or other kinds of policies, such as traditional regulatory measures on consumer protection, the environment etc.[27]

[23] ibid 12 ff.
[24] ibid 14 (original emphasis); see also Arrowsmith (n 11) 693 f.
[25] ibid (original emphasis); see also S Arrowsmith, 'Horizontal Policies in Public Procurement: A Taxonomy' (2010) 10(2) *Journal of Public Procurement* 150.
[26] C Turpin, *Government Contracts* (Penguin, 1972) 244.
[27] S Arrowsmith and P Kunzlik, 'Public procurement and horizontal policies in EC law: general principles' in Arrowsmith and Kunzlik (eds) (n 22) 9, 14.

III. Sustainable Public Procurement in the 2014 Directives

Whatever economic single-mindedness might have been still around after *Concordia Bus* was badly battered by *Max Havelaar*.[28] The case concerned the possibility to refer to specific fair-trade labels in the purchase of coffee for office coffee machines. Advocate General Kokott launched her assessment by remarking:

> For a long time the pursuit of environmental and social objectives was disapproved of in public procurement law, as was manifested not least in the use of the phase 'objectives irrelevant to the contract'. However, it is now generally recognised that contracting authorities may also take account of environmental and social factors when awarding contracts … In practical terms, however, the conditions under which, and the form in which, the contracting authorities' environmental and social views may affect a specific award procedure is fiercely disputed.[29]

Among the issues fought about in *Max Havelaar* was the link to the subject-matter requirement.[30] Following the Advocate General's Opinion, the Court of Justice held that, since 'the drafting of the award criterion at issue … covered only the ingredients to be supplied in the framework of that contract, without any bearing on the general purchasing policy of the tenderers,' it therefore 'related to products the supply of which constituted part of the subject-matter of that contract'.[31] Indeed, according to the Court, 'there is no requirement that an award criterion relates to an intrinsic characteristic of a product, that is to say something which forms part of the material substance thereof'.[32]

Public procurement law in the EU after the 2014 reform allows a much wider scope for Sustainable Public Procurement (SPP).[33] Everything happening in the life-cycle of a product or service, from production to end of life, can be considered in technical specifications (Article 42 of Directive 2014/24/EU),[34]

[28] Case C-368/10 *Commission v Netherlands* ECLI:EU:C:2012:284.

[29] Opinion of AG Kokott delivered on 15 December 2011 in Case C–368/10 *Commission v Netherlands* ECLI:EU:C:2011:840, para 37.

[30] See A Semple, 'The Link to the Subject Matter: A Glass Ceiling for Sustainable Public Contracts?' in B Sjåfjell and A Wiesbrock (eds), *Sustainable Public Procurement under EU Law* (Cambridge University Press, 2016) 99.

[31] Case C–368/10 *Commission v Netherlands* [2012] ECLI:EU:C:2012:284 para 90.

[32] ibid para 91; the Court referred to Case C-448/01 *EVN and Wienstrom* [2003] ECR I-14527, para 34.

[33] Arrowsmith (n 11) 719 f; DC Dragos and B Neamtu, 'Sustainable Public Procurement in the EU: Experiences and Prospects' in F Lichère, R Caranta and S Treumer (eds), *Modernising Public Procurement: The New Directive* (DJØF, 2014) 301; R Caranta, 'The Changes to the Public Contract Directives and the Story They Tell About How EU Law Works' (2015) 52 *CML Rev* 391, 396; Sjåfjell and Wiesbrock (eds) (n 30); M Andhov, 'Contracting Authorities and Strategic Goals of Public Procurement – A Relationship Defined by Discretion?' in S Bogojevic, X Groussot and J Hettne (eds), *Discretion in EU Public Procurement Law* (Hart Publishing, 2019) 117 ff; but room for SPP was there under the previous directives as well, and see Kunzlik (n 9) 319 ff.

[34] Directive 2014/24/EU of 26 February 2014 on public procurement and repealing Directive 2004/18/EC [2014] OJ L94/65. C Risvig Hamer, 'Article 42 Technical Specifications' in R Caranta and

award criteria (Articles 67 and 68)[35] and performance conditions (Article 70).[36] Moreover, under given conditions, labels may be required by contracting authorities (Article 43)[37] and life-cycle-costing methodologies may be developed (Article 68).[38]

The possible single most important provision is Article 67(3) of Directive 2014/24/EU. In line with *Max Havelaar*, Article 67(3) provides that award criteria are considered to

> be linked to the subject-matter of the public contract where they relate to the works, supplies or services to be provided under that contract in any respect and at any stage of their life cycle, including factors involved in:
>
> (a) the specific process of production, provision or trading of those works, supplies or services; or
>
> (b) a specific process for another stage of their life cycle,
>
> even where such factors do not form part of their material substance.

Clearly, everything taking place during the life-cycle of a product or service to be acquired under a procurement contract is linked to the subject matter, so that the latter notion becomes redundant and should be ditched.[39]

The 2014 EU public procurement and concessions directives revision clarified that SPP is permissible, but they steered clear of introducing mandatory rules.[40] It was thought better to leave sector-specific legislation to set mandatory criteria and targets.[41] Examples of sectoral EU legislation that introduced mandatory SPP provisions include Regulation (EC) No 106/2008 (the so-called 'EU Energy

A Sanchez Graells (eds), *European Public Procurement: Commentary on Directive 2014/24/EU* (Edward Elgar Publishing, 2021) 462.

35 See respectively A Semple, 'Article 67 Contract Award Criteria' in Caranta and Sanchez Graells (eds) (n 34) 705; and M Andhov, 'Article 68 Life-cycle Costing' in Caranta and Sanchez Graells (eds) (n 34) 721; see also M Andhov, R Caranta and A Wiesbrock (eds), *Cost and EU Public Procurement Law: Life-Cycle Costing for Sustainability* (Routledge, 2020).

36 M Andhov, 'Article 70 Conditions for Performance of Contracts' in Caranta and Sanchez Graells (eds) (n 34) 747; and Andhov (n 35).

37 M Andhov, 'Article 43 Labels' in Caranta and Sanchez Graells (eds) (n 34) 474; see also JJ Czarnezki, 'EU and US Discretion in Public Procurement Law: The Role of Eco-Labels and Life-Cycle Costing' in Bogojevic, Groussot and Hettne (eds) (n 33) 211.

38 See also the papers collected by Andhov, Caranta and Wiesbrock (eds) (n 35).

39 See R Caranta, 'Public Procurement and Award Criteria' in CH Bovis (ed), *Research Handbook on EU Public Procurement Law* (Edward Elgar Publishing, 2016) 149.

40 M Andhov (Andrecka) and K Peterkova Mitkidis, 'Sustainability Requirements in EU Public and Private Procurement – A Right or An Obligation?' (2017) 1 *Nordic Journal of Commercial Law* 56.

41 European Commission, 'Green Paper on the Modernisation of EU Public Procurement Policy Towards a More Efficient European Procurement Market' (2011) COM(2011) 15 final 41 ff; see the discussion by P Trepte, 'The Contracting Authority as Purchaser and Regulator: Should the Procurement Rules Regulate What We Buy?' in GS Ølykke, CR Hamer and CD Tvarnø (eds), *EU Public Procurement, Modernisation, Growth and Innovation* (DJØF, 2012) 85; see also Recital 95 of Directive 2014/24/EU and Recital 100 of Directive 2014/25/EU of 26 February 2014 on procurement by entities operating in the water, energy, transport and postal services sectors and repealing Directive 2004/17/EC [2014] OJ L94/243.

Star Regulation'),[42] which introduced obligations on contracting authorities to require in their public contracts a certain level of energy efficiency, and Directive 2019/1161 on clean vehicles, which set out targets for the number of clean vehicles that are bought by contracting authorities.[43]

IV. The European Green Deal and What is to Come

Allowing SPP is nowhere near enough to help achieve the climate objectives set by the EU and, more generally, the Sustainable Development Goals (SDGs). As the new Circular Economy Action Plan avowed, the shift towards mandatory criteria is born out of the realisation that instruments such as the EU green public procurement (GPP) criteria 'have reduced impact due to the limitations of voluntary approaches'.[44] Unsurprisingly, the EU Green Deal indicated that '[p]ublic authorities, including the EU institutions, should lead by example and ensure that their procurement is green'.[45] The Circular Economy Action Plan following the Green Deal aired the Commission's intention to 'propose minimum mandatory green public procurement (GPP) criteria and targets in sectoral legislation'.[46] Finally, the EU Green Deal Investment Plan stated:

> The Commission will propose minimum mandatory green criteria or targets for public procurements in sectoral initiatives, EU funding or product-specific legislation. Such minimum criteria will 'de facto' set a common definition of what a 'green purchase' is, allowing the collection of comparable data from public buyers and setting the basis for assessing the impact of green public procurements. Public authorities across Europe will be encouraged to integrate green criteria and use labels in their procurements.[47]

Following the Green Deal, but also the earlier European Pillar of Social Rights, which focuses on the social aspects included under the umbrella of sustainability,[48]

[42] Regulation (EC) No 106/2008 of 15 January 2008 on a Community energy-efficiency labelling programme for office equipment (recast version) [2008] OJ L39/1.

[43] Directive (EU) 2019/1161 of 20 June 2019 amending Directive 2009/33/EC on the promotion of clean and energy-efficient road transport vehicles [2019] OJ L188/116.

[44] European Commission, 'Communication from the Commission to the European Parliament, the Council, the European Economic and Social Committee and the Committee of the Regions, A New Circular Economy Action Plan for a Cleaner and More Competitive Europe' (2020) COM(2020) 98 final para 2.1.

[45] European Commission, 'Communication from the Commission, The European Green Deal' (2019) COM(2019) 640 final 8; see K Pouikli, 'Towards Mandatory Green Public Procurement (GPP) Requirements under the EU Green Deal: Reconsidering the Role of Public Procurement as an Environmental Policy Tool' 2020 21(1) *ERA Forum* 699.

[46] European Commission (n 44) para 2.2.

[47] European Commission, 'Communication from the Commission to the European Parliament, the Council, the European Economic and Social Committee and the Committee of the Regions, Sustainable Europe Investment Plan' (2020) COM (2020) 21 final 12.

[48] European Commission, 'Communication from the Commission to the European Parliament, the Council, the European Economic and Social Committee and the Committee of the Regions, Establishing a European Pillar of Social Rights' (2017) COM(2017) 250 final.

the Commission has tabled many proposals, a number of which include provisions concerning public procurement and more relevant to it. Some proposals have already been turned into legislation, and more might yet be approved before the election of the European Parliament in June 2024. An example of the first kind of measure is given by the new Regulation (EU) 2023/1115 on making available on the Union market, as well as export from the Union of, certain commodities and products associated with deforestation and forest degradation.[49] Article 23 is devoted to 'penalties' and requires the Member States to foresee penalties for operators and traders infringing the Regulation. Those penalties shall be effective, proportionate and dissuasive and shall include '(d) temporary exclusion for a maximum period of 12 months from public procurement processes and from access to public funding, including tendering procedures, grants and concessions'.

An example of indirect relevance for public procurement is given by the the Recast Energy Efficiency Directive (EED).[50] Article 5 of the EED introduces an obligation for the public sector to reduce its energy consumption; while Article 6 broadens the scope of the renovation obligation, making it applicable not just at the state level, as it is under the rules now in force, but to all public bodies at all administration levels and in all sectors of public bodies' activities, including healthcare, education and public housing, where the buildings are owned by public bodies.[51] While these provisions do not refer explicitly to public procurement, clearly more often than not 'renovation' will be managed through public procurement, so much so that the EED aligns the definition of the public bodies covered by the obligation to reduce energy consumption with the well-articulated notions defined under Directive 2014/24/EU (Recital 28).[52] Moreover, Article 7 of the EED refers explicitly to public procurement in its title already and calls on the Member States to ensure that contracting authorities and contracting entities only purchase 'products, services buildings and works with high energy-efficiency performance'.

Provisions on SPP in EU secondary law do at times extend to fully developed SPP criteria to be taken up by contracting authorities and entities in the Member States. One relevant instance is provided by the Proposal for a Regulation laying down harmonised conditions for the marketing of construction products,[53] which

[49] Regulation (EU) 2023/1115 of the European Parliament and of the Council of 31 May 2023 on the making available on the Union market and the export from the Union of certain commodities and products associated with deforestation and forest degradation and repealing Regulation (EU) No 995/2010 [2023] OJ L150/206 (Deforestation Regulation).

[50] Directive (EU) 2023/1791 of 13 September 2023 on energy efficiency and amending Regulation (EU) 2023/955 (recast) [2023] OJ L231/1.

[51] European Commission, 'Proposal for a Directive of the European Parliament and of the Council on Energy Efficiency (recast)' (2011) COM(2021) 558 final.

[52] See R Caranta, 'Towards Mandatory SPP for buildings/works' (2022) 4(1) *European Journal of Public Procurement Markets* 9, 17 f.

[53] European Commission, 'Proposal for a Regulation of the European Parliament and of the Council laying down harmonised conditions for the marketing of construction products, amending Regulation (EU) 2019/1020 and repealing Regulation (EU) 305/2011' (2022) COM(2022) 144 final.

was finally approved in April 2024. Under proposed Article 84(1), the Commission may adopt delegated acts 'establishing sustainability requirements applicable to public contracts, including implementation, monitoring and reporting of those requirements by Member States'. Under proposed Article 84(3), in setting the sustainability requirements, the Commission shall take into account (i) the value and volume of public contracts awarded for that given product family or category, or for the services or works using the given product family or category; (ii) the need to ensure sufficient demand for more environmentally sustainable products; and (iii) the economic feasibility for contracting authorities or contracting entities to buy more environmentally sustainable products, without entailing disproportionate costs. Under proposed Article 7(2), the requirements will be mandatory for contracting authorities and entities.[54]

Many more examples could be given if it were not for the constraints of space.[55] What clearly emerges is the evolution of EU public contracts law (procurement and concessions) from a 'how to buy' approach to one including instances of 'what to buy'. As was convincingly argued by Mélon, 'mandatory GPP promotes the availability of information on the market, further standardisation, and more legally certain and efficient procurement processes for the authorities. Furthermore, a mandatory GPP approach is likely to increase market demand and innovation and lower the costs of environmentally-friendly products and services.'[56]

What is specifically relevant here is that – far from being secondary – climate-change concerns and other aspects of sustainability are today at the centre of EU public procurement and concession law. Only much of the action takes place outside the procurement and concession directives, as appropriate measures may differ from sector to sector.[57]

V. The Principle of Sustainability

The new centrality of sustainability is bound to require a different reading – and possibly reform – of the general public procurement rules. A case in point is Article 18(2) of Directive 2014/24/EU. It provides:

> Member States shall take appropriate measures to ensure that in the performance of public contracts economic operators comply with applicable obligations in the fields

[54] See also D Gruyaert and V Pissierssens, 'Transforming the Construction Sector Through Minimum Requirements' in W Janssen and R Caranta (eds), *Mandatory Sustainability Requirements in EU Public Procurement Law* (Hart Publishing, 2023) 169.

[55] But see the contributions in Janssen and Caranta (eds) (n 54).

[56] L Mélon, 'More Than a Nudge? Arguments and Tools for Mandating Green Public Procurement in the EU' (2020) 12 *Sustainability* 1003; see also M Andhov et al, 'Sustainability Through Public Procurement: The Way Forward – Reform Proposals' (2020) at https://papers.ssrn.com/sol3/papers.cfm?abstract_id=3559393.

[57] See, also pointing out the need for the EU to have competence in the sector, Arrowsmith (n 11) 721.

> of environmental, social and labour law established by Union law, national law, collective agreements or by the international environmental, social and labour law provisions listed in Annex X.[58]

In *TIM*, the Court of Justice of the EU has recognised

> that Article 18 of Directive 2014/24, entitled 'Principles of procurement', is the first article of Chapter II of that directive devoted to 'general rules' on public procurement procedures. Accordingly, by providing in paragraph 2 of that article that economic operators must comply, in the performance of the contract, with obligations relating to environmental, social and labour law, the Union legislature sought to establish that requirement as a principle, like the other principles referred to in paragraph 1 of that article, namely the principles of equal treatment, non-discrimination, transparency, proportionality and prohibiting the exclusion of a contract from the scope of Directive 2014/24 or artificially narrowing competition. It follows that such a requirement constitutes, in the general scheme of that directive, a cardinal value with which the Member States must ensure compliance pursuant to the wording of Article 18(2) of that directive.[59]

While the precise implications of such a major pronouncement will have to be determined in future case law, it is clear that general EU public procurement law is empowering SPP.[60] Still, the wording in Article 18(2) might be stronger. It refers to the Member States, not to contracting authorities (even if the latter might be read as implied therein). More importantly, the article as it is written now, simply reiterates the rather obvious provision that mandatory rules concerning the environment and social and labour rights should be complied with. As a rule, non-compliance with those obligations should lead to the exclusion of potential tenderers from the award procedures. However, this is currently the case only with reference to child labour and other forms of trafficking in human beings, as defined in Article 2 of Directive 2011/36/EU[61] (Article 57(1)(f) of Directive 2014/24/EU). Otherwise, an EU non-mandatory exclusion is simply foreseen in Article 57(4)(a) of the 2014 Directive. From a legal systematic point of view, it is as if Article 18(2) were only prospective and not retrospective, ready to strike misbehaviour in the implementation of the contract rather than past breaches of environmental and social obligation. As *TIM* shows, this is not necessarily so. In *TIM*, the Court of Justice upheld the exclusion of a subcontractor for not complying with domestic rules on the mandatory employment of disabled workers.[62] Still, the shift towards mandatory SPP rules requires strengthening of the exclusion regime, as is the case

[58] M Andhov, 'Article 18(2)' in Caranta and Sanchez Graells (eds) (n 34) 199.

[59] Case C-395/18 *Tim SpA Direzione e coordinamento Vivendi SA v Consip SpA, Ministero dell'Economia e delle Finanze* ECLI:EU:C:2020:58, para 38.

[60] See Andhov (n 58).

[61] Directive 2011/36/EU of 5 April 2011 on preventing and combating trafficking in human beings and protecting its victims, and replacing Council Framework Decision 2002/629/JHA [2011] OJ L101/1.

[62] *Tim SpA* (n 59) para 13.

with the Deforestation Regulation. The concern that looking into past behaviours will too severely curtail participation and trade is easily assuaged by the possibility for economic operators to avail themselves of self-cleaning.[63]

Article 9 ('Public procurement') of Directive (EU) 2022/2041 on adequate minimum wages in the European Union[64] provides another model, as it includes an explicit reference to the award stage, which is necessarily looking to the past (retrospectively). Under Article 9:

> In accordance with Directives 2014/23/EU, 2014/24/EU and 2014/25/EU, Member States shall take appropriate measures to ensure that, in the awarding and performance of public procurement or concession contracts, economic operators and their subcontractors comply with the applicable obligations regarding wages, the right to organise and collective bargaining on wage-setting, in the field of social and labour law established by Union law, national law, collective agreements or international and labour law provisions, including ILO Freedom of Association and the Protection of the Right to Organise Convention No 87 (1948) and ILO Right to Organise and Collective Bargaining Convention No 98 (1949).

Presently, the link to the subject matter – however broadly understood according to Article 67(3) of Directive 2014/24/EU – may be read as standing in the way of allowing contracting authorities and entities to insist on dealing with economic operators and avoiding inequitable practices. The last phrase of Recital 97 indicates that

> the condition of a link with the subject-matter of the contract excludes criteria and conditions relating to general corporate policy, which cannot be considered as a factor characterising the specific process of production or provision of the purchased works, supplies or services. Contracting authorities should hence not be allowed to require tenderers to have a certain corporate social or environmental responsibility policy in place.[65]

The iterative framing of the provision betrays a raw nerve in the (recent) public procurement orthodoxy. The non-commercial considerations the Iron Lady was fighting against were local councils' policies aimed at not passing contracts with economic operators doing business with Apartheid South Africa. Thence, a very artificial distinction between the possibility of insisting on ethical behaviour when performing a specific contract by one and the same economic operator otherwise potentially engaged in unethical business dealings. Pharisees have gained a bad reputation for much less. This approach runs against the same notion of an economic operator's (un)reliability as a ground for its exclusion from public contracts award procedures. It is not just – if you can say so – an ethical problem. This approach creates a misalignment between EU procurement law and the EU efforts for strengthening corporate social responsibility (CSR).[66]

[63] Arrowsmith (n 11) 778.

[64] Directive (EU) 2022/2041 on adequate minimum wages in the European Union [2022] OJ L275/33.

[65] Directive 2014/24/EU, Recital 97, last phrase.

[66] See B Sjafjell, 'Sustainable Public Procurement as a Driver for Sustainable Companies? The Interfaces Between Company Law and Public Procurement Law' in Sjåfjell and Wiesbrock (eds) (n 30)

Indeed, the prohibition to refer to the general CSR policy of the economic operator will be overrun when the Directive on corporate sustainability due diligence (CSDD) enters into force.[67] This Directive aims to foster sustainable and responsible corporate behaviour throughout global value chains, including both social and environmental considerations. Larger companies will be required to identify and, where necessary, prevent, end or mitigate adverse impacts of their activities on human rights, such as child labour and exploitation of workers, and on the environment, for example pollution and biodiversity loss. The wide scope of the Directive basically obliterates the difference between due diligence and CSR, transforming the latter from a voluntary tool of self-regulation into a legislative mandatory standard. Under the upcoming Directive, due diligence obligations foreseen under the Directive can be contract performance conditions for economic operators that are obliged under the Directive and award criteria for economic operators who are not obliged to carry out due diligence under the Directive.[68]

Still, Article 18(2), the other SPP provisions in Directive 2014/24/EU and the corresponding rules in the other 2014 procurement and concessions directives, should be reformed to add bite to the sustainability principle through stronger exclusion clauses.[69]

VI. Conclusions: Towards Geo-Strategic Procurement

As Sue Arrowsmith very timely understood, cross-cutting political goals are in no way secondary.[70]

182; C Methven O'Brien and R Caranta, 'Due Diligence in EU Institutions' Own Account Procurement: Rules and Practices' Study for European Parliament (2024).

[67] European Commission, 'Proposal for a Directive of the European Parliament and of the Council on Corporate Sustainability Due Diligence and Amending Directive (EU) 2019/1937' (2022) COM(2022) 71 final.

[68] The same will apply with reference to the obligations flowing from Directive (EU) 2022/2464 amending Regulation (EU) No 537/2014, Directive 2004/109/EC, Directive 2006/43/EC and Directive 2013/34/EU, as regards corporate sustainability reporting [2022] OJ L322/15. See Methven O'Brien and Caranta (n 66).

[69] Holding the present exclusion regime insufficient to justify exclusions related to the lack of CSR and other business policies, Arrowsmith (n 11) 779 ff.

[70] For reference to cross-cutting goals, see the European Commission, 'Report from the Commission to the European Parliament, the Council and the Court of Auditors, Annual Management and Performance Report for the EU Budget – Financial Year 2020' (2021) COM(2021) 301 final; the Report highlights that 'The EU budget is much more than the sum of its parts. Every spending programme is designed to tackle a particular set of challenges. However, the EU budget is at its most powerful when programmes work together to unlock synergies, catalyse private and public funding, and coherently promote the overarching political priorities which are central to the headline ambitions of the von der Leyen Commission ...'

Following the COVID pandemic and the invasion of Ukraine, sustainability is going to team up with and be strengthened by new concerns – resilience and the security of supplies. And public contracts will have a role to play here as well. The new approach is the cornerstone of the recent Proposal for a Regulation on establishing a framework of measures for strengthening Europe's net-zero technology products manufacturing ecosystem (Net Zero Industry Act – NZIA).[71] The Explanatory Memorandum gives the context of the Proposal. Its first phrase highlights the opportunities coming from the transition to a climate-neutral, clean economy, 'in terms of developing the net-zero technology sectors and creating quality jobs and growth'. The 'net-zero energy technologies are at the centre of strong geostrategic interests and at the core of the global technological race'.[72] According to the Commission, 'these technologies … play a key role in the Union's open strategic autonomy, ensuring that citizens have access to clean, affordable, secure energy'.[73] As Recital 20 to the Proposal indicates, '[a] secure supply of clean energy is a prerequisite for economic development, as well as for public order and security'. There is no skirting around the matter: the security of supplies is instrumental to public order and security at large, that is, nothing less than the core aim of any political organisation.

An industrial policy for the EU is thus required. According to the Commission, facilitating access to markets for EU-based industries requires 'specific measures related to public demand through public procurement procedures and auctions, as well as through schemes to support private demand by consumers'.[74] Specifically, encouraging public demand for sustainable products requires public buyers to 'consistently apply criteria to ensure a high level of sustainability and resilience of the net-zero products they procure'.[75] The SPP measures in the proposal are 'designed to help public authorities create and maintain a stable public demand for net-zero technologies that will make it economically attractive for business to scale-up the production of tailor-made products for the European market designed with high sustainability and resilience criteria in mind'. Under the proposed rules, 'public authorities must take into account criteria related to sustainability and resilience when awarding the contracts or ranking the bids'.[76]

Recital 25 to the Proposal, avowing that the 2014 procurement and concessions directives already allow for the consideration of social, environmental and innovative characteristics, places the proposed rules squarely within the field of mandatory SPP:

[71] European Commission, 'Proposal for a Regulation of the European Parliament and of the Council, on establishing a framework of measures for strengthening Europe's net-zero technology products manufacturing ecosystem (Net Zero Industry Act)' (2023) COM(2023) 161 final.

[72] ibid Recital 6.

[73] ibid 3.

[74] ibid 4.

[75] ibid 7.

[76] ibid 14.

> When awarding contracts for net-zero technology through public procurement, contracting authorities and contracting entities should duly assess the tenders' contribution to sustainability and resilience in relation to a series of criteria relating to the tender's environmental sustainability, innovation, system integration and to resilience.

Recital 26 sharpens the bite of Article 18(2) of Directive 2014/24/EU by referring directly to contracting authorities, clarifying that they 'should contribute to social sustainability by taking the appropriate measures to ensure that in the performance of public contracts economic operators comply with applicable obligations in the fields of social and labour law'.

Article 19 is the first provision in Chapter IV ('Access to markets') of the Proposal. It is dedicated to 'Sustainability and resilience contribution in public procurement procedures'. While complying with the WTO GPA and Union's other international commitments, and with the general public procurement framework (Recital 31), when awarding contracts for the eight net-zero technologies covered under the proposed Regulation, under Article 19(1), both contracting authorities and contracting entities must have recourse to 'the most economically advantageous tender, which shall include the best price-quality ratio, comprising at least the sustainability and resilience contribution of the tender'. Under Article 19(2), the tender's sustainability and resilience contribution must be based on four objective, transparent and non-discriminatory criteria, namely:

> (a) environmental sustainability going beyond the minimum requirements in applicable legislation;
> (b) where an innovative solution needs to be developed, the impact and the quality of the implementation plan, including risk management measures;
> (c) where applicable, the tender's contribution to the energy system integration, and
> (d) the tender's contribution to resilience, taking into account the proportion of the products originating from a single source of supply … from which more than 65% of the supply for that specific net-zero technology within the Union originates in the last year for which data is available for when the tender takes place.

While the criteria are indicated as cumulative, those under (b) and (c) will not be applicable to all and every public procurement or concession. Criteria (a) and (c) focus on environmental sustainability, (b) on innovation and (d) is specific to the security of supplies.

Recital 27 to the Proposal expands on environmental sustainability, expressly adding several considerations to those already non-exhaustively listed in Article 67(2) of Directive 2014/24/EU. This is the case concerning the durability and reliability of the solution; the ease and quality of recycling; the use of substances; the consumption of energy, water and other resources in one or more life-cycle stages of the product; the environmental footprint of the product and its life-cycle environmental impacts; the carbon footprint of the product; the microplastic release; emissions to air, water or soil released in one or more life-cycle stages of the product; the amounts of waste generated.

The 'single source of supply' under (d) above is determined in accordance with Regulation (EU) No 952/2013 laying down the Union Customs Code,[77] and refers to countries and territories from outside the customs territory of the EU as defined under Article 4 thereof. To help contracting authorities and entities, Recital 29 of the Proposal entrusts the Commission with publishing an annual of relevant products/countries and territories.

Under the proposed Article 19(3), '[c]ontracting authorities and contracting entities shall give the tender's sustainability and resilience contribution a weight between 15% and 30% of the award criteria'; they can give an even higher weighting to the criteria referred under Article 19(2), points (a) and (b) (see also Recital 32). Proposed Article 19(4) gives budget-strained contracting authorities and entities some leeway. They are not obliged

> to apply the considerations relating to the sustainability and resilience contribution of net-zero technologies where their application would oblige [them] to acquire equipment having disproportionate costs, or technical characteristics different from those of existing equipment, resulting in incompatibility, technical difficulties in operation and maintenance …

To this end, cost differences above 10 per cent may be presumed disproportionate. Still, abnormally low tenders can still be excluded – and must be so in the event of breach of obligations relevant under Article 18(2) of Directive 2014/24/EU and the corresponding provisions in other directives (proposed Article 19(4)).

The NZIA is currently pending approval, and changes to the Proposal are expected. However, the bottom line is that EU is faced with enormous challenges and cannot afford to be complacent. All available tools need to be enlisted to fight climate change and to keep our planet a welcoming place for future (and present) generations. Public contracts included. The parenthesis of mechanical procurement is closed, horizontal and sustainable procurement are here to stay.

Still, there is the need to make rules requiring the exclusion of or giving preference to certain economic operators transparent and predictable in their application. As Sue Arrowsmith has indicated, that does not require abandoning sustainable considerations but simply finding adequate institutional and procedural rules, such as measures centralising the finding of breaches (as under the Deforestation Regulation) or of establishing the occurrence of some requirement (such as the 'single source of supply' under the Net-Zero Industry Act).[78]

A lot is happening in SPP, and the legislative materials are bound to increase, going well beyond the procurement and concession directives. When I first met Sue Arrowsmith in 1995, I had no clue that public procurement could have kept one scholar engaged for many decades. Now I know it can, and I can count on keeping learning from the likes of Sue and the great community of scholars she has raised from Nottingham, many of whom I count among my closest academic friends.

[77] Regulation (EU) No 952/2013 of 9 October 2013 laying down the Union Customs Code (recast) [2013] OJ L269/1.

[78] Arrowsmith (n 11) 700 f; she is obviously not referring to the examples in the text.

9

Arrowsmith and the Balanced Review System under EU Procurement Law

MARI ANN SIMOVART

I. Introduction

One of the specific features of the European Union (EU) public procurement law is the distinct system of remedies that accompanies the substantive procurement law. It is now generally recognised that without a strong and specifically suited remedies framework, the enforcement of EU public procurement law would be compromised, and its purposes – free movement, open access to the Member States' procurement markets and healthy competition – would remain mere theoretical notions. Since the creation of the system of remedies through the Remedies Directives, the transposing national laws have in general met their objectives in the Member States, allowing review options to grow and evolve into a sophisticated framework that can offer the much-needed support for the economic operators. While there are differences between national review systems – and obviously, even the best systems suffer from occasional drawbacks or unavoidable negatives – this at least was the overall conclusion of the European Commission in 2017.[1]

Sue Arrowsmith has been and continues to be the titan leading EU public procurement law research. Inter alia, she has written extensively on the topic of review in EU public procurement law cases. Her work has focused on various aspects related to the review of public procurement decisions, including the types of review available, the grounds for review and the available remedies for aggrieved bidders. Arrowsmith has also explored the relationship between EU law and national law in the context of review. She supervised remarkable doctoral theses concerning the subject of review of public purchasing, such as the effectiveness

[1] European Commission, 'Report from the Commission to the European Parliament and the Council on the Effectiveness of Directive 89/665/EEC and Directive 92/13/EEC, as Modified by Directive 2007/66/EC, Concerning Review Procedures in the Area of Public Procurement' COM(2017) 28 Final at https://eur-lex.europa.eu/legal-content/EN/TXT/PDF/?uri=CELEX:52017DC0028&from=EN (accessed 28 June 2021) 3, 4.

of remedies by Despina Pachnou[2] and on the supplier review system in China by Xinglin Zhang.[3] Her input in the field of procurement remedies cannot be underestimated, in particular the constant search for well-balanced solutions for an efficient and fair review system.

In this chapter, I will look at Sue Arrowsmith's work on the remedies system, aiming to pinpoint the expectations of legal review systems today. As Arrowsmith highlighted, next to the clearly substantial contribution of the EU Remedies Directives to improving compliance, the new reality of 'thousands of actions a year in many Member States' can potentially be disruptive for the procurement system.[4] That new reality seems to call for a reasonable and just balancing of the remedies system for it to continue to function in securing the efficient enforcement of EU procurement law. This chapter focuses on the remedies system in EU law and will not analyse or compare different national jurisdictions, despite occasionally referring to national solutions that are part of the transposition of the Remedies Directives into the legal systems of the Member States.

II. Development of the Review System in EU Procurement Law

The area of review over public purchasing is a part of legal studies where the work of Arrowsmith truly stands out. While the current statutory framework for review was only established by the Remedies Directives from the years 1989 and 1992, several issues essential to the effective functioning of the review system found the valuable attention of Sue Arrowsmith already in 1989.[5] In the outstanding book based on her doctoral thesis, Arrowsmith investigates the example of Canadian government procurement law, with the purpose 'not simply to justify, or advocate' but to suggest how to introduce judicial review over public procurement.[6] Even though analysed under a legal system different from that of the Member States under EU procurement law, the main notions underlying the modern EU review system are similar.

For today's reader, an interesting observation might be Arrowsmith's denouncing of the misguided assumption of that time, of procurement activity as a rule being excluded from review, arguing that there is 'nothing in the nature of the

[2] D Pachnou, 'The Effectiveness of Bidder Remedies for Enforcing the EC Public Procurement Rules: A Case Study of the Public Works Sector in the United Kingdom and Greece' (PhD thesis, University of Nottingham, 2003) 442.

[3] X Zhang, 'A Supplier Review System as Part of the Government Procurement System for China' (PhD thesis, University of Nottingham, 2008).

[4] S Arrowsmith, *The Law of Public and Utilities Procurement: Regulation in the EU and UK*, vol 2 (3rd edn, Sweet & Maxwell, 2018), para 22-03.

[5] S Arrowsmith, *Government Procurement and Judicial Review* (Carswell, 1988).

[6] ibid *passim*.

procurement function which makes it inappropriate to apply the usual public law principles of review' and 'no reason in principle to exclude this function from the operation of administrative law review'.[7] On the contrary, a certain nature of the power exercised by an authority should always justify review, irrespective of specific legislation to that end.[8] Any party adversely affected by an administrative decision must be entitled to some procedural protection, unless a specific good reason to the contrary exists. Without any good reason to argue against it, review over government procurement must allow for the right to be heard for the concerned party and a rule against bias, and thus guarantee procedural fairness of government contracting decisions.[9]

At the same time, however, the peculiarities of procurement procedures and the related legal rights and interests must be considered.[10] The overall purpose should thus be the introduction of a legal review system that is fit to deal with concerns specific to procurement situations, such as the need for taking decisions rapidly. Such a system would have to offer a balanced approach that protects the interests of both the parties – the contracting authority as well as the potential private party to the public contract concerned – and serves the purposes of the review in general.[11]

It is well recognised today that review systems and remedies before national review bodies are central to modern procurement systems, providing significant benefits and advantages, such as efficient protection of the parties' interests and securing compliance in the public interest.[12] Under the general principles of the EU law, Member States are bound to have an effective legal basis for enforcing substantive EU procurement law. An effective review mechanism is needed to ensure that the procurement rules are followed. That has, however, not always been clear.[13]

Historically, 'in the early days of the EU procurement regime' many Member States either ignored the duty to provide legal remedies or failed to enforce the existing ones.[14] The EU had witnessed the transposition of the first substantive procurement directives and was faced with practical difficulties in ensuring the uniform and full application of these directives in the Member States. The then existing remedies were clearly inadequate to ensure strict compliance with substantive EU public procurement law. In particular, there was no system for quick correction of violations during an ongoing public procurement procedure, when

[7] ibid 8–9, 20, 22.
[8] ibid 134, 136.
[9] ibid 147, 149.
[10] ibid 239–41, 245, 265–67, 305.
[11] ibid *passim*.
[12] Arrowsmith (n 4) para 22-35.
[13] C Ginter and MA Simovart, 'The Remedies Directives 89/665 Etc' in M Steinicke and PL Vesterdorf (eds), *EU Public Procurement Law. Brussels Commentary* (Beck, Hart, Nomos, 2018) 1377, 1384–88.
[14] Sue Arrowsmith, *The Law of Public and Utilities Procurement: Regulation in the EU and UK*, vol 1 (3rd edn, Sweet & Maxwell, 2014) para 3-24; Arrowsmith (n 4) para 22-03.

that was still effectively possible, that is, before the award of a public procurement contract.[15] Even though, like today, compliance with EU procurement law could be secured via the European Commission's monitoring and enforcement activities, that mechanism could not be effective simply due to the sheer number of procedures and the cases related to potential or actual breaches.[16]

Adopted to overcome these weaknesses and designed to provide strong antidotes for breaches, the Remedies Directives[17] were introduced to establish adequate and swift review procedures that would eliminate or sanction possible violations of the substantive rules effectively and rapidly. Overall, the Remedies Directives function successfully to this day, although there were some later amendments.[18] Similar rules with certain area-specific adaptations were introduced for defence and security procurement in the Defence and Security Directive[19] itself, therefore referred to by Trybus as the 'hidden Remedies Directive'.[20]

The right to review as well as equal access of tenderers to procurement procedures rely on the respective fundamental principles of the TFEU.[21] In fact, as Arrowsmith notes, some of the requirements stated in the Remedies Directives and the respective clauses of the Defence and Security Directive could be deduced from the principles of the TFEU. In other respects, however, the specific remedies introduced under the Directives imposed 'more stringent requirements than the Treaty itself'.[22] Therefore, unlike some other areas of EU economic law, the EU legal framework for public procurement remedies has led Member States to create effective national review systems specifically for the enforcement of public procurement law.[23]

[15] See also Ginter and Simovart (n 13) 1385.

[16] Arrowsmith (n 4) para 22-03.

[17] Council Directive 89/665/EEC of 21 December 1989 on the coordination of the laws, regulations and administrative provisions relating to the application of review procedures to the award of public supply and public works contracts [1989] OJ L395/33; Council Directive 92/13/EEC of 25 February 1992 coordinating the laws, regulations and administrative provisions relating to the application of Community rules on the procurement procedures of entities operating in the water, energy, transport and telecommunications sectors [1992] OJ L76/14.

[18] Directive 2007/66/EC of the European Parliament and of the Council of 11 December 2007 amending Council Directives 89/665/EEC and 92/13/EEC with regard to improving the effectiveness of review procedures concerning the award of public contracts [2007] OJ L335/31.

[19] Directive 2009/81/EC of the European Parliament and of the Council of 13 July 2009 on the coordination of procedures for the award of certain works contracts, supply contracts and service contracts by contracting authorities or entities in the fields of defence and security, and amending Directives 2004/17/EC and 2004/18/EC [2009] OJ L216/76, Arts 55 et seq.

[20] M Trybus, *Buying Defence and Security in Europe. The EU Defence and Security Procurement Directive in Context.* (Cambridge University Press, 2014) 455.

[21] Consolidated version of the Treaty on the Functioning of the European Union [2012] OJ C326/47 (TFEU).

[22] Arrowsmith, *The Law of Public and Utilities Procurement*, vol 1 (n 14) para 3-25.

[23] ibid para 3-25; Ginter and Simovart (n 13).

III. Characteristics of the Peer-Review System under EU Procurement Law

A. The Rationale of the Peer-Review System

The Remedies Directives require the Member States to introduce and maintain national review systems that would offer every interested party a rapid remedy against any breach of public procurement law by a contracting authority. Differently from the initial proposals that would have granted the European Commission a relatively significant power to oversee procurement matters, the Remedies Directives introduced a system of remedies that is primarily based on supplier review. It should be noted that the EU 'experimented' with other types of review systems as well, mainly in the case of utilities procurement. However, they were not adopted, at least not on the EU level.[24]

In the case of supplier review, proceedings in competent national bodies are initiated as private enforcement by interested economic operators. The review bodies can be either domestic courts or other institutions, as may be designated by the Member States.[25] As opposed to administrative or state supervision, a supplier-review system can effectively offer protection both of the public interests as well as of interests of economic operators at the same time. Since a violation of public procurement rules almost always touches on the rights or liberties of a competing economic operator, correction of any wrongful decisions of a contracting authority is most effectively conducted via supplier review.

The first reason for the supplier-review system's effectiveness is the suppliers' strong incentive to monitor the lawfulness of contracting authorities' purchasing activities and to initiate review procedures quickly when necessary for their own protection. Second, as active participants in the public procurement procedure concerned and, moreover, as practitioners in the relevant field of business, the economic operators possess insights into the area's specific economic conditions. As such, economic operators are best equipped to notice or discover any breaches in a procurement procedure.

In her doctoral thesis supervised by Arrowsmith, Xinglin Zhang highlights another important societal benefit of the supplier-review system: that of the increased trust of economic operators in the system of public procurement as a whole. Obviously, without suppliers' confidence in the fair operation of public procurement, no real competition could occur, and thus it would be difficult to guarantee the public sector's purchasing cost-effectively. An efficient set of rules for review over public procurement is one of the bases for creating such supplier confidence.[26]

[24] See, for more on the topic, Arrowsmith (n 4) para 22-04.
[25] ibid para 22-01; Ginter and Simovart (n 13) 1385.
[26] Zhang (n 3)14–15.

Of course, a supplier-review system is not without its drawbacks, such as 'reputational concerns' and – in the case of a court-based review system – the ordinary litigation risks and high costs of litigation. Such concerns can lead to the unwillingness of economic operators to initiate litigation against contracting authorities.[27] Also, any litigation undertaken in procurement cases can result in delays, leading to the loss of benefit for end-users, possibly higher prices during an interim period between contracts, as well as a related negative effect on the contracting authority's reputation. The reported drawbacks have led Heikkinen and Halonen to question the efficiency of the litigation-based remedies system and instead to recommend a review system based on alternative review bodies, such as complaints boards for public procurement.[28]

Indeed, that recommendation seems to find support in practice. For instance, the effective functioning of the Danish administrative Complaints Board system is acknowledged by Risvig Hamer.[29] Similarly, Estonian procurement practice seems to prove the benefits of a review system based on an independent complaints board. The preparatory materials for the last Estonian Public Procurement Act (in force since 2017) indicated that the practice of reviewing cases before the Public Procurement Complaints Board was more efficient both financially and time-wise, the estimated time for reviewing a case before the Board being 6.7 times shorter than that of a review in the first-instance court.[30] Even though drawbacks can also be found in the Complaints Board-based review system, and Estonia has even briefly considered changing to a litigation-based system in 2020, this idea was rejected for the benefit of continuing review by the Complaints Board. Furthermore, the 2017 conclusions of the European Commission reported the first-instance administrative review bodies of Member States to be generally more effective than the first-instance judicial instances in terms of both the duration of the review procedures and the standards of review.[31]

B. Rapid and Effective Review

Speed and effectiveness are the primary standards expected throughout the review system. As such, the speedy and effective nature of a review of procurement is

[27] R Craven and S Arrowsmith, 'Public Procurement and Access to Justice: A Legal and Empirical Study of the UK System' (2016) 6 *Public Procurement Law Review* 227; P Heikkinen and K-M Halonen, 'Is It All Worth It? Litigation Risks in Public Procurement and Role of Reputation in Particular: Evidence from Finland' (2023) 4 *Public Procurement Law Review* 171; Pachnou (n 2).

[28] Heikkinen and Halonen (n 27) 175–76.

[29] CR Hamer, 'Remedies for Breaches of the Public Procurement Rules in Denmark – Is the Danish Enforcement System Effective?' (2020) 1 *Upphandlingsrättslig Tidskrift* 1.

[30] 'RHS Seletuskiri' at https://eelnoud.valitsus.ee/main#RS4JOtIr (accessed 4 March 2024), 120–21. Based on data from 2010, the level of decision-making in the complaints board was also considered good, with four out of five cases receiving a final decision from the complaints board and entering into force without an appeal to the court.

[31] European Commission (n 1).

emphasised both in the Remedies Directives and in the case law concerning its application. National review systems must provide the interested economic operators with rapidly and effectively available options for review.[32]

The requirement that a breach of EU procurement law must be reviewed effectively is based on the general principle of effectiveness of EU law. Moreover, it has been argued, based on the *Alcatel* decision,[33] that a *specific* requirement for the effectiveness of remedies applies, as opposed to the *general* principle of effectiveness under the TFEU. Arrowsmith has questioned this understanding and argues alternatively that the requirement of effectiveness *goes beyond the requirement for effectiveness under the TFEU*. Despite the possible differences in the theoretical approach towards the nature of principles of effectiveness, the essence of the principle seems to be relatively clear: the remedies system must provide review options that are effective both from the public interest perspective and for the economic operators participating in public and utilities procurement procedures.[34]

Interestingly, in 2018 Arrowsmith predicted that

> in the future the principle may become important for dealing with obstacles to review that are created by procedural aspects of the remedies system, such as costs, that are not expressly addressed by the Remedies Directive, possibly imposing standards that go beyond those of the TFEU …[35]

Indeed, the recent judgment in *EPIC*[36] does just that, looking at obstacles to review under national law.

The case of *EPIC* concerned a procurement under a framework agreement in Austria: the Republic of Austria and the federal purchasing company Bundesbeschaffungs GmbH awarded a framework agreement for the supply of COVID-19 antigen tests. The legal question was whether the following requirements of Austrian law were in harmony with Remedies Directive 89/665: (i) the requirement that a claimant‘s application for review must identify the specific public contract award procedure and a contestable decision; and (ii) the requirement to pay the correct court fee. In the case at issue, these requirements were impossible to fulfil because the contracting authority had entered into the framework agreement concerned as a result of a negotiated procedure, without publishing the contract notice. The choice of the negotiated procedure without prior publication of a contract notice under Article 32(2)(c) of Directive 2014/24[37] was not in question in the Court, and was presumably justified to obtain the

[32] See, eg, Joined Cases C-274/21 and C-275/21 *EPIC Financial Consulting GesmbH v Republik Österreich and Bundesbeschaffung GmbH* ECLI:EU:C:2022:565, paras 72, 82, 91.

[33] Case C-81/98 *Alcatel Austria AG and Others, Siemens AG Österreich and Sag-Schrack Anlagentechnik AG v Bundesministerium für Wissenschaft und Verkehr* ECLI:EU:C:1999:534.

[34] Arrowsmith (n 4) para 22-57.

[35] ibid.

[36] *EPIC* (n 32).

[37] Directive 2014/24/EU of the European Parliament and of the Council of 26 February 2014 on public procurement and repealing Directive 2004/18/EC [2014] OJ L94/65.

supply of antigen tests as a matter of urgency.[38] However, the Court of Justice of the European Union (CJEU) decided that in the absence of prior publication of a contract notice, no litigant is in a position to determine the type of procedure and the exact contestable decisions.[39] Therefore, national legislation requiring a litigant to indicate that type of information in such situations renders the exercise of rights conferred by EU law practically impossible and, accordingly, compromises the effectiveness of Directive 89/665.[40] Thus, while the Remedies Directives do not expressly contain clauses regarding national procedural laws on court costs or contents of applications, the nature of the requirements concerned clearly created obstacles to a speedy and effective review. Therefore, such requirements were not compliant with the Directive.

It is important to note that the difficulties created by enforcing the requirements in question in *EPIC* do not only concern direct awards resulting from exceptional procedures. The potential impact of the ruling against restrictions that limit potential claimants' access to fair review is even wider, covering the availability of procurement law remedies when challenging any public contract awarded by means other than ordinary advertised procedures, including potential illegal direct awards and unlawful contract modifications.

The question of accessibility to review was also the subject matter of recent cases looking into the right to initiate review by economic operators that had been excluded from the procurement procedure. In *VZ*,[41] the case concerned a claim of an economic operator who did not satisfy a condition for participation laid down in the call for tenders, and whose claim to challenge that condition was rejected by a decision with the force of *res judicata*. The Remedies Directive does not preclude that tenderer's being refused access to a review of the award decision.[42] The situation would be different, however, if the exclusion of the operator had not been definitive[43] – such as in the case of *Randstad Italia SpA*.[44] Here, the CJEU confirmed that a Member State was not entitled to refuse review to an economic operator excluded from the procurement when the exclusion could still be legally challenged, as provided under Article 2a(2) of Directive 89/665. Such an operator could still be regarded as potentially having an interest in and a chance to be awarded the contract. Moreover, the standing of such persons could not even be tied to irrelevant factors, such as the excluded tenderer's ranking or the number of tenderers.[45]

[38] *EPIC* (n 32) para 80. See also J Taylor, 'Availability of Procurement Remedies in Situations of Extreme Urgency: EPIC Financial Consulting Ges.m.b.H. v Republic of Austria and Bundesbeschaffung GmbH (C-274/21 and C-275/21)' (2022) 6 *Public Procurement Law Review* NA176.

[39] *EPIC* (n 32) para 81.

[40] ibid 82–84, 94.

[41] Case C-53/22 *VZ (Soumissionnaire définitivement exclu)* ECLI:EU:C:2023:88.

[42] ibid para 33, 38.

[43] ibid para 39; see also Case C-355/15 *Bietergemeinschaft Technische Gebäudebetreuung GesmbH und Caverion Österreich GmbH v Universität für Bodenkultur Wien and VAMED Management und Service GmbH & Co KG* ECLI:EU:C:2016:988.

[44] Case C-497/20 *Randstad Italia SpA v Umana SpA and Others* ECLI:EU:C:2021:1037.

[45] ibid 74.

Arrowsmith also refers to speed as one of the aspects of effectiveness that may potentially develop into new obligations in relation to the review proceedings, where the national law has not already prescribed that.[46] The notion of speed is particularly important for the protection of the interests of multiple parties involved, and the public interest is always present as well. Should the response to a dispute or potential breach in a procurement procedure not be quick enough, projects can be subject to suspension or, in contrast, projects may be completed while ignoring the interests of economic operators. Speed is expected as regards both the initiation and the completion of the review proceedings.[47]

In fact, considerations of speed and the possibility to enforce remedies quickly were at issue in *EPIC*, discussed above. As regards those considerations, Directive 89/665 precludes national legislation that requires a review body to first determine certain details of the contested procedure (type of contract-award procedure, the estimated value of the public contract concerned, the total number of contestable decisions, the lots) for the sole purpose of calculating the applicable court fees, before deciding on an injunction. Otherwise, in the type of situation that was in question, it is highly likely that the review body needs to conduct long and complicated investigations, making it impossible to suspend the challenged contract and reducing any actual possibility of useful interim measures to zero.[48]

C. Procedural Autonomy versus Effectiveness and Equivalence of National Review Systems

It is important to take note of the connection between EU and national jurisdictions with regard to the scope of public procurement review. The Remedies Directives balance the established general principle of procedural autonomy of the Member States, on the one hand, and the two principles limiting the application of national procedural economy, on the other – the principles of effectiveness and equivalence.[49] Under the principle of national procedural autonomy, a Member State enjoys a wide discretion in implementing the review system, as the Remedies Directives prescribe only the minimum conditions for the review procedures that national jurisdictions must establish.[50]

For instance, as already discussed, national frameworks for review of public procurement cases are divided into two categories in one very basic respect: the first-instance review procedures can be conducted either by courts – either general courts or administrative courts, as is fitting for the Member States – or by

[46] Arrowsmith (n 4) para 22-59.
[47] ibid para 22-58.
[48] *EPIC* (n 32) 88–97.
[49] Arrowsmith (n 4) paras 22-43 et seq; Ginter and Simovart (n 13) 1385.
[50] See further Arrowsmith (n 4) para 22-72.

other review bodies.[51] Both legislative choices obviously come with benefits and drawbacks, while both are equally acceptable choices of the national legislators. However, vesting specialised independent review bodies with the exclusive power of review over procurement cases has been shown to provide specific expertise, allows the taking of the special nature of the procurement process into account, and avoids the known negatives of many judicial systems, such as high costs and slow progress, as discussed in section III.A. In fact, Arrowsmith has even referred to the possibility that jurisdictions with 'slow, cumbersome and/or costly proceedings' may be considered to 'contravene the directive's requirement for effective, including rapid, review'.[52]

However, with a view to effectiveness, to guarantee contractors and suppliers in a public procurement procedure a real chance to quickly initiate the sanctioning of breaches of law, the Remedies Directives oblige the Member States to introduce a system of remedies that corresponds to certain minimum standards. For instance, the Directives establish the minimum requirements concerning the scope and general terms of application and the circle of persons entitled to protection under the Directive (Article 1). Thus, it restricts procedural autonomy by setting the requirement of effective and no less favourable (equivalent) remedial protection and uniform application of EU procurement law.[53]

Currently, as a result of accumulating and developing CJEU case law, a vital development within the EU procurement remedies law seems to be the silent reduction of Member States' autonomy regarding their remedies systems.[54] The CJEU case law clearly indicates the complicated balancing acts surrounding the principles of equivalence and effectiveness when enforcing remedies for breaches of EU public procurement law, as well as the intricate relations between national law and EU law with regard to review issues.[55]

D. Types of Remedies under the Peer-Review System

Initially, the Remedies Directives introduced three main types of remedies that all national jurisdictions had to provide for cases of breaches of the public or utilities rules: (i) setting aside unlawful decisions; (ii) provision of interim measures; and (iii) compensation in damages for aggrieved parties. Later, certain additions were made to the remedies system, based on concepts developed in the CJEU case law, such as declaring a contract ineffective if it was awarded with a major breach.[56]

[51] For more on that topic, ibid paras 22-60 et seq.
[52] ibid para 22-60.
[53] eg, *EPIC* (n 32) paras 73, 83, 88–89.
[54] Arrowsmith (n 4) para 22-37.
[55] ibid paras 22-43–22-47.
[56] Directive 89/665/EEC, Arts 2(1), 2d.

As such, proper implementation of the Remedies Directives into national law makes the review options available to a wide range of interested parties, offers quick solutions and covers a wide field of legal relations, from the start of a procurement procedure until, occasionally, awarded contracts.

As a result of its balanced approach, as well as the gradual incorporation of the case law into the Directives, the remedies reform that started in the 1980s and 1990s has in general served its purpose very well. Major additions to the remedies system in 2007 were the introduction of the remedy of ineffectiveness of contracts for cases of major breaches of procurement law and a mandatory standstill period between contract award and conclusion, plus the expansion of the review options to concession contracts following the adoption of the Concessions Directive in 2014.[57] According to the 2017 European Commission Report, the Remedies Directives have

> generally met their objectives of increasing the guarantees of transparency and non-discrimination; allowing effective and rapid action to be taken when there is an alleged breach of the Procurement Directives; and providing economic operators with the assurance that all tender applications will be treated equally.[58]

The Remedies Directives were also highly praised in terms of efficiency, relevance, coherence with other EU policies and providing added value.[59]

However, the Remedies Directives contain uncertainties[60] and can be subject to costs and limitations.[61] Arrowsmith proposed solutions for problematic issues related to the review of public and utilities procurement. Examples of such issues include the need for effective review of contract award decisions in cases when private and public law overlap,[62] as well as the opposite problem: the questionable use of contract law remedies for the benefit of bidders in a procurement procedure;[63] the application of interim measures in the course of a review procedure, such as especially the balancing of interests for such measures;[64] subjecting public

[57] Directive 2014/23/EU of the European Parliament and of the Council of 26 February 2014 on the award of concession contracts [2014] OJ L94/1, Recital (81), Art 46.

[58] European Commission (n 1) 5.

[59] ibid 6–8.

[60] ibid 9–10.

[61] Arrowsmith (n 4) paras 22-35, 22-36.

[62] S Arrowsmith, 'Legitimate Expectations and Judicial Review in Contract Award Procedures: A Note on R v The Lord Chancellor, Ex Parte Hibbitt & Sanders' (1993) 4 *Public Procurement Law Review* CS104; S Arrowsmith and M Dischendorfer, 'Case C-212/02, Commission v Austria: The Requirement for Effective Remedies to Challenge an Award Decision' (2004) 6 *Public Procurement Law Review* NA165.

[63] Sue Arrowsmith, 'Enforcing the EC Public Procurement Rules: The Remedies System in England and Wales' (1992) 2 *Public Procurement Law Review* 92; S Arrowsmith, 'The "Blackpool" Implied Contract Governing Public Sector Tenders: A Review in the Light of Pratt and Other Recent Case Law' (2004) 5 *Public Procurement Law Review* NA125.

[64] S Arrowsmith, 'The Award of Interim Measures in Procurement Cases: Implications of the Recent Order in the Wallonia Buses Case' (1994) 4 *Public Procurement Law Review* CS130.

procurement to the general administrative law principles of judicial review;[65] and the speed and timeliness of review.[66]

The fundamental lines of argument in matters concerning the remedies system evolve from the right of economic operators to equal access to procurement markets and the question of whether such a right even exists.[67] While many of the approaches discussed may seem self-evidently logical today, at the time, Arrowsmith's work offered much-needed new conceptual guidance. This includes the interaction or overlap between jurisdictions (EU versus national) or types of law (for example, private versus public law remedies). Further, in addition to offering solutions to various procedural or legal issues that can occur and have occurred in review practice, Arrowsmith has convincingly argued for the need to balance the review system.

IV. Balancing Acts within the Public Procurement Review System

A. Purposes of the Review System versus Aims of Public Procurement

The notion of *balanced* review options for procurement can relate to different aspects. First is, of course, the underlying procedural aim of providing a suitable balance between the opposing interests present in the review proceedings between the parties representing those interests. Both the adversarial and inquisitorial aspects of a review procedure can be used to obtain a just equilibrium in any procedure. At the same time, such a balance is guided by the principle of equivalence and the prohibition of discrimination in such proceedings.

In addition, as a system, the review mechanisms under EU procurement law are designed to balance the rights and powers of the market participants and the contracting authorities, on the one hand, and for the wider benefit of the review system for the common good, on the other hand. As such, an effective review system has a preventive effect towards compliance with the EU procurement rules.[68]

[65] S Arrowsmith, 'Judicial Review of Procurement in the Supreme Court of Canada' (1994) 5 *Public Procurement Law Review* CS174; S Arrowsmith, 'Judicial Review of Public Procurement: The Recent Decisions in the National Lottery Case and R v Bristol City Council, Ex p DLBarrett' (2001) 1 *Public Procurement Law Review* NA41.

[66] S Arrowsmith, 'Time Limits for Bringing Proceedings in Public Procurement Cases in the United Kingdom: The High Court Judgment in Matra Communications v Home Office' (1999) 2 *Public Procurement Law Review* CS55; S Arrowsmith, 'The Time Limit for Instituting Proceedings under the UK Procurement Regulations: Holleran v Severn Trent Water' (2005) 2 *Public Procurement Law Review* NA44.

[67] Arrowsmith (n 5) 233–34.

[68] Hamer (n 29) 1.

It seems that while generally, the former supports the latter, the more effective individual remedies for economic operators a national remedies regime provides, the greater the public interest benefits. An important, if often overlooked, component of such influence can be the above-mentioned element of increased trust in the system on the procurement market.[69]

However, the efficiency of individual review proceedings may also require balancing the purposes of the review with the aims of the procurement procedure itself. Arrowsmith has noted that remedies can potentially be disruptive to the procurement procedure.[70] While fair review options serve a significant purpose in procurement, as shown, it cannot be excluded that excessive review actions might bring about undesirable side-effects in the way of making it impossible to make necessary purchases on time. Thus, the maximum effectiveness of the review system from an individual economic operator's point of view does not necessarily lead to the most effective review system for society.

That understanding relates to the above-mentioned issue of access to review proceedings and drawing a line regarding persons who have standing in the respective court or review body. Hypothetically, a wider circle of economic operators than is currently accepted under the CJEU case law could make a successful argument of having standing in a procurement case. For instance, a tenderer who has no chance of being awarded the relevant contract could argue standing. This challenge could then lead to the cancelling of the procurement procedure and the publication of a new procedure in which such an operator could then participate.[71] Besides being extremely difficult to establish, and containing many hypotheticals, accepting the right to review by an excluded or a clearly unsuccessful operator would disproportionally increase the volume of disruptions to procurement procedures in practice caused by review proceedings. The CJEU case law therefore rightfully rejects the standing of such clearly excluded or clearly unsuccessful tenderers, and by doing so, supports the conduct of successful and economically efficient procurement procedures in practice.

Similarly, the notion of balancing can concern the depth of review decisions: how far should a review body double-guess the substantial reasoning behind a contracting authority's decision? The Remedies Directives do not prescribe the substance of the review, leaving the question for Member States' legal systems to decide. Member States are free to vest the review bodies with extensive powers of review, including the determination of legal versus merit-based decisions. The latter can be appropriate if the reviewers possess special expertise.[72] Besides the review body's expertise, the effect on efficient procurement procedures might also either benefit or lose from extensive scrutiny of the contracting authority's decisions.

[69] Zhang (n 3) 14–15.

[70] Arrowsmith (n 4) para 22-03.

[71] ibid para 22-77. See also Case C-131/16 *Archus sp z o.o and Gama Jacek Lipik v Polskie Górnictwo Naftowe i Gazownictwo SA* ECLI:EU:C:2017:358, para 52.

[72] Arrowsmith (n 4) para 22-117.

B. Gaps in the Review System

i. Remedies (Not) Following the Material Law of Procurement

In 1988, Arrowsmith correctly identified certain types of decisions in the procurement process that would be most likely to cause legal challenges, such as the technical specifications, exclusions and (un-)fair treatment of tenderers, and contract award decisions.[73] Other topics discussed in her early publications were the impact of breaches of procurement rules on the validity of a public contract that had been awarded, the effect of review of public procurement on contractual autonomy, the standing of competing economic operators in review proceedings concerning public contracts between the winning tenderer and the contracting authority, and possible claims of restitution for the benefit of the winning tenderer in cases where the public contract turns out to be invalid.[74] Clearly, all the above-mentioned types of cases have by now become familiar through the case law of the European Court in the field of procurement.

However, while the substantive law on EU procurement has constantly been evolving, the remedies system has not always followed as quickly and comprehensively as one would hope. As already discussed, the review system was designed under EU public procurement law, based on earlier versions of the Directives. Since its creation, the remedies system has been updated to a certain extent based on the CJEU case law, the most significant change introduced by the 2007 amendments to the Remedies Directives.[75] Directive 2007/66 eliminated 'important loopholes' in the review system by both enhancing the possibility of review before the contract award via notification and standstill requirements, and introducing the new remedy of ineffectiveness and other *ex ante* control measures.[76]

After the 2007 amendments, the Remedies Directives have not been subject to any further changes corresponding to the developments in the substantive EU procurement law, which might have benefitted from better 'backing up' by the available review options.[77] Therefore, I submit that some issues relating to the remedies system need attention and possibly amendment. This concerns, for instance, the lack of specific remedies for wrongful contract modification or termination cases; specific problems relating to initiating review and the application of remedies in a joint cross-border public procurement situation; and the virtually non-existent remedy of damages. The problems with the remedy of damages in procurement cases, or at least the very diverse level of addressing public procurement breaches

[73] Arrowsmith (n 5) 229–31, 305.

[74] ibid 3–4, 24, 329–33.

[75] Directive 2007/66/EC of the European Parliament and of the Council of 11 December 2007 amending Council Directives 89/665/EEC and 92/13/EEC with regard to improving the effectiveness of review procedures concerning the award of public contracts [2007] OJ L335/31.

[76] Arrowsmith (n 4) para 22-38.

[77] MA Simovart, 'Current Issues Related to Remedies System under the EU Public Procurement Law' (2018) 1 *Upphandlingsrättslig Tidskrift* 1. Also Hamer (n 29) 12–13.

via damages, is clearly related to the fact that specific rules on damage claims are left largely within the powers of and subject to the national laws of the Member States. The preconditions for and the potential for a successful damage claim vary in Member States, reducing the effectiveness of the Remedies Directives in this respect.[78]

ii. Lack of Remedies for Unlawful Contract Modification

The Remedies Directives that originally introduced the specific supplier-review system to EU public procurement law did not address the issue of contract modifications, because the relevant substantive directives at the time did not contain any clauses on such contract modifications. Since 2014, the EU substantive directives of procurement[79] expressly regulate contract modifications, albeit without specific support from the Remedies Directives. Under the rules of contract modifications, any substantial modification to a public contract is regarded as an illegal direct award, and as such can clearly provide grounds for declaring the contract ineffective and the obligation to conduct a new award procedure as a further result of the breach.[80] However, the exact scope and details of the possible declaration of ineffectiveness are rather unclear. Furthermore, the remedy of ineffectiveness has been reported to be not so effective overall, for example with significant gaps between the practices of the Member State. That has led Arrowsmith to argue that it might be better to focus instead on possible cases of ineffectiveness where there is a fault present.[81] In cases of unlawful modifications, the application of the remedy of ineffectiveness can be subject to even more obstacles, such as the lack of publicly available information about the modification at issue, applicable time limits and questionable practical issues. For instance, would the whole contract become ineffective or only the modified part?[82]

As the current system of remedies was designed with the 'traditional' types of breaches that occur pre-contract award in mind, the option to use other remedies, such as set-aside or interim measures, in cases where the contract modification rules have been breached, can be complicated, unproductive or impossible, and may vary, depending on the choices of national legislators.[83] Therefore, to level the consequences of unlawful modifications and provide uniform protection for rights of interested third parties, the current Remedies Directives might benefit from a review in this aspect.

[78] MA Simovart, 'Old Remedies for New Violations? The Deficit of Remedies for Enforcing Public Contract Modification Rules' (2015) 1 *Upphandlingsrättslig Tidskrift* 33, 44–45.

[79] Directive 2014/23/EU; Directive 2014/24/EU; Directive 2014/25/EU of the European Parliament and of the Council of 26 February 2014 on procurement by entities operating in the water, energy, transport and postal services sectors and repealing Directive 2004/17/EC [2014] OJ L94/243.

[80] Simovart (n 78).

[81] Arrowsmith (n 4) para 22-39.

[82] Simovart (n 77) 3–5.

[83] Simovart (n 78).

iii. Gaps in Regulating Review Over Joint Cross-Border Public Procurement Decisions

Another gap noticeable in the remedies system is again related to an innovation of substantive EU law on public procurement that is not being backed up by remedies. Namely, considerable confusion can occur when the review of procurement decisions occurs as part of a joint cross-border public procurement (JCBPP). In the case of JCBPP, the collaborating contracting authorities can agree that not all parts of the procurement procedure are to be conducted jointly; some collaborators will conduct some parts of the procedure or the procurement project independently. While doing so, the contracting authority may be obliged under its law to follow the law of another Member State. For instance, that is the case under Article 39(3), 2nd subparagraph of Directive 2014/24, if most of the procurement for a framework agreement is conducted by a central purchasing body (CPB) but a collaborating authority reopens the competition and awards a contract under a framework agreement. In such a case, the contract award is subject to the national law of the CPB, even when carried out by a sole contracting authority of another Member State. Accordingly, if a review procedure is initiated against such a contracting authority, the national court or complaints board would also have to apply the national law of the country of the CPB.[84] Would a complaints board even have the necessary competence to apply a foreign law? If so, would the participants trust the board's knowledge and expertise in doing so?

In the light of the above,[85] the review of JCBPP cases seems to lack regulation on the EU level. In particular, enforcement or review of procedural steps that a collaborating contracting authority conducts pursuant to the national laws of another Member State may lack speed and efficiency, and as such may not comply with the rationale of the remedies system under EU procurement law.

V. Conclusions

Sue Arrowsmith's contribution to the field of procurement remedies cannot be overestimated. Especially, her focus on well-balanced solutions – to have a fair

[84] MA Simovart, 'Choice of Law Applicable to Joint Cross-Border Public Procurement by Central Purchasing Bodies or under Occasional Collaboration Agreements' (2021) 1 *Upphandlingsrättslig Tidskrift* 1, 15–18.

[85] See also IH Anchustegui, 'Collaborative Centralized Cross-Border Public Procurement: Where Are We And Where Are We Going To?' at https://papers.ssrn.com/sol3/papers.cfm?abstract_id=3052159 (accessed 10 August 2023) 14–15; B Heuninckx, 'Aggregated Procurement under Directive 2014/24/EU: Lessons from the Defence Sector' (2018) 5 *Public Procurement Law Review* 189, 195–96; A Sanchez-Graells, 'The Emergence of Trans-EU Collaborative Procurement: A "Living Lab" for European Public Law' (2020) 1 *Public Procurement Law Review* 16, 20, 26; MA Simovart and J Kubinec, 'Pathways for (Quasi-)Institutionalised Joint Cross Border Public Procurement in the Security Sector – Is There a Will and a Way?' (2023) 3 *Public Procurement Law Review* 157, 166–67.

system of remedies that is both speedy and efficient, finding the just equilibrium between competing interests and objectives and options – is crucial. With a view to continued balancing of the system of remedies, review options in the field of EU procurement law should be understood as a work in progress, always aiming to secure compliance with EU procurement law and adjusting to an ever-changing legal and economic environment. In this chapter, I have drawn attention to some of the issues that put a question mark over the speed and efficiency of the current functioning of the remedies system. As with every legal system, the reform, or at least maintenance, of the framework often needs to be a continuing as opposed to a final effort.

10

Exclusion and Debarment under EU Procurement Law: Of Cats and Lions

PETER TREPTE

I. Introduction

One of the most well-known false syllogisms that may be traced back to Aristotle relates to lions, namely, that whilst a lion may be a cat, it does not follow that all cats are lions. Something similar could be said of exclusion and debarment under European Union (EU) procurement law. Whilst there is a tendency to use these terms interchangeably when discussing debarment, they are separate concepts, and it is argued that this must be recognised if the scope and limitations of the treatment of debarment under EU procurement law and jurisprudence are to be properly understood. Whilst debarment may be a ground for exclusion, it does not follow that all exclusions are instances of debarment. That maybe they should be is a separate question. The modest aim of this chapter is simply to draw attention to that distinction because, as we know from Arrowsmith's work, taxonomies are important.[1] The focus is on debarment, in particular the definition of the concept itself. It will be argued that the failure properly to define debarment (and, in effect, to conflate it with exclusion) may lead to a fundamental misunderstanding of the debarment mechanism, but also of relevant EU case law. The problem stems from a poor and piecemeal introduction into the European Directives in 2014[2] of certain elements of a debarment system.[3] The European legislator did not have a clear vision of debarment and the architecture needed to implement a debarment system, and instead introduced some isolated elements that are common

[1] See, eg, her work on 'horizontal' policies: S Arrowsmith, 'Horizontal Policies in Public Procurement: a Taxonomy' (2010) 10(2) *Journal of Public Procurement* 149; S Arrowsmith, *The Law of Public and Utilities Procurement* (3rd edn, Sweet & Maxwell, 2018) 696; S Arrowsmith and P Kunzlik, 'Public procurement and horizontal policies in EC law: general principles' in S Arrowsmith and P Kunzlik, *Social and Environmental Policies in EC Procurement Law* (Cambridge University Press, 2009) 9, 13.

[2] For example, Directive 2014/24/EU of the European Parliament and of the Council of 26 February 2014 on public procurement and repealing Directive 2004/18/EC [2014] OJ L94/65.

[3] P Trepte, 'Washing Your Dirty Laundry in Public … Procurement: the New European Procurement Rules' in Grayston & Company, *State of the eUnion* (2014) at www.graystoncompany.com/docs/state-of-the-eunion.pdf.

in more sophisticated and complete debarment systems elsewhere (eg, in the United States (US)[4] and some Member States like Germany[5]). The incoherent legislation means that even discussing and seeking to improve 'debarment' in the EU context is undermined. This problem is exacerbated by the tendency of commentators[6] to equate debarment with exclusion, with the result that recent jurisprudence[7] may be misunderstood. Criticism would be justified if what the legislator had put in place was a recognisable debarment system, but the jurisprudence is entirely consistent with the current legislation, which focuses, rather, on exclusion from individual contract award procedures. The legislation and its interpretation are based on exclusion and not debarment. This chapter argues for a clearer taxonomy to help visualise a coherent debarment policy and allow recommendations for an improved EU debarment system to be made. Making such recommendations is outside the scope of the chapter, but these have been made by a number of authors, including Arrowsmith, notably given the opportunity for doing so provided by Brexit.[8]

As those familiar with existing debarment systems outside the EU have pointed out, debarment is about disqualifying individuals and firms from future contracting opportunities[9] for past misconduct, and is a concept increasingly finding its way into procurement systems around the world.[10] As Friton has stated in the context of the EU:

> Exclusion must be distinguished from debarment: exclusion concerns only an ongoing procurement procedure, while debarment prohibits tenderers from participating in an indefinite number of future procurement procedures for a specific amount of time.[11]

[4] Federal Acquisition Regulation (FAR) part 9.405.

[5] P Friton and C Wolters, 'The German Register of Competition and Its International Context' (2018) 13 *European Procurement & Public Private Partnership Law Review* 119.

[6] For example, S Schoenmaekers, 'The EU debarment rules: legal and economic rationale' (2016) 3 *Public Procurement Law Review* 91, 95; S Williams-Elegbe, *Fighting Corruption in Public Procurement – A Comparative Analysis of Disqualification or Debarment Measures* (Hart Publishing, 2012) 60; S Hawley, 'What makes a good debarment regime? Keeping corrupt and fraudulent companies out of post-Brexit procurement' (2021) 3 *Public Procurement Law Review* 124, 125.

[7] Notably, Case C-41/18 *Meca Srl v Naples* ECLI:EU:C:2019:507 (*Meca*); and Case C-267/18, *Delta Antrepriză de Construcţii şi Montaj 93 SA v Compania Naţională de Administrare a Infrastructurii Rutiere SA* ECLI:EU:C:2019:826 (*Delta*).

[8] S Arrowsmith, *Constructing Rules on Exclusions (Debarment) Under a Post-Brexit Regime on Public Procurement: A Preliminary Analysis* (2020) at https://papers.ssrn.com/sol3/papers.cfm?abstract_id=3659909, Hawley (n 6); and A Jones, 'Combatting Corruption and Collusion in UK Public Procurement: Proposals for Post-Brexit Reform' (2021) 84 *Modern Law Review* 667.

[9] See, eg, S Schooner, 'The paper tiger stirs: rethinking suspension and debarment' (2004) 13(5) *Public Procurement Law Review* 211, 212; C Yukins and M Kania, 'Suspension and Debarment in the US Government: Comparative Lessons for EU's Next Steps in Procurement' (2019) 2 *Procurement Law Journal* 47; S Harutyunyan, Risk and Expectation in exclusion from public procurement: understanding market access and harmonization between the European Union and the United States' (2016) 45 *Public Contracts Law Journal* 449.

[10] P Friton, 'International Developments in 2018 – Part II: Debarment in EU Public Procurement Law – Tentative Progress or Treading Water?' *Government Contracts Year in Review 2018 Conference Briefs* (Thomson Reuters) at https://publicprocurementinternational.com/wp-content/uploads/2019/03/YIR_session_2pt2_2019_Pascal-Friton.pdf.

[11] P Friton and J Zöll, 'Article 57: Exclusion Grounds' in R Caranta and A Sanchez-Graells, *European Public Procurement: Commentary on Directive 2014/24/EU* (Edward Elgar, 2021) 588, 592.

The key elements are 'past misconduct' and 'future disqualification'. Whilst some past misconduct (eg, convictions for corruption) may automatically disqualify persons from participation in future procurements (at least for a certain time), in the same way that convictions for dangerous driving may disqualify persons from driving until such time as the conviction is 'spent',[12] most future disqualifications (debarments) require a system that presupposes the existence of a relatively sophisticated and managed investigative process (including due process safeguards), capable of assessing the severity of any offences on the part of potential tenderers and of applying various preventative and rehabilitative measures according to the nature of the offence and the likelihood or acceptability of remedial action. This is not what was introduced into the EU legislation in 2014.

II. Exclusion under EU Law

The EU rules apply safeguards against discrimination on grounds of nationality for the benefit of tenderers from EU Member States, and do so through the application of transparent contract award procedures and objective and non-discriminatory selection and award criteria as well as technical specifications. One of the key features of the rules has always been the use of 'selection' criteria, whereby tenderers could only be disqualified for failure to meet those selection criteria that were set out and advertised in advance. These selection criteria encompass provisions relating to the general suitability of tenderers, their economic and financial standing, and their technical capacity. The criteria relating to economic and financial standing and to technical capacity might more properly be described as 'qualification' criteria, since they apply, for the most part, to the ability of tenderers to fulfil the terms of the contract, that is, whether they are financially and technically able to perform the required contractual obligations. The criteria related to general suitability are more akin to eligibility requirements, since they are not connected with the ability of the tenderers to perform the ultimate contract but with the desirability or not of the tenderer as a contracting party. In 2004, the legislator also introduced a series of mandatory exclusions in respect of criminal convictions for certain offences,[13] which also resemble eligibility criteria, since they do not relate to the performance of the contract being procured. These require conviction by final judgment, that is tenderers may be excluded only where convicted of the relevant offences. These include offences related to such things as participation

[12] See, eg, under the UK's Rehabilitation of Offenders Act 1974, under which a conviction is to be treated as spent after the end of the rehabilitation period (set at a number of years depending on the sentence and age of the offender) and the convicted person rehabilitated. Spent convictions need not be disclosed.

[13] Directive 2004/18/EC of the European Parliament and of the Council of 31 March 2004 on the coordination of procurement award of public works contracts, public supply contracts and public service contracts [2004] OJ L134/114, Art 45(1). Now contained in Directive 2014/24, Art 57(1).

in criminal organisations, corruption, money laundering, terrorist activities, etc. These offences are defined by reference to a series of EU measures and not generally comparable offences under the laws of the Members States. In addition, there were a series of 'discretionary' exclusions that allowed contracting authorities to exclude tenderers on grounds related to their conduct. Under the Directives adopted in 2014, the scope of these eligibility requirements was expanded and now includes various integrity-related criteria connected, amongst other things, to corrupt activities.

The expanded grounds for exclusion are relevant for the discussion in this chapter. The grounds for discretionary exclusion under Directive 2014/24 are now:

- Article 57(4)(a): where a contracting authority is aware of any violation of obligations established by Union or applicable international legislation in the field of social and labour law or environmental law.
- Article 57(4)(b): where a tenderer is the subject of insolvency or winding-up proceedings, etc.
- Article 57(4)(c): where the contracting authority can *demonstrate by appropriate means* that the tenderer is guilty of grave professional misconduct, which renders its integrity questionable. This ground for exclusion was previously contained in two provisions, one of which was subject to a conviction by way of final judgment (offences of professional conduct) and the other relating to grave professional misconduct (effectively the provision that has now been retained), which could be proved by any means the contracting authorities could demonstrate.
- Article 57(4)(d): where the contracting authority has *sufficiently plausible indications* to conclude that the tenderer has entered into agreements with other economic operators aimed at distorting competition.
- Article 57(4)(e): where a conflict of interest cannot be effectively remedied by other less intrusive measures. One of the innovations of the new rules is the introduction of specific provisions relating to conflicts of interest, which have not hitherto been regulated, although there has been European jurisprudence that has set out the parameters of conflicts in the context of public procurement.[14]
- Article 57(4)(f): where a distortion of competition from the prior involvement of the tenderers in the preparation of the procurement procedure cannot be remedied by other, less intrusive measures. This discretionary ground for exclusion is the corollary of this new conflict-of-interest provision, allowing disqualification where there are no other means of preserving equality of treatment. It is unlikely that it could be used as a general ground of debarment, since the existence of inequality or distortions of competition will necessarily be determined in the context of a specific contract award procedure.

[14] For example, Case C-21/03 *Fabricom* [2005] ECR I-1559.

- Article 57(4)(g): where the tenderer has shown significant or persistent deficiencies in the performance of a substantive requirement under a prior public contract, a prior contract with a contracting authority or a prior concession contract, which led to early termination of that prior contract, damages or other comparable sanctions. This ground for exclusion may be difficult to apply in practice, since it does not explicitly require any court judgment to substantiate the poor performance. Where damages or other sanctions are imposed by a court, deficient performance might be assumed, but applying the exclusion in other cases may be more problematic.
- Article 57(4)(h): where the tenderer has been guilty of serious misrepresentation in supplying the information required for the verification of the absence of grounds for exclusion or the fulfilment of the selection criteria, has withheld such information or is not able to submit the required supporting documents.
- Article 57(4)(i): where the tenderer has undertaken to unduly influence the decision-making process of the contracting authority, to obtain confidential information that may confer upon it undue advantages in the procurement procedure or to negligently provide misleading information that may have a material influence on decisions concerning exclusion, selection or award. This is another new provision and appears to provide something of a catch-all provision to cover cases of corrupt behaviour that are not otherwise caught by the ground for mandatory exclusion, above. It is rather vaguely drafted and does not seem to require any strong proof or evidence of the actions undertaken.

There are also provisions relating to the failure to pay taxes or social security contributions. This may be a ground for mandatory or discretionary exclusion depending on whether the failure is subject to a court judgment (see Article 57(2)).

Crucially, Article 56(1) of Directive 2014/24 requires contracting authorities to satisfy themselves that no grounds for exclusion exist, but there is no explicit obligation to make thorough investigations. As will be seen in section III this is to be done on a contract-by-contract basis with the onus on the contracting authorities to make the relevant enquiries to discover the grounds for exclusion. Where tenderers use the ESPD,[15] they are under a duty to make appropriate declarations confirming that they are not in one of the situations covered by Article 57 of the Directive, in which economic tenderers must or may be excluded. Otherwise, it will be difficult for contracting authorities to find evidence of compliance in the absence of some central register of firms or list of debarred firms. These will often form part of more mature national debarment systems,[16] but do not form part of the Directive's provisions on exclusion.

[15] The European Single Procurement Document (ESPD), referred to in Directive 2014/24, Art 59.

[16] For example, the relatively recent Competition Register maintained in Germany by the *Bundeskartellamt*: see at www.bundeskartellamt.de/EN/CompetitionRegister/CompReg_node.html. In the US, debarred firms are listed on the System for Award Management (SAM), a central repository of qualification and performance information maintained by the General Services Administration (GSA): see at https://sam.gov/content/home.

III. Implementation

The exclusion criteria introduced in 2004 were drafted as if they applied to single contract award procedures, that is, if a tenderer was found to fall into one or other of the identified categories, it could or must be excluded from the contract award procedure at issue. Whilst the rules did not exclude the possibility of national systems that applied a more rigorous and permanent debarment system (ie where tenderers could be excluded for a given period of time where they fell within one of the defined categories), they did not themselves foresee or provide for such a system.[17] The situation under the 2014 Directives has not changed in this regard, to the extent that the rules do not provide for an EU-wide debarment system, but they do now clearly foresee the existence of such debarment systems at a national level and, to some extent, provide for a mechanism to deal with cases where a national debarment system is incomplete. Crucially, the rules also provide for rehabilitation – a system under which tenderers can overcome disqualification by demonstrating that they have taken action to reform themselves. In respect of mandatory exclusion, until 2014, the EU rules imposed a rather blunt instrument, which consisted of the mandatory exclusion of tenderers who had been convicted of offences related to, inter alia, corruption. The consequence was, in effect, to exclude convicted tenderers permanently from participation in contract award procedures, with no possibility of rehabilitating themselves. Under the new rules, Member States are required to establish implementing mechanisms for the provisions, and a key feature of these must be determining the maximum period of exclusion. Where this is not fixed, the 2014 Directive sets the maximum at five years. As a result, mandatory exclusion is no longer permanent and became subject to the Directives' rehabilitation process. Though this would be the result of the application of a mature debarment system, that is not how the 2014 legislation operates. It is much more akin to the setting of a rehabilitation period for spent convictions.[18]

Though incomplete, these changes demonstrate that the EU legislator is beginning to see the exclusion rules as part of a bigger picture of debarment. Without fundamentally changing its approach at the EU level, some of the provisions clearly allow for (and to some extent require) the creation at national level of more

[17] Although the EU does have its own system for this applying to the European institutions. This is the Early Detection and Exclusion System (EDES), established by the European Commission to strengthen the protection of the Union's financial interests and to ensure sound financial management. The EDES rules are provided in the revised Financial Regulation (Regulation 2018/1046 of the European Parliament and of the Council of 18 July 2018 on the financial rules applicable to the general budget of the Union, amending Regulations (EU) No 1296/2013, (EU) No 1301/2013, (EU) No 1303/2013, (EU) No 1304/2013, (EU) No 1309/2013, (EU) No 1316/2013, (EU) No 223/2014, (EU) No 283/2014, and Decision No 541/2014/EU and repealing Regulation (EU, Euratom) No 966/2012 [2018] OJ L193/1). See further, the Commission Staff Working Document, Early Detection and Exclusion System (EDES) SWD(2019) 362 final, 11 October 2019.

[18] See n 12. This is supported by the jurisprudence of the EU: Case C-472/19 *Vert Marine* ECLI:EU:C:2020:468.

sophisticated debarment systems. The strengthened requirement that Member States should put in place laws, regulations or administrative provisions to implement the provision relating to discretionary exclusion means that each Member State is able to establish some form of debarment system, including one that provides for maximum periods of debarment, although the evidence on the ground suggests that this has not happened across the board.[19] The additional requirement to provide minimum conditions of rehabilitation also means that there need to be some minimum safeguards throughout the EU based on the terms of the Directive. The broad parameters of a debarment system are discernible but not much more.

The expanded grounds for discretionary exclusion contain further references to integrity and conflicts of interest, thus broadening the potential grounds for debarment. Some of these grounds for exclusion, such as those based on contractor performance, imply the ability to collect information regarding previous contracts, potentially with various authorities – the provision is not explicitly linked to previous contracts with the contracting authority in question, although that would be the obvious assumption – in the public sector.[20] This presupposes the existence of a contractor registration or performance measurement system. These grounds for exclusion may also become mandatory to the extent that the rules allow for Member States to *require* contracting authorities to exclude tenderers where these grounds are met. This enables Member States to start creating broader debarment systems, although the lack of precision in the means of proving that these conditions are met is likely to be problematic in practice. This will be entirely dependent on the implementing measures adopted by the various Member States.

The wide discretion on how to implement these provisions means, however, that implementation will be something of a patchwork throughout the EU, since Member States may choose not to apply the exclusionary grounds or to incorporate them into national law with varying degrees of rigour.[21] This may lead to the implementation of these provisions with no guarantee of consistency in any number of national systems.[22] Some Member States may opt to make grounds for discretionary exclusion mandatory; some may do so for some of the grounds and not others; some Member States may leave it entirely to the discretion of the contracting authorities.

The emergence of a move towards incorporating these exclusionary measures into a broader debarment system may be evidenced by a number of provisions that clearly indicate that exclusion is not necessarily contract-specific, that is, not based merely on the qualification criteria required to be met for the purposes of fulfilling the contract that is the subject of the contract award procedure at issue.

[19] Friton, n 10.

[20] The provision refers to 'public' contracts, suggesting that contracts performed in private markets are not covered.

[21] Case C-395/18 *Tim* ECLI:EU:C:2020:58, para 34; Case C-171/15 *Connexion Taxi Services* ECLI:EU:C:2016:948.

[22] See also A Sánchez Graells, *Public Procurement and the EU Competition Rules* (Hart Publishing, 2015) 470.

Under Article 57(7) of Directive 2014/24, contracting authorities must now *at any moment during the procedure* exclude a tenderer where it turns out that the tenderer in question falls, *in view of acts committed or omitted either before or during procedure*, within one of the grounds for mandatory exclusion. In the case of the grounds for discretionary exclusion, contracting authorities may exclude on the same basis, that is, at any time and based on facts arising before or during the procedure, although Member States may also require them to do so. This again presupposes broader knowledge than would ordinarily be possessed by a contracting authority in the context of a single contract award procedure.

Arguably, one of the most novel features of the new rules on exclusion concerns the introduction of rehabilitation measures, sometimes referred to as 'self-cleaning' measures. This is a common feature of existing comprehensive debarment systems but is a novelty within the EU rules, although many have argued that it should have been incorporated by analogy, if only to satisfy the EU principle of proportionality.[23] Under the 2014 provisions on rehabilitation, tenderers are able to offer a defence to exclusion in the form of evidence of remedial action's having been taken to remedy the offences. This possibility is, however, *retrospective*, in the sense that the tenderer must provide evidence of what it has done, not what it will do. It is thus an indicator of a much broader debarment system that presupposes the ability to take into account past behaviour outside the contract award procedure at issue. There is some lack of clarity in this respect, however, since the new rules also provide that rehabilitation is not available where exclusion is fixed by final judgment, only where the decision is made on a discretionary basis by the contracting authority. This devalues the remedial effect of rehabilitation, since, once the period of exclusion is over, the tenderer is in any event permitted to tender and is no longer excluded. Rehabilitation is then of little value if, indeed, the intention is to provide an incentive for improvement.

The provision in the 2014 Directives is retrospective in the sense that it applies to measures taken in response to a conviction or finding of misconduct *before* the contract award procedure has been concluded. It does not provide for prospective remedial action that would foresee continuing efforts to improve conduct. The 'defence' applies to action taken and not *to be* taken. Whilst Recital 102 of Directive 2014/24 suggests that the purpose of this provision is to allow for the possibility that tenderers may adopt compliance measures aimed at remedying the consequences of any criminal offences or misconduct, and at effectively preventing further occurrences of the misconduct, that is not the effect of this provision. It does not address the prevention of further occurrences of misconduct but the correction of past occurrences of misconduct. It thus fails in meeting the more general debarment objective of providing an incentive for future improvement and merely rewards the correction of a discovered offence.

[23] H-J Prieß, S Arrowsmith and P Friton, 'Self-cleaning- an emerging concept in EC public procurement law' in H Pünder, H-J Prieß and S Arrowsmith (eds), *Self-Cleaning in Public Procurement Law* (Heymanns, 2009) 1.

This approach is compounded by a further provision under which a tenderer that has been excluded by final judgment from participating in procurement award procedures will not be entitled to make use of this possibility of rehabilitation during the period of exclusion resulting from that judgment in the Member States where the judgment is effective. In the case of a mandatory exclusion, therefore, if the conviction itself refers to debarment (or if that is an automatic effect) or if debarment can only be made effective through a subsequent judgment, then rehabilitation is not available. In this respect, the EU approach is to use debarment as a punishment and not as an incentive for improvement, since mandatorily excluded tenderers are excluded for the stated period of time (no more than five years, unless the Member State provides otherwise), regardless of any remedial action they may choose to take. It is only when the exclusion is imposed by the contracting authority itself, or a third party that is not capable of making a judicial decision (ie in cases of discretionary exclusion), that rehabilitation is available. This deprives rehabilitation of any useful effect where mandatory exclusion is applied, and significantly reduces its impact. That does leave scope for rehabilitation in the case of discretionary exclusion, and given the ease with which such exclusion can be made under the new rules, that scope is broad.

It is perhaps important to point out that Recital 102 also gives Member States discretion to decide whether the authority for evaluating the self-cleaning is to be the individual contracting authority or another authority on a central or decentralised level. This implies once more a much more sophisticated debarment system that foresees multiple actors, including a centralised authority to manage the process. Arrowsmith, for example, argues strongly for such a centralised system in the United Kingdom following Brexit.[24]

Finally, under the provision in Article 57(7) of Directive 2014/24 requiring Member-State implementation of the exclusionary rules, the legislator imposes some critical minimum requirements. It requires, for example, that the national implementing rules provide for a maximum period of exclusion where no remedial measures are taken by the tenderer to demonstrate its reliability. Where maximum periods of exclusion have not been set by final judgment, the new rules provide for these maximum periods themselves: not more than five years from the date of the conviction by final judgment in the case of mandatory exclusion; and not more than three years from the date of the relevant event in the case of discretionary exclusion. At first sight, this appears to foresee some form of debarment, in that there is a period for which the exclusion is operative. However, this is once more a backwards-looking period and not a prospective one, which would be the case of debarment as defined herein. The period runs from the 'relevant event', not from the exclusion. It is the relevant event that triggers the exclusion and not the exclusion that triggers a period of debarment. The provisions are not, however, a model of clarity.

[24] Arrowsmith (n 8).

One of the challenges of the retrospection of the provisions of the Directive relates to the period of exclusion. In the case of mandatory exclusion, which requires a judgment, the date of the judgment is what triggers the period of exclusion. In the case of discretionary exclusion, it is the 'relevant event', but that is also dependent on whether a particular ground for exclusion has been adopted, and also on the specific ground for exclusion. They cannot all be treated in the same way. A number of observations may be made.

The obvious problem here is to determine how the tenderers will be aware of the ground for exclusion and, consequently, the period of exclusion. There is less difficulty in the case of a judgment, although the question of identifying a relevant judgment may be problematic in the absence of a central and catalogued repository of relevant judgments. This, of course, is a reason for arguing for some centralised form of debarment where relevant judgments could be made readily available, allowing contracting authorities to consult them as needed. The issue is more problematic in the case of discretionary grounds. In the interests of transparency and equal treatment, it is established case law that

> substantive and procedural conditions concerning participation in a contract must be clearly defined in advance, require that the period be determined with absolute certainty and made public in order that the persons concerned may know exactly the procedural requirements and be sure that the same requirements apply to all candidates. That period may be fixed by national legislation or the latter may confer that responsibility on the contracting authorities.[25]

This implies that, if the period of exclusion is not contained in national law, it must be contained in the tender documents that set out the terms and conditions of the procurement. These will establish the grounds for exclusion as well as the period of exclusion, and would also need to establish due process, that is, the mechanism by which a tenderer could demonstrate that it had resolved the problem through self-cleaning.[26] Failure to establish these in the tender documents may mean that they cannot be applied. Unless the Member State has made them mandatory, contracting authorities need to take care to include all relevant exclusions, and this requires some foresight and some planning, which may be difficult where there is no guidance to identify common and likely infringements. It is dependent on each contracting authority, which may take a view on what is important for them, including making appropriate risk assessments. Application is thus unlikely to be consistent between contracting authorities and between Members States.

Since, as we know, under Article 57(5) of Directive 2014/24, both mandatory and discretionary exclusion grounds are defined as 'acts committed before

[25] Joined Cases C-226/04 and C-228/04 *La Cascina* ECLI:EU:C:2006:94, para 32. This was decided in the context of a discretionary ground for exclusion under Art 29 of Council Directive 92/50/EEC of 18 June 1992 relating to the coordination of procedures for the award of public service contracts [1992] OJ L209/1.

[26] Case C-387/18 *RTS* ECLI:EU:C:2021:13, where the time for providing evidence for self-cleaning had not been established either by law or in the tender documents.

or during the procedure', it is necessary to identify when the periods of exclusion might begin to run. As stated above, they do not run from the date of exclusion from the contract award procedure; They run rather from the date of the 'relevant event', which must have occurred either before or during the procedure. Indeed, if the relevant date occurred sufficiently early before the contract award procedure was initiated, it may be that the exclusion period has expired and that it no longer provides grounds for exclusion from that specific procedure (even in the absence of any self-cleaning measures), although reliability will always be an issue for the contracting authority. In that regard, it is similar, by analogy, to determining past performance, which is often assessed on the basis of references for performance (Article 58(4)) on similar contracts during a period of years (eg, three years) prior to the contract's being procured. In some cases, looking at the grounds for exclusion, it is even questionable whether a period of exclusion is even relevant. It depends on the ground itself.

It is not clear, for example, how it would apply in the case of bankruptcy or similar proceedings under Article 57(4)(b). The situation pertains or it does not. It would make no sense to apply a three-year period of exclusion to a bankrupt firm. Bankruptcy is final. If, in a subsequent procedure, the tenderer has recovered, the ground would, in any event, no longer apply. In the case of conflicts under Article 57(4)(e) and (f), the grounds are contract-specific and would arise during the ongoing procedure. They are not 'events' that would arise beforehand but situations that arise in the context of the procurement at issue. Similarly, the misrepresentation and undue influence 'events' of Article 57(4)(h) and (i) would also take place during the contract award procedure itself, so that a period of exclusion is not relevant. If, contrary to the plain wording of the Article, it were possible to apply these grounds to offences committed during previous procurements, a period of three years could arguably apply in the same way as past performance assessment, that is, to any such events that occurred in the previous three years.

The exclusion grounds referred to in Article 57(4)(a), (c) and (d), non-compliance with applicable legislation, grave professional misconduct and collusion, respectively, are not contract-specific and refer to broader reasons relating to the reliability of the tenderer. Here, it is clearly possibly to set a period of exclusion, depending on the date of the 'relevant event', which could be, for example, the date of the violation or the date on which the violation was brought to an end. The poor-performance ground for exclusion set out in Article 57(4)(g) is explicitly based on a past event, and a period of exclusion could be applied from the date of the remedy applied, for example the termination of the contract or date of payment of liquidated damages. Thus, in four of the nine situations that may give rise to discretionary exclusion, a period of exclusion may be relevant. It does not appear relevant or even possible in respect of the remaining grounds, making the provisions of the Directive somewhat redundant in that regard.

Since, as previously explained, the relevant event is the trigger for exclusion in a particular contract award procedure, and that the relevant event must have taken place before or during the contract award procedure, the exclusion 'period' must also be seen as retrospective. Exclusion in the contract award procedure at issue does not trigger exclusion from future contracts by other contracting authorities. It is not debarment as defined in this chapter. As suggested, the way to consider this exclusion period is thus to work backwards from the point at which exclusion from a contract award procedure is contemplated. As with past performance, contracting authorities, in deciding (where they have discretion in their Member States) which grounds of discretionary exclusion to apply should state in their tender documents which periods (to a maximum of three years) apply to those grounds. Logically, these periods should be stated as from the date of the procurement, for example the exclusion ground applies where a relevant event occurred within the last three years.

An additional issue that arises from the setting of maximum exclusion periods is that it also implies the creation of a more graduated debarment system that provides for temporary as well as permanent debarment dependent, inter alia, on the gravity of the offence and scope of remedial actions leading to rehabilitation. This cannot be done effectively outside a full debarment system.

Notwithstanding these small steps towards focusing on or creating a framework for a debarment system, at EU or national level, the 2014 legislation is left wanting. This has been made apparent in the relevant jurisprudence. Another consequence of focusing on the contract award procedure is that any decision on exclusion is to be made by the contracting authority managing that procedure, and jurisprudence confirms that it is for the contracting authority to make the decision. This is because qualification – and thus exclusion – is tied to the reliability of a tenderer to perform a specific contract. In *Meca*,[27] the Court of Justice of the European Union (CJEU) was asked whether a legal challenge to a decision adopted by a contracting authority to terminate a public contract early, on account of major deficiencies in its performance by the operator, prevents the contracting authority that issues a further call for tender from conducting an assessment of the reliability of the operator concerned in that early termination. The CJEU stated that the legislature intended that the contracting authority must make its own assessment of the acts or omissions committed by an economic operator when it applies the discretionary exclusions in Article 57(4),[28] and that it should do so at the time of selecting tenderers in the award procedure.[29] It may not rely on the determination of another contracting authority. The CJEU also commented more generally that that a contracting authority cannot be automatically bound by an assessment made by a third party (here a Member State in legislation) on when an exclusion will apply, as it would then be difficult to apply the principle of proportionality.[30] The CJEU commented that this is because the exclusion is based on the need for a relationship of trust between the contracting authority and its supplier.[31]

[27] *Meca* (n 7).
[28] ibid para 28.
[29] ibid para 31.
[30] ibid para 32.
[31] ibid para 30.

At the same time, it may be that a third-party organisation has the exclusive competence to make determinations in respect of certain actions or offences committed by an economic operator, for example in the case of competition law where regulatory bodies have been established. In such cases, the contracting authority must respect the outcome of a procedure before the relevant authority.[32] This is not conclusive for the contracting authority, however, which retains responsibility for assessing any risks in awarding a contract to a tenderer whose integrity or reliability is in doubt.[33] As already explained, in the case of self-cleaning under Article 57(6), a third party (judicial authority in the case of a conviction) is able to make a decision on rehabilitation if that is the system set up by a Member State through its implementing measures.

In *Delta*,[34] a municipality had terminated early a contract for the restoration and modernisation of a leisure facility on the ground that the operator had used a subcontractor without the municipality's prior authorisation. The municipality also lodged a report on a national on-line platform ('the EPPS platform'), stating that that contract had been terminated early on account of misconduct by the operator and that this had caused losses to the municipality. Another contracting authority subsequently initiated an open public procurement procedure for the construction project for widening a national road in which the operator (Delta), which had been the subject of the previous early termination, was a tenderer. After searching the EPPS platform in respect of each tenderer, the contracting authority's evaluation committee became aware of the report and requested clarification in that regard from the municipality and from Delta. The evaluation committee decided to exclude Delta on the basis of the report and responses.

Following its approach in *Meca*, the CJEU in *Delta* also stated that the assessment of whether the grounds for exclusion exist must be made by the relevant contracting authority itself (that is, the contracting authority making the exclusion)[35] because of the need for assurance of the reliability of the economic operator to ensure trust in the relationship.[36] On this basis, and to ensure that the principle of proportionality can be applied in making the exclusion, the ECJ concluded that the excluding contracting authority cannot be automatically bound by an assessment made by another contracting authority in an earlier award procedure.[37]

It is for the contracting authority to carry out its own evaluation of the economic operator's conduct covered by the early termination of a prior public contract. In that regard, it must examine, diligently and impartially, on the basis of all the relevant factors, in particular the early termination decision; and in the light of the principle of proportionality, whether that operator is, from its point

[32] Case C-124/17 *Vossloh Laeis* ECLI:EU:C:2018:855, para 25.
[33] ibid para 26.
[34] *Delta* (n 7).
[35] ibid para 25.
[36] ibid para 26.
[37] ibid para 27.

of view, responsible for significant or persistent deficiencies in the performance of a substantive requirement imposed on it under that contract, those deficiencies being such as to break the relationship of trust with the economic operator in question.[38]

Under these cases, contracting authorities have both responsibility and power to decide on exclusion.[39] This is quite different, for example, to the debarment system in the US, where a decision by (the designated officer of) one contracting authority applies to future contracts to be let by all federal agencies for the defined period.[40]

This reasoning seems to suggest that assessments of the facts relating to a particular exclusion, and of whether the conduct is sufficiently serious to warrant exclusion from public contracts. cannot be made by anyone other than the contracting authority. This means that such a decision could not be made by, for example, a central authority made responsible for debarment, even on a case-by-case basis relating to specific violations. This position has been criticised,[41] because it could prevent the emergence of centralised systems of debarment, which have many advantages. These judgments are, however, entirely consistent with the legislation and show the weakness of that legislation. This militates in favour of amending the rules to complete the provisions on debarment.

IV. Concluding Remarks

The purpose of this chapter was to analyse the provisions of Directive 2014/24 on exclusion to determine whether they provide an identifiable debarment system at EU level. The answer is no. Any debarment system will be developed at national level, although there are a few provisions in the Directive that suggest the legislator did envisage some degree of debarment.

Though not intended as a review of debarment systems in general, a number of issues would need to be decided before a full-blown debarment system could be contemplated. It would be important, for example, to articulate the purpose of any debarment system. Would it be punitive, or could it be used to improve the reliability of tenderers and thus the procurement outcomes? The provisions on mandatory exclusions by way of final judgment with no possibility of rehabilitation through self-cleaning suggest a punitive intention. The introduction of self-cleaning, on the other hand, would suggest a rehabilitative effect, save that it is limited to retrospective action, so that the incentive to improve and the ability of contracting authorities to encourage such an approach is limited. A more

[38] ibid para 29.
[39] *Meca* (n 7) para 34; *Delta* (n 7) para 25.
[40] FAR (n 4) part 9.405(a).
[41] See, eg, Arrowsmith (n 8).

consistent approach to what is mandatory or discretionary would provide greater certainty; there is some overlap at present, with different means of establishing the existence of the grounds for exclusion. The poor drafting of the legislation has led to jurisprudence that appears to rule out a centralised debarment system operated by a third party, whether judicial or administrative; and the practical difficulty of ascertaining the grounds for exclusion, based on convictions or otherwise, means that exclusions, let alone debarment, will be haphazard without any central repository of key information required by contracting authorities to implement exclusions or debarment. The self-cleaning provisions, which are perhaps the clearest indication of a debarment system, are weakened by their retrospection and inapplicability in the event of exclusion by way of a judgment.

The incomplete provisions on debarment, if that is what was intended by the regulator in 2014, has led to predictable jurisprudence, which appears to hamper the development of debarment at an EU level. Significant improvement is required to make debarment a reality in the EU, other than nationally. The purpose of this chapter was not, however, to promote debarment or recommend a particular debarment system, which has been done by Arrowsmith[42] and others, but to ensure understanding of terms used to allow for that discussion to take place in a coherent manner. The discussion is currently taking place in the context of post-Brexit UK legislation, which has provided an opportunity. It is a debate, however, that is sorely required under the Directives too.

[42] See n 8.

11

The Blind Leading the Blind: The Need for Further Reform of Defence and Security Procurement in the European Union

BAUDOUIN HEUNINCKX

I. Introduction

Professor Sue Arrowsmith's work covers all aspects of public procurement, including the most arcane, such as that in the defence sector. Her so-called Blue Book has discussed defence and security procurement from its first edition, and the third edition included an entire chapter on the topic.[1] In addition, she has been the PhD supervisor of all those who ended up becoming the foremost experts on the law of defence and security procurement, in particular Professors Martin Trybus, Aris Georgopoulos and Luke Butler, as well as the author of this chapter, and their research is highly indebted to her guidance. In a way, one could argue that she is the fairy godmother to the entire defence procurement law academia in the UK.

Defence procurement law in the European Union (EU) changed drastically in 2009, when the EU adopted the Defence and Security Directive (further referred to as 'the Directive'),[2] which coordinates the defence and security procurement legislation of the EU Member States. The establishment of a common legislative framework for defence and security procurement was seen as a prerequisite for the gradual establishment of a European Defence Equipment Market (EDEM) aimed at fostering, developing and sustaining a European Defence Technological and Industrial Base (EDTIB) that is capability-driven, competent and competitive,

[1] S Arrowsmith, *The Law of Public and Utilities Procurement*, vol 2 (3rd edn, Sweet & Maxwell, 2018) ch 15 (co-authored with B Heuninckx).

[2] Directive 2009/81/EC of the European Parliament and of the Council of 13 July 2009 on the coordination of procedures for the award of certain works contracts, supply contracts and service contracts by contracting authorities or entities in the fields of defence and security, and amending Directives 2004/17/EC and 2004/18/EC [2009] OJ L216/76.

thereby allowing the development of the military capabilities required to implement the EU Common Security and Defence Policy (CSDP).[3]

As mandated by the Directive, the European Commission (further referred to as 'the Commission') reviewed its transposition by the Member States and reported thereon to the European Parliament and the Council in 2016.[4] This Report included recommendations to improve the functioning of the Directive, proposed a way forward, but made no proposals for legislative reform. The Commission in the meantime implemented an action plan to clarify the use of the Directive. The European Parliament also completed studies and adopted a resolution on the implementation of the Directive,[5] which included its own conclusions and recommendations.

In an earlier article, the author dubbed the adoption process of the Directive a game of 'trick or treat'.[6] He explained that the Member States trick-or-treated the Commission by arguing that the main reason why the Article 346 exemption of the Treaty on the Functioning of the European Union (TFEU),[7] which allows a Member State, within defined limits, to take measures contrary to EU law that it considers necessary for the protection of its essential security interests connected with the production of or trade in arms, munitions and war material, had to be invoked was because the Public Sector Directive[8] was not appropriate for the procurement of 'hard' defence equipment such as tanks, missiles or fighter aircraft. This was only partially true, as the unmentioned reason why the Member States

[3] Directive 2009/81/EC, Recitals 2–4; for a detailed analysis of the context of the Directive, see M Trybus, *Buying Defence and Security in Europe* (Cambridge University Press, 2014) ch 1.

[4] Directive 2009/81/EC, Art 73(2); European Commission, *Report from the Commission to the European Parliament and the Council on the implementation of Directive 2009/81/EC on public procurement in the fields of defence and security, to comply with Article 73(2) of that Directive*, COM(2016)762, 30/11/2016; and European Commission Staff Working Document, *Evaluation of Directive 2009/81/EC on public procurement in the fields of defence and security*, SWD(2016)407, 30/11/2016.

[5] H Masson et al, *The impact of the 'defence package' Directives on European defence* PE 549.044 (European Parliament Directorate General for External Policies, 06/2015); I Ioannides (ed), *EU Defence Package: Defence Procurement and Intra-Community Transfers Directives – European Implementation Assessment*, PE 654.171 (European Parliamentary Research Service, 10/2020); European Parliament resolution of 25 March 2021 on the implementation of Directive 2009/81/EC, concerning procurement in the fields of defence and security, and of Directive 2009/43/EC, concerning the transfer of defence-related products (2019/2204(INI)).

[6] B Heuninckx, 'The EU Defence and Security Procurement Directive: Trick or Treat?' (2011) 20(1) *Public Procurement Law Review* 9.

[7] Consolidated Version of the Treaty on the Functioning of the European Union (TFEU) [2008] OJ C115/47, Art 346; for a detailed discussion of this exemption, see B Heuninckx, '346, the Number of the Beast? A Blueprint for the Protection of Essential Security Interests in EU Defence Procurement' (2018) 27(2) *Public Procurement Law Review* 51; B Heuninckx and S Arrowsmith, 'Defence and Security Procurement' in Arrowsmith (n 1) paras 15-26 to 15-45; Trybus (n 3) ch 3; the Commission published an interpretative communication on the use of Art 346 TFEU (then Art 296 EC Treaty): European Commission, Interpretative Communication on the application of Article 296 of the Treaty in the field of defence procurement, COM(2006) 779, 7/12/2006.

[8] Directive 2004/18/EC of the European Parliament and of the Council of 31 March 2004 on the coordination of procedures for the award of public works contracts, public supply contracts and public service contracts [2004] OJ L134/114, as amended, which was then the generic EU law applicable to public procurement.

used this exemption was to advantage their domestic defence industry through direct contract awards and offsets.[9] The Commission, on the other hand, expected that, now that the concerns expressed by the Member States had been answered by the adoption of the Directive, it would be in a better position to tackle abusive discriminatory use of the exemption.

However, 10 years later, the implementation and recent evaluation of the Directive looks more and more like a case of the blind leading the blind. At least, when trick-or-treating, each party involved knows what the other wants and acts accordingly. Not here. Even though each institution of the EU may have its own agenda, their converging aims for the Directive were to open up the domestic defence and security procurement markets of the Member States. By contrast, the principal objectives of the Member States in this context are to procure the best possible military equipment and services at the lowest price, to protect their national security interests and to strengthen their domestic DTIB, to the detriment of the EDTIB as a whole and of other Member States if necessary.

Unfortunately, each of these two parties seems to be blind to the expectations of the other, so that the European institutions try to reform the EDEM through actions that are often ignored, or complied with at the barest minimum by the Member States, because such actions do not contribute to meeting the latter's objectives, and because many of these actions are not legal requirements. In the meantime, the Member States generally focus primarily on their own benefit, only cooperating when they feel they can gain from such cooperation, without much regard for the interests of the EU as a whole.

The aim of this chapter is therefore, after an introduction to the scope and contents of the Directive, to perform a critical analysis of the Commission's evaluation of the Directive and of its subsequent initiatives. Based on this analysis, this chapter makes recommendations on how the Commission's action plan could be open for improvement.

II. The Defence and Security Directive

A. Applicability and Exclusions

As mentioned in section I, the legal regime applicable to defence and security procurement in the EU currently consists principally of the Directive, as transposed in the domestic laws of the Member States,[10] which contains the substantive

[9] B Heuninckx, 'Security of Supply and Offsets in Defence Procurement: What's New in the EU?' (2014) 23(2) *Public Procurement Law Review* 33.

[10] For a more in-depth discussion of the applicability of the current EU public procurement regime to defence procurement, see B Heuninckx, 'Lurking at the Boundaries: Applicability of EU Law to Defence and Security Procurement' (2010) 19(3) *Public Procurement Law Review* 91, § 2; Report from the Commission to the European Parliament and the Council on transposition of directive 2009/81/EC on Defence and Security Procurement, COM(2012)565, 2/10/2012.

and procedural measures for the harmonisation of public procurement procedures and related remedies.

The Directive implements one prerequisite for the creation of an EDEM, namely a legislative framework ensuring the coordination of procedures for the award of contracts by the Member States.[11] By providing an adequate legal framework for defence procurement, the EU legislator hoped to reduce reliance on the TFEU exemptions in defence procurement, whereby contracts either were awarded to domestic enterprises or contained offset obligations.[12]

This Directive applies to the procurement activities of contracting authorities and entities.[13] The ministries and departments of defence of the Member States are all contracting authorities,[14] and therefore have to comply with the domestic law transposing the Directive for their procurement contracts covered by its material scope.

The Directive applies to contracts awarded for the supply of military equipment and sensitive equipment, works, supplies and services directly related to them, works and services for specifically military purposes, and sensitive works and services, subject to Articles 36, 51, 52, 62 and 346 TFEU.[15] Military equipment is further defined as equipment specifically designed or adapted for military purposes and intended for use as arms, munitions or war materiel.[16] This definition is to be understood by reference to the 1958 list of materiel to which the Article 346 TFEU exemption applies,[17] which is to be interpreted broadly, for instance on the basis of the EU Common Military List (which is a more detailed list of military equipment to which the EU rules governing control of exports of military technology and equipment apply), but also to cover products initially designed for civilian use and later adapted to military purposes.[18]

[11] Directive 2009/81/EC, Recitals 2–4.

[12] Heuninckx (n 6) 10–11; Heuninckx (n 9); D Furter, 'The Influence of Legislation and Government Policy on Patterns of International Defence Trade and Future Markets: The Case of Offset and Directive 2009/81/EC' (PhD thesis, Brunel University, 2014), pp. 227–228.

[13] Directive 2009/81/EC, Art 1(2), referring to Art 1(2)(a) of Directive 2004/17/EC and Art 1(2)(a) of Directive 2004/18/EC; Directive 2014/24/EU of the European Parliament and of the Council of 26 February 2014 on public procurement and repealing Directive 2004/18/EC, [2014] OJ L94/65, Art 1(1) and Art 2.1(1) (replacing the former); Heuninckx (n 10) §§ 2.2.1 and 2.3.1; S Arrowsmith, *The Law of Public and Utilities Procurement*, vol 1 (3rd edn, Sweet & Maxwell, 2014) paras 5-02 and 5-53 to 5-55; Heuninckx and Arrowsmith (n 7) paras 15-57 and 15-58; Trybus (n 3) section 6.2.

[14] See Directive 2014/24/EU, Annex I.

[15] Directive 2009/81/EC, Art 2 and Recitals 12, 15 and 16; Trybus (n 3) section 6.3.

[16] Directive 2009/81/EC, Art 1(6); Heuninckx and Arrowsmith (n 7) paras 15-60 to 15-64.

[17] Council Decision 255/58 of 15 April 1958 defining the list of products (arms, munitions and war material) to which the provisions of Article 223(1)(b) [now Art 346(1)(b)] of the Treaty apply (not published); the list circulates as a public but unpublished document of the Council: 'Extract of the Council Decision 255/58 of 15 April 1958', 26/11/2008, document 14538/4/08 Rev 4; Heuninckx and Arrowsmith (n 7) paras 15-36 to 15-40.

[18] Directive 2009/81/EC, Recital 10; Common Military List of the EU adopted by the Council on 20 February 2023 (equipment covered by Council Common Position 2008/944 defining common rules governing the control of exports of military technology and equipment) [2023] OJ C72/2.

The applicability of the Directive is subject to a number of exclusions, in addition to the general exemptions from EU law such as Article 346 TFEU, the invocation of which also means that the Directive does not apply.[19]

The Directive does not apply to contracts governed by specific procedural rules:

(a) pursuant to an international agreement or arrangement concluded between one or more Member States and one or more third countries;[20]
(b) of an international organisation purchasing for its purposes or contracts that must be awarded by a Member State in accordance with those rules.[21]

The last exclusion actually contains two sub-exclusions with different scopes, the first sub-exclusion being limited to purchases made 'for the purpose' of the organisation.

The Directive also does not apply to contracts awarded in the framework of a cooperative programme based on research and development, conducted jointly by at least two Member States for the development of a new product, including for the later phases of its life cycle.[22] In addition, the Directive does not apply to contracts awarded by a government to another government.[23]

Figure 11.1 EU Collaborative Equipment Procurement as a Percentage of Total Equipment Procurement Spending of the EU Member States (include R&D)

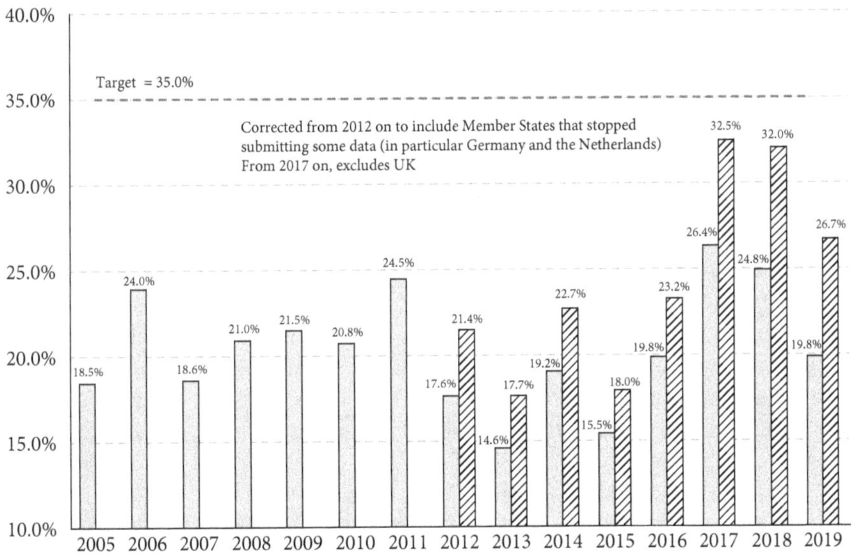

[19] Directive 2009/81/EC, Art 2. See also the detailed discussion in Heuninckx (n 10) 108–14; and in Trybus (n 3) 267–301.

[20] Directive 2009/81/EC, Art 12(a); Heuninckx and Arrowsmith (n 7) paras 15-94 and 15-95.

[21] Directive 2009/81/EC, Art 12(c); Heuninckx and Arrowsmith (n 7) paras 15-98 and 15-99.

[22] Directive 2009/81/EC, Arts 1(27) and 13(c), and Recital 28; Heuninckx and Arrowsmith (n 7) paras 15-104 to 15-106.

[23] Directive 2009/81/EC, Art 1(9) and Art 13(f); A Estrup Ippolito, 'Government to Government contracts in EU defence procurement' (2014) 23(6) *Public Procurement Law Review* 249; Heuninckx and Arrowsmith (n 7) paras 15-109 and 15-110.

These are two important exceptions for defence procurement. As show in Figure 11.1, an average of about 22.6 per cent of the defence equipment procurement and R&D expenditures of Member States (more than €8.6 billion per year) was spent collaboratively in the period 2005–19, and a significant portion of these collaborative procurement activities (about 90 per cent) was performed among states that were in majority members of the EU. However, this figure fails to meet the collective benchmark for European collaborative equipment procurement of 35 per cent.[24] At the same time, about 9 per cent of the defence equipment procurement expenditures of Member States in 2005–13 (somewhat less than €3 billion per year) was spent through government-to-government transactions, of which about 79 per cent was with the United States (US) and 17 per cent among Member States.[25]

B. Substance

In terms of substantive law, even though the Directive contains provisions similar to those in the directives applicable to the general procurement activities of the public sector, it contains a number of specificities.[26]

Probably the most significant specificity of the Directive is that the contracting authority may freely award contracts based on the negotiated procedure with publication of a contract notice. On the other hand, the open procedure is not available.[27] In addition, the negotiated procedure without publication of a contract notice may be used in some additional specific cases, such as in case of urgency resulting from a crisis such as a peacekeeping operation or a terrorist attack, and for air and maritime transport services for the armed forces or security forces deployed or to be deployed abroad.[28]

The Directive also includes additional grounds under which a candidate may be excluded, such as if it has been convicted for terrorist offences or offences linked to terrorist activities, where it has been convicted of an offence concerning its professional conduct, such as, for example, infringement of applicable legislation on the export of defence and/or security equipment, if it has been found guilty of grave professional misconduct, such as a breach of its obligations regarding security of information or security of supply in a previous contract, and if it has been

[24] Council Recommendation of 15 October 2018 concerning the sequencing of the fulfilment of the more binding commitments undertaken in the framework of permanent structured cooperation (PESCO) and specifying more precise objectives [2018] OJ C374/01; EDA Ministerial Steering Board, Adjusted List of Indicators for Defence Data (EDA Doc No 2007/12) and Collective Benchmarks (EDA Doc No 2007/13), 19/11/2007; see B Heuninckx, 'Permanent Structured Cooperation within the scope of the EU Common Security and Defence Policy – The Ride Begins?' (2019) 28(4) *Public Procurement Law Review* 140, §§ 4 and 6.3.

[25] L Retter et al, *Study and analysis of 'government-to-government sales' of defence materiel – Executive Summary* (RAND Europe, July 2014) 2.

[26] For more details, see Heuninckx (n 6); and Trybus (n 3) ch 7.

[27] Directive 2009/81/EC, Art 25; Heuninckx and Arrowsmith (n 7) paras 15-125 and 15-129.

[28] Directive 2009/81/EC, Art 28(1)(c) and Recitals 53–54, and Art 28(5) respectively; Heuninckx and Arrowsmith, (n 7) paras 15-130 to 15-133.

found not to possess the reliability necessary to exclude risks to the security of the Member State concerned.[29]

The Directive includes specific rules on subcontracting.[30] Specifically, the contracting authority may ask the successful tenderer to subcontract to third parties a share of the contract, with a maximum of 30 per cent of the value of the contract.[31] The successful tenderer may also be required award subcontracts based on competitive and non-discriminatory procedures.[32] Lastly, contracting authorities may reject the subcontractors selected by the tenderer based on criteria applied for the selection of the tenderers for the main contract.[33]

When the contract involves, requires and/or contains classified information, the contracting authority must specify in the contract documentation the measures and requirements, in particular contract performance conditions, with which the tenderers have to comply to ensure the security of such information at the requisite level during the tendering process, for the duration of the contract and after.[34]

The Directive also defines what the contracting authority may require from tenderers to ensure security of supply, for instance evidence that the tenderer will be able to honour its obligations regarding export, transfer and transit, that the organisation and location of the tenderer's supply chain will allow it to comply with the security of supply requirements, as well as commitments to maintain the capacity required to meet additional needs required as a result of a crisis, to carry out in the future the maintenance, modernisation or adaptation of the equipment provided under the contract, and to inform the contracting authority of any change in its organisation, supply chain or industrial strategy that may affect its obligations.[35]

The Directive also includes specific provisions on reviews, standstill and remedies.[36]

III. The Commission's 2016 Evaluation

As mentioned in section I, at the end of 2016, the Commission published an evaluation of the operation of the Directive that included proposals for the way forward.[37]

According to the Commission, the Directive's adoption led to a more than twofold increase in the value of defence and security contracts published EU-wide

[29] Directive 2009/81/EC, Art 39 and Recitals 65 and 67; Heuninckx and Arrowsmith (n 7) paras 15-134 to 15-136.

[30] See the detailed discussion in Trybus (n 3) ch 9.

[31] Directive 2009/81/EC, Art 21(4); Heuninckx and Arrowsmith (n 7) paras 15-141 and 15-142.

[32] Directive 2009/81/EC, Arts 50–53; Heuninckx and Arrowsmith (n 7) paras 15-140 and 15-143 to 15-146.

[33] Directive 2009/81/EC, Art 21(5); Heuninckx and Arrowsmith (n 7) para 15-148.

[34] Directive 2009/81/EC, Arts 1(8), 7 and 22, and Recitals 20 and 42–43; Heuninckx and Arrowsmith (n 7) paras 15-149 to 15-152; Trybus (n 3) ch 8.

[35] Directive 2009/81/EC, Art 23 and Recitals 42 and 44; Heuninckx and Arrowsmith (n 7) paras 15-153 to 15-156; Trybus (n 3) ch 8.

[36] Directive 2009/81/EC, Arts 55–64; Heuninckx and Arrowsmith (n 7) para 22-292; Trybus (n 3) ch 10.

[37] European Commission, *Report from the Commission to the European Parliament and the Council on the implementation of Directive 2009/81/EC on public procurement in the fields of defence and security,*

and awarded competitively. Between 7.6 per cent and 9.5 per cent of the total value of defence procurement expenditure seems now to be awarded on the basis of the Directive, although the figure varies widely between Member States. The Commission sees this as a significant increase, showing that the Directive has at least partially met its objectives. However, a very significant share of defence procurement expenditure still occurs outside the Directive, especially for high-value, strategic, complex defence systems, in particular because of use of the Article 346 TFEU exemption and offsets requirements.[38] The European Parliament regretted this situation.[39]

The Commission also found that about 10 per cent of the value of contracts awarded under the Directive was won directly cross-border by foreign enterprises (to be compared with 3.5 per cent under the 2014 Public Contracts Directive), of which 6 per cent were awarded to EU-based enterprises and 4 per cent to enterprises from outside the EU. The total value of indirect cross-border awards (the award of a contract to a domestic enterprise that is a subsidiary of a foreign enterprise and where the latter performs an important part of the contract), equalled approximately 40 per cent of the total value of awarded contracts, of which about 22 per cent were EU-based enterprises and slightly less than 18 per cent were US-based enterprises, the participation of enterprises based in other non-Member States being negligible.[40]

Figure 11.2 Cross-border and Domestic Contract Awards under Directive 2009/81/EC

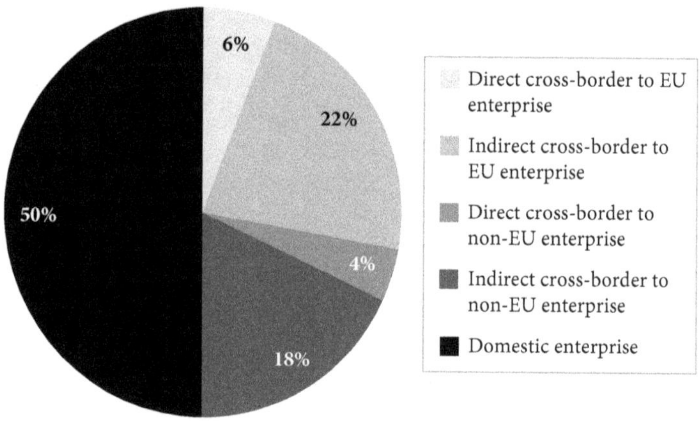

to comply with Article 73(2) of that Directive, COM(2016) 762, 30/11/2016; European Commission Staff Working Document, *Evaluation of Directive 2009/81/EC on public procurement in the fields of defence and security*, SWD(2016) 407, 30/11/2016; see also I Ioannides (ed), *EU Defence Package: Defence Procurement and Intra-Community Transfers Directives – European Implementation Assessment*, PE 654.171 (European Parliamentary Research Service, 10/2020).

[38] European Commission, *Report on the implementation of Directive 2009/81/EC*, 4; European Commission, *Evaluation of Directive 2009/81/EC*, section 5.3.

[39] European Parliament resolution of 25 March 2021 on the implementation of Directive 2009/81/EC, concerning procurement in the fields of defence and security, and of Directive 2009/43/EC, concerning the transfer of defence-related products (2019/2204(INI)) paras 5–7.

[40] European Commission, *Report on the implementation of Directive 2009/81/EC*, 5; European Commission, *Evaluation of Directive 2009/81/EC*, 55–60.

The Commission also found that the negotiated procedure with publication (27 per cent of notices, but 55 per cent in value) and the restricted procedure (32 per cent of notices, 19 per cent in value) were the most used competitive procedures and that the use of the competitive dialogue was only 'marginal'. The negotiated procedure without publication was used in 38 per cent of cases (24 per cent in value), which the Commission sees as quite significant.[41] Some Member States and non-governmental organisations suggested including in the Directive the one-phase open procedure, which is the most used procedure under the 2014 Public Contracts Directive because it is quicker to run and more transparent, but industry representatives suggested that this was not appropriate,[42] which is somewhat surprising.

Figure 11.3 Used Contract Award Procedures under Directive 2009/81/EC

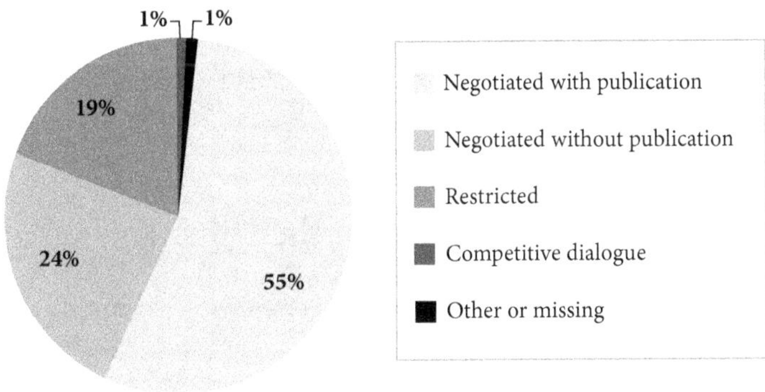

The Commission found that the provisions on security of information and security of supply were appropriate.[43] It also concluded that the Directive does not hinder collaborative procurement,[44] which is anyways performed outside the scope of the Directive.

Small and medium-sized enterprises (SMEs) were awarded slightly more than 6 per cent of the total value of contracts, to be compared with about 29 per cent under the 2014 Public Contracts Directive.[45] Therefore, SMEs seem less competitive in the defence and security sector. Moreover, the Commission and all stakeholders consulted agreed that the subcontracting provisions of the Directive are too complex. They are, on the one hand difficult to apply by prime contractors, and on the other hand difficult to effectively monitor for contracting authorities. Some

[41] European Commission, *Evaluation of Directive 2009/81/EC*, 39–40; Heuninckx and Arrowsmith (n 7) para 15-126.

[42] European Commission, *Evaluation of Directive 2009/81/EC*, 109.

[43] European Commission, *Report on the implementation of Directive 2009/81/EC*, 6.

[44] ibid 9.

[45] European Commission, *Evaluation of Directive 2009/81/EC*, 89.

of the subcontracting provisions of the Directives are actually little used, raising doubts over their utility or effectiveness.[46] As subcontracting could be a means to facilitate the penetration of SMEs in the supply chains of major defence companies, the ineffectiveness of the subcontracting provisions is even more problematic.

Nevertheless, the Commission concluded that no substantive amendment of the Directive was needed, a view shared by the Parliament.[47] One might have expected that the 2016 review would at least have led to the revision of the Directive to introduce amendments parallel to those that were made to the general public-sector regime with the adoption of the 2014 Public Procurement Directive, including by codifying the case law in important areas such as modifications to concluded contracts, but the Commission concluded that it was not appropriate to do this in the foreseeable future. However, the Commission indicated that it would develop additional guidance on use of the Directive, in particular regarding the exclusions,[48] especially since a large number of defence and security contracts were awarded either without competition (about 31 per cent in number, 13–15 per cent in value) or with some form of competition but outside of the scope of the Directive (about 55 per cent in number, 71–76 per cent in value).[49]

IV. Clarifications of the Directive

Just after the publication of the Directive, the Commission produced a number of guidance notes presenting its interpretation of the Directive's provisions.[50] These guidance notes were definitely useful but, as they were drafted by the Commission without consulting the Member States, they reflected only the point of view of the Commission, and the practice and the Commission's evaluation showed that more detailed guidance was needed on some specific issues, in particular some exclusions from the Directive.

The first of these more detailed guidance notes, published in 2016, concerned government-to-government contracts.[51] It clarified under which conditions a contracting authority from an EU government may directly award a contract to another government based on the Article 13(f) exclusion of the Directive. It requires

[46] European Commission, *Report on the implementation of Directive 2009/81/EC*, 7; European Commission, *Evaluation of Directive 2009/81/EC*, 87–93.

[47] European Commission, *Report on the implementation of Directive 2009/81/EC*, 10; European Parliament resolution of 25 March 2021 on the implementation of Directive 2009/81/EC and of Directive 2009/43/EC, para 10.

[48] European Commission, *Report on the implementation of Directive 2009/81/EC*, 10–11; European Commission, *Evaluation of Directive 2009/81/EC*, para 6.4.1.3.

[49] European Commission, *Evaluation of Directive 2009/81/EC*, 70–75.

[50] European Commission, 'Directive 2009/81/EC on the award of contracts in the fields of defence and security – Guidance Notes', 1/10/2010: 'Field of application', 'Exclusions', 'Research and Development', 'Security of Information', 'Security of Supply', 'Subcontracting', 'Offsets', all at https://defence-industry-space.ec.europa.eu/eu-defence-industry/defence-procurement_en (accessed 25 February 2023).

[51] Commission Notice of 30 November 2016, Guidance on the award of government-to-government contracts in the fields of defence and security (Article 13(f) of Directive 2009/81/EC), [2016] OJ C450/01.

the contracting authority to perform a market analysis to identify if competition is absent or impracticable, or alternatively if competition appears to be possible. In the latter case, the Commission recommends pre-procurement advertising and a deeper market analysis before finalising the procurement strategy.

The second recommendation concerned cross-border market access for sub-suppliers and SMEs in the defence sector and was published in 2018.[52] The Parliament also strongly supports measures to facilitate the access of SMEs to defence procurement.[53] It included a number of proposed measures to increase transparency, to promote the division into lots, to simplify qualitative selection, to enhance training and capacity building, and proposed measures linked to industrial policy. This document has been discussed in details in another publication,[54] which concludes that the recommendation did not make many new proposals and was likely to have little effect.

The third guidance note dated from 2019, and covered various aspects of the Directive related to collaborative procurement.[55] It discussed the application and limitations of joint procurement with and without the use of a central purchasing body, the Article 13(c) exclusion of the Directive for cooperative programmes based on research and development, the Article 12(c) exclusion for procurement through international organisations, and the use of the negotiated procedure without publication to ensure convergence of existing capabilities between Member States.

In 2019, another guidance note was produced, dealing with the participation of third-country bidders and goods in the EU procurement market.[56] It clarified that defence and security procurement is not covered by the Government Procurement Agreement (GPA) of the World Trade Organization or by existing bilateral agreements, and that therefore EU law does not give access to the defence and security procurement procedure to third-country operators, even though national legislation may do so.

V. What Should Be Done

A. A Review of the Directive

As we have seen, the view of the Commission and of the Parliament is that no substantive amendment of the Directive is currently needed. Therefore, the

[52] Commission Recommendation (EU) 2018/624 of 20 April 2018 on cross-border market access for sub-suppliers and SMEs in the defence sector [2018] OJ L102/87.

[53] European Parliament resolution of 25 March 2021 on the implementation of Directive 2009/81/EC and of Directive 2009/43/EC, paras 28–38.

[54] M Trybus and B Heuninckx, 'Small and Medium-size Enterprises and EU defence procurement law: The soft impact of Recommendation 2018/624/EU' (2023) 32(3) *Public Procurement Law Review* 115.

[55] Commission notice on guidance on cooperative procurement in the fields of defence and security (Defence and Security Procurement Directive 2009/81/EC) [2019] OJ C157/01.

[56] Communication from the Commission: Guidance on the participation of third-country bidders and goods in the EU procurement market [2019] OJ C271/43.

required clarifications have been provided through guidance and recommendations, as explained in section IV, some of which are quite detailed and provide useful guidance to the procurement practitioners. However, this way of working raises a number of issues whilst leaving some others unresolved.

First, these guidance notes and recommendations are not legislative instruments and represent only the view of the Commission. Therefore, a Member State that fully complies with them has no guarantee that the Court of Justice of the EU will not declare its actions contrary to EU law. This is especially true since some of the views taken by the Commission are somewhat borderline, such as allowing the use of the negotiated procedure without publication to purchase directly from the manufacturer to ensure convergence of existing capabilities between the armed forces of different Member States.[57]

Second, these guidance notes and recommendations are non-legally binding. Even though they were discussed with representatives of the Member States in the Commission Experts Group on Defence and Security Procurement,[58] they do not necessarily reflect a consensus amongst Member States. The latter can therefore ignore some, or even all, of them, which could lead to different application of the Directive's provisions across Member States. Actually, these publications do not bind the Commission either: the author is aware that the current staff of the Commission does not necessarily agree with some of the clarifications provided by their predecessors. The legal certainty of this type of document is therefore limited.

Third, some of the issues identified with the Directive are not resolved by the Commission's clarifications, namely:

- The award procedures under the Directive and those under the 2014 Public Contracts Directive are similar but have different names and somewhat different descriptions. This means that they are, strictly speaking, different procedures. This creates difficulties for the practitioners using the two regimes.
- The single-phase open procedure, often considered the simplest and most transparent award procedure, is not available under the Directive. Even though the Commission sometimes says (only orally) that using the procedure for the award of defence and security contracts would not breach EU law, there is no certainty for this. As the negotiated procedure with publication is a standard procedure under the Directive, it could also be appropriate to introduce the possibility to perform this procedure in one phase.[59]

[57] Commission notice on guidance on cooperative procurement, section 5.2, on the basis of Directive 2009/81/EC, Art 28(1)(e).

[58] Group E02389 in the Register of Commission Expert Groups and Other Similar Entities at https://ec.europa.eu/transparency/expert-groups-register/screen/expert-groups/consult?lang=en&groupID=2389 (accessed 28 February 2023).

[59] As has been done in Belgium under the EU thresholds: Arrêté royal du 23 janvier 2012 relatif à la passation des marchés publics et de certains marchés de travaux, de fournitures et de services dans les domaines de la défense et de la sécurité, Art 4, 4°, MB 01/02/2012.

- The Directive's rules on subcontracting are not used by the Member States. The main stated reason is that they are too complex to apply in practice, but it is likely that the real reason is that they cannot meet the actual objectives of the Member States: opening supply chains to the benefit of their domestic enterprises, not of EU-based enterprises in general. Therefore, the Article 346 TFEU exemption remains widely used.

These issues can only be resolved through a revision of the Directive. In addition, such revision should also include the clarifications provided by the Commission in its guidance notes and recommendations, which would help resolve the problems that the nature of these documents generate.

B. An EU-wide Global Balance

As stated previously, the actual objectives of the Member States is to ensure the participation of their domestic enterprises in their procurement contracts. Obviously, this objective is not officially mentioned in the EU context, and the Commission feigns not to be aware of it. However, even though this objective is contradictory to the development of an integrated EDTIB, it cannot be ignored. A possible solution could be to embrace the issue at the EU level and ensure a fair societal return to the domestic DTIB of each Member State. This could be achieved by an EU-wide global balance.

Collaborative defence procurement programmes, where a number of States agree to procure defence equipment and fund non-recurring costs in common,[60] usually apply the so-called *juste retour* work allocation principle or variations thereof. Under this principle of 'fair industrial return', the proportion of industrial activities allocated to the domestic industry of a participating State within the scope of the programme (work-share) is calculated to match the latter's financial contribution to the programme (cost-share). This principle is actually a multinational version of offsets.[61]

However, this principle, usually applied on a programme-by-programme basis (and sometimes even independently for each phase of the programme), is applied in a wider fashion by some organisations.

The Joint Organisation for Armaments Cooperation (OCCAR), an international organisation whose mission consists of the management of collaborative

[60] See B Heuninckx, *The Law of Collaborative Defence Procurement in the European Union* (Cambridge University Press, 2016).

[61] ibid 4–5, 28 and 216–17; J Bourn, *Maximizing the Benefits of Defence Equipment Co-Operation*, HC 300 Session 2000–2001 (UK National Audit Office, 2007) 20–26; J Michel and J Rivière, *Rapport d'Information sur les nouveaux défis de la construction de l'Europe de la défense* (French National Assembly, 2005) 40–41; M Trybus, *European Defence Procurement Law* (Kluwer, 1999) 39–42; J Bourn, *Ministry of Defence: Collaborative Projects*, doc 1990/91 HC 247 (UK House of Commons, 1991), §§ 3.32–3.34; Trybus (n 3) 352–54.

defence procurement programmes,[62] applies an overall multi-programme/multi-year work-share rule called 'global balance', which, as a more flexible version of *juste retour*, is expected to bring about increased efficiency.[63] Should there be a global imbalance, the latter can be rectified by awarding contracts to enterprises located in the States suffering from the imbalance, by providing guidance on work allocation to a prime contractor or tenderer, or by requesting a prime contractor to award subcontracts to enterprises from the State concerned.[64]

Likewise, a similar system is applied by the European Space Agency (ESA),[65] an international organisation whose objective is to provide for and to promote cooperation among European states in space research and technology and in their operational space applications. To achieve this, the ESA must, among other objectives, elaborate and implement an industrial policy.[66]

This industrial policy aims not only to meet the requirements of the European and national space programmes in a cost-effective manner, but also to improve the worldwide competitiveness of the European space industry by encouraging the rationalisation and development of an industrial structure appropriate to market requirements, whilst ensuring that all ESA member states participate in an equitable manner, having regard to their financial contribution.[67] For that purpose, the ESA places contracts to enterprises and organisations of its member states to ensure a geographical distribution of contract awards, on the basis of a return coefficient calculated as the ratio between the percentage share of each ESA member state in the total value of all contracts awarded by the ESA and the total percentage contribution of that member state to the ESA financing, also taking into account weighting factors based on the technological interest of the activity concerned. Ideally, this return coefficient should be equal to one for each ESA member state.[68] This is a similar form of global balance to the one used by OCCAR.

[62] Convention on the Establishment of the Organisation for Joint Armament Cooperation (Organisation Conjointe de Coopération en matière d'Armement – OCCAR), done at Farnborough on 9 September 1998, JORF N° 69 of 22/03/2001, 4468, Art 8; see also Heuninckx (n 60) 91–95; A Georgopoulos, 'The European Armaments Policy: A *conditio sine qua non* for the European Security and Defence Policy?' in M Trybus and ND White (eds), *European Security Law* (Oxford University Press, 2007) 198, 209–12; Trybus (n 3) 222–25.

[63] OCCAR Convention, ch II; Heuninckx (n 60) 183–84; F Heisbourg et al, *European Defence: Making it Work*, Chaillot Paper No 42 (Institute for Security Studies, 2000) 104; J-P Darnis et al, *Lessons Learned from European Defence Equipment Programmes*, Occasional Paper No 69 (Institute for Security Studies, 2007) 25; A Georgopoulos, 'European Defence Procurement Integration: Proposals for Action within the European Union' (PhD thesis, University of Nottingham, 2004) 72.

[64] OCCAR Convention, Art 5 and Annex III; Heuninckx (n 60) 184; M Trybus, 'Defence Procurement: The New Public Sector Directive and Beyond' (2004) 13(4) *Public Procurement Law Review* 198, 207.

[65] G Stjernevi, 'Fair return and the European Space Agency', Conference Paper for the Public Procurement: Global Revolution VIII conference, 12–13 June 2017; Trybus (n 61) 218 already envisioned the ESA rules as a possible model for an EU defence procurement regime.

[66] ESA Convention at www.esa.int/About_Us/Law_at_ESA/ESA_Convention (accessed 9 March 2023) Art II.

[67] ibid Art VII; Trybus (n 3) 352–54.

[68] ESA Convention, Annex V (in particular its Art IV); see also ESA Procurement Regulations and related Implementing Instructions, ESA/REG/001, rev 5, 10 July 2019, and ESA Industrial Policy Rules and Regulations, ESA/REG/009, 1 Jul 2015, at www.esa.int/About_Us/Law_at_ESA/Highlights_of_ESA_rules_and_regulations (accessed 4 March 2023).

Without some form of return to the society of the purchasing State, major defence contracts are politically very hard to 'sell' to public opinion, especially in times of austerity. This is one of the likely reasons for the continued use of offsets. Moreover, there is some evidence that offsets actually tend to strengthen cooperation and mutual dependencies,[69] both at the State and industrial level, thereby contributing to an form of EDTIB integration that ensures that not only the dominant enterprises of large Member States benefit from the EDEM. Offsets could be seen as increasing the integration of the EDTIB whilst keeping it diverse and avoiding the creation of monopolies.

One could therefore imagine a form of global balance managed at the EU level and applying to all defence procurement activities of the Member States. Under that scheme, an independent entity, such as the Commission or the European Defence Agency (EDA),[70] would act as 'EU global balance manager' and make sure that the work being performed in the execution of all defence contracts awarded by Member States or international organisations in the EU is distributed amongst the defence industry of each Member State proportionally to its defence procurement expenditures over the years. This 'guiding' of the market should be performed centrally and, especially, transparently.[71] Indeed, a large majority of public- and private-sector defence experts consider that the current lack of official offset rules leads to less transparency.[72] When rules are neither formal nor public, offset agreements are negotiated behind closed doors, which can lead to unequal treatment of economic operators and is prone to corruption. Managing global balance at the EU level would provide more transparency and reduce the use of surreptitious offset deals.

Such a scheme would guarantee a fair return to the society of each Member State, but could be quite complex to manage. However, it would be much better than the current situation, where many smaller Member States require offsets in an uncoordinated and often non-transparent manner, whilst larger Member States procure directly from their domestic industry. If adequately handled by the EU global balance manager in line with the strengths and weaknesses of the DTIB of each Member State, it could help develop synergies between the domestic defence industries and lead to more supply-chain integration, thereby making the defence supply chains more diverse, efficient and resilient, and contributing to a stronger and more competitive EDTIB. The European Defence Fund (EDF), which aims to foster the competitiveness, efficiency and innovation capacity of the EDTIB by supporting with EU funds cross-border cooperation between enterprises established in the EU,[73] is based on a similar principle.

[69] DE Schoeni, 'Defence Offsets and Public Policy: Beyond Economic Efficiency' (2016) 76 *Air Force Law Review* 95, 122–25.

[70] Heuninckx and Arrowsmith (n 7) paras 15-168 to 15-171; Trybus (n 3) section 5.2.

[71] See L Fluker, J Muravska and M Pyman, *Due diligence and corruption risk in defence industry offset programmes* (Transparency International UK, 2012); RJ Lambrecht, 'The Big Payback: How Corruption Taints Offset Agreements in International Defense Trade' (Master of Laws thesis, Washington University Law School, 2012); Schoeni (n 69) 126–32, 152 and 157.

[72] Furter (n 12) 374.

[73] Regulation (EU) 2021/697 of the European Parliament and of the Council of 29 April 2021 establishing the European Defence Fund and repealing Regulation (EU) 2018/1092, [2021] OJ L170/149.

In addition, such a scheme would obviate one of the reasons why offsets are requested by Member States: supporting the domestic defence industry and creating domestic employment. As work allocation to the DTIB of each Member State would be fairly and transparently ensured centrally, national initiatives to boost the domestic defence industry, in addition to being impossible to justify under EU law, would become largely useless, as they would be 'compensated' in the future through the EU-wide global balance. Offsets and related measures would then only be used for their single justifiable purpose under EU law: to protect the essential security interests of the Member State concerned, for instance security of supply in critical military equipment.

In an earlier article, the author made a number of proposals to implement an EU-wide global balance in practice.[74]

VI. Conclusions

The Directive has proved to be a useful instrument for effective defence procurement, but some parts of it require clarification, such as the use of the exclusions, and others need modifications, for instance to align the Directive with the 2014 Public Contracts Directive, to introduce the open procedure and a single-phase negotiated procedure with publication, and to improve the rules related to subcontracting. These changes require a review of the Directive, as the current approach of the Commission, using guidance notes and recommendations, is not sufficient. The fact that the Commission fears opening Pandora's box by launching a modification process of the Directive is understandable, but fear should not prevent it from doing the right thing.

In addition, the Commission should stop being blind to the issue of offsets and direct procurement from domestic enterprises, and the Member States should stop being blind to the fact that such uncoordinated practices actually weaken the EDTIB and the competitiveness of the EU defence industry in general. No integrated and efficient EDTIB will ever be created if some domestic DTIBs find themselves being the losers of such integration. As long as this risk exists, the Member States will resist any further integration of the EDTIB. Therefore, an EU-wide global balance system must be managed centrally to ensure that the domestic DTIB of each Member State receives a return that is proportionate to the defence procurement expenditures of the Member State concerned. This would in addition constitute an incentive for the Member States to increase their defence investment expenditures, which should collectively reach at least 20 per cent of their total defence spending.[75] Such measure could also help provide more incentives to the participation of SMEs.

[74] Heuninckx (n 7) section 5.2.

[75] Council Decision (CFSP) 2017/2315 of 11 December 2017 establishing permanent structured cooperation (PESCO) and determining the list of participating Member States, Annex, Commitment 2; Heuninckx (n 24) section 6.3.

However, this approach would require a major shift from the current internal market doctrine. Only the Commission can deliver such change. Even though the EDA could act as global balance manager, any legislative action would have to be initiated by the Commission. Both the EU institutions and its Member States should realise that the EDTIB operates in an EDEM that is not a market like any other, and that the 'invisible hand of the market', which up to now has generally failed to build a really competitive and efficient EDTIB, should be, at least for a time, replaced by a more directed industrial policy. This scheme could initially be limited to contracts that are currently excluded from complying with the Directive, such as collaborative procurement and government-to-government contracts. This could make this scheme more palatable for the Commission.

Once these measures are in place, they must be accompanied by a more assertive enforcement by the Commission. If the Member States are effectively given what they want, they should be expected to comply with the rules. The European Parliament urged the Commission to step up its efforts and take bold and proactive measures to prevent the misuse of exceptions and adopt a more assertive enforcement policy, in particular by ensuring the effectiveness of infringement procedures.[76] However, such assertive enforcement of the rules (the stick) should be paired with an EU-wide global balance that makes sure that no domestic DTIB ends up losing to the more integrated EDTIB (the carrot).

[76] European Parliament resolution of 25 March 2021 on the implementation of Directive 2009/81/EC and of Directive 2009/43/EC, paras 5–7.

PART III

International Public Procurement Law

12

Globalising Procurement Law and Policy: The Early Period

JOHN LINARELLI

I. Introduction

To the best of my recollection, I first came to know Sue in the mid-1990s. I cannot remember the details of how we connected. Surely it was through my old Professor at Georgetown, Don Wallace, Jr. At the time, Sue was already quite the phenomenon on the public procurement law and policy scene. She was the youngest woman ever to earn a chair in the British legal academy. At that time, I was a seasoned United States (US) government contracts lawyer, having practised in the field in the Washington DC area. I had large swathes of the US Federal Acquisition Regulation and the Defense Federal Acquisition Regulation Supplement (DFARS) memorised from repeated references in counselling and representing government contractor clients. I taught US Government Contracts Law at the Catholic University Columbus School of Law for a number of years while in practice, as an adjunct professor. I also co-taught with Don Wallace Jr a course on International Procurement Law and Policy, and then a Global Infrastructure Projects seminar course at the Georgetown University Law Center in the 1990s.

What was most auspicious about our meeting in the 1990s was its connection to the end of the Cold War. It is unclear whether we understood the significance of our work at the time. Suddenly, the distinction between public and private contracting mattered for so many newly independent states, and it mattered a lot. I began consulting work with the International Law Institute (ILI) in Washington, DC, writing proposals for procurement law reform and training for countries. Don Wallace was ILI Chairman. Don was a key leader, particularly in the early years on the internationalisation of all questions relating to procurement law, and served as the first US delegate to UNCITRAL in the development of the Model Law on Procurement. This was a time when the three of us joined forces to write *Regulating Public Procurement: National and International Perspectives*,[1] which

[1] S Arrowsmith, J Linarelli and D Wallace Jr, *Regulating Public Procurement: National and International Perspectives* (Kluwer Law International, 2000).

was the first or one of the first books ever to cover procurement from international and comparative perspectives. After writing this book, I joined Sue on the academic staff at Aberystwyth.

This summary of some personal history is offered only to give the reader some context. This early collaboration was at a time of an intellectual paradigm change for public procurement law. Sue aptly titled her successive conferences 'Public Procurement: Global Revolution'. I have fond memories of working with her on the very first of these conferences. And indeed, a revolution it has been.

This chapter offers only a partial accounting of that revolution. Section II reconstructs the earliest days for public procurement law to come to international attention. It was very different then. There was almost no research at the international and comparative level. There was no possibility of Googling and finding a mass of information. More on this in section II. Section III extends outwards to the rise of procurement law in the 1990s and a set of core global norms to govern procurement law, as part of the phenomenon of the end of the Cold War and primacy of markets at the global level. Markets need law. Markets are constituted by law. And public procurement law played an essential role at the time in setting the ground rules for markets for goods and services needed by the public sector. Section IV offers an assessment of what came next, after paradigm changes of the 1990s in procurement law. It provides an explanation of how public procurement law has stabilised as a set of accepted common set of standards and values that are non-controversially accepted at a global scale. Sue played a big role in bringing all this to be.

II. The 1990s: De-nationalising Procurement Law and Policy

Up to sometime in the early 1990s, public procurement law was understood mainly as a national affair. The US had a well-developed body of rules at the federal and State level to govern public procurement. The tradition in the US has been a very rule-based legal order for public procurement, in which formation of a public contract was governed by a mix of administrative law and contract law, and post-award was in the form of a contract law dominated by standard contract clauses. At the federal level at least in the US, these standard contract clauses developed legal meanings in an extensive administrative case law generated in the federal boards of contract appeals. As well at the federal level, and perhaps most relevant for procurement law, a substantial bid protest corpus of cases and case law exists, generated by both the federal courts and the US Government Accountability Office, which forms part of the extensive legalisation of the procurement process. The US approach to government procurement was no doubt influenced by the significant defence expenditures the country made during the Cold War. The United Kingdom maintained a very different system, a model based on negotiation between a contractor community and government. Europe was a system of national enclaves for favoured national companies until the procurement directives liberalised procurement in the European Union (EU; then European Community).

What was most striking in this period was the state of public procurement law, or perhaps more important, its absence, in developing countries. Developing countries had mainly legacy institutions in place designed by and for former colonisers, which had little to nothing to do with good procurement practices. Colonisers put these laws in place not to promote good public procurement in any sense in which we might understand this concept today. Their objective, rather, was to promote extractive practices by colonisers from the colonised. Their aim was efficient colonial administration. This legacy produced a precarious institutional culture for promoting good public procurement practices in the post-colonial period. Add to this that many of these countries, after achieving independence, lacked the institutional capability and the resources to reform their procurement systems. In the 1990s, either the institutional infrastructure in these countries was practically non-existent or what was in place was a hindrance to reform.

There did not appear to be much concern in the then-communist countries about public procurement law, probably because these countries for the most part limited private contracts to the small-scale sale of consumer goods and the state, through state planning, accounted for what would be contracting in a market-oriented economy. In such cases it might be better to study how state planning worked in these countries.[2] Comparing the institutions of these countries with what would exist in a market-oriented economy has to be done with great care.

The General Agreement on Tariffs and Trade (GATT) maintained a plurilateral Agreement on Government Procurement as a result of the Tokyo Round. This Agreement remained after the Uruguay Rounds. While a longstanding and important agreement of the World Trade Organization (WTO), it has had limited membership and sets basic norms for the opening of select markets, though these markets are major ones that comprise a significant proportion of global GDP.[3]

Partly the result of all of this was that procurement was a purely national affair. This was the institutional background in which the UNCITRAL Model Law on Procurement came into existence. Section II.A explains how this institutional context affected research on public procurement law and policy.

A. The Dearth of Research on International and Comparative Public Procurement Law and Policy

Before the publication of *Regulating Public Procurement: National and International Perspectives*, research on public procurement law and policy, to the extent there

[2] See JN Hazard, *Communists and their Law* (University of Chicago Press, 1969) 312, 343.

[3] J Linarelli, 'The WTO Transparency Agenda: Law, Economics and International Relations Theory' in S Arrowsmith and M Trybus (eds), *Public Procurement: The Continuing Revolution* (Kluwer Law International, 2003) 235.

was much, was national in scope. *Regulating Public Procurement* was one of the first books to be written about public procurement law and policy that was international and comparative in scope. Another book, by Arie Reich, *International Public Procurement Law: The Evolution of International Regimes on Public Purchasing*, also came out at about the same time.[4] Both books were published by Kluwer Law International. These two books, to my knowledge, were the first to 'de-nationalise' public procurement law, to take a global focus and to go beyond national limits. *Regulating Public Procurement* was the first significantly comparative text and in its use of a cases and materials approach to the subject. I hope I am not being too immodest to say that it has been by far the most influential of the two works.

In an American context, at the time, the two major scholarly works on public procurement law were *Formation of Government Contracts* and *Administration of Government Contracts*, by John Cibinic and Ralph Nash at George Washington University Law School.[5] Of course, there was plenty of other work that a practitioner or an academic could rely upon, but these books served as essential scholarly reference points in the field. There were few academics at the time in the US taking procurement law seriously beyond John Cibinic and Ralph Nash. This of course changed with the rise of the Nash and Cibinic legacy at George Washington University Law School. These books, excellent as they are, are entirely about US federal government contracts law. They are an example of the best work to be done in a field that is national in scope. Others can speak to work in European or other national (or supranational) traditions. Sue's book, *The Law of Public and Utilities Procurement*, has achieved a similar stature in the British and EU context.[6]

Regulating Public Procurement was very different in orientation. As a comparative and international text, it had to be conceptual in scope. We had to cover the major concepts in procurement law, and how the law differs across various jurisdictions. In a good deal of the book, we looked beyond terminology and searched for differences and commonalities in terms of function. The most challenging aspect of the book, however, was not in writing it but in finding adequate source materials, a subject covered next.

B. Researching and Writing *Regulating Public Procurement: National and International Perspectives*

Researching and writing a book on international and comparative public procurement law in the 1990s was a very different endeavour than it is today. It was easy

[4] A Reich, *International Public Procurement Law: The Evolution of International Regimes on Public Purchasing* (Kluwer Law International, 1999). Arie Reich informed me at an International Academy of Commercial and Consumer Law conference dinner at Durham University several years ago that he lost interest in public procurement law.

[5] These texts are now in later editions: J Cibinic Jr, R Nash Jr and CR Yukins, *Formation of Government Contracts* (4th edn, CCH, 2011); J Cibinic Jr, R Nash Jr and JF Nagle, *Administration of Government Contracts* (4th edn, CCH, 2006).

[6] S Arrowsmith, *The Law of Public and Utilities Procurement* (3rd edn, Sweet & Maxwell, 2011).

to find law and regulation for the US, given its long tradition with extensive legality in public procurement. The UNCITRAL Model Procurement Law at the time, along with its negotiating history and Guide to Enactment, was of course a major source of information. The EU Directives were very important to the work, but as an American lawyer steeped in legal realism, I tended to find the early EU procurement law research to be primarily descriptive of the rules, with no explanation of national rules and no discussion about how the Directives actually worked in action. Early EU procurement law research had this odd 'law on the books' feel to it. This of course changed as the years progressed and procurement law research has advanced.

To find anything out about developing countries was a monumental task. Georgetown University Law Center generously funded a research assistant for Don Wallace, whom we put to task in searching for public procurement law. The Internet was in its relative infancy, so it was of little help. This research assistant (I wish I remembered his name) mailed and called many embassies and international organisations for guidance. He kept a rather significant spreadsheet of the information he received. What he did receive informed us of the very low quality of public procurement law across the world. This was a world in dire need of public procurement law norms and best practices.

Sometime in the mid-1990s, I cannot remember precisely when, the late Raghavan Srinivasan (Srini), then World Bank Chief Procurement Advisor, called me to his office to discuss Country Procurement Assessment Reports (CPARs). He wanted to hear ideas from me about how to produce and distribute these Reports more effectively. He took me into a room of metal file cabinets full of CPARs. As I recall at the time, CPARs were for internal use in the World Bank. Srini, if I am recalling correctly, wanted to rejuvenate and open up CPAR production to the procurement community beyond the World Bank. This has happened, with CPARs now freely available on the World Bank website.[7] The oldest CPAR on the website is dated 1985, for Sierra Leone. For many countries, CPARs are now a matter of course and freely available. Srini was a great influence on good practices in public procurement. He was also a great influence on my thinking about procurement.

III. Post-Cold War Procurement Institutional Reform Starting in the 1980s

While the EU Procurement Directives figured prominently in the late twentieth century, there was a parallel movement that was ongoing at the time, in procurement law reform in developing countries and in countries in transition to market orientation at the end of the Cold War. These were heady times for procurement law and policy, thus Sue's concept of a series of conferences on the global revolution in procurement law and policy was so relevant.

[7] Country Procurement Assessment at https://openknowledge.worldbank.org/handle/10986/2165.

A. The UNCITRAL Model Procurement Law

In 1993, UNCITRAL completed its work on the UNICITRAL Model Law on Procurement of Goods and Construction.[8] One year later, UNCITRAL added services to the scope of the law, which led to the characterisation of the Model Law as the Model Law on Procurement of Goods, Construction, and Services. Since 2011 it has simply been called the UNCITRAL Model Law on Public Procurement.[9] The Model Law came at an auspicious time. In the 1990s, it may be an understatement to say that procurement law and practice in many countries were in a dismal state. But we have to understand the context of the Model Law's production at its start in the mid-1980s. The book that Sue, Don and I wrote in the late 1990s really built on the foundational work of the UNCITRAL Model Law. Let us take a peek, to the extent we can, at what was happening at UNCITRAL in the mid-1980s.

Start with the 1986 UNCITRAL Yearbook.[10] This is where we see the first discussion of the UNCITRAL Model Law in UNCITRAL public records. Procurement was included as a possible area of work in a note entitled 'Future Work in the Area of the New International Economic Order'.[11] The opinion expressed in the 1986 UNCITRAL Yearbook was that there was 'very wide support for the view that work on procurement should be given priority'.[12] The Yearbook noted the great importance of procurement to developing countries.[13] It was proposed to proceed expeditiously.[14]

The 1987 UNCITRAL Yearbook[15] included 'International Procurement: Note by the Secretariat'.[16] The Note explained that UNCITRAL had been collecting materials from a wide variety of sources on procurement law and was in the process of preparing a study. The Note referenced a meeting set for 7–11 December 1987 to prepare the study.

The 1988 UNCITRAL Yearbook[17] noted that a group of experts was scheduled to commence work on procurement in Vienna on 17–28 October 1988. The Yearbook stated that the work product might be a set of principles on procurement that states could adapt or use for guidance in preparing their own legislation. But principles were not to be, and instead what happened in the following year was considerable initial work towards the development of the Model Law. In the

[8] See at https://uncitral.un.org/en/texts/procurement/modellaw/procurement_of_goods_construction (last viewed 28 June 2023).

[9] UNCITRAL Model Law on Public Procurement at https://uncitral.un.org/en/texts/procurement/modellaw/public_procurement (last accessed 27 June 2023).

[10] Vol XVII UNCITRAL Yearbook, A/CN.9/SER.A/1986.

[11] A/CN.9/277.

[12] ibid para 240.

[13] ibid paras 237, 240.

[14] ibid para 240.

[15] Vol XVIII UNCITRAL Yearbook, A/CN.9/Ser.A/1987.

[16] A/CN.7/291.

[17] Vol XIX UNCITRAL Yearbook, A/CN.9/Ser.A/1988.

1989 UNCITRAL Yearbook[18] we see the first major report on the Working Group taking on the Model Law.[19] It is a report on the Working Group's meeting in late October 1988. This report explains that the Working Group decided in favour of a model law rather than a set of principles. What is most significant about the report, however, is its identification of a set of disciplines and values that would continue on in the procurement community and, when fused into the Model Law, become a set of normative standards for procurement law that continue to this day. In a section of the report entitled 'Nature of Model Procurement Law', we see the explication of these procurement disciplines and values to be incorporated into the Model Law. These include discussions of the methods of procurement, with a strong preference for competitive tendering under conditions of open competition, and how to use qualification and prequalification procedures so as not to limit competition but to ensure quality in procurement. The clear focus here is towards efficiency, market discipline, transparency, the lowering of transaction costs and, to use a phrase probably adopted by Sue at some later time, 'value for money'. These moves may not be significant today but they were then. They set the standard, to be able to say that favouritism, restricting competition, limiting suppliers to national entities, and use of discretion to deviate from transparency and market discipline were all 'bads' to be eradicated and not to be tolerated.

Following on from this report we see another Report of the Secretary General that provided a detailed study of procurement law.[20] Here we see a major focus on the details of procurement law on a comparative and de-nationalised basis. In the 1990 UNCITRAL Yearbook we then see the initial drafts of the Model Procurement Law.[21]

The development of the UNCITRAL Model Procurement Law must be understood in the context of the interests of the World Bank and the regional development banks in government procurement. About 90 per cent of all World Bank loans are disbursed through government procurement. The World Bank must take procurement very seriously as a result. It has maintained procurement guidelines and policies that must be followed and standard bidding documents that must be used in World Bank-financed procurements.[22] Without good procurement, there is the very real risk that loan funds will sit undisbursed and unavailable to borrower countries, but which are still accruing interest owed by the borrower countries. This outcome can produce hardship on poor countries with scarce resources and can frustrate development objectives. Procurement is the 'plumbing' of development assistance. Experts can plan for all sorts of laudable development projects,

[18] Vol XX UNCITRAL Yearbook, A/CN.9.Ser.A/1989.

[19] *Report of the Working Group on the Work of its Tenth Session* (Vienna, 17–25 October 1988) A/CN.9/315.

[20] Procurement: Report of the Secretary General A/CN.9/WG.V/WP.22.

[21] Vol XXI UNCITRAL Yearbook, A/CN.9/SER.A/1990.

[22] Procurement for Projects and Programs at www.worldbank.org/en/projects-operations/products-and-services/procurement-projects-programs (last accessed 22 June 2023).

but without procurement, these projects cannot get off the ground. Moreover, as explained in section III.B, reform of government procurement is a relatively straightforward and inexpensive way to promote good governance in developing countries, a longstanding objective of the World Bank.[23] The World Bank and other regional development banks have therefore invested in procurement reform in developing countries and in countries in transition to market orientation. The Bank's funding documents for these efforts specify the UNCITRAL Model Law as the standard for reform. The World Bank played a key role in the deliberations toward the drafting of the Model Law.

B. Procurement Law Reform and the 'New International Economic Order'

Work on the Model Procurement Law and on procurement law reform after the end of the Cold War locates its normative stance in something called the New International Economic Order (NIEO). It is standard for UNCITRAL to work under the auspices of the NIEO. This brings up some compelling insights on the role of the Model Procurement Law, and law reform for public procurement more generally, for developing states and states that were transitioning to market orientation at the end of the Cold War in the 1990s and into the early 2000s.

The NIEO has its origins in the 1970s and was primarily a response from developing countries to address inequalities in the post-colonial global economy that the international legal order created or perpetuated. With the NIEO, developing countries sought to restructure international law to provide for their greater control over their own resources. In the 1970s, developing countries, especially in Africa, Asia and Latin America, articulated concerns about their limited participation in global economic decision-making and the unfavourable terms of trade they faced in relation to developed countries. They argued that the existing economic order, dominated by Western industrialised countries, perpetuated their economic dependence and hindered their development. The key principles associated with the NIEO are dealt with in greater depth elsewhere.[24] While the NIEO concept gained significant support among developing countries, it faced considerable opposition from developed countries. Over time, the NIEO waned as an idea. The global economy underwent significant transformations since the 1970s. The liberalisation of trade in the Uruguay Round, the rise of bilateral investment treaties and the opening of capital markets moved the global economy towards a very different order. The 1980s and 1990s witnessed a shift towards neoliberal policies,

[23] Understanding Poverty/Topics/Good Governance at www.worldbank.org/en/topic/governance/overview (last accessed 22 June 2023).

[24] See authorities cited in n 26.

emphasising free markets, deregulation and privatisation. This ideological shift diminished the influence of the NIEO and led to the adoption of market-oriented reforms in many developing countries.

Where we were when procurement reforms were on the rise in the 1990s and early 2000s was at a time when the NIEO had no real normative pull and the Washington Consensus was in ascendancy. The NIEO and the Washington Consensus offer two distinct sets of ordering concepts that emerged at different times and represent radically different perspectives on economic development. The Washington Consensus emerged in the 1980s and early 1990s as a set of policy recommendations advocated by international financial institutions, particularly the International Monetary Fund (IMF) and the World Bank.[25] These recommendations were intended to guide economic policy in developing countries, especially those facing financial crises or seeking to implement structural reforms. The Washington Consensus promoted market-oriented policies, including fiscal discipline, privatisation, deregulation, trade liberalisation and the promotion of foreign investment.

While both the NIEO and the Washington Consensus addressed issues related to economic development, they differed significantly in their approach and underlying principles. The NIEO focused on challenging the existing global economic order and advocating for greater control and benefits for developing countries. The Washington Consensus, on the other hand, emphasised market-oriented reforms and the adoption of neoliberal policies to promote economic growth and stability.[26]

I would place the Model Procurement Law and procurement law reform in the Washington Consensus camp and not in the NIEO camp. While its focus is not on liberalised trade in procurement but on the substance of procurement law itself, it was clear from the beginning that the Model Law would be designed to be complementary to the goal of liberalised procurement markets. The Uruguay Round was happening at the same time as the drafting of the Model Law. One of the earliest statements on the drafting aims of the Model Law was to 'take into account the particular needs of foreign participants in procurement proceedings and their opportunity to participate in such proceedings'.[27] The signals were clear. Procurement preferences favouring domestic tenderers or to assist in building domestic industry were to be discouraged. And procurement needed to be

[25] So much has been written about the Washington Consensus. See J Williamson, 'A Short Hiistory of the Washington Consensus' in N Serra and J Stiglitz (eds), *The Washington Consensus Reconsidered: Towards a New Global Order* (Oxford University Press, 2008). On new moves towards abandoning the Washington Consensus and towards economic nationalism at least in the US, see F Foer, 'The New Washington Consensus' *The Atlantic* (9 May 2023).

[26] S Arrowsmith, 'Horizontal Policies in Public Procurement: A Taxonomy' (2010) 10 *Journal of Public Procurement* 149; S Arrowsmith and P Kunzlik (eds), *Social and Environmental Policies in EC Procurement Law* (Cambridge University Press, 2009); C McCrudden, *Buyng Social Justice: Equality, Goverment Procurement, and Legal Change* (Oxford University Press, 2007).

[27] Vol XX UNCITRAL Yearbook, A/CN.9/WG.V/WP.22, para 9.

transparent, with the key emphasis on sealing bidding as the 'better' or 'preferred' method of procurement. Of course, countries can and do favour domestic tenderers and maintain policies to use procurement to assist in the development of domestic industry. These are well-known secondary or horizontal policies.[28] But the key point here is about policy: secondary or horizontal policies should be instantiated in some form of public law and be supportable in the form of a rational and transparent national objective, readily knowable and accessible to citizens as well as foreign firms interested in bidding on procurements in the country in question. And they were still clearly disfavoured. Of course, a country would need market power in its government procurement sector to be able to join the WTO Agreement on Government Procurement and maintain these secondary and horizontal policies, which presents an issue about how equality actually operates in global trade.[29]

C. Good Governance on the Cheap

Most procurement law reform of the time was 'conservative' in its approach. By conservative, I mean that the presumption was to limit the discretion of government officials. As I have explained elsewhere,[30] an important question for governments and taxpayers – whom we may call principals – is whether procurement officials – the agents of these principals, are not, in American parlance, committing 'fraud, waste and abuse' or, to use different terminology more familiar to the development community, engaging in corruption. Principals may find it difficult to monitor agents to determine whether the agents are making good procurement decisions. Rigid and detailed procurement rules are a way to solve this problem. For example, do we actually know whether a procurement is conducted in an optimal way when the sealed-bid method of procurement is used? Not really. What we know is bid prices relevant to a published specification, and we can easily see the lowest bid. Sealed bidding is easier to monitor than methods of procurement such as negotiated procurement or requests for proposals. This is good governance on the cheap. Developing country governments and development banks lack the resources to run a comprehensive and sophisticated set of institutions to conduct oversight in the form of audits, evaluations and investigations. Another way to conceptualise these notions is the promotion of transparency in government procurement.

This, we may say, serves as an important policy framework for the UNCITRAL Model Law and procurement reform in developing and transitioning countries. I have previously classified models of procurement systems along two lines.[31]

[28] See n 24.

[29] J Linarelli. 'The WTO Agreement on Procurement and the UNCITRAL Model Law: A View from Outside the Region' (2006) 1 *Asian Journal of WTO and Health Law and Policy* 317.

[30] Linarelli (n 3).

[31] ibid.

The terminology may be used to classify procurement systems according to the level of sophistication of the procurement regulatory regime in a country. The two models can be described as a 'mature' procurement systems model, which I designate as model 1, and an 'emerging' procurement systems model, which I designate as model 2.[32] In model 1 systems, a high degree of professionalisation of the procurement workforce exists, and there is adequate remuneration for procurement officials through an established civil service system. The professionalisation of the workforce is due in substantial part to years of costly investment in the human capital of civil service employees. Model 1 systems include substantial criminal and quasi-criminal investigative institutions complementing significant procurement regulatory institutions. In countries with model 1 systems, substantial levels of monitors exist in the form of internal enforcement bodies whose functions are to deter corruption. In addition to such internal enforcement institutions, some countries have privatised enforcement in bid-challenge or bid-protest systems that permit interested parties (typically disappointed offerors) to protest procurement actions that they claim violate procurement law. In model 1 systems, effective enforcement institutions and a well-trained and well-compensated bureaucracy make less transparency a worthwhile tradeoff for enhanced discretion and flexibility. Model 2 procurement systems differ in substantial ways from model 1 systems. Many of the features of procurement law and practice in model 1 systems tend either not to exist in model 2 systems, or to exist at only the early stages. The implementation of a model 1 system would require the fundamental reform of judiciaries, legislatures and bureaucracies. Enforcement institutions do not exist or are deficient in model 2 systems. Model 2 systems have to rely relatively more on the transparency of procurement procedures to facilitate monitoring of procuring entities and contractors. Much of the procurement reform of the 1990s and early 2000s occurred in model 2 systems.

IV. The Common Core and Function of Procurement Law Rules

Much of what happened in the 'early' period of procurement law development and reform from about the mid-1990s to the early 2000s would benefit from more explicit study using the methods of comparative law. In this study, we will find that Sue did a great deal to advance the comparative study of procurement law.

We can break out comparative law methods along several lines. Two common themes come to mind in public procurement law research at the inter-country

[32] My model 1 and 2 approach has been confirmed empirically. See E Bosio et al, 'Public Procurement in Law and Practice' (2022) 112 *American Economic Review* 1091 (regulation effective in countries with low public-sector capacity but not in countries with high public-sector capacity where it can impede exercise of discretion).

level. First, it falls within what is known as the functional method in comparative law. In the functional method, comparativists examine actual problems in a country and the way they are solved from a legal point of view in different countries, looking for similar or different results. In the functional method, the focus is on the actual social problem at hand and not on terminology or formal legal concepts removed from their actual social context. In the common-core method of comparative law, a comparative legal scholar looks for commonalities and differences among legal systems and asks whether harmonisation might be possible across these legal systems.[33] There are other methods at work in comparative law but let us stay with these two for this chapter.

Both these methods are at work in the study of procurement law.[34] There are so many examples.[35] The *Public Procurement Law Review*, which Sue founded, is inherently comparative, and its mission makes comparison one of its key objectives. You will see these two methods at work in abundance in the pages of the *Review*.

Perhaps the best example of the advances that have been made in procurement law since the early 1990s lies in the ability of procurement specialists (lawyers and non-lawyers) to be able to agree on a set of fundamental principles that undergird contemporary procurement as it has advanced to this day. Take a look at Sue's recent work on post-Brexit procurement.[36] This work identifies eight key objectives for a sound public procurement legal system: value for money; integrity; accountability; equal treatment; fair treatment of suppliers; effective implementation of industrial, social and environmental objectives; opening markets; and an efficient procurement process. Compare this to Steve Schooner's nine goals for a public procurement legal system: (i) competition; (ii) integrity; (iii) transparency; (iv) efficiency; (v) customer satisfaction; (vi) best value; (vii) wealth distribution; (viii) risk avoidance; and (ix) uniformity.[37] The details of procurement law – the finer-grained legal rules we find in sound procurement legal systems – all fall within and promote one or more of Sue's objectives and Steve's goals. It is very

[33] See M Van Hoecke, 'Methodology of Comparative Legal Research,' *Law and Method* (December 2015) www.lawandmethod.nl/tijdschrift/lawandmethod/2015/12/RENM-D-14-00001 (last accessed 27 June 2023). The common-core method has been used primarily to study European private law, but its reference seems apt here. See M Bussani and U Mattei, 'The Common Core Approach to European Private Law' (1997) 3 *Columbia Journal of European Law* 339.

[34] A good example of the common-core approach at work might be CR Yukins, 'A Case Study in Comparative Procurement Law: Assessing UNCITRAL's Lessons for US Procurement' (2006) 35 *Public Contract Law Journal* 457.

[35] See eg, CR Yukins, 'Are IDIQs Inefficient?: Sharing Lessons with European Framework Contracts' (2008) 37 *Public Contract Law Journal* 545; DI Gordon, 'Constructing a Bid Protest Process: Choices Every Procurement Challenge System Must Make' (2006) 35 *Public Contract Law Journal* at https://ssrn.com/abstract=892781.

[36] S Arrowsmith, 'Reimagining Public Procurement Law After Brexit: Seven Core Principles for Reform and Their Practical Implementation, Part 1' at https://ssrn.com/abstract=3523172; S Arrowsmith, 'Reimagining Public Procurement Law after Brexit: Seven Core Principles for Reform and Their Practical Implementation: Part 2' at https://ssrn.com/abstract=3672421.

[37] SL Schooner, ' Desiderata: Objectives for a System of Government Contract Law' (2002) 11 *Public Procurement Law Review* 103.

doubtful that, in the early period of procurement law reform, lawyers, policy makers, procurement specialists and officials in intergovernmental organisations would have been able to articulate these goals and objectives without some degree of difficulty. What seems uncontroversial today would have been knowledge in the hands of an elite few in the past, 'in the know' about procurement law and policy. What has happened is that procurement law has been democratised from an epistemological point of view. Now, no one would take issue with the goals and objectives that Sue and Steve have articulated. If you have a sense of the history of public procurement law reform, you will not take this for granted.

Really, what has happened is that the normative values for the soundness of procurement legal systems have evolved and cemented in the minds of procurement professionals. The reform and advancement of procurement law has changed the professional and legal culture of procurement. This is not a case of culture's determining law but of law's determining culture. Surely, no one disagrees that local and national cultures can and do determine the content of the finer-grained procurement rules and procurement practices. But all these finer-grained rules and practices comport, at least aim to comport, with the normative values that Sue and Steve have identified. Procurement law now has a common core.

V. Conclusion

What is the future for procurement law and its change and reform? UNCITRAL has been a bellwether for things to come. It is the grand-norm entrepreneur for public procurement law. UNCITRAL Working Group I completed its work on the Model Procurement Law in 2012.[38] It then moved on to continue work it had done previously on privately financed infrastructure projects, to develop the UNCITRAL Model Legislative Provisions on Public–Private Partnerships, which it finalised in 2019.[39] The World Bank has developed an impressive Global Suspension and Debarment Directory, containing the results of a global survey launched in March 2020 that makes accessible information on the exclusion systems of 23 jurisdictions and institutions.[40] Surely other important advances have been made or are ongoing in the more recent years that are being missed here, particularly with all that goes on in the EU with the consolidation of its Procurement Directives. The focus of this chapter is plainly outside of Europe.[41]

[38] 2004–2012 Procurement at https://uncitral.un.org/en/working_groups/1/procurement (last accessed 27 June 2023).

[39] UNCITRAL Model Legislative Provisions on Public–Private Partnerships at https://uncitral.un.org/en/mlpppp#:~:text=Public%2DPrivate%20Partnerships%20cover%20a,achieve%20the%20Sustainable%20Development%20Goals (last accessed 27 June 2023).

[40] Global Suspension and Debarment Directory at www.worldbank.org/en/about/unit/sanctions-system/osd/brief/exclusion-survey (last accessed 27 June 2023).

[41] See S Arrowsmith, Modernizing the EU's Public Procurement Regime: A Blueprint for Real Simplicity and Flexibility' (2012) 21 *Public Procurement Law Review* 71.

One plausible prediction is that the grand international legal projects are basically over for government procurement. Change will be incremental, though it is hard to predict what those changes might be. It will be interesting to see what happens, and whether procurement will be affected by the trend toward localism and away from offshoring.[42]

One thing is certain: public procurement is law is now a thoroughly international and comparative law subject. Sue had a great deal to do with this. She was instrumental in globalising and cosmopolitanising the field.

[42] See, eg, D Rodrik, 'The New Productivism Paradigm' *Project Syndicate* (1 July 2022) at www.project-syndicate.org/commentary/new-productivism-economic-policy-paradigm-by-dani-rodrik-2022-07 (last accessed 28 June 2023); S Walters, 'The Backlash Against Globalization' (2021) 24 *Annual Review of Political Science* 421.

13

The WTO Agreement on Government Procurement as a Multipurpose Trade Instrument: A Vision for the Future

ROBERT D ANDERSON*

I. Introduction

From January 2005 through March 2019, I had the honour to serve as Counsellor and Team Leader for Government Procurement and Competition Policy in the Secretariat of the World Trade Organization (WTO), in Geneva, Switzerland. In that capacity, I headed a small but dynamic team of dedicated professionals responsible for servicing the WTO's Agreement on Government Procurement (GPA, 'GPA 2012' or 'the Agreement') and supporting the work of the Organization's Committee on Government Procurement (CGP or the Committee), the body of WTO member state representatives that is responsible for the administration of the Agreement. Throughout this time, I benefited immensely from the support and collaboration of Professor Sue Arrowsmith, the leading academic authority on the Agreement, worldwide, in her capacities as a colleague, mentor and expert contributor to multiple related Secretariat technical assistance programs and fora. Her original treatise on the Agreement, published in 2003, remains the leading treatment of foundational aspects of the Agreement as an instrument of international economic law.[1] Separately, in 2011, Professor Arrowsmith and I co-edited a research volume[2] that galvanised growing interest in the Agreement and helped set the stage for adoption of important amendments to it in 2012.[3]

* The expert assistance of Antonella Salgueiro in preparing this chapter is gratefully acknowledged.

[1] See, S Arrowsmith, *Government Procurement in the WTO* (Kluwer Law International, 2003).

[2] S Arrowsmith and RD Anderson (eds), *The WTO Regime on Government Procurement: Challenge and Reform* (Cambridge University Press and the WTO, 2011).

[3] See the text of the 2012 Revised Agreement on Government Procurement at www.wto.org/english/tratop_e/gproc_e/gp_gpa_e.htm. For related commentary, RD Anderson, 'The Conclusion of the Renegotiation of the WTO Agreement on Government Procurement: What it Means for the Agreement and for the World Economy' (2012) 21 *Public Procurement Law Review* 83; and

Over time, Professor Arrowsmith's writings and contributions to WTO Symposia and technical assistance activities in the area of government procurement, together with those of other eminent scholars and practitioners, have contributed to a progressive deepening of public and scholarly understanding of the GPA 2012 and growth in its importance for international trade, national procurement reforms and the global struggle for good governance. The GPA 2012's heightened importance and influence were evident, inter alia, in Professor Arrowsmith's own pathbreaking work on the overhaul of the United Kingdom's (UK's) national procurement legislation in the aftermath of Brexit[4] (prior to, during and following the UK's timely accession to the GPA 2012 in its own right[5]) and in the accession of several other major economies to the Agreement during the past decade, including Australia, New Zealand and Ukraine.[6]

Since retiring from the WTO Secretariat in March 2019, I have continued to lecture and write on the GPA and related topics.[7] These and other activities have provided me with extensive occasion for reflection, over time, on both the evolving role of the GPA over the past two decades and its future prospects. This chapter sets out my reflections. The argument is made that the GPA, originally conceived as a relatively narrow instrument of market access and transparency covering a select group of developed economies, is increasingly serving larger purposes.

RD Anderson, S Schooner and C Swan, 'Feature Comment: The WTO's Revised Government Procurement Agreement: An Important Milestone Toward Greater Market Access and Transparency in Global Public Procurement Markets' (2012) 54(1) *The Government Contractor* 1. A valuable synthesis of related developments is provided in A Davies, 'The Evolving GPA: Lessons of Experience and Prospects for the Future' in A Georgopoulos, B Hoekman and P Mavroidis (eds), *The Internationalization of Government Procurement Regulation* (Oxford University Press, 2017) ch 1.

[4] See, eg, S Arrowsmith, 'Transforming Public Procurement Law After Brexit: Some Reflections on the Government's Green Paper' (2021) 30 *Public Procurement Law Review* 103; S Arrowsmith, 'Reimagining Public Procurement Law After Brexit: Seven Core Principles for Reform and Their Practical Implementation, Part 1' (2020) at https://ssrn.com/abstract=3523172 or http://dx.doi.org/10.2139/ssrn.3523172 (last accessed 28 February 2024); and S Arrowsmith, 'Reimagining Public Procurement Law after Brexit: Seven Core Principles for Reform and Their Practical Implementation: Part 2' (2020) at https://ssrn.com/abstract=3672421 or http://dx.doi.org/10.2139/ssrn.3672421 (last accessed 28 February 2024). A key premise of the last two references is that 'the GPA will … provide the main constraint for [public procurement] regulation' in the UK post-Brexit.

[5] See RD Anderson, 'The UK's New Role in the WTO Agreement on Government Procurement: Understanding the Story and Seizing the Opportunity' (2021) 30(3) *Public Procurement Law Review* 159.

[6] See RD Anderson and N Sporysheva, 'The Revised WTO Agreement on Government Procurement: Evolving Global Footprint, Economic Impact and Policy Significance' (2019) 28(3) *Public Procurement Law Review* 71.

[7] ibid; Anderson (n 5); RD Anderson and AC Müller, 'Keeping Markets Open While Ensuring Due Flexibility for Governments in a Time of Economic and Public Health Crisis: The Role of the WTO Agreement on Government Procurement (GPA)' (2020) 29(4) *Public Procurement Law Review* 189; RD Anderson, WE Kovacic and A Salgueiro, 'Competition policy in relation to public procurement: an essential element of the policy framework for addressing COVID-19 and its aftermath' in S Arrowsmith et al (eds), *Public Procurement in (a) Crisis: Global Lessons from the COVID-19 Pandemic* (Hart Publishing, 2022); and RD Anderson et al, 'Deploying the WTO Agreement on Government Procurement (GPA) to Enhance Sustainability and Accelerate Climate Change Mitigation' (2023) 32(5) *Public Procurement Law Review* 223.

In addition to its original (trade-focused) purposes, these include: (i) complementing and reinforcing the global struggle for good governance and against corruption in an area of public administration with particular vulnerability to corrupt practices (ie, public procurement);[8] (ii) supporting the implementation of procurement reforms in a number of significant transition economies around the world;[9] and (iii) serving as a focal point for vital discussions on sustainability (and, in the future, mitigation of the effects of global climate change) in public procurement internationally.[10]

In serving these disparate aims, the GPA 2012 provides a paradigmatic example of a 'multipurpose trade agreement' or instrument.[11] The latter refers to, or should (in my submission) refer to, an instrument that, *while founded on and embracing the norms of liberal trade policy*, also serves to advance, directly or indirectly, and without disproportionate costs, other 'horizontal' policy objectives including human rights, good governance, sustainability and development. As a key proponent (and former WTO Appellate Body official), Nicholas Lamp, has stated:

> Inspired by competing narratives about globalization that bring different values to the fore, this approach no longer just tries to achieve an efficient international division of labour through trade liberalization. Rather, it tasks trade policy with achieving other substantive policy objectives as well, which include bolstering labour rights, addressing inequality, building resilient supply chains, safeguarding national security, and mitigating the climate crisis.[12]

Two key words in the foregoing quotation are 'as well'. In other words, multipurpose trade policy is not intended to neglect or (still less) come in the way of efficient trade consistent with the requirements and the values embodied in relevant agreements. Rather, it is intended to respond to additional concerns and provide complementary benefits. Still, as will be discussed below, it is important not to overlook possible tradeoffs between relevant objectives, if and when they arise.

In any case, the full potential of the GPA 2012 will *not* be realised if international interest in the Agreement lapses and appropriate leadership is absent.

[8] See RD Anderson and AC Müller, 'The revised WTO Agreement on Government Procurement (GPA): key design features and significance for global trade and development' (2017) 48(4) *Georgetown Journal of International Law* 949; and RD Anderson, A Jones and WE Kovacic, *Combatting Corruption and Collusion in Public Procurement: A Challenge for Governments Worldwide* (Oxford University Press, 2024).

[9] Anderson and Sporysheva (n 6).

[10] Anderson et al, 'Deploying the WTO Agreement' (n 7) and related discussion in section III.

[11] See N Lamp, 'Toward Multipurpose Trade Policy? How competing narratives about globalization are reshaping international trade cooperation' (International Institute for Sustainable Development, 2023) at www.iisd.org/articles/policy-analysis/multipurpose-trade-policy; A Roberts and N Lamp, *Six Faces of Globalization: Who Wins, Who Loses, and Why It Matters* (Harvard University Press, 2021); E Cima, *From Exception to Promotion: Re-Thinking the Relationship between International Trade and Environmental Law* (Koninklijke Brill NV, 2021); 'Partner Session: Toward Multipurpose Trade Policy' at www.youtube.com/watch?v=oTmT-8UiV70 (last accessed 28 February 2024); and related discussion in section II.

[12] Lamp (n 11).

Until recently, there appeared to be some risk of this.[13] Work in the Committee on Government Procurement was stalled during 2022 when it was, unusually, without a Chairman. Subsequently, Brazil took the unusual step of withdrawing its market access offer pursuant to its ongoing GPA 2012 accession process.[14] Thankfully, the situation regarding the chairmanship was remedied early in 2023 with the selection of Mr Martin Zbinden of Switzerland as the Committee's Chair.[15] Moreover, in the same year, North Macedonia became the 49th WTO member to be covered by the Agreement, Albania reinitiated its long-paused accession negotiation and Costa Rica submitted its own accession application. On this basis, and given the stakes involved, there are renewed grounds for hope. Furthermore, it is posited that the appeal of the GPA, and therefore its survival and flourishing as an element of the global trade framework, will be buttressed when its multiple purposes are embraced and given due recognition and weight.

The remainder of this chapter is organised as follows: section II elaborates on the concept of 'multipurpose trade policy'; section III explains how the GPA 2012 fits within this paradigm, looking back (in a selective and summary fashion) on the evolving role of the GPA from its inception through to the end of 2023; section IV sets out a vision of the GPA 2012's future prospects, *if* its Parties are able to come together for a further round of negotiations and summon the requisite engagement and willingness to compromise. Section V provides concluding remarks.

II. The Concept of 'Multipurpose Trade Policy'

Currently, the concepts of 'multipurpose trade policy' and/or 'multifunction trade agreements' are receiving growing attention in policy-making circles.[16] These ideas presuppose that international trade and trade policy can legitimately and appropriately advance important objectives beyond those of reducing tariff and non-tariff trade barriers, establishing conditions for efficient trade and managing related conflicts. Moreover, in contrast to earlier literature, which tended to be based on perceptions of WTO rules as potential threats to human rights and related values and, therefore, as needing to be subjected to corrective disciplines,[17] according to the new approach, concern over the protection of human

[13] See, for an important recent assessment, J Heilman Grier, *The International Procurement System: Liberalization & Protectionism* (Dalston Press of Djaghe LLC, 3 November 2022).

[14] See J Heilman Grier, 'WTO Procurement Pact: North Macedonia Joins, Brazil Pulls Offer' *Perspectives on Trade* (8 June 2023) at www.trade.djaghe.com/?p=7763 (last accessed 28 February 2024).

[15] See 'North Macedonia set to become new party to government procurement pact' at www.wto.org/english/news_e/news23_e/gpro_07jun23_e.htm (last accessed 28 February 2024).

[16] See, generally, Lamp (n 11); Roberts and Lamp (n 11).

[17] See, eg, C Dommen, 'Raising Human Rights Concerns in the World Trade Organization: Actors, Processes and Possible Strategies' (2002) 24(1) *Human Rights Quarterly* 1; and J Harrison, *The Human Rights Impact of the World Trade Organisation* (Hart Publishing, 2007).

rights, environmental values and the promotion of good governance need not be seen merely as 'exceptions' to be safeguarded from the core principles of the WTO but as complementary objectives that can be embraced and directly supported by the system.[18] As summarised aptly in a recent publication for the International Institute for Sustainable Development (IISD):

> Trade officials have long been attentive to the effects of trade on other policy objectives, often portraying them as either positive or negative externalities of trade liberalization … Since the early 1990s, trade agreements have also often featured provisions regarding labour rights and the environment to ensure that greater international competition does not take place on 'unfair' terms. … *The key distinguishing feature of the more recent shift to multipurpose trade policy is that other policy objectives no longer come into the picture as externalities of trade liberalization or as safeguards against unfair competition. Instead, those other policy objectives have taken a place alongside, and in some cases the place of, trade liberalization as the immediate objectives that trade policy is supposed to pursue.*[19]

Interest in the use of trade policy and trade agreements to support complementary policy objectives is fast becoming a new norm of global policymaking. For example, as European Union (EU) Director-General for Trade Sabine Weyand has recently written, it is now 'normal to ask what trade can do to address the big tests of our time. How can it help combat climate change? How can it promote labour rights globally? How does it impact security'?[20] In the United States (US), President Biden's 2022 Trade Policy Agenda issued a broad call for a 'Worker-Centered Trade Policy' that encompasses objectives concerning the protection of workers' rights; the acceleration of decarbonisation and the promotion of sustainability; agricultural and supply-chain resiliency; and pandemic readiness/amelioration.[21] This built upon calls by US Trade Representative Katherine Tai for the construction of a 'Globalization 2.0', which would 'adapt the rules of trade to incentivise firm behaviour to take into account more than just efficiency, but to promote and to reward decisions that are made to pursue sustainability for our people and our planet'.[22]

It must be acknowledged, nonetheless, that trade-offs can be involved even amongst broadly complementary policy objectives and, consequently, there will inevitably be limits to the new approach. Lamp himself observes:

[18] See, Cima (n 11) and, for an early contribution, RD Anderson and H Wager, 'Human Rights, Development, and the WTO: The Cases of Intellectual Property and Competition Policy' (2006) 9(3) *Journal of International Economic Law* 707.

[19] See Lamp (n 11) (emphasis added). See also 'Partner Session: Toward Multipurpose Trade Policy' (n 11).

[20] See S Weyand, 'Sabine Weyand on role of trade policy in fighting climate change' *The Economist* (16 October 2021) at www.economist.com/by-invitation/2021/10/16/sabine-weyand-on-role-of-trade-policy-in-fighting-climate-change (last accessed 28 February 2024).

[21] See United States Trade Representative, 2022 Trade Policy Agenda and 2021 Annual Report of the President of the United States on the Trade Agreements Program (March 2022) at www.ustr.gov/sites/default/files/2022%20Trade%20Policy%20Agenda%20and%202021%20Annual%20Report%20(1).pdf (last accessed 28 February 2024).

[22] Quoted in Lamp (n 11).

> Trade negotiators have always had to navigate trade-offs – for example, they needed to balance export interests that were looking for trade liberalization against import-competing industries that favoured protection … Multipurpose trade negotiators face trade-offs of [demonstrably] greater complexity … How do you find the right balance not just between the economic interests of different domestic constituencies but between economic efficiency, security concerns, climate objectives, and resilience? … To a greater extent than their predecessors, multipurpose trade negotiators have to develop frameworks for integrating and balancing radically different and incommensurable goals.[23]

Scholars of government procurement are, perhaps, particularly aware of the risks and trade-offs involved in loading additional objectives onto policies or international agreements that are fundamentally intended to promote efficiency and best value for money in public policies. Sue Arrowsmith, herself, is the author of a seminal contribution in this area, introducing important distinctions between categories of related instruments and favouring a nuanced approach to policy development.[24] In an earlier but, in many respects, complementary contribution, Schooner argues explicitly that excessive loading of additional objectives onto national or international procurement systems, for example concerning wealth redistribution, is likely to undermine their effectiveness in promoting the attainment of best value for money.[25]

Still, in my view and that of other contemporary observers, scope exists to find a 'sweet spot' where international agreements can promote both trade liberalisation *and* other important social and economic objectives. In addition to international trade generally, this is true, in my view, of agreements or chapters in international agreements that deal with government procurement policy.[26] As a practical matter, and as already noted, in the GPA 2012 amendments, the Parties to the Agreement placed considerable emphasis on the Agreement's role in reinforcing the global struggle for good governance and against corruption.[27] Expectations are growing regarding the GPA 2012's ability to serve as a tool of sustainability and, in the future, global climate change mitigation.[28] And, in my view, the Agreement still has a vital role to play in guiding procurement policy reforms in transition economies around the globe.[29] All three 'complementary objectives' of the Agreement are discussed further in section IV.

To be sure, this embracing of complementary objectives for trade liberalisation is *not* entirely new to the trading system, nor to its practitioners. For example, the

[23] Lamp (n 11).

[24] S Arrowsmith, 'Horizontal policies in public procurement: a taxonomy' (2010) 10(2) *Journal of Public Procurement* 149.

[25] See SL Schooner, 'Desiderata: Objectives for a System of Government Contract Law' (2002) 11 *Public Procurement Law Review* 103, esp at section 3, 'Competing Aspirations'.

[26] See also Anderson and Sporysheva (n 6).

[27] See Anderson and Müller (n 8); and Anderson, Jones and Kovacic (n 8).

[28] Anderson et al, 'Deploying the WTO Agreement' (n 7) and related discussion in section IV.

[29] Anderson and Sporysheva (n 6).

Preamble to the Marrakesh Agreement – the foundational agreement of the WTO – refers specifically to the objectives of

> [r]aising standards of living, ensuring full employment and a large and steadily growing volume of real income and effective demand, and expanding the production of and trade in goods and services, while allowing for the *optimal use of the world's resources in accordance with the objective of sustainable development, seeking both to protect and preserve the environment* …[30]

As such, the Marrakesh Agreement itself embodied a nascent commitment to the notion of multipurpose trade policy and the current (very appropriate) concern over sustainability. In a related vein, already in 2006, Anderson and Wager argued that the promotion of human rights and development, rather than being most appropriately seen as mere 'exceptions' to the WTO's rules, are important (and intended), if imperfectly realised, objectives and outcomes of the system.[31]

III. The GPA 2012 as a 'Multipurpose Trade Agreement': Relevance of the 2012 Amendments

The WTO Agreement on Government Procurement, especially as embodied in the 2012 amended version of the Agreement, is broadly congruent with the above-outlined paradigm of multipurpose trade policy. As has been well documented, the Agreement had its origins in work undertaken initially in the Organisation for Economic Cooperation and Development (OECD) that identified extensive patterns of discrimination in government procurement activities of that Organisation's members.[32] Such discriminatory practices were, moreover, intended to be effectively excluded from the ambit of the main non-discrimination provisions of the General Agreement on Tariffs and Trade (GATT) (and the subsequent General Agreement on Trade in Services (GATS)). The OECD work suggested further that, while, in some cases, discrimination was based on explicit statutory mandates, in other cases it was not. A clear implication was that general non-discrimination rules by themselves (as in the GATT and GATS) would be insufficient to remedy discriminatory practices in the field of public procurement.[33]

[30] Marrakesh Agreement Establishing the World Trade Organization, Preamble, First Recital at www.wto.org/english/docs_e/legal_e/04-wto_e.htm (emphasis added) (last accessed 28 February 2024).

[31] Anderson and Wager (n 18). See also P Lamy (former Director-General of the WTO), 'Lamy calls for mindset change to align trade and human rights' (13 January 2010) at www.wto.org/english/news_e/sppl_e/sppl146_e.htm (last accessed 28 February 2024).

[32] A Blank and G Marceau, 'The History of the Government Procurement Negotiations Since 1945' (1996) 4 *Public Procurement Law Review* 79; see also S Arrowsmith and RD Anderson, 'The WTO Regime on Government Procurement: Past, Present and Future' in Arrowsmith and Anderson (eds) (n 2) ch 1. In fairness, the OECD's work at that time already showed a clear awareness of the potential contribution of liberalised public procurement markets to global growth and development.

[33] Arrowsmith (n 1); also Anderson and Müller (n 8).

The foregoing insight, effectively, gave rise to the need for a more subject-specific agreement, incorporating minimum standards with respect to procedural and transparency rules.[34] Despite being sometimes overlooked, this insight remains relevant today: appropriate transparency and other procedural rules are essential both to prevent corrupt practices and to ensure that public procurement serves its ultimate purpose of ensuring good value for money in goods, services and public works that are purchased/commissioned by governments. They can help shape substantive approaches to public procurement policy, in addition to ensuring fair and non-discriminatory procedures. As such, the GPA has always had relevance for important aspects of good governance and the allocation of scarce resources.[35] Nonetheless, with the adoption and coming into force of the 2012 version of the Agreement, significantly greater emphasis was placed on such complementary objectives. The following documents key aspects of the evolution that took place.

A. The 2012 Amendments and the New, Explicit Focus on the Prevention of Corruption

To begin with, in the 2012 amendments to the GPA, significantly greater emphasis was placed on the Agreement's importance for good governance. Specifically, the revised GPA 2012 incorporates, in its Article IV, a new substantive provision providing that '[a] procuring entity shall conduct covered procurement in a transparent and impartial manner that … avoids conflicts of interest … and … prevents corrupt practices'.[36] Furthermore, a new recital to the Agreement's Preamble recognises 'the importance of transparent measures regarding government procurement, of carrying out procurements in a transparent and impartial manner and of avoiding conflicts of interest and corrupt practices in accordance with applicable international instruments, such as the United Nations Convention Against Corruption'.[37] It is important to note that these are the first explicit references to the problem of corruption in any of the WTO Agreements. The 2012 amendments thereby broke important new ground in the WTO system.

As documented by Anderson and Sporysheva, the new emphasis on good governance and the prevention of corruption has been embraced by several recently acceded GPA Parties, and cited as a reason for joining the Agreement:

> Increasingly, new GPA accession candidates explain their interest in joining the Agreement by reference not only to 'mercantilist' considerations (ie, export market opportunities) but to the utility of the GPA as an instrument for motivating, guiding

[34] See Anderson and Müller (n 8).
[35] Anderson and Arrowsmith (eds) (n 2).
[36] GPA 2012 (n 3) Art IV.
[37] See, for related discussion, Anderson and Müller (n 8).

> and 'locking in' policy reforms and initiatives, including anti-corruption campaigns. Such interests are salient particularly in the case of the 'transition' economies of Central and Eastern Europe and Central Asia … The accession of Ukraine in 2016 was a clear example of this phenomenon. As stated by Ukraine's Deputy Minister of the Economy and Trade, at the time of the conclusion of Ukraine's GPA accession negotiation, 'participation in the GPA would help Ukraine strengthen good governance in the area of public procurement, assist in its fight against corruption, and increase the transparency of government procurement practices' … Similar motivations, in addition to a desire for alignment with global best practices and models, [have been] cited by responsible officials in regard to the accessions of Montenegro in 2015 and Moldova in 2016, … and appear to underlie the related efforts of Tajikistan.[38]

B. A New, Explicit Focus on the Efficient and Effective Management of Public Resources

As a further illustration of the revised GPA 2012's 'multipurpose' nature, the Preamble to the revised Agreement contains an *entirely new recital* making clear that, in addition to its more directly trade-focused objectives (already largely set out in the 1994 text), the revised Agreement is built upon a perception that

> the integrity and predictability of government procurement systems are integral to the efficient and effective management of public resources, the performance of the Parties' economies and the functioning of the multilateral trading system.[39]

For me, this reference to the 'efficient and effective management of public resources' is, perhaps, the most important and satisfying new element in the 2012 Agreement's Preamble: it explicitly acknowledges the complementary triad that exists between the GPA 2012, well-conceived policy reforms, and good results for governments and citizens in the public procurement field.

C. Sustainability as a Complementary Objective of the GPA 2012

The GPA amendments of 2012 also did not overlook the growing salience of the Agreement for the promotion of sustainability (at least, with respect to its environmental aspects). As discussed by Anderson et al, the most explicit examples of new language incorporated in the GPA 2012 text that references environmental concerns are found in Article X of the Agreement regarding technical specifications and tender documentation in bidding processes.[40] In particular, Article X:6 of the 2012 text provides as follows (emphasis added):

[38] Anderson and Sporysheva (n 6).
[39] GPA 2012 (n 3) third Recital.
[40] Anderson et al, 'Deploying the WTO Agreement' (n 7).

Technical Specifications

...

6. For greater certainty, a Party, including its procuring entities, *may, in accordance with this Article, prepare, adopt or apply technical specifications to promote the conservation of natural resources or protect the environment.*

In addition, Article X:9 of the 2012 text provides as follows (emphasis added):

Tender Documentation

...

9. The evaluation criteria set out in the notice of intended procurement or tender documentation may include, among others, price and other cost factors, quality, technical merit, *environmental characteristics* and terms of delivery.

The intent of these provisions is plain enough. Article X:6 makes clear that the GPA Parties/their procuring entities may employ technical specifications to promote the conservation of natural resources or protect the environment. While arguably this was not precluded under the 1994 Agreement, the forthright new language sends a useful signal to the Parties and their entities. Article X:9 provides the additional helpful clarification that environmental characteristics, together with quality, technical merit, price and other cost factors, may be included in the evaluation criteria that are set out in tenders governed by the Agreement. All of this is powerfully congruent with the idea of a multipurpose trade agreement.

Beyond the foregoing, the revisions resulting in the GPA 2012 put in motion a further important process concerning the potential role of the Agreement in relation to sustainability and, by extension, global climate change. As explained by Anderson et al:

> The negotiations to revise the GPA that culminated in 2012 also resulted in the adoption, by the WTO Committee on Government Procurement, of an important package of work programmes and a built-in mandate for further negotiations/possible amendments 'with a view to improving this Agreement, progressively reducing and eliminating discriminatory measures, and achieving the greatest possible extension of its coverage among all parties on the basis of mutual reciprocity, taking into consideration the needs of developing countries'. This mandate offers an attractive and flexible vehicle for addressing issues concerning the nexus of public procurement with sustainability and climate change mitigation.[41]

While work on the Work Programme on Sustainable Procurement of the WTO Committee on Government Procurement appeared to have stalled in the course of 2021–22, recently, related activity has resumed. In particular, a new 'Transatlantic Initiative on Sustainable Trade', sponsored jointly by EU and the US, has provided new hope that work in the Committee can now move forward with due urgency.[42] It should be noted that the WTO Work Programme is not

[41] ibid (internal citations omitted).

[42] See 'Transatlantic Initiative on Sustainable Trade' work programme in Joint Statement EU–US Trade and Technology Council of 31 May 2023 in Lulea, Sweden, Annex 1 (31 May 2023) at

strictly limited to the environmental aspects of sustainability; rather, it potentially also encompasses the 'social dimensions' of sustainability envisioned by the UN Sustainable Development Goals (SDGs). Nevertheless, a higher degree of convergence has generally been manifested with respect to the former aspects (ie the concept of green procurement).[43]

D. A Further Critical Element Reinforcing the Scope for Addressing Sustainability Concerns: The GPA's Broad Language Concerning Contract Awards

Of possibly even greater significance than the foregoing, the GPA 2012's language concerning the critical issue of contract award criteria, while not referring specifically to environmental concerns, unambiguously provides appropriate scope for them to be taken into account. Specifically, Article XV:5 of the 2012 Agreement provides as follows (emphasis added):

> **Article XV Treatment of Tenders and Awarding of Contracts**
>
> **Awarding of Contracts**
>
> …
>
> 5. Unless a procuring entity determines that it is not in the public interest to award a contract, the entity shall award the contract to the supplier that the entity has determined to be capable of fulfilling the terms of the contract and that, based solely on the *evaluation criteria specified in the notices and tender documentation*, has submitted:
>
> (a) the *most advantageous tender*; or
> (b) where price is the sole criterion, the lowest price.

As observed by Anderson et al:

> First, the reference in Article XV:5 to 'evaluation criteria specified in the notices and tender documentation' clearly implicates the set of possible criteria referenced in Article X:9 (discussed above) which, as we have seen, include possible 'environmental characteristics'. As such, the evaluation of submitted bids on the basis of predetermined environmental criteria may be facilitated by the application of a price-quality ratio, where environmental advantages are considered as a part of the quality of the intended good or service. On this basis, there can be no doubt that the GPA provides broad scope for contracts covered by the Agreement to be awarded on the basis of environmental characteristics or criteria.

https://ec.europa.eu/commission/presscorner/detail/en/statement_23_2992 (last accessed 28 February 2024). For related commentary, Anderson et al, 'Deploying the WTO Agreement' (n 7); and J Heilman Grier, 'US-EU Green Public Procurement Initiative' (15 June 2023) at https://trade.djaghe.com/?p=7782 (last accessed 28 February 2024). The documentation refers specifically to the EU and US hope that the new initiative will facilitate related progress in the WTO Committee.

[43] Anderson et al, 'Deploying the WTO Agreement' (n 7).

> More generally, it should be noted that the GPA in no way privileges or favours the award of contracts based on lowest price. This is important in that the awarding of contracts based solely on lowest price is clearly a practice that can undervalue environmental considerations in the acquisition process. The alternative concept of 'most advantageous tender' is clearly intended to permit a broader approach.[44]

IV. A Vision for the Future

The GPA 2012 was conceived as and remains a work in progress. The 2012 Agreement (Article XXII:7) embodies a built-in commitment for its Parties to

> undertake further negotiations, with a view to improving this Agreement, progressively reducing and eliminating discriminatory measures, and achieving the greatest possible extension of its coverage among all Parties on the basis of mutual reciprocity, taking into consideration the needs of developing countries.[45]

Furthermore, to facilitate the expected negotiations, the Agreement commits the Parties to undertaking a series of Work Programmes, inter alia on the following topics of interest:

(i) the treatment of small and medium-sized enterprises;
(ii) the collection and dissemination of statistical data;
(iii) the treatment of sustainable procurement;
(iv) exclusions and restrictions in Parties' Annexes; and
(v) safety standards in international procurement.[46]

These work programmes are currently in progress, with the exception of the anticipated work programme on safety standards, which appears to have been rendered moot by developments subsequent to the 2012 renegotiation.

This section of the chapter sets out various suggestions for elements that could be included in the mandated negotiations. Subsections IV.A and IV.B focus on two substantive areas of concern, each consonant with this chapter's vision of the GPA 2012 as an multipurpose trade agreement: (i) deepening and broadening the GPA 2012's usefulness as a tool of sustainability and climate change mitigation; and (ii) complementing the explicit anti-corruption provisions that were incorporated in the 2012 Agreement with a new, explicit focus on preventing supplier collusion (and thereby broadening and further highlighting its significance for good governance). Subsection IV.C brings together additional ideas of a more technical nature that could contribute to the optimal functioning of the Agreement.

[44] ibid (internal citations omitted).
[45] GPA 2012 (n 3) Art XXII:7.
[46] GPA 2012 (n 3) Art XXII:8.

A. Carrying Forward the GPA's Potential as a Tool of Sustainability and Climate Change Mitigation

As noted, the GPA 2012 already incorporated important new references to environmental concerns in Article X of the Agreement regarding technical specifications and tender documentation in bidding processes. Nonetheless, given the dire need,[47] more can and should be done to deepen and make more explicit the Agreement's significance in this area.[48]

Possible additional elements could include:

- Inserting additional language in the GPA 2012's Preamble, to call attention to the importance of a sustainability/climate change mitigation focus in framing public procurement policy and activities.
- Additional operative (substantive) provisions, for example relating to environmental considerations in: (i) contract award criteria; (ii) contractor selection procedures and/or conditions for participation; and/or (iii) contract management.
- A possible need for negotiations to address the coverage of the Agreement with respect to government procurement of environmental goods, services and works, and 'Buy National' requirements that are being imposed in tandem with new initiatives in this area.
- If the GPA Parties are prepared to be ambitious, consideration could be given to an approach for giving 'credit' to GPA accession candidates, in the course of their market access negotiations, for measures taken to promote green public procurement (on the ground that these will eventually provide benefits not only to the acceding country but to all members of the global commons).

To be sure, the foregoing is only a very preliminary list, and each of the above-suggested elements will require further consideration.

B. Deepening the GPA 2012's Relevance for Good Governance, by Incorporating Additional Appropriate References to the Problem of Supplier Collusion

As already noted, the GPA 2012 incorporated path-breaking new requirements for participating member governments to prevent/avoid corrupt acts and conflicts of interest. The Agreement also contains a passing reference to the related problem of supplier collusion – the rigging of bids in secret meetings of suppliers, which

[47] SL Schooner, 'No Time to Waste: Embracing Sustainable Procurement to Mitigate the Accelerating Climate Crisis' (2021) 61 *Contract Management* 24.

[48] See Anderson et al, 'Deploying the WTO Agreement' (n 7), on which this subsection builds.

may occur with or without the knowledge of procurement officials.[49] Specifically, it includes, as a possible justification for the use of limited tendering, a situation where tenders submitted have been collusive.[50]

While the foregoing reference is useful and apropos, it scarcely amounts to a systematic or satisfactory treatment of the issue. Both economic evidence and the experience of competition agencies, worldwide, make clear that supplier collusion is widespread in public procurement markets and, where it occurs, imposes very substantial costs on governments and taxpayers.[51] Typically, its successful deterrence requires the vigorous application of competition laws and a range of related (complementary) measures.[52] Successful collusion among national suppliers can, moreover, be facilitated by (and thereby incentivise) the exclusion of foreign competitors from markets. It is therefore worth considering whether the GPA 2012 should be amended to impose an obligation on participating national governments to implement measures to prevent or deter collusive tendering.

C. Additional Technical Tweaks and Extension of Coverage

Beyond the foregoing, a number of other useful tweaks to the Agreement can be identified. Some of these would include:

- Explicit extension of the Agreement to framework agreements. Currently, these are not mentioned specifically, though they arguably are permitted and, to an extent, regulated by the Agreement's general provisions.[53] The adoption of relevant explicit provisions could address the particular challenges that are posed by such agreements, from the perspectives of competition and transparency.[54]
- Coverage of public–private partnerships (PPPs), which are another important vehicle for public provision, particularly of infrastructure projects, that is not explicitly addressed by the GPA 2012, though concession contracts (a related concept) are covered by the Agreement in the case of some Parties. In any case, PPPs are certain to play an important role both in meeting future

[49] RD Anderson, A Jones and WE Kovacic, 'Preventing Corruption, Supplier Collusion and the Corrosion of Civic Trust: A Procompetitive Program to Improve the Effectiveness and Legitimacy of Public Procurement' (2019) 26(4) *George Mason Law Review* 1233; TLI Think! Paper 5/2019, King's College London Law School Research Paper No 19-14 at www.ssrn.com/abstract=3289170 (last accessed 28 February 2024). See also Anderson, Jones and Kovacic (n 8).

[50] GPA 2012 (n 3) Art XIII:1(a)(iii).

[51] Anderson, Jones and Kovacic (n 49); and Anderson, Jones and Kovacic (n 8).

[52] Anderson, Jones and Kovacic (n 49); and Anderson, Jones and Kovacic (n 8).

[53] Art IV:4 of the GPA 2012 (n 3) provides that a procuring entity shall conduct covered procurement in a transparent and impartial manner that 'is consistent with this Agreement, using methods *such as* open tendering, selective tendering and limited tendering' (emphasis added).

[54] See, for pertinent background, GL Albano and C Nicholas, *The Law and Economics of Framework Agreements: Designing Flexible Solutions for Public Procurement* (Cambridge University Press, 2016).

infrastructure needs and in the transition to a green economy. As such, they serve to be explicitly treated by the Agreement.

- A possible general extension of coverage, as mandated by the Agreement itself in Article XXII:7.

Again, the above is only a preliminary list; no doubt, the GPA Parties' own discussions will identify additional needs and concerns.

V. Concluding Remarks

The GPA 2012, originally conceived as a relatively narrow instrument of market access and transparency covering a select group of developed economies, is increasingly serving larger purposes. In addition to its original (trade-focused) purposes, these include: (i) complementing and reinforcing the global struggle for good governance and against corruption in a particularly salient policy area; (ii) supporting the implementation of procurement reforms in a number of transition economies around the world; and (iii) serving as a focal point for vital discussions on sustainability and, potentially, mitigation of the effects of global climate change. In serving these disparate aims, the GPA 2012 provides a paradigm example of a 'multipurpose trade agreement' or instrument. As such, and if appropriately supported by the international community, it can be a central element of the legal and policy architecture for the global economy *and* the struggle for sustainability and climate change mitigation in the twenty-first century.

To be sure, this potential will *not* be realised if international interest in the Agreement lapses and appropriate leadership is absent.[55] Thankfully, the GPA Committee's chairmanship was filled in 2023 and important work on accessions to the Agreement has resumed. No doubt, the survival and flourishing of the GPA as an element of the global trade framework will be buttressed when its multiple purposes are more universally embraced and given due recognition and weight.

In pursuing these issues, the WTO Committee on Government Procurement and the broader international community will be well served if they follow the example and channel the intellectual acuity and creativity of Sue Arrowsmith. Sue, as is well known, is scrupulous in her insistence on policy-relevance, rigour and clarity of thought in legal and policy research. Indeed, her own clarity of thought and commitment to the field of public procurement law and policy – including, very much, its international dimensions – have been completely critical to the expansion of interest and understanding and the proliferation of relevant international models that have occurred in the field over the past three decades (and to my own thinking on related issues). Without her, we would not be where we are. In moving ahead, we must be ever mindful of her wisdom and counsel.

[55] See Grier (n 14).

14

Discrimination in Government Procurement: Delimiting Multilateral and Plurilateral National Treatment Obligations

ARWEL DAVIES

I. Introduction

As academics, we naturally start with the seminal contributions when compiling our reading lists. Which works should appear first by reason of their accessibility, coverage, depth and rigour? In the broad field of public procurement law and regulation, the name Sue Arrowsmith is conspicuous by its repetition. This applies whether the focus is on the domestic, regional or international landscape. Within the sub-field of international procurement regulation, Arrowsmith's works are a reference point when studying the development and evolution of the main instruments, as well as their relationship with domestic and regional rules. The hallmark of this work is that it keeps in sight the broad picture, while also addressing issues of important detail. This chapter focuses on one such issue, using as one of its reference points Arrowsmith's thoughts as set out in her book *Government Procurement in the WTO*.[1] In international procurement regulation, national treatment is perhaps the most sensitive obligation. When it applies, discrimination against imported products in the procurement process is prohibited. As between members of the World Trade Organization (WTO), the multilateral national treatment obligation in Article III of the General Agreement on Tariffs and Trade (GATT) does *not* apply as procurement is carved out by a derogation within this provision. National treatment only applies to procurement that is covered by the plurilateral Agreement on Government Procurement. However, the precise point at which the reach of the multilateral obligation ends, and the plurilateral obligation takes over, is a matter of interpretation. This chapter discusses why the point

[1] S Arrowsmith, *Government Procurement in the WTO* (Kluwer Law International, 2003).

of delimitation matters, and appraises the WTO Appellate Body's location of this point. It is argued that the Appellate Body's interpretation is difficult to reconcile with the principles of treaty interpretation and contrary to the reasonable expectations of WTO members.

Discrimination in government procurement in favour of national goods, services and suppliers amounts to a significant barrier to international trade. It cannot be assumed that 'free-trade' or market access has been achieved when border tariffs on imported goods have been substantially reduced or eliminated. A portion of the market will remain closed to the extent that government procurement is subject to 'buy-national' policies. The question of whether and how to regulate discrimination in government procurement at the international level has always been a sensitive issue. Bilateral and regional free-trade agreements frequently involve some level of commitment to procurement market liberalisation up to and including full procurement chapters.[2] However, for trade agreements that are less than comprehensive in their policy area coverage, procurement tends to be among the excluded areas. For example, procurement is excluded from all but one of Africa's eight subregional preferential trade agreements.[3] Procurement is also excluded from the China–Australia free-trade agreement, which can reasonably be described as otherwise comprehensive in its coverage, including, for example, intellectual property and investment.[4] At the WTO, negotiations on multilateral rules on government procurement are in abeyance,[5] while the Agreement on Government Procurement (GPA), as the foremost international instrument, has plurilateral or optional status. This is primarily because procurement power is an instrument of industrial, social and environmental policy, which often involves directly or indirectly preferences for national suppliers and products.[6] The more flexibility states wish to retain here, the less able they are to accede to international rules with national treatment obligations at their core.

[2] See RD Anderson et al, 'Government Procurement Provisions in Regional Trade Agreements: A Stepping Stone to GPA Accession' in S Arrowsmith and RD Anderson (eds), *The WTO Regime on Government Procurement: Challenge and Reform* (Cambridge University Press, 2011) ch 20.

[3] See M Maliszewska and M Ruta, The African Continental Free Trade Area Economic and Distributional Effects, World Bank Group (2020) at www.worldbank.org/en/topic/trade/publication/the-african-continental-free-trade-area, 2.

[4] China–Australia Free Trade Agreement, entered into force on 20 December 2015, at www.dfat.gov.au/trade/agreements/in-force/chafta/official-documents/Pages/official-documents (accessed 6 March 2024).

[5] The history of the multilateral work between 1996 and 2004 is provided on the WTO's website at www.wto.org/english/tratop_e/gproc_e/gp_dda_e.htm (accessed 6 March 2024). See S Arrowsmith, 'Towards a Multilateral Agreement on Transparency in Government Procurement' (2008) 47(4) *International and Comparative Law Quarterly* 793; SJ Evenett, 'Is There a Case for New Multilateral Rules on Transparency in Government Procurement?' in SJ Evenett and Swiss Secretariat for Economic Affairs (eds), *The Singapore Issues and The World Trading System: The Road to Cancun and Beyond* (Seco, 2003) 169.

[6] See S Arrowsmith, 'Public Procurement as an Instrument of Policy and the Impact of Market Liberalization' (1995) 111 *Law Quarterly Review* 235; S Arrowsmith, 'Horizontal Policies in Public Procurement: A Taxonomy' (2010) 10(2) *Journal of Public Procurement* 149; S Morettini, Public Procurement and Secondary Policies in EU and Global Administrative Law' in E Chiti and BG Mattarella (eds), *Global Administrative and EU Administrative Law* (Springer, 2011) 187.

The desire to carve out procurement from the reach of multilateral national-treatment obligations became evident at an early point in the post-war negotiations, during which there was a sharp U-turn. The Suggested Charter for an International Trade Organisation, drafted by the United States (US) and published in September 1946, originally proposed that government procurement should be subject to the general national-treatment obligation.[7] However, it quickly became apparent that this would not be possible. In the leading account of the negotiations, Blanc and Marceau refer to the realisation that national treatment would require the elimination of 'buy-national' laws involving preferences for domestic products.[8] The authors refer to 'consensus that an attempt to reach agreement on such a commitment would lead to exceptions almost as broad as the commitment itself'.[9] They also identify agreement among delegations that an express exclusion of government procurement was preferable to merely omitting any reference to procurement in the national-treatment obligation. Without an exclusion, the obligation might otherwise be interpreted as applying to government procurement. The Charter's initial inclusion of procurement was therefore substituted[10] with the derogation eventually expressed in GATT Article III:8(a):

> The provisions of this Article shall not apply to laws, regulations or requirements governing the procurement by governmental agencies of products purchased for governmental purposes and not with a view to commercial resale or with a view to use in the production of goods for commercial sale.

This contribution focuses on this derogation. In WTO dispute settlement, it has been interpreted by panels and the Appellate Body in three cases. *Canada – Certain Measures Affecting the Renewable Energy Generation Sector*[11] was brought against Canada by EU, while *Canada – Measures Relating to the Feed-In Tariff Programme*[12] was brought by Japan. The complaints related to the same matter, with panels established in 2011 and 2012 respectively. For both disputes, the Appellate Body Reports were adopted in 2013. The third case, *India – Certain Measures Related to Solar Cells and Solar Modules*,[13] was brought by the US. The panel was established in 2014 and the Appellate Body report was adopted in 2016. The three cases are factually indistinguishable for the purposes of this contribution. Canada and India conditioned the

[7] Art 9(1) covered 'laws and regulations governing the procurement by governmental agencies of supplies for public use other than by or for the military establishment'; see at www.worldtradelaw.net/document.php?id=misc/Suggested%20Charter.pdf (accessed 6 March 2024).

[8] See A Blanc and G Marceau, 'The History of Government Procurement Negotiations Since 1945' (1996) 5 *Public Procurement Law Review* 77, 82–83.

[9] ibid.

[10] The derogation first appeared in Art 2(5) of the 'Tentative and Non-Committal Draft Suggested by the Delegation of the United States' of 7 February 1947, E/PC/T/C.6/W.53, at www.worldtradelaw.net/document.php?id=misc/Draft%202.pdf (accessed 6 March 2024).

[11] WT/DS412/AB/R, *Canada – Certain Measures Affecting the Renewable Energy Generation Sector*, adopted 24 May 2013.

[12] WT/DS426/AB/R, *Canada – Measures Relating to the Feed-In Tariff Programme*, adopted 24 May 2013.

[13] WT/DS456/AB/R, *India – Certain Measures Related to Solar Cells and Solar Modules* (*India – Solar Cells*), adopted 14 October 2016.

award of a long-term electricity supply contract on suppliers' having to meet domestic content requirements on wind- and solar-electricity-generating equipment.

The question is whether the WTO Appellate Body has interpreted the derogation in an overly narrow manner, thereby expanding the reach of GATT Article III into the domain of government procurement. Such an outcome, if it has emerged, is unlikely to be consistent with the expectations of WTO members. The decision of most WTO members not to accede to the plurilateral GPA is undermined via an effective strengthening of the multilateral national treatment obligation. The WTO members who are GPA parties may wonder what their protracted negotiations on coverage commitments were for if the procurement in question is, in any event, covered by GATT Article III. In sum, the more narrowly the derogation is interpreted, the more likely it becomes that obligations to which only some WTO members have acceded under the GPA, or even obligations to which no GPA Party has acceded, are multilateralised.

The chapter proceeds as follows. Section II provides an explanation of GATT Article III. It is important for readers to understand how this provision covers discrimination in government procurement when the derogation is not available. Section III offers a view on the likely expectations of WTO members in this area. These are to the effect that the gradual removal of discrimination in government procurement will occur on a plurilateral basis under the GPA, rather than on a multilateral basis under GATT Article III. Section IV describes Professor Arrowsmith's treatment of the procurement derogation. While this pre-dates the relevant WTO cases, the analysis offered is consistent with the reasonable expectations of WTO members. Section V proceeds to contrast the panel and Appellate Body interpretations of the derogation. The Appellate Body envisaged a narrower interpretation of the derogation than the panel, and, therefore, a greater reach for GATT Article III:4 to cover discrimination in the context of government procurement. Section VI considers whether the Appellate Body's approach can be defended as a matter of treaty interpretation. Section VII discusses the difficulties of applying the Appellate Body's approach to a hypothetical example – a procurement of electric vehicles subject to the use of domestic batteries. It is questioned whether the availability of the derogation can be taken for granted here. Section VIII re-caps on the areas of legal certainty and uncertainty, while section IX concludes.

II. Article III of the General Agreement on Tariffs and Trade

Article III is entitled 'National Treatment on Internal Taxation and Regulation'.[14] Article III:1 provides a general statement about what is prohibited. Internal

[14] For a full introduction of GATT Art III, see S Lester, B Mercurio and A Davies, *World Trade Law: Text, Materials and Commentary* (Bloomsbury Publishing, 2018) ch 7. Leading contributions include,

measures 'should not be applied to imported or domestic products so as to afford protection to domestic production'. The provision therefore prohibits protectionism, which can also be termed as nationality or origin-based discrimination between domestic and imported products. Discrimination in government procurement falls under internal regulation rather than internal taxation. As such, the relevant part, if the provision applied to government procurement, would be GATT Article III:4:

> The products of the territory of any contracting party imported into the territory of any other contracting party shall be accorded treatment no less favourable than that accorded to like products of national origin in respect of all laws, regulations and requirements affecting their internal sale, offering for sale, purchase, transportation, distribution or use.

The prohibition against discrimination is expressed in the obligation to accord 'treatment no less favourable' to imported products relative to domestic products. This would clearly be breached if the government only purchased domestic products, or provided a price preference for domestic products, or imposed offset requirements under which, for example, products purchased must incorporate domestic components. Such measures adversely affect the 'internal sale, offering for sale' and 'purchase' of imported products.

Article III:4 is breached only when the domestic and imported products are 'like'. This may be termed the 'comparator element' or 'likeness analysis'. However, this element is uncontentious and self-evidently satisfied in cases of *de jure* discrimination, understood as discrimination that is indisputable from the face of the measure. The examples in the previous paragraph fall under this classification because the imported and domestic products concerned, whatever they may be, are distinguished on the basis of a prohibited criterion – their nationality or origin. In contrast, the comparator element becomes relevant when the measure is origin-neutral on its face, drawing a regulatory distinction on the basis of something other than origin. Thus if a government were to specify that it will purchase any electric vehicles, provided the batteries do not contain a certain chemical, it cannot automatically be concluded that there is discrimination here, even if only domestic batteries satisfy the regulatory distinction. This is an example of possible *de facto* discrimination, with the outcome depending on the content and application of likeness criteria in relation to domestic and imported batteries. We would need to know what these criteria are.[15] However, if the government specifies that

JY Qin, 'Defining Nondiscrimination under the Law of the World Trade Organization' (2005) 23 *Boston University International Law Journal* 215; DH Regan, 'Regulatory Purpose and "Like Products" in Article III:4 of the GATT (with Additional Remarks on Article III:2)' (2002) 36 *Journal of World Trade* 443; F Ortino, 'From "Non-discrimination" to "Reasonableness": a Paradigm Shift in International Economic Law', Jean Monnet Working Paper 01/2005; RE Hudec, 'GATT/WTO Constraints on National Regulation: Requiem for an Aim and Effects Test' (1998) 32 *International Lawyer* 619.

[15] The headline test for likeness throughout WTO law is that it requires 'a determination about the nature and extent of a competitive relationship between and among products'. Appellate Body Report,

it will only purchase domestic batteries, this is *de jure* discrimination, regardless of what approach to the comparator element is used.

Of course, provisions such as GATT Article III:4 can only be breached if they apply. If the GATT Article III:8(a) derogation is available, any discrimination will be outside the reach of the GATT. As between WTO members, the question is then whether the plurilateral non-discrimination obligations in Article IV of the GPA apply.[16] Article IV only applies as between GPA Parties, and only to 'covered procurement' as defined in GPA Article II. It is relevant here, for example, to consider whether the 'goods, services, or any combination thereof' are 'specified' in the relevant coverage Annex of the respondent GPA Party.[17]

III. The Expectations of WTO Members

It is clear that WTO members consider the locus of procurement market liberalisation to be the plurilateral GPA, rather than GATT Article III:4. The origin and development of the GPA indicate that WTO Members (previously GATT contracting parties) think long and hard before acceding to the GPA. Membership remains limited and imbalanced towards developed countries. It covers 48 of the WTO's 164 members, with 27 of these being the EU Member States.[18] The WTO reports that 11 WTO members are currently in the process of acceding to the GPA. These members include China, which submitted its first coverage offer in 2007.

The conditions of accession to the GPA in terms of contract coverage are also hard fought. Contract coverage does not operate on a most-favoured-nation basis. It is not the position that when a supplier of a particular GPA Party is entitled to participate in a contract award of another GPA Party, the suppliers of all GPA Parties are entitled to participate. Rather, the entitlement to participate depends on the content of the coverage schedules, comprising seven annexes, maintained by each GPA Party.[19] The content of these annexes depends on the outcome of bilateral negotiations conducted with reciprocity considerations in mind. Country-specific derogations are therefore common. As Professor Arrowsmith notes, 'coverage of the GPA is very complex'.[20]

European Communities – Measures Affecting Asbestos and Asbestos-Containing Products, WTO Doc, WT/DS135/R (adopted 5 April 2001) para 99. Beyond this, likeness is determined on a case-by-case basis, taking account of considerations such as the physical characteristics of the products, their end-uses and tariff classification.

[16] The plural 'non-discrimination obligations' is used here because GPA Art IV:1 is formulated as a combined national treatment and most-favoured-Party provision. Under the latter, the focus is on favourable treatment given to the goods, services or suppliers of any Party, rather than to domestic goods, services or suppliers as under national treatment.

[17] GPA Art II:2.

[18] For the list of Parties, see www.wto.org/english/tratop_e/gproc_e/memobs_e.htm (accessed 6 March 2024).

[19] The coverage schedules of each GPA Party may be viewed at www.wto.org/english/tratop_e/gproc_e/gp_app_agree_e.htm (accessed 6 March 2024).

[20] Arrowsmith (n 1) 100.

Whether a particular contract is covered can usually be determined via the relevant annex. However, the question of whether a coverage commitment has been given can also be highly contentious. The only case decided under the Uruguay Round GPA involved alleged violations of the GPA by South Korea.[21] The panel found that South Korea had not committed to coverage of the airport construction contract in question and did not therefore proceed to the alleged GPA breaches.

The interpretation of the derogation is therefore a sensitive matter. If it is interpreted restrictively, such that GATT Article III:4 applies to domestic content requirements in the government procurement, the consequence is that obligations to which only some WTO members have acceded under the GPA, or even obligations to which no GPA Party has acceded, are multilateralised. Put differently, the carefully considered decisions of WTO members on whether to join the GPA at all, and if so, on what contracts should be open to the suppliers of different parties, would be at least undermined if not undone.

IV. Professor Arrowsmith's Treatment of the Article III:8(a) Procurement Derogation

Before coming to the relevant case law, it is helpful to refer to Professor Arrowsmith's treatment of the GATT Article III:8(a) procurement derogation in her book, *Government Procurement in the WTO*.[22] Professor Arrowsmith's eye for detail is evident in this part of the book and throughout. The approach is to anticipate the questions of interpretation raised by the treaty text. As set out over several sections, the provision above raises a number of difficult issues. It is a hallmark of Arrowsmith's work that a preferred interpretation is always identified and defended. I shall not describe the coverage of these issues in the book. My focus is rather on the passage that precedes these issues, in which Arrowsmith sets out what the derogation almost self-evidently excludes from the reach of GATT Article III. Having set out the provision, Arrowsmith continues:

> This clearly excludes from national treatment, procurement measures by the traditional state apparatus – such as federal government departments, and regional and local authorities – where the products concerned are for use in providing non-commercial public services. This covers the vast majority of government procurement. For example, procurements of equipment such as computers and office suppliers [*sic*] for government departments are exempt. Requirements relating to products that are contained in services contracts are also exempt – for example, requirements for products of national origin to be used in the office buildings of government departments, or for private companies providing refuse collection services to use vehicles manufactured domestically.[23]

[21] WT/DS163/R, *Korea – Measures Affecting Government Procurement*, adopted 19 June 2000.
[22] Arrowsmith (n 1).
[23] ibid 50.

It is unlikely that any WTO member, practitioner or legal scholar would be troubled by these examples. As Arrowsmith proceeds to explain, the derogation means that 'most WTO members enjoy substantial freedom to use procurement measures to promote national economic and other objectives'.[24] Only the WTO members who are Parties to the optional GPA undertake to limit their flexibility. It is also important to understand that the examples in the passage above may still apply once a WTO member accedes to the GPA. As explained in section III, the obligations in the GPA, including national treatment, apply only if the contract in question is covered. When the contract is not covered, GPA Parties remain free to favour domestic products.

In light of the Appellate Body's subsequent interpretation of the derogation,[25] the question is whether the examples offered in the book can continue to be accepted as plainly correct. An affirmative answer would, it is submitted, correspond with the expectations of WTO members. Discrimination in government procurement would be generally permitted, other than when the contract in question is covered by the GPA. In contrast, if the Appellate Body's interpretation creates some uncertainty on whether these examples fall under the derogation, this could undermine the plurilateral GPA. There would be less incentive for a WTO member to accede to the GPA, and carefully delineate its contract coverage, if government procurement might already be covered by the multilateral GATT national treatment obligation. To reiterate, the more narrowly the derogation is interpreted, the more likely it becomes that obligations to which only some WTO members have acceded under the GPA, or even obligations to which no GPA Party has acceded, are multilateralised.

V. Contrasting the Panel and Appellate Body Reports

The procurement derogation has been interpreted in three cases, as identified in section I. Given the closeness of these cases in terms of the types of measures involved and the Appellate Body's reasoning, it is sufficient to outline the two cases with Canada as respondent. In *Canada – Renewable Energy/Feed-in Tariff*,[26] the EU and Japan complained of domestic content requirements applicable in the

[24] ibid.

[25] See nn 11–13.

[26] On the subsidy dimension of this case, see L Rubini, '*Ain't Wastin' Time No More*: Subsidies for Renewable Energy, The SCM Agreement, Policy Space, and Law Reform' (2012) 15 *Journal of International Economic Law* 525; A Cosbey and PC Mavroidis 'A Turquoise Mess: Green Subsidies, Blue Industrial Policy and Renewable Energy: The Case for Redrafting the Subsidies Agreement of the WTO' (2014) 17 *Journal of International Economic Law* 11; R Pal, 'Has the Appellate Body's Decision in *Canada – Renewable Energy/Canada – Feed-in Tariff Program* Opened the Door for Production Subsidies?' (2014) 17 *Journal of International Economic Law* 125; I Espa and GM Durán, 'Renewable Energy Subsidies and WTO Law: Time to Rethink the Case for Reform Beyond *Canada – Renewable Energy/Fit Program*' (2018) 21(3) *Journal of International Economic Law* 621.

construction of solar- and wind-power-generation facilities in the Feed-in Tariff Programme (FIT Programme) established by the Ontario Power Authority.[27] Under the FIT Programme, generators of electricity via renewable sources delivered into the Ontarian system were paid a guaranteed price under 20-year or 40-year contracts. The meeting of minimum domestic content levels for energy-generation equipment was among the conditions for being offered a contract. Both Japan and the EU argued that the domestic content requirements breached the GATT Article III:4 national-treatment obligation,[28] on the basis that their energy-generation equipment was being treated less favourably than like products of Ontarian origin.[29] Canada countered that the procurement derogation applied. For Canada, the FIT Programme constituted 'laws and requirements that govern the procurement of renewable electricity for the governmental purpose of securing an electricity supply for Ontario from clean sources, and "not with a view to commercial resale or with a view to use in the production of goods for commercial sale"'.[30] No complaint was brought under the GPA. This would not have been possible, partly because the Ontario Power Authority was not a covered entity under the Uruguay Round GPA.[31]

The panel ultimately found that the derogation was not available because the electricity was purchased 'with a view to commercial resale', by reason of the profit made by the government of Ontario from resale of FIT Programme electricity to consumers, and because the resales were made in competition with licensed electricity retailers.[32] As the derogation was ultimately not available, the domestic content

[27] This body was established under Ontario's Electricity Restructuring Act of 2004 as a government agency responsible for managing Ontario's electricity supply.

[28] GATT Art III:4 provides in relevant part 'The products of the territory of any contracting party imported into the territory of any other contracting party shall be accorded treatment no less favourable than that accorded to like products of national origin in respect of all laws, regulations and requirements affecting their internal sale, offering for sale, purchase, transportation, distribution or use.'

[29] Both complainants argued that there was a 'stand-alone' GATT Art III:4 violation (see WT/DS412//R, *Canada – Certain Measures Affecting the Renewable Energy Generation Sector*, adopted 24 May 2013, paras 3.1–4.3).The complainants also supplemented this claim with an alleged violation of Art 2.1 of the Agreement on Trade-related Investment Measures (TRIMS). The Appellate Body confirmed that the GATT Art III:8(a) procurement derogation applies to measures 'that fall within the scope of Article 2.2 of the TRIMs Agreement and the Illustrative List annexed thereto' (Appellate Body report (n 11) para 5.33). Therefore, if GATT Art III:4 does not apply to a measure by reason of the Art III:8(a) procurement derogation, then Art 2.1 of the TRIMs Agreement also does not apply to this measure.

[30] Appellate Body report (n 11) para 1.10.

[31] Canada's commitments under the Uruguay Round GPA and the Revised GPA at the sub-central (Annex 2) level may be viewed at www.wto.org/english/tratop_e/gproc_e/gp_app_agree_e.htm (accessed 6 March 2024). Notably, a new entity, known as the Integrated Electricity System Operator (IESO) absorbed the old Ontario Power Authority as of January 2015. The IESO falls under the Ontario Ministry of Energy. The Revised GPA covers 'All Ministries of the Province' of Ontario. Therefore, it is reasonably clear that the IESO is now a covered entity. This does not, in itself, mean that FIT contracts are now covered by the GPA. This is because goods or services 'procured with a view to commercial sale or resale' are not covered (Revised GPA, Art II:2).

[32] However, the panel also noted that 'commercial resale' would not always necessarily involve profit, stating that 'loss-making sales can be, and often are, a part of ordinary commercial activity'(Panel

requirement was confirmed as a GATT Article III:4 violation.[33] Of greater significance for this contribution are the panel's earlier findings, which were favourable towards the availability of the derogation, and which were overruled by the Appellate Body. The issue, according to the panel, was whether the challenged measures could be characterised as 'laws regulations or requirements *governing* procurement'.[34] The panel focused on the domestic content requirements, emphasising that this measure compelled the purchase and use of equipment sourced in Ontario 'as a necessary prerequisite for the alleged procurement … to take place'.[35] As there could not be any procurement of electricity without meeting the domestic content requirement, this requirement governed procurement for the purposes of the derogation.

The crucial insight here is that there need not be any connection between the products discriminated against and the products procured in order for the derogation to apply. The products need not be in a competitive relationship, and it is also irrelevant that the products might otherwise be in a close relationship in the sense that electricity cannot be generated, and then procured, without electricity-generating equipment. To illustrate this point using an example not used by the panel, requirements to buy buffalo meat sourced in Ontario as a prerequisite for gaining an electricity-supply contract would still have governed the procurement of electricity. The panel therefore proceeded to dismiss the EU's alternative understanding under which the derogation should be understood as referring only to measures that directly affect a product identical to the product procured.[36] This position is the opposite extreme to that preferred by the panel. While rejecting this understanding, and indeed the need for any degree of similarity between the products at issue, the panel nevertheless noted a 'close relationship' between the products subject to the domestic content requirements (generating equipment) and the product allegedly procured (electricity).[37]

In sum, for the panel, the domestic content requirements were laws 'governing' procurement, indicating the availability of the Article III:8(a) derogation. This was

report (n 29) para 7.151). The Appellate Body seemed to broadly agree with this understanding in elaborating its own view of the 'not with a view to commercial resale' language (Appellate Body Report (n 11) para 5.71). However, it did not apply this aspect of the derogation to the facts. As explained in the main text, the Appellate Body considered the derogation to be unavailable independently of the 'commercial resale' test.

[33] Panel report (n 29) para 7.167.

[34] *Canada – Renewable Energy*, Panel report (n 29) para 7.122.

[35] ibid para 7.124.

[36] ibid para 7.126.

[37] ibid para 7.127. The panel's interpretation has sometimes been understood as being dependent upon the noted 'close relationship'. However, it is reasonably clear that the panel considered that the measure governed procurement independently of this close relationship between electricity and generating equipment. The panel commenced (ibid para. 7.127) by noting that 'the "Minimum Required Domestic Content Level" is a necessary prerequisite for the alleged procurement by the Government of Ontario to take place, and to this extent, we are of the view that such requirements "govern" the alleged procurement'. The subsequent reference to the 'close relationship' is therefore an *obiter dictum*, rather than a condition for the derogation to apply. Hence, it is submitted that the reference to buffalo meat is a correct example of the panel's understanding of the derogation.

on the basis that meeting the domestic content requirements was a condition for any contract award.

In contrast to the panel, the Appellate Body paid particular attention to the phrase 'products purchased' when deciding whether the domestic content requirements governed the procurement. The core idea here was that the derogation had to be understood in relation to the obligations of Article III. The derogation 'becomes relevant only if there is discriminatory treatment of foreign products that are covered by the obligations in Article III, and this discriminatory treatment results from laws, regulations, or requirements governing procurement by governmental agencies of products purchased'.[38] The 'same discriminatory treatment' had to be considered both under Article III and its derogation. It followed that the term 'products purchased' in the derogation was tied to the scope of the 'products' covered by Article III. This led to the conclusion that, for the derogation to apply, 'the product of foreign origin [electricity-generating equipment] must be in a competitive relationship with the product purchased [electricity]'.[39] The competitive relationship encompassed products that were either identical, or like, or directly competitive or substitutable.[40] As there was no competitive relationship, the domestic content requirements were not 'laws, regulations or requirements governing the procurement by governmental agencies' of electricity within the meaning of Article III:8(a).[41] As such, the discrimination relating to generating equipment in the FIT contracts was not covered by the derogation.

VI. Evaluation of the Appellate Body's Interpretation

The Appellate Body's interpretation could be defended on the basis that it pays more attention to context than the panel's interpretation. This, it might be argued, gives effect to the 'General rule of interpretation' in Article 31 of the Vienna Convention on the Law of Treaties,[42] which begins as follows:

> 1. A treaty shall be interpreted in good faith in accordance with the ordinary meaning to be given to the terms of the treaty in their context and in the light of its object and purpose.

The panel, it might be argued, interpreted the derogation in isolation from its immediate context as part of GATT Article III. In contrast, the Appellate Body located the derogation in the context of a provision that prohibits discrimination between like domestic and imported products. In much the same way as Article III:1 informs the interpretation of the more substantive obligations in

[38] *Canada – Renewable Energy*, Appellate Body report (n 11) para 5.63.
[39] ibid para 5.74.
[40] ibid para 5.63.
[41] ibid para 5.79.
[42] Vienna Convention on the Law of Treaties 1155 UNTS 331.

Articles III:2 and III:4,[43] so does Article III:4 inform the interpretation of the Article III:8 derogation.

The problem is that this thinking conceals the conceptual difference between a rule and a derogation from a rule. If a provision establishes a rule, the interpretive challenge is to work out whether the rule has been breached. Parts of Article III establish rules. As outlined, GATT Article III:4 prohibits national treatment-type discrimination in relation to internal regulatory measures. GATT Article III:1 does not itself set out a rule that can be breached independently of GATT Article III:4.[44] However, Article III:1 does provide important interpretive context as a general statement about what is prohibited within the more substantive paragraphs, such as Article III:4.[45] The two provisions can naturally be grouped together.

In contrast, the interpretive challenge with a derogation is not to work out whether a rule has been breached, but rather to work out whether the rule applies at all. In principle, this is a question that can be asked and answered without a definitive answer on whether the relevant rule has been breached. A conclusion to the effect that the rule may or may not have been breached, but that this does not matter because the derogation is available, is, it is submitted, coherent.[46] It only becomes strictly necessary to decide whether the rule is breached if it is first decided that the derogation is not available.[47] This suggests that derogations can

[43] The Appellate Body has explored the relationship between the different paragraphs of Art III in several cases, including WT/DS8, 10, 11/AB/R *Japan – Taxes on Alcoholic Beverages*, 17–18; and WT/DS135/AB/R *European Communities – Measures Affecting Asbestos and Asbestos Containing Products*, paras 97–98.

[44] Panel report WT/DS2/R *United States – Standards for Reformulated and Conventional Gasoline*, adopted 20 May 1996, para 6.17.

[45] 'Article III:1 articulates a general principle that internal measures should not be applied so as to afford protection to domestic production. This general principle informs the rest of Article III. The purpose of Article III:1 is to establish this general principle as a guide to understanding and interpreting the specific obligations contained in Article III:2 and in the other paragraphs of Article III, while respecting, and not diminishing in any way, the meaning of the words actually used in the texts of those other paragraphs.' *Japan – Alcoholic Beverage* (n 43) 18.

[46] This is not to suggest that a panel should leave unaddressed the question of whether a measure potentially covered by a derogation to a rule breaches that rule. Even if a panel is confident that a derogation is available, it should proceed on the basis that it could be wrong and address whether the rule has been breached. A failure to do so would increase the burden for the Appellate Body were it to decide that a derogation is not available. The panel report would lack the factual and legal findings on the question of whether a rule has been breached, thereby making it more difficult for the Appellate Body to complete the analysis. Conversely, if a panel were to decide that a derogation is not available, and were the Appellate Body to overrule this, the Appellate Body's analysis could end at this point without in any way being incomplete. There would be no strict need for the Appellate Body to review the panel's findings on the compatibility of a measure with a rule that does not apply.

[47] Readers who consider this proposition to be incorrect will probably have mind GATT Art XX. This provision is entitled 'General Exceptions'. It provides an affirmative defence against established violations of other GATT provisions. It is not possible to apply Art XX without first having established a violation of another provision. For one reason, the Appellate Body has found that 'the aspects of a measure to be justified under the subparagraphs of Article XX are those that give rise to the finding of inconsistency under the GATT'. WT/DS400, 401/AB/R *European Communities – Measures Prohibiting Importation and Marketing of Seal Products*, adopted 18 June 2014, para 5.185. In contrast, there is no conceptual difficulty in applying the procurement derogation as the first analytical step to decide whether GATT Art III applies.

be interpreted independently from the rule to which the derogation pertains. Put differently, GATT Article III:1 and III:4 provide natural interpretive context for each other. Both provisions speak to what is prohibited. In contrast, these two provisions do not provide natural interpretive context for the Article III:8 derogation, which speaks to whether the prohibition applies at all.

It might be argued in response that the proposed distinction between whether a rule applies at all and whether it has been breached is illusory or merely semantics. If, under Article III:4, the domestic and imported products are not like, the provision is not breached. Interchangeably, it might be argued, we could say that the provision does not apply when the products are not like. But which phrase better captures what has happened in the legal analysis? The likeness analysis, which is usually contentious in possible cases of *de facto* discrimination, has occurred in the context of a provision that applies. The provision applies because of an earlier finding that there is no available derogation. Upon applying the provision, the outcome is that it has not been breached. It is therefore submitted that there is nothing strained or artificial about the proposed distinction.

Based on this distinction, the Appellate Body's starting point for its interpretation can be questioned. The derogation, according to the Appellate Body, 'becomes relevant only if there is discriminatory treatment of foreign products that are covered by the obligations in Article III'.[48] It is more accurate to state that it becomes relevant whenever a respondent state invokes it to establish that Article III does not apply. The availability of the derogation can be determined without knowing whether there is any discrimination against foreign products.

What might need to be conceded, however, is the potential for overlap between the analysis of whether the provision applies at all and whether it has been breached. In principle, these are separate questions. However, if the derogation contains terms that repeat those in the rule to which the derogation pertains, overlap would reasonably be expected. Thus, if the Article III:8 contained the phrase 'like products', or some other phrase indicating a comparator element, it would be natural for the interpreter to engage with this concept.

Of course, the derogation does not refer to 'like products' and it does not otherwise contain any explicit instruction that it might require a likeness analysis. As indicated in *Canada – Renewable Energy*, the Appellate Body nevertheless interpreted the derogation as requiring a comparator element. This was achieved by noting the phrase 'products purchased' in the derogation, and determining that the scope of this phrase was tied to the scope of products covered by the preceding paragraphs of Article III – that is products that are identical, like or directly competitive or substitutable. It is submitted that this is a thin textual and contextual basis to incorporate a comparator element into the derogation. It amounts to little more than an assertion that the derogation has a comparator element, because other parts of Article III require this assessment. This can be challenged by asking why some parts of Article III explicitly require this assessment. The

[48] *Canada – Renewable Energy* (n 11) para 5.63.

purpose of the likeness analysis is to reveal whether or not there is discrimination. As already explained, this is uncontentious when the domestic and imported products being compared are practically identical, but increasingly contentious the more the products can be distinguished. The nature and extent of the actual or potential competitive relationship between the products must then be considered. But the key point is that the purpose of this exercise is to reveal whether there is *de facto* discrimination between non-identical products. In contrast, the derogation is not about whether there is discrimination; it is rather about whether the prohibition against discrimination applies at all. This is a question that can be asked and answered without a definitive answer on whether there is discrimination. In sum, it seems incongruous for the availability of a carve-out from an obligation to be conditioned on a test the purpose of which is to reveal whether the obligation itself has been breached.

The Appellate Body's interpretation of the derogation can also be challenged from another angle. As already referred to, and to provide the full sentence here, the Appellate Body considered:

> Because Article III:8(a) is a derogation from the obligations contained in other paragraphs of Article III, we consider that *the same discriminatory treatment* must be considered both with respect to the obligations of Article III and with respect to the derogation of Article III:8(a).[49]

The problem here is that the Appellate Body did not follow its idea of considering the 'same discriminatory treatment' under Article III and its derogation. The discrimination under GATT Article III:4 is in relation to domestic versus foreign electricity-generating equipment. These are clearly like products, and the requirement to use the domestic product amounts to a *de jure* violation – one which is indisputable from the face of the measure. Considering the same discrimination under the derogation would involve the same two products, and the derogation would then be available based on the competitive relationship between these products. Under the derogation, however, there is clearly a shift by the Appellate Body from domestic versus foreign generating equipment to generating equipment versus electricity. Moreover, if the last two products were compared under Article III:4, there would be no violation and no derogation would be required. Therefore, had the analysis actually been about the 'same discriminatory treatment', there would have been two possible outcomes. Either the competitive relationship test would have been satisfied under the derogation, or there would have been no GATT Article III:4 violation for which a derogation would be required.

Thus far, two problems have been explained. First, as a matter of treaty interpretation, it is difficult to accept that the availability of a derogation can turn upon a concept (likeness) that is not explicitly or implicitly referred to in the derogation itself, and the purpose of which is to reveal whether a rule has been breached rather than whether the rule applies at all. Second, if it is nevertheless accepted that

[49] ibid para 5.63 (emphasis added).

the derogation incorporates a comparator element, and upon working through the Appellate Body's own explicit explanation of how it works, the outcome is either than the derogation is available or that it is not required. It is only because the Appellate Body did *not* follow its own explanation around 'the same discriminatory treatment' that it arrived at the conclusion that the derogation was not available.

VII. Implications of the Appellate Body's Interpretation for a Different Scenario

From *Canada – Renewable Energy* it is known that if a WTO member were to procure electricity, it is not permissible to require the use of domestically produced electricity-generating equipment. The procurement derogation is not available because there is no competitive relationship between electricity (the product purchased) and generating equipment (the product discriminated against). It follows that GATT Article III:4 applies. This provision is clearly breached on a *de jure* basis. Imported generating equipment is treated less favourably than domestic equipment and these are like products. The analysis in section VI has questioned the introduction of a likeness or comparator element into the derogation.

This section proceeds to consider the implications of this interpretation for a different scenario. Specifically, would the derogation apply to the procurement of electric vehicles, subject to the use of domestic batteries? At first glance, the derogation might not be available. There is no competitive relationship between electric vehicles (the product purchased) and batteries (the product discriminated against). However, this answer perhaps misidentifies either the product that is purchased or the product that is discriminated against.

The batteries are being purchased as part of the electric vehicles. Imported batteries are also being discriminated against. If this is the correct understanding, the competitive relationship test is satisfied and the derogation would be available. The batteries here can at least be distinguished from generating equipment, in that the government takes possession of the batteries and will gain a proprietary interest in relation to them. However, it can be questioned how much weight should be given to possession and proprietary interest here. While the government will not gain any proprietary interest in the generating equipment, it will pay for it over time through its purchase of electricity. This is analogous to paying for the batteries via the purchase of the electric vehicle. There is also the problem that it is more natural to think of what is being purchased as the finished product of an electric vehicle, rather than all of its separate components.[50]

[50] Canada argued to this effect in the NAFTA Chapter 11 claim challenging the same Canadian measures at issue in the *Canada – Renewable Energy/Feed-in Tariff* WTO dispute (nn 11 and 12). With reference to a previous case, Canada noted that 'the state of Virginia was not procuring steel, and it certainly was not procuring the process by which steel was manufactured; it was procuring the construction of a highway interchange'. *Mesa Power v Canada*, Canada's Rejoinder on the Merits, 2 July 2014, para 77 at https://pca-cpa.org/en/cases/51/ (accessed 6 March 2024).

This problem of artificial thinking is merely moved, rather than solved, if the product purchased is identified as electric vehicles. It might be argued that imported electric vehicles are being discriminated against via the discrimination against foreign batteries. This again achieves a match between the product purchased and the product discriminated against – both electric vehicles. But why is it realistic to equate the discrimination against foreign batteries with discrimination against foreign electric vehicles as a whole? This is only realistic because the battery contributes a high proportion of the overall value. Of course, this invites us to identify the point at which the equation would no longer be realistic. Are foreign electric vehicles as a finished product discriminated against when domestic windshields must be used? What about indicator stalks or the valves through which the tyres are inflated? In all the examples, including the battery, the contracts could be fulfilled with electric vehicles of entirely foreign origin other than the component that must of domestic origin. It would most naturally be stated here that the equivalent foreign component is being discriminated against, in the context of procuring vehicles as a finished product. As the component and electric vehicles are not in a competitive relationship, the derogation is not available, and the discrimination is prohibited by GATT Article III:4.

This would be an extraordinary outcome. The derogation surely ought to cover the discrimination in the examples provided. Yet with the Appellate Body's competitive relationship test, the application of the derogation can only be secured via artificial thinking, either about what is purchased or about what is discriminated against.

That the derogation must be available in the examples (notwithstanding the artificial thinking) is revealed by increasing the level of discrimination. Suppose that the government specifies that it will only purchase wholly domestically produced electric vehicles. As this single product is both the product purchased and the product discriminated against, the competitive relationship test is satisfied and the derogation would be available. It would be paradoxical if the derogation covered the higher level of discrimination in this example but not the lesser level of discrimination in the requirement to use domestic batteries, or the other components referred to. This would amount to a perverse incentive to avoid GATT Article III by completely shutting out foreign products and their components. Put differently, the derogation would be rendered inutile if it did not cover total discrimination against foreign vehicles. As it covers this discrimination, it must also cover the lesser discrimination against foreign components. However, to reiterate and emphasise, the required outcome can only be achieved via artificial thinking. In a procurement of electric vehicles subject to the use of domestic valves, the discrimination against foreign valves must be equated with discrimination against foreign electric vehicles as finished products in order for the derogation to be available.

It can therefore be seen that the competitive relationship test produces a definite outcome without any artificial thinking in the type of situation present in the cases; that is, where the government does not, in any direct sense, purchase the product (generating equipment) that is discriminated against.

In a procurement of electricity subject to the use of domestic generating equipment, the derogation is not available because of the absence of a competitive relationship between electricity and generating equipment. In contrast, it is more difficult to apply the competitive relationship test when the government does purchase the product that is discriminated against. In a procurement of electric vehicles subject to the use of domestic batteries (or any other component), the derogation must be available. Were it not available to cover discrimination against foreign valves, it would also not be available to cover complete discrimination against foreign electric vehicles. The derogation would be rendered inutile. The problem is that discrimination against foreign valves is only covered by the derogation if this discrimination is equated with discrimination against foreign electric vehicles as a whole. This is quite a stretch, and leads to the question of whether the Appellate Body offered any indication of how it might apply the derogation to a procurement of electric vehicles subject to the use of domestic batteries or other components. The following passage may be considered:

> We have found above that, under Article III:8(a), the product purchased by way of procurement must necessarily be 'like', or 'directly competitive' with or 'substitutable' for – in other words, in a 'competitive relationship' with – the foreign product subject to discrimination. Although a consideration of inputs and processes of production may inform the question of whether the product purchased is in a competitive relationship with the product being discriminated against, it does not displace the competitive relationship standard. The question of whether the cover of Article III:8(a) may also extend to discrimination relating to inputs and processes of production used in respect of products purchased arises only after the product purchased has been found to be in a competitive relationship with the product subject to discrimination.[51]

There are two references here to 'inputs and processes of production'. This raises the question of whether batteries and other components are 'inputs' for electric vehicles. However, does the answer to this question have any bearing on the availability of the derogation under the current scenario – a procurement of electric vehicles subject to the use of domestic batteries? The answer is no if we adopt the most natural understanding of what is being purchased and what is being discriminated against – respectively, electric vehicles and foreign batteries. These two products are not in a competitive relationship. This is not a situation in which 'a consideration of inputs', 'may inform' the competitive relationship. Electric vehicles contain batteries, but the two products do not have similar end uses. Under the extract reproduced above, this means that the derogation is not available. The analysis ends here, without any consideration of 'inputs'.

Conversely, the consideration of inputs *might* be relevant if the competitive relationship test is satisfied (as above) by changing the identification of the product

[51] *Canada – Renewable* Energy (n 11) para 5.40.

discriminated against to foreign electric vehicles. This would satisfy the competitive relationship test. However, the extract above now presents legal uncertainty. As the competitive relationship test has been satisfied, should it be concluded that the derogation is available without any consideration of inputs? Or is the further question whether 'the cover of Article III:8(a) may also extend to discrimination relating to inputs and processes of production used in respect of products purchased'?

It would be rather odd here for batteries to be regarded as 'inputs'. This is because the competitive relationship test has been satisfied by identifying the product discriminated against as imported electric vehicles, rather than the specific component targeted for discrimination. It would be odd to take this artificial step only to revert to the specific component as an input under a subsequent stage of the analysis. Perhaps, more generally, the battery is not an input at all. Perhaps the Appellate Body had in mind inputs that are consumed in a production process, rather than components capable of being installed and removed. These consumed inputs might be physically incorporated, such as grapes for wine, or not physically incorporated, such as electricity consumed by a factory. Without any examples from the Appellate Body, it is difficult to know.

Working through the electricity example involves layers of uncertainty. Suppose that the procurement is for electric vehicles subject to the use of domestic electricity in the manufacturing process. The product purchased here is clearly electric vehicles, but is the product discriminated against foreign electricity or foreign electric vehicles? If the former, the derogation is not available, because the competitive relationship test is not satisfied. It the latter, the competitive relationship test is satisfied, but is the derogation now available, or is there the further question of whether the derogation extends to discrimination against foreign electricity as an input?

VIII. Revisiting Areas of Legal Certainty and Uncertainty

This is a good point to revisit the areas of legal certainty and uncertainty. If a government specifies that it will purchase electricity subject to the use of domestic generating equipment, the procurement derogation does not apply. This is based on the lack of a competitive relationship between electricity and generating equipment. As a matter of treaty interpretation, it is difficult to see how the competitive relationship test belongs under the derogation. However, the test at least produces a definite outcome for these products, because there is no suggestion that the government is purchasing generating equipment in any direct sense. The test is more difficult to apply to the main example in this chapter – the purchase of electric vehicles subject to the use of domestic batteries. The difficulty stems from the difference that the government is here, in a direct sense, purchasing the batteries.

There is legal uncertainty about what product is purchased and what product is discriminated against. We would most naturally say that electric vehicles are being purchased and that foreign batteries are being discriminated against. However, this would prevent the application of the derogation. This cannot be the correct outcome. As the derogation is unequivocally available to cover total discrimination against foreign electric vehicles, it must also be available to cover the lesser discrimination against foreign batteries. The availability of the derogation for the lesser discrimination can be secured via identity between the product purchased (electric vehicles) and the product discriminated against (foreign electric vehicles). However, this involves an artificial identification of the product discriminated against; a point that becomes obvious when batteries are substituted with valves. It is regrettable that overall coherence as between the greater and lesser levels of discrimination can only be achieved via the artificial identification of the products. Even when this is done, there is possibly the further question of whether the derogation covers discrimination against inputs.

IX. Conclusion

It is difficult to accept that there should be a competitive relationship test in the GATT Article III:8(a) procurement derogation. This test is the essence of the likeness analysis or comparator element under the rules within Article III that can be breached. However, the derogation is not among the rules that can be breached. It is rather about whether the rule applies at all. The Appellate Body has conditioned the availability of a derogation from a rule, on a test the purpose of which is to reveal whether the rule has been breached. The Appellate Body has also not clearly explained the parameters of this test. The report advises that 'the same discrimination' must be considered under Article III and its derogation. However, the Appellate Body did not actually do this. Had it done so, then either the competitive relationship test in the derogation would have been satisfied or there would have been no Article III breach for which the derogation would be required. In sum, the presence and explanation of the competitive relationship test in the derogation lack a clear and coherent basis.

As applied in the WTO cases to date, the competitive relationship test would not be satisfied in the procurement of electricity subject to the use of domestic electricity-generating equipment. As such, the *de jure* discrimination here is prohibited by GATT Article III:4. In this fact pattern, GATT Article III has been strengthened. This is unlikely to be consistent with the expectations of WTO members to the effect that discrimination in government procurement is permitted other than when the contract in question is covered by the plurilateral GPA.

The competitive relationship test also results in legal uncertainty for other scenarios. According to the Appellate Body, the test must always be applied without exception under the derogation. There must be a competitive relationship between the product purchased and the product discriminated against. This test is not obviously satisfied in the procurement of electric vehicles subject to the use of domestic batteries and other lesser components. The chapter has argued that the derogation must be available in this situation, but that this can only be achieved via the artificial identification of the product discriminated against as foreign electric vehicles, rather than just their batteries or other identified components. Without this thinking, the derogation would not apply. In turn, this would call into question whether it would even apply to cover more pronounced discrimination were the government to specify that it will purchase only wholly domestically produced electric vehicles.

Given these criticisms, it is advised that a future embodiment of the/an Appellate Body should affirm the panel's interpretation of the derogation. It is recalled that, under this approach, discriminatory domestic content requirements can be regarded as 'governing procurement' when their fulfilment is a 'necessary prerequisite' for the procurement to take place. This applies notwithstanding the absence of a competitive relationship between the product discriminated against and the product procured, and even if the two products are completely unrelated. This test is straightforward to understand and apply. It does not raise any problems of coherence, nor lack of legal certainty. Moreover, it is entirely consistent with the treaty language to find that a measure governs procurement when the contract cannot be awarded unless domestic content requirements are fulfilled. While the panel's interpretation expands the scope of the derogation, its availability does not depend solely on whether the measure governs procurement. Furthermore, when the derogation applies, the discrimination does not fall into a legal vacuum. While GATT Article III:4 will not apply, the GPA may apply depending on contract coverage; a matter that is the subject of hard-fought concessions.

The Appellate Body ceased to function in December 2019, having lost its quorum after sustained blocking of (re)appointments by the US. Part of the background here is the perception of overreach in the interpretation of treaty norms, whether through the narrowing of exceptions and derogations or overly expansive understandings of the trade remedy agreements that strike down the preferred methodologies of national authorities. It is alleged that policy space, and the exit options offered by trade remedies, have been excessively curtailed.

Of course, claims of judicial overreach must be carefully and individually evaluated, including the criteria applied to reach a conclusion. This chapter has sought to identify and substantiate an example of overreach that, contrary to WTO rules, adds to the obligations of the members.[52] GATT Article III has been strengthened using questionable legal reasoning, which results in pronounced legal uncertainty. Readers will have their own views on the separate matter of whether the decisions are sensible as a matter of policy; the question is whether the response to climate

[52] Dispute Settlement Understanding, Art 3:2 Recommendations and rulings of the DSB cannot add to or diminish the rights and obligations provided in the covered agreements.

change is helped or hindered by limiting the scope for governments to favour domestically produced energy-generating equipment.

Naturally, the Appellate Body's demise is generating a significant body of commentary.[53] One of the recommendations is to reinvigorate political oversight of the dispute-settlement process via informal authoritative interpretations formulated during special sessions of the Dispute Settlement Body (DSB).[54] Of course, WTO members have always been able to express views on panel and Appellate Body reports in the regular DSB meetings at which reports are adopted under the negative consensus rule. One of Canada's comments in the meeting during which *Canada – Renewable Energy* was considered is noteworthy:

> Canada was surprised by the manner in which the Appellate Body had arrived at the finding that Article III:8(a) applied to the purchase of a product that competed with the product against which discrimination was alleged. None of the parties had made submissions on such an interpretation of Article III:8(a). Nor had any questions been put to the parties regarding such an interpretation. As a result, the parties had not had the opportunity to address this particular issue, which formed the crux of the conclusions in respect of Canada's obligations under the GATT 1994 and the TRIMs Agreement.[55]

This is perhaps a cautionary statement is relation to how to minimise the risk of overreach. This problem was not corrected in *India – Solar Cells*.[56] The Appellate Body considered that India had not argued that there were 'cogent reasons' for the panel to depart from previous Appellate Body findings on the same legal issue, and had not argued that the competitive relationship test should be set aside. It had rather sought, unsuccessfully, to distinguish fact patterns from *Canada – Renewable Energy* that were materially identical.[57]

When assessing claims of overreach, it is equally important to consider views from the other side – successful claimant members. If they too express reservations, this strengthens the claim of overreach. However, such a claim can also be objectively substantiated when complainants express their approval. In the DSB during which *India – Solar Cells* was considered, the US noted that 'discriminatory policies in the clean energy sector – such as India's domestic content requirements – undermined efforts to promote the generation of clean energy by requiring the

[53] GC Shaffer, 'A Tragedy in the Making?: The Decline of Law and the Return of Power in International Trade Relations' (2019) 43 *Yale Journal of International Law* 37; T Cottier, 'Recalibrating the WTO Dispute Settlement System: Towards New Standards of Appellate Review' (2021) 24 *Journal of International Economic Law* 1; E-U Petersmann, 'Between "Member-Driven" WTO Governance and "Constitutional Justice": Judicial Dilemmas in GATT/WTO Dispute Settlement' (2018) 21 *Journal of International Economic Law* 103; O Suttle, 'Rules and values in international adjudication: the case of the WTO Appellate Body' (2018) 68(2) *ICLQ* 399.

[54] CD Creamer, 'From the WTO's Crown Jewel To Its Crown Of Thorns' (2019) 113 *AJIL Unbound* 51, 54.

[55] WT/DSB/M/332, 24 May 2013, para 8.4.

[56] *India – Solar Cells* (n 13).

[57] ibid para 5.39.

use of more expensive and less efficient equipment'.[58] The weight accorded to such a statement depends, in some measure, on the extent to which a member abides by it. The most recent renewable energy case at the WTO involved a successful challenge by India against local content requirements embedded in US State government measures.[59] The case did not have a procurement dimension but is a further illustration of the connection between clean energy measures and local content requirements.[60] If and when the Appellate Body is reconstituted, it is perhaps just a matter of time before the opportunity arises to revisit the procurement derogation.

[58] WT/DSB/M/386, 14 October 2016, para 1.3.

[59] WT/DS510/R, *United States – Certain Measures Relating to the Renewable Energy Sector*, Final Report Circulated 27 June 2019.

[60] It is becoming increasingly apparent that local content requirements associated with clean energy measures are not compatible with WTO law, whether this involves the procurement derogation, the Agreement on Subsidies and Countervailing Measures or possible justification under GATT Art XX. Whether this is a realistic position in terms of what WTO members will accept, and whether this position helps or hinders responses to climate change, is an important theme of the literature: Rubini (n 26) 530, 551, 568, 569; Cosbey and Mavroidis (n 26) 29–33; T Meyer, 'A Political Theory of Legal Exceptions' Vanderbilt University Law School, Legal Studies Research Paper Series, Working Paper No 21-18.

15

Sue Arrowsmith and the Reform of the UNCITRAL Model Law on Public Procurement: An Appreciation

CAROLINE NICHOLAS AND CHRISTOPHER YUKINS

I. The History of the UNCITRAL Model Law in Public Procurement Reform

The UNCITRAL Model Law on the Procurement of Goods, Construction and Services was adopted in 1994.[1] Sue Arrowsmith was an early user of the text, as she records in the 'Introduction' to *Reform of the UNCITRAL Model Law on Procurement: Public Procurement Regulation in the 21st Century*.[2] Indeed, as soon as it was adopted, Arrowsmith based her then undergraduate module on international public procurement on the 1994 Model Law and its accompanying Guide to Enactment,[3] later based her subsequent postgraduate modules around its provisions and those of the 2011 UNCITRAL Model Law on Public Procurement, and has used these texts as reference tools in her own consultancy work. As this chapter explains, through her scholarship and her work around the globe, Arrowsmith has played a significant role in the success of the UNCITRAL Model Laws, and in reforming public procurement laws and driving up standards in over 30 countries.[4]

[1] For ease of reference, this chapter will generally use the term 'Model Law' to refer to the current 2011 text and 'the 1994 Model Law' to refer to its earlier iteration.

[2] S Arrowsmith (ed), *Reform of the UNCITRAL Model Law on Procurement: Public Procurement Regulation in the 21st Century* (West, 2009). The book considered then ongoing reforms of the UNCITRAL Model Law on Procurement of Goods, Construction and Services (1994), which led to the UNCITRAL Model Law on Public Procurement (2011).

[3] Each iteration of the Model Law is accompanied by a Guide to Enactment, which contains a detailed explanation of the policy objectives reflected in the text, how to use its provisions, commentary on individual articles, and recommendations for additional regulations, guidance and institutions to support the effective use of the Model Law in practice.

[4] See at https://uncitral.un.org/en/texts/procurement/modellaw/public_procurement/status (accessed 31 October 2022). For the remainder of this chapter, references to the Model Law are to the 2011 text, unless otherwise indicated.

A. Iterations of the Model Law

The first UNCITRAL text on procurement was the UNCITRAL Model Law on Procurement of Goods and Construction (1993). It was superseded by the 1994 Model Law, which added provisions on services and which, as Arrowsmith has noted, was 'one of the most successful of UNCITRAL's instruments … and has been used in numerous states worldwide as the basis for legal reform'.[5] After an eight-year review process, UNCITRAL adopted the Model Law on Public Procurement in 2011, and in 2012 its accompanying Guide to Enactment.

B. Notion of the UNCITRAL Model Law as a Tool of Harmonisation and International Private Law and of Economic and Social Development

The Model Law is an example of an international 'private law' instrument issued by the United Nations Commission on International Trade Law (UNCITRAL). These instruments, which may take the form of Conventions, Model Laws, Legislative Guides or contractual texts, are 'international' in the sense that they provide rules for countries to use in their domestic law. They are 'private law' instruments in that they address business-to-business or business-to-government commercial relations, rather than state-to-state relations (as, for example, the World Trade Organization's (WTO's) agreements do).[6] UNCITRAL texts are also *non-binding* instruments in the sense that no state or other entity is bound to use them; adoption and implementation are entirely voluntary. Having a champion attesting to their quality, as UNCITRAL's procurement instruments were fortunate enough to do, is a critical success factor, and a champion with Arrowsmith's considerable reputation was arguably the critical success factor.

The Guide to Enactment of the 1994 Model Law explains the importance of this instrument: it comments that for developing and transition countries, much 'procurement is in connection with projects that are part of the essential process of economic and social development'.[7] In addition, harmonising public procurement laws could help reduce obstacles to international trade and, thus, enhance 'the extent to which Governments [could] access the competitive price and quality benefits available through procurement on an international basis', and could allow suppliers and contractors to access commercial opportunities beyond their

[5] Arrowsmith (n 2) Preface.

[6] Nonetheless, it should be noted that governments in many common law systems contract in the same capacity as private commercial entities, and so procurement contracts are also private law contracts at the national level, whereas, in other mainly civil law systems, the contracts are governed by public administrative law.

[7] Guide to Enactment of the 1994 Model Law, 'Introduction', para 3. This reflects the Preamble to the United Nations Charter (1945), which states that the Organisation 'will employ international machinery for the promotion of the economic and social advancement of all peoples'.

domestic markets, activities that were then 'hampered by the inadequate or divergent state of national procurement legislation in many countries'.[8] Improving standards continues to be at the core of UNCITRAL's public procurement reforms, given procurement's importance to sustainable development. 'Inadequacy' is nowadays (rather less diplomatically) discussed in terms of fraud, corruption and waste of resources.

The Model Law is often referred to as a 'harmonisation' text. 'Harmonisation' in the UNCITRAL context refers to a 'process through which domestic laws may be modified to enhance predictability in cross-border commercial transactions',[9] through reducing divergences rather than imposing detailed legislative rules. Arrowsmith has long recognised an ongoing process of convergence in the public procurement context, saying that the 'formal rules on procurement procedures considered appropriate for opening international markets are similar to those often adopted to implement national objectives of value for money and probity. One consequence is that [these] parallel developments … have to a certain degree supported and reinforced each other.'[10] Indeed, through parallel reform programmes in the WTO and UNCITRAL in the 2000s and 2010s, and information-sharing between these institutions, the WTO's Agreement on Government Procurement (WTO GPA)[11] and the Model Law both seek to encourage greater cross-border procurement trade in practice through the convergence of rules at the national level, preventing discrimination against overseas suppliers and highly similar procedures.[12]

Nonetheless, the harmonisation objective is not designed to generate identical procurement laws, let alone systems, all over the world, but to lead to systems based on the same principles, with similar desired outcomes.[13] Although the Model Law provides a template for a national procurement law, it is a 'framework law', intended to be complemented by more detailed regulations, rules and guidance, and supported by suitably-resourced institutions.[14] The Guide to Enactment to the 2011 Model Law notes that the Model Law provides significant flexibility

[8] ibid para 4.

[9] See at http://www.uncitral.org/uncitral/en/about_us.html.

[10] S Arrowsmith, J Linarelli and D Wallace Jr, *Regulating Public Procurement: National and International Perspectives* (Kluwer Law International, 2000) 233; see also S Arrowsmith, 'The Past and Future Evolution of EC Procurement Law: From Framework to Common Code?' (2006) 35 *Public Contract Law Journal* 337.

[11] The current version of the GPA was adopted in 2012 and is available at www.wto.org/english/tratop_e/gproc_e/gpa_1994_e.htm.

[12] C Nicholas, 'UNCITRAL and the Internationalisation of Government Procurement Regulation' in AC Georgopulos, B Hoekman and PC Mavroidis (eds), *The Internationalisation of Government Procurement Regulation* (Oxford University Press, 2017) ch 3.

[13] See D Gordon, 'Anti-Corruption Internationally: Challenges In Procurement Markets Abroad – Part II: The Path Forward for Using Procurement Law to Help with Development and the Fight Against Corruption' paper delivered at West Government Contracts Year in Review Conference Covering 2012 (Thomson Reuters, 2013) at http://scholarship.law.gwu.edu/cgi/viewcontent.cgi?article=1329&context=faculty_publications.

[14] See the Guide to Enactment, section entitled 'The Model Law as a "framework" law: elements of a procurement system' paras 58 et seq.

as regards the manner in which its provisions might be implemented to suit local circumstances.[15] Early experience with the Model Law indicated that there were differences in the way countries were using its provisions. Legal reform in public procurement in the countries of operation of the European Bank for Reconstruction and Development (EBRD) and in the Caribbean region follow the Model Law,[16] and similar efforts are underway elsewhere.[17] In Africa, by contrast, the more innovative provisions and electronic tools, including framework agreements, have been less used (perhaps reflecting capacity considerations).[18] On the other hand, in Latin America, extensive use has been made of these very provisions, despite the fact that the procurement laws in those countries are not otherwise closely based on the Model Law.[19] This varied approach accords with commentary that the UNCITRAL process is an iterative one towards 'unification over time';[20] and even if 'the world procurement market is evolving toward a unified, open model' and to 'a common procurement market, based on common instruments', it may be at least a generation away.[21]

II. Influence of the UNCITRAL Model Law in its Various Iterations

In a Note to UNCITRAL in 2003, the UNCITRAL Secretariat highlighted that the use of the 1994 Model Law had 'resulted in widespread harmonisation of procurement rules and procedures';[22] the World Bank and other international donors' use of the text in their own programmes had extended its influence to far beyond the numbers of countries declaring their procurement laws to be based on the Model Law.[23] Even though the World Bank and other international

[15] See, eg, Guide to Enactment, Part II, commentary to Chapter VIII, 'Challenge proceedings', 268 ff.

[16] ibid. See also at http://uk.practicallaw.com/4-573-7465?source=relatedcontent.

[17] Notably under the EBRD–UNCITRAL Initiative. See at www.ppi-ebrd-uncitral.com/ (accessed 4 March 2024).

[18] See, eg, E Caborn and S Arrowsmith, 'Procurement methods in the public procurement systems of Africa' in G Quinot and S Arrowsmith (eds), *Public Procurement Regulation in Africa* (Cambridge University Press, 2013) ch 12, 267–68.

[19] See at www.sela.org/attach/258/EDOCS/SRed/2014/09/T023600006062-0-Di_11_Compras_publicas.pdf and www.slideshare.net/denirose/03-javier-davilamexicosubastasjdp (Spanish language texts). This may reflect that UNCITRAL is the first international legal text on public procurement to address framework agreements in detail.

[20] S Block-Lieb and T Halliday, 'Harmonization and Modernization in UNCITRAL's Legislative Guide on Insolvency Law' (2007) 42 *Texas International Law Journal* 475.

[21] S Schooner and C Yukins, 'Incrementalism: eroding the impediments to a global public procurement market' (2007) 23 *Georgetown Journal of International Law* 529.

[22] Note by the Secretariat: Current activities of international organizations in the area of public procurement: possible future work, A/CN.9/539, at https://undocs.org/en/A/CN.9/539; and A/CN/9/539/Add.1 at https://undocs.org/en/A/CN.9/539/Add.1, para 2 (accessed 31 October 2022).

[23] See, eg, R Hunja, 'The UNCITRAL Model Law on Procurement of Goods, Construction and Services and its Impact on Procurement Reform' in S Arrowsmith and A Davies (eds), *Public*

financial institutions (IFIs) had rejected elements of the 1994 Model Law (such as simultaneous negotiations and the use of 'standardised trade terms' in descriptions and contract terms),[24] its procedures determined to a significant extent what they accepted as good practice.[25]

The 2011 iteration, over a dozen years old at the time of writing, has also had a significant influence, which should again be assessed not just in terms of numbers of users, but also for the influence of the UNCITRAL negotiation process on contemporaneous and subsequent reforms in the WTO, the European Union (EU) and in the World Bank and other IFIs. Indeed, this influence went both ways: provisions in the texts of these other bodies reflect both the deliberations in UNCITRAL during the reform process and the eventual instrument.[26]

This influence reflects the success of the Model Law in operating as a harmonisation text. A first aspect of harmonisation is that the Model Law's provisions must be able to work everywhere. Accordingly, they must (and do) contain tools suitable for and acceptable in all countries, reflect international standards and shared challenges, practice from all regions, and accommodate different economic, legal and administrative systems, capacity levels and levels of development. To this end, UNCITRAL's texts are developed through an inclusive and multilingual intergovernmental process, which is explained in more detail in section IV.A, but the upshot is that its tools achieve these objectives, without compromising the quality of the tools themselves. As the Guide to Enactment emphasises, the Model Law was not 'designed with any particular groups of countries or particular state of development in mind, and … it does not promote the experience in or approach of any one region',[27] and it was intended to be 'flexibly implemented to accord with local circumstances, while preserving the desired outcomes'.[28]

Procurement: Global Revolution (Kluwer Law International, 1999) ch 5; Arrowsmith, Linarelli and Wallace (n 10); and S Arrowsmith, 'Public Procurement: An Appraisal of the UNCITRAL Model Law as a Global Standard' (2004) 53 *International & Comparative Law Quarterly* 17.

[24] UNCITRAL, *Yearbook: Volume XXV: 1994* (1994) UN Doc A/CN.9/SER.A/1994, 361, para 64 at https://uncitral.un.org/sites/uncitral.un.org/files/media-documents/uncitral/en/yb_1994e.pdf (accessed 31 October 2022).

[25] Arrowsmith, 'Public Procurement: An Appraisal' (n 23) section B.

[26] The UNCITRAL Model Law's adoption of a multilateral competitive method ('requests for proposal with negotiation', analogous to 'competitive dialogue' under the EU's procurement directives (and to 'competitive negotiations' under pt 15 of the US Federal Acquisition Regulation)), for example, helped set the stage for 2016 changes to the World Bank Procurement Framework, which specifically allowed for competitive dialogues in World Bank-financed projects. This sharing of best practices between the UNCITRAL Model Law and other instruments was assisted by various cooperative initiatives, such as working groups and training, which drew together experts and officials from around the world. Ongoing discussions and debate of the Model Law, through academic forums led by Sue Arrowsmith and others, facilitated this sharing of best practices and ideas across the international procurement community.

[27] See Guide to Enactment, Part I, 'General Remarks', 2, para 5.

[28] C Nicholas, 'Framework agreements and the UNCITRAL model law on procurement' (2012) 2 *Public Procurement Law Review* 19, 23, drawing on A/59/17, paras 80–82.

A second aspect requires the harmonisation of the Model Law's provisions, so far as possible, with those of other international texts, so that their parties can use the Model Law for their national laws without major amendment. How the Model Law achieves this is explained in the Guide to Enactment.[29] The United Nations Office on Drugs and Crime, custodians of the United Nations Convention against Corruption (UNCAC),[30] highlights the benefits of using the Model Law in the *Legislative Guide for the Implementation of the United Nations Convention against* Corruption.[31] Commentaries on the Model Law and WTO GPA note that the Model Law can be used to fulfil the legal requirements of the GPA,[32] providing a further example of its integration into the law of international trade (state-to-state relations) and international agreements.

III. Seminal Importance of Arrowsmith's Review in Prompting Reform of the 1994 Model Law and Development of the 2011 Model Law

In her ground-breaking article, 'Public Procurement: An Appraisal of the UNCITRAL Model Law as a Global Standard',[33] Arrowsmith analysed the terms of the 1994 Model Law and some lessons from its use in practice. Arrowsmith proposed reforms to provisions on procurement methods (some streamlining and limited dilution of open tendering as a default method), on advertising (better transparency), on the introduction of suppliers' lists and framework agreements, e-procurement, on strengthening supplier review and enforcement, on introducing provisions on contract administration and what are now known as 'sustainability' policies.[34]

In 2003, against the background of Arrowsmith's article and UNCITRAL's adoption of a *Legislative Guide on Privately-Financed Infrastructure Projects* that had given light to important developments internationally in the regulation of procurement, the UNCITRAL Secretariat proposed a review (and possible update) of the 1994 text.[35] The Secretariat's proposal drew on the activities of other organisations in the field, notably 'the preparation of an international convention against

[29] See Part I, 'General Remarks', section A.6, 'International context of the Model Law and promotion of international participation in procurement proceedings'.

[30] UN General Assembly, United Nations Convention Against Corruption 2349 UNTS 41.

[31] United Nations (New York, 2006) at www.unodc.org/pdf/corruption/CoC_LegislativeGuide.pdf (accessed 31 October 2022).

[32] See, eg, C Nicholas and AC Müller, 'SME Participation in Government Procurement Markets – Legal and Policy Considerations under the WTO Agreement on Government Procurement and the UNCITRAL Model Law on Public Procurement' in T Rensmann (ed), *Small and Medium-Sized Enterprises in International Economic Law* (Oxford University Press, 2017) ch 5.

[33] Arrowsmith, 'Public Procurement: An Appraisal' (n 23).

[34] See also Arrowsmith (n 2) ch 1.

[35] Note by the Secretariat (n 22) A/CN.9/539, and A/CN/9/539/Add.1.

corruption by the Ad Hoc Committee established by the General Assembly in its resolution 56/260 of 31 January 2002 and the negotiations under the auspices of the World Trade Organization and other international and regional organizations'.[36]

There were two important limbs to the proposal: to allow for the then-emerging use of e-procurement; and to take account of practical experience gained in the use of the Model Law. UNCITRAL endorsed the proposal, suggested that UNCITRAL could formulate 'best practices, model contractual clauses and other forms of practical advice, in addition or as an alternative to legislative guidance', and underscored the importance of collaboration with other organisations engaged in public procurement law reform.[37]

A further, and critical, insight in Arrowsmith's article, which has, however, attracted less attention, came from her analysis of the character of the 1994 Model Law and its status as text developed to harmonise public procurement laws around the world.

Arrowsmith noted that other international rules promoting cross-border procurement (notably the WTO GPA) 'merely prohibit discrimination and establish a procedural framework for making foreign suppliers aware of opportunities and ensuring that entities cannot hide discrimination. However, they do not offer a blueprint for achieving domestic objectives, such as value for money'.[38] She continued that they also did not offer a regulatory framework for all procurement, focusing naturally on higher-value contracts more likely to attract cross-border interest: hence, there was no need for harmonisation in areas not tackled by the GPA, but a standard approach to common issues and a careful check on compatibility should be undertaken. Where there were departures, such as in domestic preferences, UNCITRAL might remain neutral but could offer guidance on the pros and cons; where tools were then considered too 'sophisticated' for the Model Law, the GPA could provide guidance that UNCITRAL might eventually follow (such as for suppliers' lists).

Thus, she concluded, encouraging greater harmonisation between the Model Law and the GPA would benefit potential GPA parties, and the Model Law should not exclude provisions unacceptable to the development banks, since they would presumably be of appropriate quality and useful for more developed countries. The UNCITRAL process to reform the 1994 Model Law would demonstrate, however, that harmonisation between the Model Law, the GPA, the EU Directives, the US Federal procurement system, and the then rules of the World Bank and other IFIs would not be straightforward.

[36] Report of the United Nations Commission on International Trade Law on its thirty-sixth session, 30 June–11 July 2003, A/58/17, para 30 at https://undocs.org/en/A/58/17(SUPP) (accessed 31 October 2022).

[37] ibid.

[38] Referring to S Arrowsmith, 'National and international perspectives on the regulation of public procurement: harmony or conflict?' in Arrowsmith and Davies (eds) (n 23) ch 1.

IV. Development of an UNCITRAL Model Law: UNCITRAL's Working Methods

A topic may reach UNCITRAL's agenda from different sources, including government proposals, consultations with stakeholders and within the UNCITRAL Secretariat based on experience in technical assistance programmes.[39] The proposal to reform the 1994 Model Law was based on Arrowsmith's analysis, as noted in section III, and, as an important indicator of the quality of the analysis, it was supported by many governments, stakeholders, such as the World Bank, and experts in UNCITRAL delegations. This level of buy-in was crucial both in terms of securing a mandate for reform and for the eventual success of the reform project.

A. The UNCITRAL Reform Process (2003–12): Expert Contributions, Intellectual Leadership and State-to-State Negotiations

In 2004, UNCITRAL decided that the 1994 Model Law 'would benefit from being updated to reflect new practices, in particular those resulting from the use of electronic communications in public procurement, and the experience gained in the use of the [Model Law] as a basis for law reform'.[40] Intergovernmental meetings known as 'Working Groups' develop an UNCITRAL text under a mandate from UNCITRAL's member States: Working Group I was given a flexible mandate in this case.[41] Following normal practice, the Working Group met twice a year, for week-long sessions alternating between New York and Vienna, and considered proposals and drafting provisions from the UNCITRAL Secretariat. Echoing the recommendations of Arrowsmith, the Working Group considered new provisions on: (i) the use of electronic communications in public procurement; (ii) electronic reverse auctions; (iii) abnormally low bids; and (iv) framework agreements, which were the emphasis from 2004–08. Later sessions focussed on (v) procurement of services; (vi) alternative procurement methods; (vii) simplification and standardisation of the 1994 Model Law; and (viii) conflicts of interest. Because UNCITRAL's member states agreed with Arrowsmith's conclusion that the Model Law was a high-quality instrument whose worth had been proved, and was not in need of major reform, the Working Group's mandate included the statement that 'care

[39] See also Section B.1, United Nations document A/CN.9/752 at https://uncitral.un.org/en/about/methods/officialdocs.

[40] Official Records of the General Assembly, Fifty-ninth Session, Supplement No 17 (A/59/17), para 81.

[41] ibid para 82.

should be taken not to depart from the basic principles of the Model Law and not to modify the provisions whose usefulness had been proven'.[42]

The UNCITRAL reform process generated not only the Model Law and Guide to Enactment, but a resolution of the United Nations General Assembly encouraging states to use the Model Law, via the following recommendation:

> *Recommends* that all States use the UNCITRAL Model Law on Public Procurement in assessing their public procurement legal regime and give favourable consideration to the UNCITRAL Model Law on Public Procurement when they enact or revise their laws.[43]

B. Factors for Developing Successful Texts in the UNCITRAL Process: Sharing Experience: Practice to Policy

In undertaking reform of the 1994 Model Law, delegations were invited from all UN member states (whether members of UNCITRAL or not) and from interested international organisations (international organisations and international non-governmental organisations). The participation of the EU, the World Bank and regional development banks and IFIs, the WTO Secretariat and other relevant organisations meant that UNCITRAL could take account of the rules and ongoing reforms in these other international systems, as well as national experience. John Honnold, Secretary of UNCITRAL from 1969–74, explained how UNCITRAL moves from discussions of practical issues to policy: delegates focus on 'concrete factual examples at the crossroads of crucial choices (there seem to be words in most languages for "facts", as contrasted with disembodied legal concepts) … [and then] the group could usually agree on what result was best'.[44] Only once 'facts' are identified (in this case, good procurement practice), would the legal drafting start.

C. Substantive Contribution from All Regions

The 'group' referred to by Honnold requires sufficiently wide, balanced and coherent participation in UNCITRAL to allow transferable best practice to be identified. UNCITRAL's membership is structured to ensure that all regions and legal and economic systems are fairly represented; and non-member UN member states,

[42] Official Records of the General Assembly, Sixty-Fourth Session, Supplement No 17 (A/64/17), para 29.

[43] UN General Assembly Resolution 66/95 of 9 December 2011.

[44] J Honnold, '3. Goals of unification' in *Uniform Commercial Law in the Twenty-First Century: Proceedings of the Congress of the United Nations Commission on International Trade Law*, New York, 18–22 May 1992, 11 at https://uncitral.un.org/sites/uncitral.un.org/files/media-documents/EN/Colloquia/uniform_commercial_law_congress_1992_e.pdf.

interested intergovernmental organisations and international non-governmental organisations with relevant expertise are invited to the sessions.[45] A review of the materials generated in the reform of the 1994 Model Law[46] shows that the Working Group concerned was highly influenced by Professor Arrowsmith's work: she had expanded on her analysis in her *Appraisal* article[47] in a report for UNCITRAL,[48] and the topics taken up and included in the (2011) Model Law largely reflect that analysis.

D. Building Consensus and Avoiding the Lowest-Common-Denominator Approach

UNCITRAL decisions are taken by consensus. Consensus here is a flexible concept, generally understood to mean that there is no formal objection to the decision concerned, and in practice it means that participants can adopt the proposed solution, even if it might not be their ideal choice. The process of finding appropriate practical solutions to common procurement problems, through experts from all delegations sharing their experience, is vital to move beyond the lowest common denominator and develop consensus on high-quality and up-to-date solutions. In addition, the use of the Model Law format (ie a non-binding template rather than a treaty with binding provisions) allows different but high-quality practical solutions to be accommodated.

E. Some Challenges in the Process

Commentators and UNCITRAL member states have noted that UNCITRAL's working methods pose challenges to effective participation: in addition to the costs of attending week-long meetings in Vienna and New York (participation is self-funded), delegates should survey practice in their home countries and be prepared to debate it with other delegates, tasks that could easily overwhelm the limited numbers of policy experts, especially where the policy experts are also those running the procurement system and in developing countries.[49] A key role

[45] For further detail, see at https://uncitral.un.org/en/about/faq/mandate_composition.

[46] See https://uncitral.un.org/en/working_groups/1/procurement, and section V.

[47] Arrowsmith, 'Public Procurement: An Appraisal' (n 23).

[48] Summaries of that report are available on the UNCITRAL website at https://uncitral.un.org/en/commission#36, A/CN.9/539 and A/CN.9/539/Add.1 – Current activities of international organizations in the area of public procurement: possible future work.

[49] The commentaries are discussed in C Nicholas, 'Negotiations and the Development of International standards in Public Procurement: Let the Best Team Win?' (2015) VII: 1 *Trade, Law and Development Journal, Government Procurement: Special Issue* (Jodhpur) 63; Nicholas (n 12); and C Nicholas, 'UNCITRAL's Role in Commercial Law Reform; History and Future Prospects' in O Akseli and J Linarelli (eds), *The Future of Commercial Law: Ways Forward for Change and Reform* (Bloomsbury Publishing, 2019) 11.

of the UNCITRAL Secretariat and external experts (including Arrowsmith in the Model Law development) is to survey international practice and engage with experts from all regions, or the Secretariat as the case may be, so as to ensure that all relevant experience can be taken into account. From this perspective, the inclusion of practices from all regions and many international organisations in Arrowsmith's papers made considerable inroads towards addressing this challenge.[50]

The conference time available to UNCITRAL Working Groups is relatively limited, and reflects pressure in UNCITRAL to tackle an ever-lengthening list of projects. This translates into pressure to make progress, soft time limits on mandates and a need for compromise, further underscoring that an UNCITRAL Model Law will operate at a framework level. Thus, for example, Article 14 of the Model Law does not set a minimum time period for the preparation of tenders but defers the issue to enacting states, with the caveat that the period be reasonable, allowing sufficient time for the preparation and for local circumstances to be reflected in national enactments or regulations.

F. A View from a Member of a State Delegation

Because of the various pressures already outlined in this section – relatively limited time to achieve consensus on difficult technical questions regarding international best practices – it was important for the delegations from the various member states to be alert to possible 'short-cuts' to effective compromise. One state delegate, for example, served as a 'monitor' for the Working Group, to ensure that the Model Law remained consistent with the demands of the WTO GPA. Another delegate stepped away from his home country's very cumbersome procurement rules, to advocate from international best practices reflected in the EU procurement directives – a quick pathway to common ground among the delegations. Thanks to goodwill and cooperation among the delegations, and patient guidance from the UNCITRAL Secretariat, it became increasingly easy over the years to make good progress on the Model Law.

V. Factors for Developing Successful Texts from Beyond the UNCITRAL Process

A. Transparency for Non-participants

All written materials for Working Group sessions are posted on the UNCITRAL website (in all six official UN languages) in advance of each session, as is a report of the main points raised and decisions taken as soon as possible after the

[50] See A/CN/9/539 (n 22).

session. The papers analyse substantive reform proposals, survey practical experience and critiques, and propose draft legislative provisions. As a general rule, digital recordings of the sessions are also uploaded. These materials enable interested non-participants to follow the deliberations leading to the adoption of an UNCITRAL text and the reasons for the policy decisions and drafting it contains.[51] UNCITRAL's transparency commitment is also designed to facilitate broader debate and understanding of the issues considered in its deliberations, which can generate academic commentary and so contribute to the deliberations themselves. Arrowsmith's book published in 2009, *Reform of the UNCITRAL Model Law on Procurement: Procurement Regulation for the 21st Century*, is an outstanding example of this phenomenon.[52]

B. The Critical Role of Intellectual Leadership: Ongoing Influence of Debate in Academia and Policy Circles

i. Arrowsmith's Leadership in Nurturing the Reforms in the Academic Sphere

The importance of Arrowsmith's leadership in stirring academic interest in the Model Law, both in the United Kingdom and abroad, cannot be overstated. She is broadly recognised as the leading academic in procurement law internationally, and her engagement with – and ongoing support of – reform of the Model Law was critical to the reform effort's success. As noted, her articles on potential reforms of the Model Law helped set the stage for a decade of meetings, papers and seminars, many of them hosted by Arrowsmith and her colleagues at the University of Nottingham, which helped propel a thoroughgoing review of the Model Law. Her leadership, and the successful revision of the Model Law, proved that academics can and do play a pivotal role in law reform.

ii. Interaction with Other Stakeholders in Policy Discussions

The Working Group Reports on the UNCITRAL website record the participation of these organisations in the Model Law's reform process.[53] In addition, their representatives took part in expert consultations throughout the process, and the UNCITRAL Secretariat participated in technical assistance meetings with the World Bank, WTO and UN Office on Drugs and Crime, to explain

[51] See at https://uncitral.un.org/en/about/faq/methods.

[52] Arrowsmith (n 2).

[53] The Model Law's Working Group materials are available at https://uncitral.un.org/en/working_groups/1/procurement; and a broad array of research materials on public procurement-related initiatives at UNCITRAL are available at https://uncitral.un.org/en/texts/procurement.

the policy debates in UNCITRAL and hear views both of the organisations and users of their own instruments. As has been explained with regard to the GPA, the result was that definitions were harmonised;[54] the term 'lowest evaluated tender' was revised to 'most advantageous tender'; Article 6 of the Model Law introduced a requirement for publication of a broader range of procurement-related texts and rulings; and the optional publication of planned and possible forthcoming procurement and opportunities,[55] requirements for specifications and descriptions, confidentiality and abnormally low tenders were aligned with those of the GPA.[56] The 2014 EU Directives also contain provisions that in part parallel those of the Model Law, such as (as discussed in section VI) an expanded acceptance of multilateral competitive negotiations as an approved method.

iii. A Diverse and Intellectual Foundation to Help Advance Progress, Built on Best Practices from Around the World

A keystone to the Model Law's success was its foundation in diverse best practices from around the world. By giving respectful attention to lessons learned in the developing world – lessons, for example, in the practical dangers of 'walling off' defence procurement from mainstream procurement requirements – the Working Group was able to shape the Model Law into an instrument that can be relied upon by governments around the world, regardless of their levels of development or legal traditions (common law versus civil law, for example). The Model Law was built on a richly diverse intellectual foundation, which has made it a more useful tool in many different countries and systems.

VI. Key Issues of Debate During the 2004–2011 Reforms

In 2009, the Working Group turned from the more technical amendments introducing electronic procurement tools and framework agreements, to procurement of services, alternative procurement methods, and their impact on the question of simplification and standardisation of the Model Law.[57] The

[54] For example, the definition of 'public procurement' in Art 2 follows the references to leasing, hire-purchasing and so forth set out in Art XV.5(a) of the 2012 GPA.

[55] Following Arts VII and XI of the GPA.

[56] See A/CN.9/575, para 79; A/CN.590, para 57; A/CN.9/664, paras 28 and 59; A/CN.9/668, paras 78, 264 and 273; A/CN.9/687, paras 63 and 153–55; and A/CN.9/690, paras 72 and 129. More generally, C Nicholas, 'Work of UNCITRAL in Government Procurement: Purpose, Objectives and Complementarity with the Work of the WTO' in S Arrowsmith and R Anderson (eds), *The WTO Regime on Government Procurement* (WTO, 2011) 746.

[57] A summary of the reforms can be found in C Nicholas, 'The 2011 UNCITRAL Model Law on Public Procurement' (2012) 21(3) *Public Procurement Law Review* 111.

background to the Working Group's activities had also shifted: first, with the financial crisis of 2008 onwards; and, second, following a proposal from some states to consider a new procurement method. As UNCITRAL noted, the review of procurement methods and simplification and standardisation then became the main element of the later discussions:

> The preliminary decision of the Working Group was to retain all options for the procurement of services, with enhanced guidance for their use. In the course of consideration, it became apparent however that services procedures contained in different articles of the 1994 Model Law were substantially the same and that only one services selection procedure – the selection procedure with consecutive negotiations – was distinct. In the light of such a significant overlap, the Working Group had reconsidered whether all methods should be retained.[58]

In Spring 2009, three countries proposed a new 'competitive negotiations' procurement method to the Working Group.[59] The proposal started from the standpoint that 'in practice requests for proposals were typically the solicitations used to launch competitive negotiations',[60] and the proposed new method was designed to

> provid[e] sufficient flexibility … (considered to facilitate achieving best value for money) while building in procedures to avoid the risk that the discretion conferred would be abused; ensuring sufficient transparency without removing all flexibility; and specifying ways for the procuring entity to control the number of suppliers with which it would negotiate (for example, through pre-selection, an assessment of responsiveness or exclusion of solutions).[61]

The deliberations on this method offer a window into the key issues of debate during the reform process, coalescing around:

(a) how to handle different capacity levels among potential Model Law users;
(b) how to balance transparency and related safeguards to prevent fraud and corruption (a key consideration in the early stages of the reform process, coinciding as it did with UNCAC's coming into force in 2005) with more flexibility to improve economic outcomes and efficiency in the process (key issues with the onset of the financial crisis).

The debate is therefore set out in some detail in section VII. This debate was part of an ongoing international and public discussion of multilateral competitive negotiations, and Professor Arrowsmith and her colleagues at the University of Nottingham were instrumental in advancing it.

[58] A/64/17 (n 42) para 37.
[59] See Document A/CN.9/WG.I/XVI/CRP.2 – Proposed Article 40: Competitive negotiations – Proposal submitted by Austria, the United Kingdom and the United States, at https://uncitral.un.org/sites/uncitral.un.org/files/16-crp2.e.pdf.
[60] ibid para 3.
[61] ibid para 38.

VII. Capacity Differences Among Potential Model Law Users, Transparency and Discretion: New Facets of Old Problems

The first issue discussed was whether the use of the proposed new method should be subject to prior approval from outside the procuring entity to mitigate the capacity and transparency challenges described in the preceding section. The Working Group agreed that the method 'presupposed significant discretion on the part of procuring entities in decision-making, and therefore it raised higher risks of corruption and abuse than might be present in other less flexible procedures'.[62]

The question revolved around whether prior approval mechanisms facilitate the detection of errors, capacity issues and integrity risks at an early stage, enhance uniformity and support capacity-development through the justification and consideration of the actions or decisions concerned when seeking approval, or whether they are an unnecessary administrative burden, prevent the longer-term acquisition of decision-making capacity and dilute accountability, largely without significant gain.[63] Delegations disagreed on the issue: those from more developed countries, including the proponents, pointed out the declining use of prior approvals; others said that they remained important stages in their systems.[64] Eventually, the mechanism was retained as an option for enacting states for the use of this method (and also for the use of single-source procurement to promote other government policies and for actions bringing the procurement contract into force). The Guide to Enactment noted that existing capacity might be the deciding factor, and that any approval requirement should be in the procurement law (to avoid the corruption risk of 'unofficial' requirements for approvals), the need for independence in the approving body, and appropriate procedures.[65]

As noted, Arrowsmith's public work as the Model Law reform began had drawn attention to comments that the 1994 Model Law was considered not to be suitable for developing countries. This point was discussed in the Working Group with regard to whether the new proposed procurement method (a form of multilateral negotiations) and similar approaches should be available only to more sophisticated users or even excluded from the Model Law, and whether the Model Law should provide simpler methods for those with lesser capacity.

[62] A/CN.9/672, para 16.

[63] Guide to Enactment, Part I, 'General Remarks', section C.1.(c), 'Institutional support', 20, paras 71–72.

[64] A/CN.9/668, Report of Working Group I (Procurement) on the work of its fifteenth session, paras 52 and 112; and A/CN.9/672, Report of Working Group I (Procurement) on the work of its sixteenth session, para 33.

[65] Guide to Enactment, Part I, 'General Remarks', section C.1.(c), 'Institutional support', 20, paras 73–78.

Developing countries responded that the proposal to remove more sophisticated methods would patronise and under-serve them.[66] Subsequent remarks included that the

> value of this procurement method had resulted in benefits to the procuring entity in enabling it to obtain the best solution to its procurement needs, and thus that there would be advantages to developed and developing countries alike in its use. It was also stressed that the opportunity cost of not providing for such negotiations should be taken into account.[67]

As use of the method would require levels of capacity, experience and governance that were not yet in place everywhere, the Guide to Enactment would 'stress that sufficient capacity to operate [this and similar] methods would be critical for their successful use',[68] and would encourage a phased approach to the introduction of procurement methods requiring higher capacity to operate successfully.[69] For example, they might start with

> tendering methods for all other than urgent and very low-value procurement (for which less structured or regulated methods are presented in the Model Law); the capacity acquired in operating these methods will allow the introduction at a later stage of methods involving negotiations or dialogue, including request for proposals.[70]

During the discussions, the World Bank also signalled to the Working Group that it was uncomfortable with allowing some of the features – notably simultaneous negotiations with multiple bidders – involved in this method.[71] This concern was reflected in the Guide to Enactment, which states that

> enacting States may wish to take into account that, historically, the procurement rules of some multilateral development banks have not included procurement methods equivalent to request for proposals with dialogue or competitive negotiations as provided for in the Model Law. These multilateral donors have included methods with the features of the Model Law's request for proposals without negotiation and request for proposals with consecutive negotiations only for the procurement of consulting (eg advisory) services. Consequently, and in the light of possible developments, enacting States – potential borrowers from the multilateral development banks – should verify the public procurement policies of those donors at the relevant time that will be applicable to procurement projects financed by such donors.[72]

[66] This discussion is available in the digital recordings of the Working Group. The Working Group's reports record the final decision with lesser detail.

[67] A/CN.9/672, para 16.

[68] See A/CN.9/WG.I/WP.71, paras 21–22; A/CN.9/WG.I/WP.71/Add.5; and A/CN.9/672, paras 14–30.

[69] See, eg, phased introduction of electronic reverse auctions, discussed in the Model Law's Guide to Enactment at 231, and the phased introduction of framework agreements, discussed at 257.

[70] See the Guide to Enactment, Part II, Chapter II, 'Enactment: policy considerations', 128, para 6.

[71] See also Document A/CN.9/718, para 69.

[72] Guide to Enactment, 130, para 9, discussing 'Enactment: policy considerations' in the context of procurement methods and conditions for use.

The final caveat replaced an earlier suggestion that the Guide should alert potential Model Law users that 'Some multilateral development banks may not authorize the use of this method in projects financed by them.'[73] This caveat echoed the World Bank's reservations expressed about the use of competitive negotiations when the 1994 Model Law was adopted: the then observer to UNCITRAL stated that the Bank would generally not recommend this method.[74]

Subsequently, however, the World Bank itself adopted competitive dialogue as an accepted procedure (with special protections because of the risks of misuse and corruption) in the World Bank's 2016 Procurement Framework.[75]

After several iterations,[76] and in-depth debates on the extent to which evaluation criteria and descriptions (including specifications) could be modified during the procedure, and the nature of the interaction between the dialogue-based methods and procurement planning (whether the method should follow detailed planning or whether it might include an 'advisory multi-step process'), the final text of the 'Request-for-proposals with dialogue' was agreed and is now set out in Articles 30(2) (conditions for use) and 49 (procedures). In including this new and sophisticated method, UNCITRAL showed that a harmonisation text could tackle capacity variations and provide opportunities to allow countries with lesser procurement capabilities to develop and start to use modern and innovative tools.

VIII. Safeguards: Transparency and Digital Tools to Enable More Commercial Attitudes and the Pursuit of Broader Policy Objectives

One of the main motivations for revising the 1994 Model Law was to enable the use of e-procurement.[77] As the reform process began in the early 2000s, this embrace of e-procurement reflected changing business practices, as government

[73] See also Document A/CN.9/718, para 69.

[74] See UNCITRAL (n 24) para 64: 'In recent years, the World Bank … recommended the Model Law with some reservations. For example, it suggested that the method of competitive negotiation should not be applied, and once the draft was approved, the Bank would probably also recommend against application of article 16, paragraph 3(b) [in that iteration, the rules governing the use of the default method for the procurement of services].'

[75] See, eg, World Bank, 'Competitive Dialogue: How to undertake a Competitive Dialogue Procurement Process' (October 2017). See Document A/CN.9/718, para 69.

[76] See, eg, at www.uncitral.org/pdf/english/commissiondocs/a-cn9-XLII-crp-2-e.pdf and www.uncitral.org/pdf/english/workinggroups/wg_1/wp.71.add5-e.pdf.

[77] As noted, the need to update the 1994 Model Law to reflect emerging e-procurement practices was a critical part of the member states' support for a revision of the Model Law. For an important report on a risk-based approach to public procurement, see Organisation for Economic Co-operation and Development, *Managing risks in the public procurement of goods, services and infrastructure* (OECD, 2023).

purchasers shifted from paper-based procurement systems. By the time review concluded in 2011, however, the stage was set for the next phase in digitally-based procurement: a more aggressive use of digital resources not simply to save administrative resources and time, but to reduce risk and improve outcomes. The 2011 text encourages 'the procurement of goods, works and services through Internet-based information technologies'.[78] It includes provisions on Internet-based publication of advertisements and notices, submission of tenders and other offers electronically, e-framework agreements and e-reverse auctions (including e-catalogues), and it enables e-communications throughout the procurement process. The provisions are based on a 'technologically neutral' approach, so that they do not refer to any particular technology,[79] to avoid technical obsolescence and to allow for flexibility in implementation. The Guide also highlights the potential of e-procurement to enhance a procurement system in terms of meeting the objectives of the Model Law: value for money; avoiding corruption and promoting the integrity of the system; ensuring participation and competition for the opportunity to supply the government; applying objectivity and fair treatment (or non-discrimination) in the procurement process; and achieving efficiency and transparency in procurement procedures and the system as a whole. It further notes the internal opportunities, from the perspective of the procurement system, arising from standardising, streamlining and automating of procedures, which should reduce the administrative burden on procurement officials and allow them to focus on outcomes, and which can facilitate the oversight of procedures (whether ex ante or ex post), playing a role, too, in prevention of procurement disputes and post-contract failures. Detailed guidance to support the effective introduction and use of e-procurement is found in the Guide to Enactment.[80]

IX. Addressing Criticisms of the 1994 Model Law

The pragmatism and compromise required in the UNCITRAL process had arguably led to the (undesirable) exclusion of defence procurement and a timid approach to supplier review in the 1994 text. Both these issues were addressed in the reform process and are now included in the Model Law.

[78] See Guide to Enactment, Part I 'General Remarks', Section A.4, 'The potential of electronic procurement (e-procurement) as a tool to promote public procurement policy objectives in the context of the Model Law', para 29.

[79] From this perspective, the text follows the approach of the UNCITRAL Model Law on Electronic Commerce (1996) and the United Nations Convention on Electronic Contracting (2005), both available at https://uncitral.un.org/en/texts/ecommerce.

[80] See Guide to Enactment, Part I, 'The potential of electronic procurement as a tool to promote public procurement objectives in the context of the Model Law' (at 9) and 'Specific issues arising in the implementation and use of e-procurement' (at 26).

A. Defence Procurement

The 1994 Model Law included limited exemptions from its coverage, the most significant of which was defence procurement, though it did allow the procuring entity to choose to apply the Model Law to a given procurement. Concerns about this exemption included that such procurement forms a significant sector of the domestic procurement market, the blanket exclusion had led to very poor results for certain goods and services (whose supply was not sensitive), and that the defence sector was commonly innovative and offered lessons for the broader procurement market. The Working Group considered that the broad variety of procedures available under the 2011 Model Law made it unnecessary to exclude the application of the Model Law from any sector of the economy, and there was consensus that the blanket exemption for defence procurement should be removed. As the Guide to Enactment highlights, including defence procurement 'promote[s] a harmonized legal procurement regime across all sectors in enacting States, and … enable[s] all procurement to benefit from the Model Law's provisions'.[81]

Several Articles of the Model Law contain provisions to accommodate defence procurement (or any form of procurement raising essential national security interests). For example, procurement involving classified information will require transparency mechanisms to be relaxed (as provided for in Articles 7(3)(b) and 24), and procurement methods such as request for proposals with dialogue, competitive negotiations and single-source procurement are specifically available for such procurement if the procuring entity determines they would be the most appropriate in the circumstances. However, any decision not to apply the full ambit of the Model Law to any procurement needs to be justified in the record of the procurement under Article 25: there is no blanket exemption from the Model Law's procedures.

B. Remedies and Challenge Mechanisms

A footnote to Chapter VI of the 1994 Model Law, which addressed remedies, provided that enacting states might choose not to incorporate some or all the Articles. There was also a list of exemptions from review, of which the most significant was the choice of procurement method, on the basis that the decisions exempted did not give rise to individual supplier rights and were more properly aspects of the system amenable to administrative oversight.[82] This gentle approach was much criticised: it was rooted in a concern that the remedies issue raised the legality of government acts, could affect the separation of powers between the executive and the judicial branches of a particular state and was therefore beyond UNCITRAL's remit, and choice should not be made among the broad range of approaches to the topic in different legal systems.[83]

[81] Guide to Enactment, Part I, 'Inclusion of defence and security-related procurement', para 47.
[82] Art 52(2) of the 1994 text.
[83] Nicholas, 'UNCITRAL's Role in Commercial Law Reform' (n 49).

In its first session, the Working Group agreed that: (i) it would be useful to provide further guidance on review provisions that national laws could incorporate; (ii) recognising the fact that there were different systems, some of which favoured review through the courts while others favoured independent administrative review, the Working Group should leave various options open for states; (iii) provisions related to the judicial review process should be left for enacting states; and (iv) the list of exceptions in Article 52(2) should be deleted. However, the Guide to Enactment should indicate that enacting states might wish to exclude some matters from the review process.[84] The Working Group's consensus was based on identified good practice and on the requirements of the mandatory language of Article 9(1)(e) of UNCAC, which required an effective system of review and appeal in procurement proceedings.[85] Behind the Working Group's reasoning was that most procurement laws enacted at that time did indeed include remedies provisions, and the policy debate had simply moved on.

The provisions broadening remedies are contained in Chapter VIII of the 2011 Model Law and implement this early decision of the Working Group. The Working Group considered it particularly important, as part of effective oversight of the use of the toolbox approach to the selection of the procurement method under the Model Law, that this decision, as all others, should be subject to challenge. Reversing the 1994 position, enacting states are encouraged in the Guide to Enactment to incorporate all the provisions of the chapter to the extent that their legal systems so permit. The provisions themselves allow three types of review – optional reconsideration by the procuring entity; review by an independent review body; and judicial review – allowing the national system to determine its form and structure in accordance with their legal and administrative traditions, and importantly take account of the procurement context in setting out time limits for submission and review, and recommending procurement-appropriate remedies.[86]

C. Use of the UNCITRAL Model Law Once Adopted: Ensuring the Model Law's Provisions are Understood – Key Role of the Guide to Enactment and UNCITRAL Secretariat and Expert Outreach

This chapter has made extensive reference to the policy explanations and implementation advice set out in the Guide to Enactment. The Guide itself sets out the reasons for accompanying the 70-page Model Law with a 400-page explanatory

[84] See A/CN.9/568, para 112.

[85] See Report of Working Group I (Procurement) on the work of its fourteenth session, Vienna, 8–12 September 2008; UNCITRAL, Forty-second session, Vienna, 29 June–17 July 2009 (A/CN.9/664) at https://uncitral.un.org/en/commission.

[86] The Guide to Enactment to Chapter VIII of the Model Law contains a comprehensive explanation of policy and legislative considerations, and issues of implementation and use of the provisions themselves.

document, a reference tool for policymakers and legislators, regulators and those providing guidance to users of a procurement system based on the Model Law:

- To explain objectives of the Model Law and how its provisions are designed to achieve them.
- To enhance the effectiveness of the Model Law as tool for modernising and reforming procurement systems, particularly in countries unused to modern procurement systems.
- To explain how practical experiences from all regions have contributed to identifying the best practices it reflects.
- To allow the provisions to be universally applicable.
- To explain issues that may be taken into account in deciding how the Model Law's options may be exercised and whether variations to the provisions are needed to accommodate local practices.
- To discuss the need for and points to be included in regulations, rules and additional guidance to support legislation based on the Model Law, and the types of legal and other infrastructure that will be needed to support the effective implementation of the text.
- To assist users of the 1994 Model Law updating their legislation to meet the standards of the 2011 text.[87]

The UNCITRAL Secretariat also engages in technical assistance activities to support users of the Model Law, through:

(a) raising awareness and promoting the adoption of the Model Law;
(b) providing gap analyses and similar reviews to help countries to assess needs for procurement reform and legislative drafting;
(c) building capacity to use and implement the Model Law through training activities.

Reports to UNCITRAL each year set out the relevant activities, many of which are undertaken with partners such as the EBRD and other multilateral institutions, the International Anti-Corruption Academy, the WTO and through bilateral national aid programmes.[88] These activities are the practical expression of the Guide's objectives, and have generated both interest in and use of the Model Law in practice.[89] Arrowsmith's own analyses of the policy discussions in the process to reform the Model Law, and as expressed in the Model Law and Guide to Enactment, have also provided much material to support these technical assistance activities of the UNCITRAL Secretariat.

[87] See Guide to Enactment, Preface.
[88] See, eg, A/CN.9/1099 – Technical cooperation and assistance, at https://uncitral.un.org/en/commission.
[89] For information on the use of the Model Law in practice, see at https://uncitral.un.org/en/texts/procurement/modellaw/public_procurement/status.

Arrowsmith also established a bi-annual 'Global Revolution' series of conferences at the University of Nottingham in 1997. Global Revolution has become a major forum at which experts, policy makers and government officials, procurement professionals, lawyers and academics from all over the world review and discuss reforms, innovations and challenges in procurement law, policy and practice. The breadth and depth of expertise in attendance, reflecting Professor Arrowsmith's own power to convene, has allowed the exchange of good (and less good) experiences that themselves are helping to drive up standards in public procurement worldwide.

X. Concluding Observations and an Appreciation

Today the UNCITRAL Model Law is a key topic of study in universities around the globe, including at the University of Nottingham (UK), the International Training Centre of the International Labour Organization/University of Turin (Italy), the University of Rome Tor Vergata (Italy), King's College, London, the University of London (UK) and George Washington University (US).

As Arrowsmith acknowledged in 2007, when establishing a consortium to develop a global academic network on public procurement, the academic study of the topic was then a relatively recent innovation.[90] It should be added that it was essentially *her* innovation, and her work internationally has helped bridge the gaps – many of them decades old – between academic programmes in different countries around the world.

The reform of the UNCITRAL Model Law, and continuing academic work built on the revised Model Law, reflects the extraordinary contribution that Sue Arrowsmith has helped make to public procurement studies globally.

As the preceding discussion reflects, although the UNCITRAL reform process seemed natural, almost inevitable, without Arrowsmith's intercession the reform could well have been stuck at the commonplace level. Instead, it was revolutionary – avoiding top-down, structural reforms in favour of a 'toolbox' of best practices gathered from a rapidly evolving, global public procurement community. Her intellectual leadership, her surefooted analysis and her thoughtful recommendations helped launch and then guide a critical reform; one that built both a better Model Law and an enduring international procurement community committed to better outcomes for citizens around the world.

[90] Developing a global academic network on public procurement, University of Nottingham, Grant and Award Announcement at www.eurekalert.org/news-releases/463579.

16

The UNCITRAL Model Law and the Past and Future of Procurement Regulation in Africa

GEO QUINOT

I. Introduction

Sue Arrowsmith has always been a staunch proponent of the United Nations Commission on International Trade Law (UNCITRAL) Model Law on Procurement of Goods, Construction and Services. In her own words, the Model Law was 'a considerable achievement' in formulating an international view on public procurement regulation and generally 'an excellent template for procurement regulation'.[1] Her views on the value of the Model Law pointedly also included its usefulness in shaping nascent procurement law systems across Africa. I vividly recall her spirited promotion of the Model Law as the ideal vehicle for public procurement reform in Africa at the first international conference on public procurement regulation in Africa, hosted in Stellenbosch in October 2011. This is a theme that Sue has consistently taken up in subsequent engagements on public procurement law in Africa. At a subsequent international conference on public procurement law in Africa, held in November 2016, she presented on the revised remedies regime under the 2011 Model Law, noting that the topic would be of prime interest in the African context given the significant influence of the Model Law on the continent.

The Model Law was first adopted in 1993/4, and a revised version, the UNCITRAL Model Law on Public Procurement, was adopted in 2011. The Model Law has had significant impact on the evolution of public procurement law regimes especially in developing countries. As Arrowsmith has noted (writing with Elinor Caborn):

> Whilst the original conception of the Model Law was as an instrument for all countries – and indeed it can be an instrument of trade from a truly global perspective

[1] S Arrowsmith, 'Public Procurement: an Appraisal of the UNCITRAL Model Law as a Global Standard' (2004) 53 *International and Comparative Law Quarterly* 17.

only through such an approach – in practice it has been used by, and perceived as relevant for, mainly developing countries and transition economies.[2]

In Africa, in particular, the Model Law provided the basis for consecutive waves of public procurement law reform, starting in the early 1990s.[3] The Model Law's influence in Africa has been both direct and indirect. Especially during the earlier reforms, many countries simply transplanted the Model Law directly into their own statute books by way of cut and paste. But the Model Law has also had notable indirect influence on the African continent by way of its effect on regional procurement law reform projects and the influence of African countries' procurement law reform on those in neighbouring states.

This impact of the Model Law stands in stark contrast to other international instruments in public procurement regulation, notably the World Trade Organization's Agreement on Government Procurement (WTO GPA), which has had virtually no effect in Africa. This chapter tracks the influence of the UNCITRAL Model Law on public procurement law development and reform in Africa. It analyses the nature of that impact and the choices made by individual African systems when using the Model Law to frame their own procurement laws, under both the 1994 and 2011 versions of the Model Law. The chapter concludes by reflecting on the effect and potential of this single, international regulatory instrument to align public procurement practices on the African continent in light of market integration under the African Continental Free Trade Area, which at present excludes public procurement.

II. Background to the UNCITRAL Model Law on Public Procurement

The UNCITRAL Model Law on Public Procurement is one of the leading international regulatory standards in this area of law.

The Model Law is the product of UNCITRAL in furtherance of its general mission of advancing the progressive harmonisation and unification of the law of international trade.[4] Like all UNCITRAL's model laws, it aims to remove barriers to cross-border trade created by divergent national legal rules applicable to

[2] E Caborn and S Arrowsmith, 'Procurement methods in the public procurement systems of Africa' in G Quinot and S Arrowsmith (eds), *Public Procurement Regulation in Africa* (Cambridge University Press, 2013) 261, 264–65.

[3] G Quinot and S Arrowsmith, 'Introduction' in Quinot and Arrowsmith (eds) (n 2) 1–6; Caborn and Arrowsmith (n 2) 261–68.

[4] UN General Assembly Resolution 2205 (XXI) (17 December 1966); C Nicholas, 'UNCITRAL and the internationalization of government procurement regulation' in A Georgopoulos, B Hoekman and PC Mavroidis (eds), *The Internationalization of Government Procurement Regulation* (Oxford University Press, 2017) 86, 88.

particular types of commercial activity,[5] in this case, acquisitions by public entities from private suppliers.[6] In essence, the Model Law aims to bring some convergence to domestic procurement law, which, in Christopher Yukins and Steven Schooner's pithy words, 'often erects a dense, twisted web of rules, which may impede (and frequently intimidates) potential foreign entrants'.[7]

The original Model Law on Public Procurement was adopted in 1993[8] and replaced by an extended version in 1994 ('the 1994 Model Law').[9] Ten years later, in 2004, UNCITRAL launched a revision of the Model Law,[10] which resulted in the adoption of a revised Model Law in 2011 ('the 2011 Model Law').[11]

As UNCITRAL's Caroline Nicholas has stated, 'the Model Law is an example of a harmonization text: that is, one that can be flexibly implemented to accord with local circumstances, while preserving the desired outcomes, rather than a unification text such as a treaty or convention (in which the opportunities for derogations are limited)'.[12]

The Model Law sets out general principles governing the procurement process, such as rules on communication, supplier qualification, description of goods and services, tender securities, exclusions, confidentiality and solicitation documents. The bulk of the Model Law contains rules on procurement methods. These are set out in Chapters II to VII of the 2011 Model Law, comprising 37 of the 2011 Model Law's 69 Articles. The 2011 Model Law provides for the following procurement procedures:

- Open tendering
- Restricted tendering
- Request for quotations
- Request for proposals without negotiation
- Two-stage tendering

[5] United Nations, *A Guide to UNCITRAL* (2013) 13–16; UNCITRAL, *Guide to Enactment of the UNCITRAL Model Law on Public Procurement* (2014) 2.

[6] Nicholas (n 4) 87.

[7] CR Yukins and SL Schooner, 'Incrementalism: Eroding the impediments to a global public procurement market' (2007) 38 *Georgetown Journal International Law* 529, 530–31; S Arrowsmith and C Nicholas, 'The UNCITRAL Model Law on Procurement: Past, Present, and Future' in S Arrowsmith (ed), *Reform of the UNCITRAL Model Law on Procurement: Procurement Regulation for the 21st Century* (West, 2009) 9.

[8] Report of the UNCITRAL Commission on its twenty-sixth session, A/48/17, 1993, para 217.

[9] Report of the UNCITRAL Commission on its twenty-seventh session, A/49/17, 1994, para 97; S Arrowsmith, 'Public Procurement: an Appraisal of the UNCITRAL Model Law as a Global Standard' (2004) 53 *International and Comparative Law Quarterly* 17.

[10] Report of the UNCITRAL Commission on its thirty-seventh session, A/59/7, para 82.

[11] Report of the UNCITRAL Commission on its forty-fourth session, A/66/17, 2011 para 192; C Nicholas, 'The 2011 UNCITRAL Model Law on Public Procurement' (2012) 21 *Public Procurement Law Review* NA111.

[12] C Nicholas, 'Work of UNCITRAL on government procurement: purpose, objectives and complementarity with the work of the WTO' in S Arrowsmith and R Anderson (eds), *The WTO Regime on Government Procurement: Challenge and Reform* (Cambridge University Press, 2011) 746, 748.

- Request for proposals with dialogue
- Request for proposals with consecutive negotiations
- Competitive negotiations
- Electronic reverse auction
- Single-source procurement
- Framework agreement procedure.[13]

As the footnote to Article 27 of the 2011 Model Law and the *Guide to Enactment*[14] that accompanies the Model Law explain, it is not the intention of the drafters that this entire list of procurement methods will be enacted by all states making use of the Model Law. Rather, the intention is that domestic procurement law should incorporate a context-appropriate range of methods, but always including open tendering. The *Guide to Enactment* explains that states should adopt procurement procedures for at least four scenarios: open tendering (as default); low-value and simple procurement; emergency and urgent procurement; and specialised and complex procurement.[15] In providing guidance on how to select the appropriate methods to incorporate into domestic law, the *Guide to Enactment* places emphasis on capacity and maturity within the local procurement system, as well as the prevalent levels of integrity.[16]

Nicholas lists the following four areas as representing the main changes introduced in the 2011 Model Law:

(a) the introduction of e-procurement, including electronic reverse auctions;
(b) a strengthening of the general principles;
(c) a more structured approach to the choice and use of procurement methods and the introduction of several new procurement methods and related techniques; and
(d) a strengthening of the rules on review.[17]

It is evident that the revision of the original Model Law also focused heavily on procurement methods. Apart from refinement of specific rules and approaches based on experience in implementing the 1994 Model Law, the revisions were largely influenced by the evolution of procurement procedures, such as e-procurement and framework agreements, and the obligations imposed by the UN Convention Against Corruption,[18] adopted after the 1994 Model Law.[19]

[13] 2011 Model Law, Art 27.
[14] UNCITRAL, *Guide to Enactment* (n 5) 128–32.
[15] ibid 128–29.
[16] ibid 130.
[17] Nicholas (n 11) NA111.
[18] United Nations Convention against Corruption, 9 December 2003, UN Doc A/58/422 (2003).
[19] UNCITRAL, *Guide to Enactment* (n 5) 2; Nicholas (n 11) NA111, NA115; C Nicholas, 'A critical evaluation of the revised UNCITRAL Model Law provisions on regulating framework agreements' (2012) (21) *Public Procurement Law Review* 19, 22–23.

III. Influence of the 1994 Model Law in Africa

The 1994 Model Law was quite influential and served as the direct template for local procurement laws in about 30 countries worldwide.[20] Of these, 11 were in Africa,[21] the largest geographical concentration of the 1994 Model Law's impact, which nevertheless extended quite a bit beyond these 11 systems. This is due to the indirect influence of the 1994 Model Law. A number of African systems thus borrowed heavily from other African systems that relied in turn on the 1994 Model Law. A good example is Botswana, where the 2006 Public Procurement and Asset Disposal Regulations were based on the Ugandan procurement regulations, which in turn were premised on the 1994 Model Law. The result was that although Botswana did not rely on the 1994 Model Law for its own procurement law, there were nevertheless clear signs of the influence of the 1994 Model Law on particular aspects of Botswanan procurement law, such as procurement methods.[22]

As Sue Arrowsmith and myself have noted, a more extensive indirect influence of the 1994 Model Law in Africa occurred via regional procurement law reform, specifically that of the Common Market for Eastern and Southern Africa (COMESA).[23] This trade bloc consists of 21 African states, making it the largest regional bloc on the continent. Starting in 2001, COMESA embarked on a procurement law reform project that resulted in the creation of a regulatory model for its member states, as well as a standard set of procurement regulations for public procurement above set thresholds within the bloc.[24] These instruments were significantly influenced by the 1994 Model Law.[25] Under the project, COMESA adopted a procurement directive, binding on all its members, explicitly advising members to align their procurement law systems to the 1994 Model Law.[26] Via COMESA, the 1994 Model Law thus considerably extended its influence in Africa.

For the most part, the direct influence of the 1994 Model Law in Africa resulted in domestic procurement laws that closely mirrored the 1994 Model

[20] UNCITRAL, Status: UNCITRAL Model Law on Procurement of Goods, Construction and Services (1994) at https://uncitral.un.org/en/texts/procurement/modellaw/procurement_of_goods_construction_and_services/status (accessed 27 February 2024). These are states that have notified UNCITRAL of their direct use of the Model Law in their domestic procurement law reform.

[21] Gambia, Ghana, Kenya, Madagascar, Malawi, Mauritius, Nigeria, Rwanda, Uganda, United Republic of Tanzania, Zambia.

[22] RA Kumar and E Caborn, 'The regulatory framework for public procurement in Botswana' in Quinot and Arrowsmith (eds) (n 2) 25, 34, 36–37; Caborn and Arrowsmith (n 2) 265.

[23] Quinot and Arrowsmith (n 3) 4.

[24] ibid; L Jiang, 'An evaluation of soft law as a method for regulating public procurement from a trade perspective' (PhD thesis, University of Nottingham, 2009) 137–38; S Karangizi, 'The COMESA Public Procurement Reform Initiative' (2005) 14 *Public Procurement Law Review* NA51; African Development Bank Group, *COMESA Public Procurement Reform and Capacity Building Projects, Project Performance Evaluation Report* (2012).

[25] S de La Harpe, 'Procurement under the UNCITRAL Model Law: A Southern Africa perspective' (2015) 18(5) *Potchefstroom Electronic Law Journal* 1572, 1583.

[26] COMESA Public Procurement Framework Directive by the Authority of Heads of States and Governments (2003).

Law in their operational provisions. That is, in many of these systems the national legislation followed the 1994 Model Law virtually verbatim in respect of operational provisions such as those governing procurement methods. In these systems, the standard suite of UNCITRAL procurement methods is set out with little or no variation in the domestic law: domestic or national tendering, two-stage tendering, restricted tendering, request for quotations and single-source procurement. This is hardly surprising given that these laws were the first comprehensive regulatory instruments governing procurement in the relevant systems. There was thus little prior local experience in procurement law that would guide departures or variations from the standard list of procedures.

Notably absent from these regimes is the 1994 Model Law's provision for competitive negotiation. This procedure was not taken up in most of the systems. It thus seems that at least in this respect, African states utilised the inherent flexibility of the 1994 Model Law and exercised a choice between the three options provided for in the 1994 Model Law to cater for scenarios where upfront setting of specifications are challenging. The choice of two-stage tendering and requests for proposals rather than competitive negotiations suggests that these states wanted to keep the level of discretion in the hands of procurement officers low, even where circumstances dictated a measure of discretion. As Caborn and Arrowsmith have argued, this can be understood against the low levels of procurement capacity in these systems when the laws were enacted, as well as major concerns with integrity.[27]

Where capacity across the procurement system is low and where there are serious integrity concerns, it is common to limit discretion in procurement decisions, especially regarding award decisions, by way of strict rules. Procurement law systems are thus continuously balancing discretion and flexibility in the hands of the procurement official to acquire goods and services on the best possible terms against the concerns that officials may not have the ability or capacity to determine or achieve best value or may take decisions for ulterior motives that do not amount to best public value.[28] Within the context that the 1994 Model Law influenced African procurement law systems, it is accordingly not surprising that strictly rule-bound procurement methods were favoured above ones granting more discretion. In fact, many of the domestic procurement statutes either explicitly prohibited or narrowly limited discretionary award practices, such as

[27] Caborn and Arrowsmith (n 2) 288.

[28] S Kelman, *Procurement and Public Management* (AEI Press, 1990) 13–18; SL Schooner, 'Desiderata: objectives for a system of government contract law' (2002) 11 *Public Procurement Law Review* 103, 110; SL Schooner, 'Fear of Oversight: The Fundamental Failure of Businesslike Government' (2001) 50 *American University Law Review* 627, 660–64; O Soudry, 'A Principal-Agent Analysis of Accountability in Public Procurement' in G Piga and KV Thai (eds), *Advancing Public Procurement: Practices, Innovation and Knowledge* (PrAcad Press, 2007) 432; CR Yukins, 'A Versatile Prism: Assessing Procurement Law through the Principal–Agent Model' (2010) 40 *Public Contract Law Journal* 63.

negotiations with bidders.[29] The Ghanian Public Procurement Act of 2003, for example, provided in section 63(1):

> Pursuant to the exception in this section no negotiations shall take place between the procurement entity and a supplier or contractor with respect to a tender submitted by the supplier or contractor.

Two areas where the African domestic laws go beyond the 1994 Model Law in a strikingly common way are in relation to community participation in procurement methods and schemes of preferential procurement. Community participation provisions typically provide ways in which the standard procurement methods and rules may be adapted where the participation of a local community in a project is desirable. For example, the Seychelles Public Procurement Act of 2008 and the 2008 Zambian Public Procurement Act directly incorporated the provision on community participation in procurement contained in the World Bank's procurement rules[30] and the African Development Bank's procurement rules of the time.[31] Section 36 of the Zambian Act thus provided:

> Where, in the interest of project sustainability, or to achieve certain specific social objectives of the project, it is desirable in selected project components to—
>
> (a) call for participation of local communities and nongovernmental organisations;
> (b) increase the utilisation of local know-how and materials; and
> (c) employ labour-intensive and other appropriate technologies;
>
> the procurement procedures, specifications, and contract packaging shall be suitably adapted by the Authority to reflect these considerations, provided these are efficient.

Another example is found in section 58 of the 2007 Rwandan Law on Public Procurement:

> The beneficiary community may participate in delivery of services within the context to be defined by the procurement regulations. This method shall be used if it is established that, it will contribute to the economy, create employment and involvement of the beneficiary community.[32]

The 2008 Regulations promulgated under the Rwandan Procurement Law provided more detail on such community participation.[33] Article 19 of the Regulations

[29] See Ghana Public Procurement Act 2001, s 63; Malawi Public Procurement Act 2003, s 31; Mauritius Public Procurement Act 2006, s 40; Uganda Public Procurement and Disposal of Public Assets Act 2003, s 74; Zambia Public Procurement Act 2008, s 51.

[30] The World Bank, *Guidelines Procurement under IBRD Loans and IDA Credits* (2006), cl 3.17.

[31] African Development Bank, *Rules of Procedure for Procurement of Goods and Works* (2000), cl 4.12.

[32] Rwanda No 12/2007 of 29/03/2007, Law on Public Procurement. See also Mauritius Public Procurement Act 2006, s 22; Madagascar Loi no 2004–009 du 26 juillet 2004 portant Code des Marchés Publics, Art 23; Décret no 2009-156 du 20 mai 2009 portant Code des Marchés Publics Congo Braza, Art 85; Liberia Public Procurement and Concessions Act 2005, s 46.

[33] Ministerial Order No 001/08/10/Min of 16/01/2008 Establishing Regulations on Public Procurement and Standard Bidding Documents, Arts 19–21.

recognised community participation as a distinct method of procurement, involving the conclusion of a contract between the procuring entity and the beneficiary community itself. In such procurements, the community is represented by two elected committees, the execution committee and the inspection committee. The Regulations also determined that the procuring entity must procure the services of an expert to assist the community in certain types of procurement.[34]

The absence of a community participation method of procurement in the 1994 Model Law suggests that it is not considered a standard practice within the international consensus on procurement rules, despite the existence of such mechanisms in multilateral development banks' procurement rules.[35] The prevalence of community mechanisms in African procurement laws suggests that there may be a fair level of consensus among African states on such practices. This may hint at a more communitarian approach to public procurement in the African context.

The second fairly common feature of African procurement laws, absent from the 1994 Model Law, was provision for a range of preferences in procurement. Rules governing such preferences, whether for local goods or suppliers or particular groupings, such as female suppliers or economically marginalised groups, are commonly found in African procurement laws.[36] While preferences for local suppliers, as an industrial development tool, are common worldwide,[37] the distinct social dimension of such preference schemes in many African procurement law regimes is noticeable. These included the regulatory systems developed under the influence of the 1994 Model Law. For example, while the 2005 Kenyan Public Procurement and Disposal Act followed the 1994 Model Law closely, it nevertheless created the framework for an extensive preferencing scheme in section 39.[38] In terms of this section, the detailed Public Procurement and Disposal (Preference and Reservations) Regulations 2011, set out to 'promote local, national and regional industry and support socio-economic development'.[39]

The absence of preference rules in the 1994 Model Law can perhaps best be understood against the main objective of the Model Law, at least as understood at the time, namely to open up cross-border procurement trade. This objective could be viewed as in tension with rules granting preferences to particular groupings, especially since such preferences commonly have a domestic element, thus reducing international participation.

[34] I Rugema, 'The regulatory framework for public procurement in Rwanda' in Quinot and Arrowsmith (eds) (n 2) 173.

[35] Community participation was raised in the UNCITRAL Working Group during the revision of the 1994 Model Law. However, the Working Group did not consider it appropriate to include community participation in the Model Law, inter alia because it did not consider community participation to be a distinct method of procurement. Report of Working Group I (Procurement) on the work of its sixth session (Vienna, 30 August–3 September 2004) paras 119–122; Arrowsmith and Nicholas (n 7) 91.

[36] G Quinot, 'Promotion of social policy through public procurement in Africa' in Quinot and Arrowsmith (eds) (n 2) 370.

[37] C McCrudden, *Buying Social Justice* (Oxford University Press, 2007).

[38] Quinot (n 36) 386–93.

[39] Reg 4.

IV. The Influence of the 2011 Model Law

The 2011 Model Law directly influenced the procurement laws of 26 countries worldwide,[40] of which eight are African.[41] There is also a fair level of indirect influence, especially via the work of the multilateral development banks, which use the Model Law as a benchmark for public procurement law reform in countries where they operate, which include many African countries. Thus, while not listed as countries that followed the 2011 Model Law in developing their own procurement laws, there are nevertheless clear indications of the 2011 Model Law's influence on new procurement statutes in, for example, Namibia,[42] Zimbabwe[43] and Lesotho.[44]

One of the most pervasive and visible influences of the 2011 Model Law in African systems has been the introduction of e-procurement, which, as noted in section II, was also one of the main drivers in the revision of the 1994 Model Law. Some of the revisions in African procurement statutes regarding e-procurement have been small. For example, the Tanzanian Public Procurement (Amendment) Act of 2016 added the obligation on accounting officers to 'ensure that all procurement information is promptly posted electronically' and the single provision stating that '[p]rocuring entities shall ensure that procurement or disposal by tender is implemented and reported through electronic procedures or manually where electronic facility is not available'. Others have been more extensive. For example, the 2015 Kenyan Public Procurement and Asset Disposal Act and amendments to the 2003 Ugandan Public Procurement and Asset Disposal Act introduced electronic reverse auctions into Kenyan and Ugandan procurement law respectively, supplemented in both systems by extensive provision for e-procurement across all procurement methods.

It is notable that both Kenya and Uganda have since made considerable strides in implementing e-procurement strategies, a dimension of public procurement in Africa that is seriously lagging behind global practice.[45] In Kenya, the Public Procurement Regulatory Authority introduced a new Public Procurement Information Portal in 2021 that allows for online tender invitations and notices, including data on awards, the procurement methods used and contract values.[46] The Authority also automated procurement dispute resolution mechanisms by way of online case management systems for both the Administrative Review Board and

[40] UNCITRAL, Status: UNCITRAL Model Law on Public Procurement (2011) at https://uncitral.un.org/en/texts/procurement/modellaw/public_procurement/status (accessed 27 February 2024). These are the countries that informed UNCITRAL of their usage of the 2011 Model Law.

[41] Egypt, Ghana, Kenya, Rwanda, Tunisia, Uganda, United Republic of Tanzania, Zambia.

[42] Public Procurement Act, 2015. See especially the provisions on electronic reverse auctions.

[43] Public Procurement and Disposal of Public Assets Act, 2017.

[44] Public Procurement Act, 2023.

[45] C Nicholas, 'Electronic procurement in Africa' in S Williams-Elegbe and G Quinot (eds), *Public Procurement Regulation for 21st Century Africa* (Juta, 2018) 204, 211.

[46] Public Procurement Regulatory Authority, *Annual Report 2020–2021* at https://ppra.go.ke/annual-reports/, 94 (accessed 27 February 2024).

its own Complaints and Investigations Department. In Uganda, the Ministry of Finance, Planning and Economic Development and the Public Procurement and Disposal of Public Assets Authority spearheaded the introduction of an online E-Government Procurement portal in 2021. The system aims to fully automate the complete procurement process, from procurement planning to bid invitations, submissions, adjudication, award, notices and contract management.[47]

While it would certainly be overly simplistic to claim that there is a direct, linear causal link between the revision of the regulatory regimes to provide for e-procurement and greater practical reliance on e-procurement, these systems certainly support the argument that explicit provision for e-procurement in the regulatory regime is an important enabler for actual practical realisation of e-procurement in a given system.[48] Conversely, these systems support the argument that in less mature procurement systems, which would include most if not all African procurement systems, the absence of explicit provision for e-procurement in the regulatory regime may act as a barrier or brake to the roll-out of e-procurement strategies. These developments thus bear out Caborn and Arrowsmith's proposition that the 2011 Model Law may 'serve as an early driver to the change that – in the area of electronic procurement, at least – seems ultimately inevitable'.[49]

The 2011 Model Law's revised rules on challenge proceedings had a more mixed impact. A number of African systems influenced by the 1994 Model Law provided for independent review *prior* to the revisions of the Model Law. These include Kenya,[50] Rwanda,[51] Tanzania[52] and Zambia.[53] Others, like Uganda, introduced independent review in post-2011 amendments of their original Acts,[54] evidently under the influence of the 2011 Model Law. Another interesting development in this area, is that a number of African systems opted not to follow the 2011 Model Law's revision of the exclusions from review. In the 1994 Model Law, a number of procurement decisions were excluded from review.[55] These included the selection of procurement method, the limitation of participation in procurement proceedings on the basis of nationality and a decision to reject all tenders,

[47] PPDA Uganda, *eGP Want to know more!* at https://ict.go.ug/wp-content/uploads/2021/07/e-GP-UPDATES.pdf (accessed 27 February 2024).

[48] Nicholas (n 45) 218; K Bala and A Dahiru, 'Identification of barriers and enablers of e-procurement processes in PPP projects delivery in Nigeria' in A Akintoye, C Liyanage and J Goulding (eds), *PPP International Conference 2013 Body of Knowledge* (University of Central Lancashire, 2013) 423; Asian Development Bank, *e-Government Procurement Handbook* (2013) 28–29.

[49] Caborn and Arrowsmith (n 2) 307.

[50] The Kenyan Public Procurement and Disposal Act, 2005 created the Public Procurement Administrative Review Board to decide requests for review of procurement decisions.

[51] The Rwandan Law on Public Procurement of 2007 provided for independent review panels at district and national levels to consider requests for review of procurement decisions.

[52] The Tanzanian Public Procurement Act, 2001 created the Public Procurement Appeals Authority to entertain appeals and reviews of procurement decisions.

[53] The Zambian Public Procurement Act, 2008 allowed for appeals against procurement decisions to the Zambia Public Procurement Authority.

[54] The Public Procurement and Disposal of Public Assets Appeals Tribunal was created by the addition of ss 91B–91M to the Ugandan Public Procurement and Disposal of Public Assets Act, 2003.

[55] Art 52(2) of the 1994 Model Law.

thereby bringing the solicitation to an end. The 2011 Model Law removed this list of exceptions, making all decisions subject to review.[56] The *Guide to Enactment* noted that UNCITRAL considered this change necessary to improve accountability and to align the Model Law to the UN Convention against Corruption.[57] Neither Kenya nor Ghana nor Tanzania followed this omission in their revised laws. That is, they all retained the list of exclusions.

V. The Model Law and the African Continental Free Trade Area

The influence of the Model Law in Africa raises the question as to its potential impact on increasing intra-Africa trade in procurement markets. After all, as noted at the outset, UNCITRAL's very mission in drafting model laws is to remove barriers to cross-border trade created by divergent national legal rules applicable to particular types of commercial activity.[58] Caborn and Arrowsmith have accordingly noted in this regard that '[a]s regional integration continues [in Africa] and increasingly addresses public procurement issues, further harmonisation is likely, with regional agreements both influencing national regulatory frameworks and building on existing commonalities'.[59] The question is thus whether the Model Law can serve the purpose of removing barriers in cross-border procurement trade on the African continent in light of its established African influence.

This is currently a pertinent question given the strong push for increased intra-continental trade in light of the Agreement establishing the African Continental Free Trade Area ('the AfCFTA'). The notion of the AfCFTA came to life with the adoption of the Agreement by the African Union Assembly in 2018.[60] The objectives of the AfCFTA include the creation of 'a single market for goods, services, facilitated by movement of persons in order to deepen the economic integration of the African continent', to 'promote and attain sustainable and inclusive socio-economic development, gender equality and structural transformation of the State Parties', to 'enhance the competitiveness of the economies of State Parties within the continent and the global market' and to 'promote industrial development through diversification and regional value chain development, agricultural development and food security'.[61] The Agreement entered into force, giving birth to the AfCFTA, following the deposit of the 22nd instrument of ratification (by the

[56] Art 64 of the 2011 Model Law.
[57] UNCITRAL, *Guide to Enactment* (n 5) 378.
[58] United Nations (n 5) 13–16; UNCITRAL (n 5) 2.
[59] Caborn and Arrowsmith (n 2) 307.
[60] About the AfCFTA at https://au-afcfta.org/about/ (accessed 27 February 2024).
[61] Agreement establishing the African Continental Free Trade Area, Art 3 at https://au-afcfta.org/wp-content/uploads/2022/06/AfCFTA-Agreement-Legally-scrubbed-signed-16-May-2018.pdf (accessed 27 February 2024).

Saharawi Republic) in 2019.[62] To date, 54 of the 55 African states have signed the Agreement.[63] Trade under the AfCFTA started on 1 January 2021.[64]

While the AfCFTA Agreement and Protocol on trade in goods are silent on public procurement, the Protocol on trade in services explicitly excludes from its scope 'procurement by governmental agencies purchased for governmental purposes and not with a view to commercial re-sale'. Generally, public procurement is not currently subjected to the AfCFTA regime. However, as has been the case in other market integration initiatives, the EU being a prime example, it is only natural that the question of adding public procurement to the single market will emerge in due course. In the African context, the very significant role that public procurement plays in domestic markets,[65] compared to private acquisition, would serve as a strong motivator for bringing public procurement in under the AfCFTA regime.

When the inclusion of public procurement in the AfCFTA is considered, the harmonisation of the domestic rules governing procurement will become a key issue, as has also been the experience in other single markets.[66] This is where the Model Law can play an important role. It is unrealistic to think that a continental code on public procurement could be created. Legal systems (and traditions) generally, and public procurement laws specifically, vary too much across the African continent to make a single code feasible. The best approach would probably be a two-tier one. At the continental level, a broad public procurement framework could be created to set out the basic principles to which all domestic procurement systems should adhere. This would be similar in approach (although not necessarily content) to the WTO GPA. That is, effectively an African GPA. Below the continental level, highly harmonised model laws within the various regional economic communities could be created. This is already the case in most African regions, making such a step a logical and viable approach. Examples of varying levels of regional procurement-law integration can be found in COMESA, the Union Economique et Monétaire Ouest-Africaine (WAEMU/UEMOA)[67] and the East African Community.[68]

The Model Law could play a key role in developing the instruments at both tiers. At the continental level, an abstraction of the essential principles underlying the Model Law would be a good starting point to design an African GPA. At the

[62] About the AfCFTA (n 60).

[63] ibid.

[64] ibid.

[65] African countries typically spend a very large proportion of funds via public procurement, in many instances more than 20% of the relevant country's GDP, which is well above the global average of 12% of GDP. E Bosio and S Djankov, 'How large is public procurement' *World Bank Blogs* at https://blogs.worldbank.org/developmenttalk/how-large-public-procurement (accessed 27 February 2024).

[66] See C Bovis, 'The regulation of public procurement as a key element of European economic law' (1998) 4(2) *European Law Journal* 220; EA Boykin, 'Public procurement and European Union integration: a systematic review' (2022) *Journal of European Integration* 1 doi:10.1080/07036337.2022.2112035.

[67] G Quinot and S Arrowsmith, 'Introduction' in Quinot and Arrowsmith (eds) (n 2) 4–5.

[68] JA Omolo and EJ Akinyi, 'The national treatment rule and the regulation of public procurement under the East African Community common market protocol' (2019) 5(1) *Journal of Corporate and Commercial Law & Practice* 115.

regional level, the influence of the Model Law in many of the regions will go a long way towards the creation of a regional model law. However, in both instances, and especially for regional model laws, the 2011 Model Law will have to be supplemented and tweaked to accommodate the elements of procurement laws in Africa that show high levels of convergence, but which depart from the 2011 Model Law. As noted in the previous sections, these include limiting discretion in negotiations (eg, by excluding competitive negotiation procurement methods) and limiting challenge proceedings.

VI. Conclusion

It is quite clear that the UNCITRAL Model Law on Public Procurement has had a significant influence on public procurement law in Africa. This applies particularly to the operational provisions, such as the rules governing procurement methods. This influence is also evident in respect of both the 1994 and 2011 texts of the Model Law. However, there are further clear areas where African systems have not followed the Model Law, including not consistently following the 2011 revisions to the Model Law. In some of these areas there is nevertheless commonality, or at least comparability, between various African systems.

The African continent will inevitably have to start considering greater alignment between its national procurement systems in support of increased intra-continental trade. Such trade integration on a continental scale became a reality in 2021 when the first trade under the AfCFTA commenced. At present, public procurement is not included in the AfCFTA regime, but given the trade integration policy aim behind this development and the enormous size of procurement in most African systems, public procurement will have to appear on the agenda at some point. When it does, the UNCITRAL Model Law will provide the single most significant model law to consider in respect of alignment of procurement rules across Africa. As Sue Arrowsmith has noted, 'the Model Law in principle supports … open market objectives'[69] and is thus conceptually ideally placed to fulfil this role. The discussion in this chapter has, however, indicated that there are distinct tweaks to the Model Law commonly found in African systems. It will accordingly be a Model Law Plus that will be the best candidate to pursue procurement law alignment, with the Plus representing those aspects where there are clear signs that African systems comparably did not follow the Model Law or developed similar rules outside of the Model Law. When the time comes for the drafting of such Model Law(s) Plus, the work of Sue Arrowsmith will be of material significance, given the unparalleled breadth and depth of her scholarship on the general principles informing the Model Law, its specific solutions for particular procurement challenges, and the Model Law's relationship with other instruments and other regulatory options.

[69] Arrowsmith (n 1) 25.

17

Twenty Years of Government Procurement Reform in China: Lessons and the Way Forward

PING WANG

I. Introduction

Public procurement as defined by Sue Arrowsmith (purchasing goods, services and works in a competitive market) did not exist in the centrally planned Chinese economy (1949–78). Since the launching of economic reform in 1978, competitive tendering, as well as the concept of open, fair and accountable public procurement, has been gradually introduced into China. Numerous government procurement-related regulations have been enacted over the last 20 years, including two national laws – the *Tendering Law* (TL) and the *Government Procurement Law* (GPL) – two State Council Regulations, a large number of ministerial decrees and provincial or sub-provincial regulatory documents.[1] The Chinese government procurement market, even without taking into account procurement of major infrastructure projects by state-owned enterprises (SOEs), such as the high-speed railway network, has grown to around 3.7 trillion Yuan in 2020, around 40 per cent of that of the European Union (EU).[2] However, the 2020 Chinese government procurement figure accounts for only 10.2 per cent of annual fiscal expenditure and 3.6 per cent of GDP, largely due to the narrow definition of government procurement

[1] The Chinese Legislation Law (enacted on 15 March 2000, entered into force on 1 July 2000, as amended in March 2015 and March 2023) has established the hierarchy of regulatory norms in the Chinese legal system. The Constitution is at the top, followed by primary legislation, namely national laws enacted by the National People's Congress (NPC) and its Standing Committee. The third level consists of implementing Ordinances and Administrative Regulations enacted by the State Council. The fourth level contains not only Ministerial Decrees/Measures but also local legislation adopted by regional People's Congresses. The third and fourth levels contain so-called secondary/implementing legislation.

[2] Author's calculation based on the relevant EU statistics available at https://european-union.europa.eu/principles-countries-history/key-facts-and-figures/economy_en (accessed 20 March 2023).

in Chinese law, which excludes the procurement of SOEs.[3] The combined value of procurement by Chinese government agencies, public bodies and SOEs is likely to be equal to or even larger than that of the EU.[4]

For historical reasons and due to conflicts between central government departments, namely the National Development and Reform Commission (NDRC) and the Ministry of Finance (MOF), China's public procurement legal framework and institutional framework are complex, segregated and fragmented. Tendering (open, selective, two-stage), as a group of procurement methods, is the subject of the TL – the brainchild of the NDRC – which in practice has become a law applying exclusively to works procurement by public entities, including SOEs. On the other hand, the GPL regulates all aspects of government procurement but excludes procurement by SOEs and works procurement where a tendering procedure is used. Such a complex and inconsistent regulatory environment is a significant barrier to market access.

It is submitted that Chinese government procurement reform started off on the wrong foot: from the regulation of open (and selective) tendering activities by both public and private entities, instead of government procurement in the comprehensive sense. The GPL failed to absorb the TL at the drafting stage due to the unwillingness of the NDRC to give up its regulatory authority. Ever since then, competition between – instead of coordination of – various procurement rules has become the norm in the evolution of the Chinese legal framework for public procurement.

Since 2018, Chinese public procurement reform has reached a new phase and is now at an important crossroads. With the momentum and mandate provided by the top leadership in 2018, a major revision of the legal framework is currently underway, with the amendment of the TL and the GPL having undergone one or two rounds of public consultation in 2020 and 2022.

The draft of the revised TL has surprisingly introduced negotiation into open tendering, similar to that provided in the World Trade Organization Agreement on Government Procurement (WTO GPA). On the other hand, the drafts of the revised GPL are more ambitious: procurement of SOEs serving public interests operating in utility sectors, as well as public–private partnership (PPP) projects, are to be added to the GPL's coverage. However, the current amendment proposals arguably remain insufficient, as two pieces of primary legislation will continue to co-exist, leaving several practical issues unresolved.

[3] It should be noted from the outset that, in China, official data are only available regarding 'government procurement' in its narrow sense. The term 'government procurement' is defined narrowly in the GPL as 'procurement of goods, works and services that are listed in the Centralised Procurement Catalogue or above prescribed thresholds; by state organs at all levels, public institutions and social organisations while using fiscal funds'. See further section III.A.i.

[4] It is reported that the value of procurement of Chinese central SOEs (those affiliated to the central Government) alone has reached 12.1 trillion Yuan in 2018, accounting for 13.16 % of the GDP.

Sue Arrowsmith has devoted a significant part of her career to providing guidance (most notably her influential work on the UNCITRAL Model Law and organising the Public Procurement Global Revolution Conference series) for developing countries to conduct their own public procurement reform. As one of her PhD students then colleague, the current author has benefited greatly from her teaching about adopting a principled and pragmatic, instead of a one-size-fits-all, approach to procurement regulation in different jurisdictions. With her teaching in mind, section II below provides a brief historical account of the evolution of this reform. Section III then elucidates the main contents of GPL and TL respectively, with notes on proposed amendments. Section IV discusses the underlying reasons for the slow progress of the current round of reform. Section V presents some proposals for moving forward. Section VI concludes.

II. The Evolution of Public Procurement Regulation in China

The evolution of public procurement regulation in China so far can be divided into five phases. The first phase is marked by the enactment of the TL in 1999. The focus of the regulation at this stage was mainly on tendering procedures rather than public procurement in general. The TL applies to tendering activities of *both public and private* sectors but lacks many features of a classic public procurement law, such as a clear definition of public procurement, procurement methods other than open and selective tendering (two-stage tendering was added later), or a supplier-review mechanism. However, it is nevertheless the first milestone of public procurement reform since certain public procurement projects (those involving publicly funded infrastructure) started being regulated by detailed rules on tendering procedures. Experiences and knowledge gained from regulating tendering activities by public entities have contributed to the acceptance of the modern concept of public procurement by legislators, government officials and the general public.

From the mid-1990s, the MOF initiated a new wave of government procurement reform, expanding beyond regulation of tendering activities. This resulted in the enactment of the GPL in 2002, marking the second phase of evolution.

However, since the very beginning, the NDRC and MOF have been competing over the authority to regulate public procurement, with the NDRC having a head start and the MOF having a more advantageous position as it controls the budget. They often concurrently enact competing rules on tendering proceedings, selection of evaluation experts, certified procuring agencies, designated media, publicity, review procedure, etc. This has caused not only duplication but also inconsistency, detrimental to legal certainty.

The third phase saw the enactment by the State Council of the Implementing Regulation of the Tendering Law (IRTL) in 2011 and the Implementing Regulation of the Government Procurement Law (IRGPL) in 2015. These two implementing Regulations have more legal authority than Ministerial Orders and local legislation. However, while they provide practical guidance and clarifications, they did not reconcile the conflicts resulting from the co-existence of TL and GPL.

In the fourth phase, China's public procurement reform embraced several new initiatives, including electronic government procurement/e-tendering and the introduction of Public Resources Trading Platforms at the local level. Although these initiatives integrated to a certain extent the institutional framework for contract publication and awards, they failed to harmonise the separate regulations of government procurement and tendering activities.

The current, fifth phase is signalled by the Chinese Communist Party's (CCP's) Plan for Deepening Government Procurement Reform 2018 ('CCP's Reform Plan') and the pending amendment of TL and GPL. The Deepening Reform Committee of the CCP, chaired by President Xi Jinping, adopted the Plan on 14 November 2018. Unusually, this document is not in the public domain, possibly because it was adopted by the CCP instead of the central Government (State Council).[5] According to the limited news coverage, this Plan identified several areas for further reform/improvement:

(a) to (re-)establish the key role of the procuring entity assuming the primary responsibility, for example by allowing procuring entities free choice of procuring methods (except single-source), procurement agencies and evaluating experts (in case of standard items), guaranteeing their say in the award process, etc;
(b) steering towards value for money, for example by raising the threshold for mandatory open tendering; most economically advantageous tender (MEAT) over lowest price; the use of whole-life-cycle costing; promoting centralised procurement; the link between technical specification, award criteria and the subject matter, etc;
(c) enhancing the role of government procurement as a policy tool;
(d) equal treatment of suppliers with different geographical origins and ownership structures,
(e) Internet + government procurement: the electronic government procurement initiative;
(f) changing the role of procurement agencies and experts: sector associations, self-regulation, and enhanced supervision.

Amendments of the TL and the GPL are already underway with the first round of public consultation on the drafts concluded in 2020. A second round of public consultation on the amendment of the GPL was started on 15 July 2022 and ended on 14 August 2022.

[5] Available in Chinese at www.ccgp.gov.cn/news/201811/t20181115_11112110.htm (accessed 15 December 2018).

III. The National Laws and their Respective Implementing Instruments

As explained above in section I, the reform of public procurement in China has resulted in a dual regulatory regime. Two national laws (TL and GPL), two respective State Council Implementing Regulations, and various ministerial measures operate in parallel. This section will explain and examine the main aspects of the legal and institutional framework established by the GPL, the TL and their respective implementing regulations, paying particular attention to potential conflicts as well as considering the current proposal for revision.

A. Overview of GPL and its Implementing Instruments

Although the GPL lost the race to become the first procurement law, it could be argued that it was the first to set up a comprehensive legal framework for government procurement in China. It goes beyond mere regulation of tendering activities by providing comprehensive rules covering all aspects of government procurement. It is implemented by the IRGPL and various measures adopted at ministerial and local level.

i. Coverage

Article 2 GPL defines 'government procurement' as 'procurement of goods, works and services that are listed in the Centralised Procurement Catalogue or above prescribed thresholds; by state organs at all levels, public institutions and social organisations while using fiscal funds'. Procurement is defined as 'acquisition of goods, construction and services through contractual means, including purchase, lease, trust, hire, etc'.

a. Entity Coverage

Unlike in the EU Directives, the definition of 'government procurement' in the GPL does not provide a general definition of 'contracting authority' but simply lists 'state organs', 'public institutions' and 'social organisations' without further clarification. As SOEs are not mentioned at all, their procurement is excluded from GPL coverage.

In practice, the social organisations covered by the GPL normally include associations for women, youths, disabled people and merchants, and trade unions controlled by the CCP and fully funded by the state.

'Public institutions' refer to 'social service organisations established using state assets by the state or other organisations to pursue educational, technological, cultural and health activities serving general public interests'.[6] However, in practice, these institutions engage in a wide range of activities, including administrative (eg vehicle registration) and commercial (eg hotels) activities, which, by their nature, go far beyond this definition. In 2008 the Chinese Government introduced a reform aimed at converting those institutions carrying out administrative functions back into state organs, and turning those providing goods and services under market conditions not involving the public interest into commercial enterprises.[7] Given that certain public institutions can generate income through services provided to the public, the key issue, as far as GPL coverage is concerned, is how to determine whether procurement undertaken by such institutions is funded by their own funds or from fiscal funds.

b. The Subject Matter of Government Procurement: Goods, Services and Works

In China, the division between the scope of works, on the one hand, and goods/services, on the other, becomes a contentious issue because of the co-existence of the GPL and TL and potential conflicts as to what they cover.

Article 2 GPL provides the following definitions:

- 'goods' – 'goods of various kinds and in various states, including raw materials, fuel, equipment, products, etc'
- 'works' – 'construction works, including the construction, renovation, expansion, decoration, demolition and repair of buildings etc'
- 'services' – 'subject matter of government procurement other than goods and works'.

Article 2 IRGPL further stipulates that the services covered include services performed to meet the Government's own needs and those provided by the Government to the general public.

With the TL covering all (public or private) tendering proceedings and the GPL covering government procurement, clashes arise where government procurement of works, goods and services is conducted through tendering procedures. The GPL tried to address this conflict by providing (in Article 4) that the '[T]endering Law shall apply to tendering proceedings in government procurement of works'. This provision implies that: (i) the TL does not apply to tendering procedures in the government procurement of goods and services; and (ii) the TL does not even apply to the government procurement of works where procurement methods other than open and selective tendering are used. It may be argued

[6] State Council, *Interim Regulation on the Registration and Administration of Public Institutions*, State Council Order No 252, 25 October 1998, as amended on 27 June 2004, available in Chinese at www.gov.cn/zwgk/2005-05/23/content_227.htm (accessed 19 August 2019).

[7] State Council Secretariat, Notice on the Reform of Public Institutions based on different categories, (2011) No 37, 24 July 2011. The Chinese text is available at www.zjhrss.gov.cn/art/2014/12/24/art_1389549_14287130.html (accessed 19 August 2019).

that although the doctrine of *lex posterior derogat legi priori* has been established in legal interpretation by the Legislation Law (Article 103), it remains difficult to reconcile the limitation imposed by the GPL with the directly conflicting provision of the TL (namely, that the TL is applicable to *all tendering activities* within the territory). The provision of the GPL is a mere patchwork instead of a real solution. Furthermore, in practice, procuring entities often follow the TL in works procurement, regardless of the method used.

The need to provide further clarification was explicitly recognised by the note prepared by the State Council Legislation Office accompanying the draft of the Implementing Regulations for the TL and GPL.[8] Article 7 IRGPL provides that government procurement of works and related goods and services through (open and selective) tendering should be subject to the TL; government procurement of works using procurement methods other than tendering procedures should be subject to the GPL and IRGPL; government procurement of works (regardless of whether tendering is involved) should follow government policy objectives (such as the 'Buy Chinese' provision).[9] Furthermore, the IRTL (Article 2) and IRGPL (Article 7) adopted identical definitions of works-related goods and services. Works-related goods are defined as 'equipment and materials … that are *inseverable parts*, and *essential* for attaining the fundamental functions of works' (emphasis added). Works-related services are defined as 'services needed to complete works, eg survey, design and supervision'. These provisions represent an attempt by the Chinese authorities to resolve the clash between the GPL and TL. However, it made little difference in practice. Furthermore, the IRGPL and IRTL, as implementing Regulations, arguably cannot substantially alter the scope of primary laws.[10]

A more principled approach, that is, the harmonisation of the GPL and TL, remains necessary. In its reply to the enquiry by a member of the NPC, the MOF admits that, despite the clarification regarding the scope of application of national laws provided in the IRGPL and IRTL, 'in practice, due to divergence in understanding of the scope of GPL and TL by procuring entities, obstacles remain with regard to the application of these laws'.[11]

[8] See www.lawtime.cn/info/gongcheng/gczbtbdt/2010090113069.html (accessed 20 March 2023).

[9] Art 7 IRGPL differs from previous drafts where works-related goods were not expressly mentioned. In addition, Art 4 IRTL states that finance departments (MOF and its local departments) are responsible for supervising government procurement of works through tendering and must follow government (secondary) policies in such procurement. Art 84 IRTL states that government procurement of *goods and services* through tendering is subject to the GPL and the IRGPL.

[10] Although the doctrine of ultra vires is enshrined in Arts 107–108 of the Chinese Legislation Law, Chinese courts do not have the power to strike down measures in violation of this doctrine. For ultra vires in general, see M Elliott, 'The Ultra Vires Doctrine in a Constitutional Setting: Still the Central Principle of Administrative Law' (1999) 58(1) *Cambridge Law Journal* 129 at doi:10.1017/S0008197399001075; P Craig, 'Ultra Vires and the Foundations of Judicial Review' (1998) *Articles by Maurer Faculty* 2756 at www.repository.law.indiana.edu/facpub/2756.

[11] MOF, Reply to NPC Enquiry No 7402, 19 July 2019, available in Chinese at http://tfs.mof.gov.cn/jytafwgk_8383/2017jytafwgk_9467/2018rddbjyfwgk/201909/t20190903_3379536.html (accessed 24 October 2019).

c. Mixed Goods and Services Contracts

It is necessary to determine whether a mixed contract is a goods or services contract, not for the purpose of coverage but for determining the use of award criteria, since the price must carry a minimum 30 per cent weighting in award criteria for goods procurement, but only 10 per cent for services. The MOF *Measures on Government Procurement of Goods and Services through Tendering* 2017 provides (in Article 7) that the 'procuring entity shall decide the nature of the procurement project in accordance with the Government Procurement Subject Matter Catalogue adopted by the MOF; where that is not possible, the decision shall be made with a view to facilitating the implementation of the procurement'.[12] It is hard to see how this provision, by subjectively measuring whether it will be beneficial to the execution of the procurement, can help to categorise a mixed goods and services contract.

d. Centralised Procurement Catalogue/Thresholds

The subject matter of procurement covered by the GPL must either be listed in Centralised Procurement Catalogues *or* have a value that exceeds prescribed thresholds. In other words, if a product is included in such a catalogue, its procurement, *regardless of its value*, falls within the scope of the GPL and must be undertaken by a centralised procurement agency.

However, it is important to note that there are no uniform, nationally applicable catalogues or thresholds. These are adopted by the central and provincial organs separately, depending on the source of funding. As a result, coverage varies between the central and provincial levels, as well as between the provinces.[13] Such divergence and disparities may encourage local protectionism detrimental to the functioning of a uniform government procurement market. This issue has been noted and is likely to be addressed in the revision of the GPL. The second draft of the revised GPL 2022 (Articles 6 and 7) states that a Centralised Procurement Catalogue and thresholds should be enacted by the State Council.

e. A Note on the Proposed Revision of the GPL with Regard to Coverage

With a view to implementing the CCP's Reform Plan, on 4 December 2020, the MOF proposed a major revision of the GPL containing 146 Articles (compared to 88 in the current law). A second draft of the revised GPL was published in July 2022.

The first draft of the revised GPL expands its coverage by adding 'other procuring entities' (to be specified by the State Council) and 'public resources' (in addition

[12] Adopted on 11 July 2017, entered into force on 1 October 2017, available in Chinese at http://tfs.mof.gov.cn/zhengwuxinxi/caizhengbuling/201707/t20170718_2652603.html (accessed 20 March 2023).

[13] Arts 7 and 8 GPL.

to fiscal funds) to the definition of 'government procurement'. This change may open the door for procurement by SOEs and PPP/concession contracts to be covered by the GPL. The intention was made clear by the second draft published in 2022. Its Article 12 provides that 'other procuring entities' means 'SOEs that serve the public interest by carrying out public utility services or operating public infrastructure or public service networks … SOEs eligible to be listed will be subsequently ascertained by the State Council'. However, based on meetings attended by the author, the resistance from SOEs to such a change seems strong.

Procurement of PPPs is also brought under the scope of the GPL in both the first and second drafts of the revised Law, despite the ongoing conflict between the MOF and NDRC as regards the regulatory authority covering PPPs. However, in July 2023, the former head of the MOF PPP Office was arrested and prosecuted for corruption and 'causing hidden debt problems'.[14] Soon after, in November 2023, the State Council Secretariat endorsed a Guiding Opinion jointly issued by the NDRC and MOF regarding a 'new mechanism for the regulation of PPPs', which effectively restricts new PPPs to user-pay concessions and confers the regulatory authority on the NDRC.[15] In light of this recent development, it is highly unlikely that adding PPP projects to the coverage of the revised GPL will stand.

ii. Objectives and Principles

It is important to note that Chinese courts, unlike the Court of Justice of the EU (CJEU), do not have the power to adopt expansive interpretations in accordance with objectives and principles provided in the law to fill gaps and/or provide clarification. Instead, they must refer to in-force provisions in laws, administrative regulations, ministerial rules or regulatory documents.[16]

The objectives of the GPL include 'regulation of government procurement activities, enhancing the efficiency of government procurement funds, safeguarding the national and public interests, protection of the legitimate rights and interests of the parties involved in government procurement, and promotion of clean government'.[17] The GPL also requires that government procurement should be conducted in conformity with the principles of 'openness and transparency, fair competition, justice, and good faith'.[18]

Two issues are worthy of note. First, Chinese authorities, including the MOF and the NDRC, are traditionally reluctant to give discretion to procuring entities

[14] See the news report (in Chinese) available at the official website: www.ccdi.gov.cn/yaowenn/202307/t20230727_278512_m.html (accessed 20 August 2023).

[15] Available in Chinese at www.gov.cn/zhengce/zhengceku/202311/content_6914162.htm (accessed 20 December 2023).

[16] For the role of the CJEU in pushing the boundaries of EU procurement rules (especially coverage), see S Arrowsmith, *The Law of Public and Utilities Procurement: Regulation in the EU and UK* (3rd edn, Sweet & Maxwell, vol 1 2014; vol 2 2018) ch 2.

[17] Art 1 GPL.

[18] Art 3 GPL.

because of the widespread and systematic corruption. Therefore, the objective of integrity/clean government often trumps other objectives. A significant shift may be detected in the CCP's 2018 Reform Plan, which, inter alia, emphasises the role of procuring entities in deciding the outcome of the procurement, implying discretion and clear-cut responsibilities. Furthermore, the proposed amendment of the GPL 2020 (Article 3) adds a new principle: cost-effectiveness.

Second, although the GPL does not make explicit reference to equal treatment or non-discrimination, these may arguably be derived from the objective of protecting the legitimate rights and interests of parties (especially suppliers), the principle of fair competition and the principle of justice. The second draft of the revised GPL, published in 2022, adds a new objective: 'to promote the construction of a unified national market'. This is in line with the Chinese central Government's current initiative to remove market access barriers introduced by local administrative measures.

iii. The Organisation of Public Procurement

The organisation of tendering activities is relatively simple under the TL: a two-tier structure consisting of procuring entities and tendering agencies. A tendering agency is defined as a lawfully established intermediary organisation undertaking tendering business, providing relevant services, and having a suitable place of business, capital and expertise.[19] Procuring entities are free to choose or not choose tendering agencies to conduct tendering activities.[20]

The GPL requires that the procurement of goods, services and works, both those listed and those not listed in the Centralised Procurement Catalogue, *must* be entrusted to centralised procurement institutions.[21] Centralised procurement institutions are procurement intermediaries with the status of not-for-profit institutional legal entities operating independently from the government procurement supervisory authority (the finance department).[22] The GPL also provides that procuring entities may employ other accredited procurement agencies for procurement outside of the Centralised Procurement Catalogue.[23] However, given that provincial-level governments have the power to create centralised procurement catalogues and exempt single government procurement contracts from centralised procurement, it could be argued that locally established centralised procurement institutions are not immune from political influence to 'buy local', undermining the functioning of a nationwide public procurement market.

The CCP 2018 Reform Plan explicitly gives procuring entities the opportunity to 'shop around' when choosing centralised procurement agencies. In practice,

[19] Art 13 TL.
[20] Art 12 TL.
[21] Art 18 GPL.
[22] Arts 16 and 60 GPL.
[23] Art 19 GPL.

however, since the electronic government procurement platforms that local procuring entities are often required to use remain under the control of individual regions, it is difficult to see how this option could be exercised.

Another important organisational aspect under the GPL is the use of evaluation panels, consisting of experts randomly selected from an official registry, to evaluate bids. The discretion of the procuring entity/agency is significantly limited by the rigid requirement to follow the expert panel's recommendation. This issue has been explicitly recognised by the CCP's Reform Plan, in which the procuring entity's right to participate in and lead the evaluation panel is emphasised. However, in practice, as an evaluation expert for the provincial government, the author has seen little change.

iv. Methods of Public Procurement

A range of modern procurement methods has been provided by the GPL, and this could be seen as major progress in comparison with the TL. These methods include open tendering, selective tendering, competitive negotiation, single-source procurement, requests for quotations, or any other method approved by the MOF. Competitive dialogue and framework agreements were added through subsequent ministerial measures.[24] The 2020 proposal for the revised GPL codifies and consolidates these methods by merging competitive negotiation and competitive dialogue, and by introducing electronic reverse auctions.

Open tendering is the default procedure under the GPL. Any deviation from open tendering needs to be justified and given *ex ante* approval by the relevant authorities. Instead of looking at the nature, type and characteristics of the contract, Article 71 GPL, unlike the TL's proposed amendment (which allows negotiation in open tendering), states that negotiation with bidders in tendering procedures, along with other illegal activities, should be subject to fines and administrative penalties.

Although open procedures are preferred because of the degree of competition they promote, the EU also recognises that they are not suitable for certain types of contracts (eg, complex or highly specialised ones) and can 'entail a greater administrative burden'.[25] In China, the procurement of PPPs, such as BOT ('build–operate–transfer') projects and concessions, was subject to open tendering during the early days. This is mainly because the TL requires infrastructure

[24] The new MOF Interim Measure on Framework Agreement Procurement was enacted on 14 January 2022 and entered into force on 1 March 2022, see at www.ccgp.gov.cn/news/202201/t20220127_17561511.htm. However, its significance is undermined by its limited scope: only applying to repeated, low-value and/or small-quantity goods and services procurement, such as spare parts; legal, accounting, auditing and evaluation services; and outsourced social services.

[25] European Commission, DG REGIO, Stock-taking of administrative capacity, systems, and practices across the EU to ensure the compliance and quality of public procurement involving European Structural and Investment (ESI) Funds (January 2016) at http://ec.europa.eu/regional_policy/en/policy/how/improving-investment/public-procurement/study/ (accessed 10 October 2020).

projects funded by public finance or involving the public interest to be procured through open or restricted tendering. In practice, however, the inadequacies of open tendering for procuring PPPs have meant that local governments have tried to circumvent this requirement by using open tendering to select the partner and subsequently negotiate with them. Although the NDRC is traditionally in favour of using open tendering to procure PPP projects, in the most recent joint proposal (with both the NDRC and MOF involved) for regulating concessions published for public consultation in November 2023, 'tendering, negotiation and other competitive methods' are allowed to be used for the procurement of concessions – the only form of PPPs now allowed.[26]

Article 30 GPL provides for competitive negotiations under the following conditions: the failure of a tender procedure; the complexity or special characteristics of the subject matter that make it impossible to set specifications; an inability to estimate the overall price; and the impossibility of meeting the emergency requirements of the procuring entities through tendering procedures due to the amount of time required. Article 26 IRGPL states that this does not apply when the emergency was foreseeable or caused by the procuring entity's own negligence. As regards the award criteria to be applied in competitive negotiation procedures, the GPL states that the procuring entity should examine the qualified candidates recommended by the negotiation working group and select the supplier offering the lowest price while at the same time matching the quality and service levels offered by the other candidates.[27] However, price is not normally the decisive factor in contract awards in competitive negotiations, and it is hard to see how this criterion could apply when the 'quality and service level' is not equal among candidates.

The second draft of the revised GPL brought some fundamental changes to this procurement method. It merged competitive negotiation and competitive dialogue procedures under the title 'competitive negotiation'. The draft provides for only two circumstances when competitive negotiation can be used, that is, 'where negotiation is needed to: (i) provide details of the solution, clarify detailed technical specifications or requirement of services or other commercial requirements; and (ii) allow suppliers to provide solutions, select the final solution and provide details'. The grounds relating to the failure of the tender procedure and emergency procurement have been removed.

The revised competitive negotiation procedure requires the remaining suppliers to submit their best and final offers in a final round. However, it does not provide a mechanism for making any adjustments that may be necessary after the confirmation of the winning supplier. Moreover, the minimum time frame for suppliers to submit their best and final offers appears unrealistic (no more than

[26] See https://yyglxxbsgw.ndrc.gov.cn/htmls/article/article.html?articleId=2c97d16b-8678801b-018c-153aeaf4-006b (accessed 12 December 2023).

[27] Art 38 GPL.

one day for single-subject procurements and no more than three days for multiple-subject procurements).

B. Note on the TL's Proposed Revision

While Article 2 TL states that it applies to all tendering activities within the territory of China, which could mean little to private procurement, Article 3 provides that the TL applies to procurement of works concerning the public interest or public security; works fully or partially invested in or financed by the state; and services and equipment related to these works to be procured by tendering. This means that government agencies, as well as SOEs, must comply with the TL when procuring through tendering certain works/construction projects, related services (such as ground exploration, design and monitoring) and goods incidental to these construction projects (important materials and equipment). Such works/construction projects include: (i) projects that concern the public interest or security, such as large infrastructure and public utilities; (ii) projects funded wholly or partly by state-owned or state-borrowed capital; and (iii) projects funded by loans or aid from international organisations or foreign governments. Tendering procedures specified or required by international institutions or foreign governments are applicable in projects sponsored or funded by those institutions, provided that the public interest would not be negatively affected by their application.[28] Since it is highly improbable that any private entity would voluntarily follow the rigid procedural rules set out in the TL, it could be argued that, in practical terms, the TL's coverage only goes as far as a compulsory requirement found in Ministerial Orders.

The major changes in the 2020 draft of the revised text of the TL include:

1. The removal from its scope of application of 'large-scale infrastructure, public utilities and other projects that have a bearing on social public interest and public safety'.
2. Enhanced transparency with regards to tender notices.
3. Introduction of a two-stage tendering procedure (although already included in the IRTL).
4. More discretion given to the procuring entity in terms of evaluation reports with recommendations but without rankings; negotiation allowed; the right to challenge the report of the evaluation panel, etc. This reflects the significant shift detected in the CCP's Reform Plan, which emphasises the role of procuring entities in deciding the outcome of the procurement process, reflecting their inherent responsibilities and preferences.
5. Restricted use of the lowest price as the award criterion; rejection of abnormally low tenders.

[28] Art 67 TL.

6. The right of bidders (though not obligatory) to attend the bid opening (more friendly treatment of non-local bidders).
7. Dispute settlement: the introduction of arbitration and mediation.

C. Enforcement and Supplier Remedies

The enforcement mechanism designed by the TL and GPL relies heavily on administrative supervisory bodies. Nevertheless, the supplier-review mechanism, despite its omission by the TL, has grown in significance since its introduction by the GPL as an effective means to detect breaches and secure compliance.[29]

However, because it is not clear from the GPL and TL whether the GPL's rules on supplier review apply to complaints about government procurement of works regulated by the TL, on 21 June 2004 the NDRC and other central government departments,[30] acting on the basis of Article 65 TL, issued the Measures on the Handling of Complaints on Tendering Proceedings in Construction Projects.[31] This ministerial regulation provides detailed rules on the general principles for handling complaints, review forums, the procedural rules for the filing and handling of complaints, decision-making and legal liabilities. On 11 August 2004, the MOF, acting on the basis of the GPL, adopted the Measures on the Handling of Complaints of Government Procurement Suppliers.[32] The timing of the introduction of these ministerial regulations indicates that little effort was made to coordinate, and the co-existence of the GPL and TL had a profound impact on the public procurement reform. Although both ministerial regulations have been largely succeeded by, and codified in, the IRTL and IRGPL,[33] certain inconsistencies remain regarding, inter alia, the scope of coverage, review forums and legal standing.

In China, the main body responsible for supplier review is the designated administrative review body, which has the power to halt the procurement process and even to set aside concluded contracts. There is arguably no real alternative to this tiered system.

The role of the Chinese judiciary in developing Chinese public procurement rules is rather limited. This is because, first, although the current laws and regulations regard government procurement contracts as *civil contracts*, they are silent about whether aggrieved suppliers can bring a civil litigation case directly against the procuring entity before the civil branch of the courts. In practice, civil courts

[29] See X Zhang, 'Supplier Review as a Mechanism for Securing Compliance with Government Procurement Rules: A Critical Perspective' (2007) 5 *Public Procurement Law Review* 325.

[30] They are the Ministry of Construction, the Ministry of Railways, the Ministry of Communications, the Ministry of Information Industry, the Ministry of Water Resources, and the General Administration of Civil Aviation of China.

[31] Effective on 1 August 2004.

[32] Effective on 11 September 2004.

[33] See Arts 57–61 IRTL; Arts 64–83 IRGPL.

often refuse to accept such cases. Second, despite the presumption of certain civil judges, the procurement decisions of government agencies are not regarded as 'administrative acts' that can be challenged directly before the administrative division of the court.[34] The jurisdiction of the court is limited to hearing appeals against decisions of administrative review bodies (or administrative appeal bodies) on points of law. As the court is arguably deprived of the power to issue interim measures, to set aside concluded contracts or to award adequate damages, it is difficult to see any incentive for aggrieved suppliers to engage in the judicial process.

More problematic is the jurisdiction of the various designated administrative review bodies. The co-existence of overlapping national procurement rules, including those covering remedies, makes jurisdictional conflicts among review bodies almost inevitable.

With a view to addressing such conflicts or failures to act, the IRTL simply provides in Article 61 that 'when any bidder or interested party files complaints regarding the *same* issue with two or more competent administrative review bodies, the complaint shall be handled by the administrative review body which received the complaint first' (emphasis added). Contrary to the IRTL, the IRGPL are silent on this important issue.[35] The IRTL provision arguably gives rise to, or even encourages, forum shopping. It is not clear what would happen if multiple complaints were to be lodged by different bidders regarding different aspects of the same procurement process. There is no procedural rule regarding time limits, transfers of documentation or communication in such cases.

IV. Analysis of Obstacles to Deepening Chinese Procurement Reform

It is fair to say that the Chinese government procurement reform has made significant achievements, with a regulatory framework in place and the need for open,

[34] Chinese Taipei takes a similar point of view. See *Taiwan Yutong Information Technology Limited v Taiwan Highway Authority and Yuantong Limited*, Taiwan Supreme Administrative Court [2006] 01239.

[35] This provision was criticised by the author in 2013 in the report presented to the MOF, which seems to have had an effect. The argument is that, under such a provision, it is not clear what would happen if the finance department in question declined to exercise the discretion (as indicated by the use of 'may' instead of 'shall'). Even if the finance department is more than happy to relinquish its jurisdiction in favour of any other administrative department to reduce its workload, as the MOF has done in the *Modern Wo'er* case (*Beijing Modern Wo'er Trading Co Ltd v Ministry of Finance of the People's Republic of China*, No 1 Intermediate People's Court of Beijing Municipality, First Level Administration Division Decisions Nos 432 and 433, 2005), such a referral is arguably illegal, since Art 13 GPL explicitly designates finance departments as the competent authority for handling supplier review in the context of government procurement. See P Wang, CH Bovis and X Tu, *A Comparative Analysis of Utilities Procurement in the EU and China*, report prepared for the EU–China Trade Project II (2013); D Mitterhoff, 'Beijing Court Orders Ministry of Finance to Rule on Supplier's Complaints, But Skirts Broader Issues of Schism in China's Procurement Supervision' (2006) 3(12) *International Government Contractor* 98.

transparent, efficient, clean and accountable public procurement widely accepted by stakeholders. However, many key aspects of the legal and institutional framework remain ambiguous, inconsistent or incoherent. The CCP's Reform Plan has arguably failed to produce the desired outcome, that is, with the revision of the GPL and the TL, as well as the institutional layout's falling short of achieving uniformity and remaining uncertain. This section will analyse the obstacles and misconceptions inhibiting the reform from making significant and real changes.

A. Lack of a Holistic View and a Principled Approach Towards the Reform

The first and foremost obstacle to Chinese government procurement reform is the lack of a holistic vision and principled approach towards a master plan. If that was not possible at the beginning of the reform back in the 1990s, due to the lack of understanding of what a modern procurement regime should look like, it has certainly become apparent over the past 20 years with domestic practice, as well as in international engagement such as the WTO GPA accession negotiations.

As a matter of principle, it is odd to delineate the coverage of two pieces of primary procurement legislation (ie the TL and the GPL) based not only on the subject matter of the procurement contract (works or works-related) but also on *the procurement method used.* On the one hand, using the type of procurement contract to define the scope of coverage, that is regulating works procurement separately, can find some support given the special nature and complexity of works procurement. On the other hand, however, it is an obsolete approach. For example, although the EU initially introduced directives on the procurement of supplies, works and services separately for historical reasons, it quickly merged them into a single instrument for reasons of simplification and clarity. Currently, China has an urgent need for such consolidation.

Furthermore, defining the scope of procurement laws by reference to the procurement method used (whether tendering is involved) is absurd. No justification can be found to support such an approach and, as far as the author is aware, no other jurisdiction in the world has opted for such an approach. The current legal framework seems to be the result of a patching-up approach, instead of a principled approach fully appreciating how a sound procurement regulatory framework should be set up.

Therefore, it is disappointing that the CCP's 2018 Reform Plan ignored the 'elephant in the room': there is arguably no rationale for the TL and the GPL to co-exist. There is no sign of a comprehensive consolidation, as the revision of the TL and the GPL has been proposed separately by the NDRC and the MOF. It can be argued that the CCP's Reform Plan falls short of providing a complete road map for reform, despite addressing several important issues, as explained in section II.

B. Lack of Determination to Suppress Individual Institutions' Interest when Institutional Conflicts Emerge

There is an argument that the reason why the CCP did not mandate harmonisation between the GPL and the TL in the 2018 Reform Plan is not due to ignorance of the logic or rationale but due to its reluctance to suppress certain individual institutions' interests when institutional conflicts emerge. Numerous Chinese state and local organs are involved in regulating public procurement. It could be argued that conflicts over procurement regulations are inevitable at various levels given this fragmented institutional framework. The MOF is the state's 'bookkeeper' and the 'Guardian of the GPL'; the NDRC is the 'investor' for infrastructure on behalf of the state and the 'Guardian of the TL'. They are both building their own 'fortresses of regulation' on public procurement. This has led not only to duplication and a waste of resources but also to inconsistencies that jeopardise the creation of legal certainty as China's legal framework covering public procurement evolves. Other line ministries, such as those in charge of international trade and transport, are also involved in implementing and enforcing the rules within their respective areas. The central Government, that is the State Council, became aware of this problem from the outset of the reform. It issued an *Opinion on Further Regulating Tendering Activities* on 12 July 2004,[36] which mandated the establishment of an inter-ministerial coordination mechanism, with the NDRC serving as the secretariat.

It is encouraging to see that all 'major players' are involved in this mechanism, and coordinating the coverage of the different regulations has been identified as one of its main objectives. On the other hand, it is doubtful whether the scheduled six-monthly liaison meetings or the annual summit[37] will fundamentally resolve the issue. Since then, various reform initiatives, such as that of the public resources trading platform, e-procurement/e-tendering and PPPs,[38] as well as China's GPA accession, have often been hijacked and undermined by regulatory competition.

At this point, the special status of the NDRC is worth noting. Like its predecessor – the State Planning Commission under the centrally planned economy – the NDRC is arguably the most powerful and influential ministry in regulating the market economy. In practice, the NDRC, often referred to as the 'mini-state council', oversees coordinating, producing and implementing major strategic policies such as the Five-Year Plan. It works closely with the leaders of government at various levels and often gains a head-start in taking up new areas subject to regulation, for example the establishment of public resources trading platforms. However, the legal basis for its authority, the TL, has its inherent limitations, in that it can only be relied upon when both tendering procedures and works-related

[36] State Council Secretariat [2004] No 56.

[37] ibid Arts 6 and 10.

[38] For further discussion of PPPs regulation, see P Wang, 'Regulation of Public–Private Partnership in China: The Search for Coherence, Consistency and Certainty' in O Akseli and J Linarelli (eds), *The Future of Commercial Law* (Hart Publishing, 2020) ch 16.

procurement are involved. To compensate for this disadvantage and fight off the attempt by the MOF to harmonise procurement rules, the NDRC formed an alliance with other line ministries also reluctant to give up their respective authority over public procurement, by holding high the banner of decentralised regulation. This has caused the phenomenon of so-called 'nine dragons handling the water' (according to Chinese myth, the dragon is bringing rain), reflecting the general public's dissatisfaction with such decentralised, inconsistent regulation of public procurement.

President Xi Jinping, in his opening address at the Bo'ao Forum in April 2018, commented on the creation of State Administration for Market Regulation (SAMR), stating that 'China is determined to remove any systematic defects restricting the ability of the government to use the market to determine the allocation of resources'.[39] This certainly raises hopes that the CCP's Reform Plan may provide fresh impetus for public procurement reform and bring about the harmonisation of the GPL and TL, as well as achieving real integration of the institutional framework at all levels. However, with that result in mind, the leadership must drop its favourite 'trouble shooter', that is an inter-institutional coordination mechanism, and show resolve by adopting a principled approach to meet the issue of institutional conflict head on.

C. Lack of a Transparent and Stakeholder-engaging Rule-making Process

The concept of transparency is important in all public procurement regimes but is difficult to define with precision. According to Sue Arrowsmith, the concept can, in fact, be broken down into four distinct aspects: (i) publicity about contract opportunities; (ii) publicity about the rules governing each procedure; (iii) a principle of rule-based decision-making that limits the discretion of procuring entities or officers; and (iv) the possibility to verify that the rules have been followed and the ability to enforce when they have not. It is submitted that transparency in the rule- and policy-making process is also of vital importance to the success of procurement regulation reform. Such process in China is essentially led by the administrative organs of the state, that is by various government ministries. Although the NPC is the legislative organ of the state with the highest authority in accordance with the Constitution, it does not table legislative packages on its own initiative; instead, all laws are drafted by the competent ministries, albeit that the idea for such laws may come from NPC representatives. In this process,

[39] President Xi Jinping, Opening Address to Bo'ao Forum, 10 April 2018, available in Chinese at www.gov.cn/xinwen/2018-04/10/content_5281303.htm (accessed 15 January 2024). President Xi, in the same speech, also called for the acceleration of China's WTO GPA accession, which led to the tabling of China's 6th revised offer in October 2019 after a standstill of five years.

the ministries now engage the public through public consultations, asking for comments on draft legislation.

However, it can be argued that the transparency and effectiveness of this process remain unsatisfactory, at least as far as the adoption of procurement rules is concerned. Firstly, the 'master' Reform Plan adopted by the CCP in 2018 is not available in the public domain. It is hard for commentators to grasp the essence, direction and unaddressed issues of this plan if the detailed wording cannot be assessed. Second, the public consultations lasted for a month, did not produce any Green Paper or White Paper summarising the comments received, from whichever sector/entity, nor explain how the subsequent version had taken such comments into account. Third, the official statistics on public procurement available on the official website present only a summary instead of a full data set. It is therefore difficult to make any proposal or suggestion for improvement based on concrete evidence. The same criticism applies to the third-party evaluation report of transparency in Chinese government procurement, the full text of which is not available to the public, a disappointing and absurd situation for a report dedicated to enhancing transparency in public procurement. Fourth, it is also noteworthy that it is particularly difficult to gather information about the procurement rules and practice of SOEs, as the material is often not available on their official websites or electronic procurement platforms.[40] On the one hand, as explained in section III, the procurement of SOEs is largely excluded from the coverage of the GPL; only their works procurement above a certain threshold is subject to the TL. On the other hand, procurement of SOEs is often an area most infected by corruption, arguably due to the lack of adequate regulation. How on earth can the rules on SOE procurement be assessed and then improved if the legal basis and practice on and data of SOE procurement remain in the dark? Finally, over the years, not only scholars but also members of NPC have raised concerns about the fragmented legal and institutional framework for public procurement in China. However, such voices have made little impact on the behaviour of the government organs. For example, the enquiry made by a member of the NPC in July 2019 raised the issue of merging the GPL and TL. In its reply, the MOF admitted that, despite the provisions made to clarify and coordinate the IRGPL and IRTL discussed in section III, 'in practice, due to divergence in understanding of the boundary of GPL and TL by procuring entities, obstacles remain regarding the application of these laws'.[41]

[40] 'Bidding and tendering information' provided by SOEs are considered statutory 'trade secrets', prohibited from disclosure to the public, according to the Interim Provision on Protection of Trade Secrets of Central SOEs issued on 25 March 2010; available in Chinese at www.gov.cn/gongbao/content/2010/content_1702214.htm (accessed 25 June 2023).

[41] MOF, Reply to NPC Enquiry No 7402, 19 July 2019, author's own translation available in Chinese at http://tfs.mof.gov.cn/jytafwgk_8383/2017jytafwgk_9467/2018rddbjyfwgk/201909/t20190903_3379536.html (accessed 24 October 2023).

D. Misconceptions about the Place where the Right Balance Needs to be Struck in Regulating Procurement

Sue Arrowsmith instructed the author, in LLM teaching, PhD supervision and through her publications, that the key to formulating sound procurement rules is about striking the right balance between conflicting objectives and principles. However, in China, regulators often jump from one end of the spectrum to the other end when designing the procurement rules. One example is the use of evaluation experts in the award procedure. To mitigate the risk of bribery and unfairness in the procuring entity, some local authorities have adopted an extreme approach: evaluation experts included in an official database maintained by respective local finance bureaux will be selected randomly and invited/notified (via telephone) only a few hours before the actual evaluation process. The author, as an evaluation expert for the provincial authority, has been notified a dozen times but had to turn down nearly all of the invitations, as it is virtually impossible to be available at such short notice. On one occasion, where the author happened to be available and did attend (mainly out of curiosity) an evaluation process with four other experts, the panel had only three hours to read a large pile of documents (thousands of pages) and make recommendations – an ordeal few people would like to go through a second time. The procuring entity merely provided logistical support without sending its own representative to join the panel, which is clearly inconsistent with the instructions in the CCP's Reform Plan.

The (over-) use of the open tendering procedure is also a typical example. Although open tendering is (rightly so) the default procedure as provided in the UNCITRAL Model Law, as explained in section III, it is arguably not suitable for procuring complex projects such as PPPs. The NDRC's insistence on using open tendering for PPP procurement is arguably due to its need to maintain regulatory authority over such projects, rather than any conviction as to the open tendering procedure's being suitable. There is a misconception that open tendering will always ensure transparency and integrity, and prevent corruption. This is highlighted by the procurement of the local theatre by the Ningbo municipal government between 2000 and 2004. The open procedure was run a dozen times; the project was 500 million Yuan over budget; and the head of the procurement office and several high-ranking local officials were convicted for corruption.[42]

Another example is the use of procurement as a tool to promote secondary policy objectives unrelated to value for money, such as environmental protection, innovation, the promotion of small and medium-sized enterprises, etc.[43] The

[42] See the news report in 2005, available in Chinese at https://finance.sina.com.cn/stock/s/20051124/09262144302.shtml?from=wap (accessed 20 March 2023).

[43] Art 10 GPL contains a buy-national policy and Art 9 requires that 'government procurement shall assist in achieving such national policy objectives of economic and social development as environment protection, development of less-developed and minority-populated areas, and development of small and medium-sized enterprises, etc'.

function of procurement in promoting other (secondary) national policy objectives received renewed attention and emphasis in the CCP's 2018 Reform Plan. Article 30 of the 2020 proposal for revising the GPL also stated that policy objectives can be achieved in procurement through initial purchase/pre-commercial ordering, set aside, technical specifications, preferential pricing, priority procurement and by encouraging sub-contracting, etc. However, it does not distinguish these methods based upon their impact on competition and value for money. Using procurement to achieve such objectives involves the careful and balanced design of procurement/industrial policies, and it may be restricted by China's GPA accession. For example, Article 23 IRGPL provides that the pursuit of other policy objectives can be used as grounds for the procuring entity to apply for the approval to use procurement methods other than open tendering, even if the value of the goods or services to be purchased is above the threshold for the mandatory use of open tendering. Such a provision, involving a trade-off between primary policy objectives (such as value for money, integrity) and secondary ones, requires careful consideration regarding its rationale and design, even if it contains a built-in safeguard of an *ex ante* approval procedure. Consideration is needed whether, instead of opting for less transparent procurement methods, it will suffice to allow such policies to be pursued in open tendering through technical specifications, conditions for participation or award criteria. Furthermore, the current regime does not provide any guidance on how to apply these secondary policy objectives in the same procurement, since these measures were adopted separately with no regard to coordination. In practice, procuring entities need to find solutions themselves. For example, the tendering notice for the procurement of medical equipment by a public hospital provides that, where the supplier also qualifies as an SME, a prison workshop, or a disabled persons' workshop (they all enjoy preference pricing but with different margins), the largest price preference margin should be applied.[44]

V. Proposal for the Way Forward

The revision of the law is not progressing; not providing for consistent, coherent and properly balanced rules as well as the mechanism to implement and enforce them. Those powerful ministries with a regulatory interest in public procurement, such as the NDRC and the MOF, do not resist harmonisation or integration; they just resist initiatives that are not led by them. Reform initiatives, for example the creation of a single electronic public procurement gateway (which could be the public resources trading platforms after adequate integration), have merits but have been stalled by putting institutional interests ahead of public interests and

[44] See Jilin People's Hospital, Procurement Notice on Medical Equipment, 11 October 2021, available in Chinese at www.ccgp.gov.cn/cggg/dfgg/gkzb/202110/t20211011_16990773.htm (accessed 12 January 2022).

legal certainty. The discussion in previous sections made the right way forward arguably quite clear:

- There should be one overarching primary procurement law, harmonising the GPL and the TL, covering the procurement of goods, services and construction works by all government agencies and public bodies, as well as SOEs serving the general interests and not subject to market competition.
- A comprehensive and thorough review of existing procurement rules through, inter alia, adequate public consultation should be conducted before the enactment of the single procurement instrument to ensure consistency and coherence.
- There should be one uniform institutional framework implementing the harmonised rules. The State Council may set up a Committee on Public Procurement (like the Committee on Anti-Monopoly), serving as the main policy maker and the 'mastermind' for procurement reform. It is recommended that the Secretariat of the Committee second its personnel from the NDRC and the MOF – officials who have been working in this field, with adequate professional knowledge and training.
- There should be one electronic public procurement gateway creating a one-stop shop for all procurement opportunities, award decisions, outcomes of supplier reviews, as well as the performance record of procurement contracts. The suppliers should be able to register without difficulty. The gateway should allow supervisory bodies such as the Audit Office to gain access to the procurement process discreetly.
- There should be uniform and effective administrative and judicial redress for misconduct and crimes (eg, bid rigging), with adequate provision for the supplier review. It is recommended that the administrative review body is placed outside and independent from the authority supervising the procuring entity, preferably at regional or national level, not closely related to any individual local authority. The specialised judicial body hearing the appeal against such administrative review body should be organised in the same fashion, detached from local interests, and should consist of procurement experts.

VI. Conclusions

The momentum and mandate provided by the top leadership in the CCP's 2018 Reform Plan has led Chinese public procurement reform into a new era and located it at an important crossroads. The major revision of the legal framework is currently underway, with amendments to the TL and GPL having undergone one or two rounds of public consultation in 2020 and 2022. The draft of the revised TL has surprisingly introduced negotiation into open tendering, similar to that provided for in the GPA. On the other hand, the drafts of the revised GPL are more ambitious: for example, procurement by SOEs serving the public interest and operating in utility sectors, as well as PPP projects, are to be added to the GPL's coverage; and provisions on framework agreements, albeit with very limited scope for application, are to be introduced, codifying the relevant ministerial measure enacted at the beginning of 2022.

However, it might be argued that the proposal to amend the GPL tabled by the MOF remains insufficient, since the TL and GPL will continue to co-exist, leaving several practical issues identified in the past unresolved.

Several underlying obstacles have been identified to explain the reason why Chinese public procurement reform has not fully achieved uniformity, consistency and coherence over the past 20 years. These include the lack of a holistic view and a principled approach at the top level; the lack of determination to suppress individual ministries' interests and opt for inter-institutional coordination mechanisms rather than simply delineating the scope of their authority; the lack of a transparent and stakeholder-engaging rule-making process; as well as misconceptions about the right place where the right balance should be struck. Therefore, the right way forward is arguably for China's top leadership to show resolve in setting aside individual institutions' vested interests, providing much needed uniformity, consistency and coherence through: harmonising the GPL and the TL, integrating the institutional framework while keeping a professional workforce, and creating a one-stop shop for electronic public procurement and a reliable and effective administrative/judicial review mechanism.

The evolution of Chinese public procurement reform largely coincides in time with the successful organisation of the Global Revolution series of international conferences on public procurement law and policy by Sue Arrowsmith. The author remembers well that she once, in her opening address to the Global Revolution Conference, quoted EF Schumacher: 'Any intelligent fool can make things bigger, more complex, and more violent. It takes a touch of genius – and a lot of courage to move in the opposite direction.'[45] This also reflects the future direction that Chinese public procurement reform should take: simplification, harmonisation and integration.

[45] EF Schumacher, 'Small is Beautiful' (1973) 37(5) *The Radical Humanist* 16, 22.

INDEX